BIOLOGY
OF THE
REPTILIA

BIOLOGY OF THE REPTILIA

Edited by

CARL GANS

*State University of New York at Buffalo
Buffalo, N.Y., U.S.A.*

VOLUME 3

MORPHOLOGY C

Coeditor for this volume

THOMAS S. PARSONS

*University of Toronto
Toronto, Ontario
Canada*

1970

ACADEMIC PRESS
LONDON AND NEW YORK

ACADEMIC PRESS INC. (LONDON) LTD
Berkeley Square House
Berkeley Square
London, W1X 6BA

U.S. Edition published by

ACADEMIC PRESS INC.
111 Fifth Avenue
New York, New York 10003

598.1
G15h
V-3
1970

Library of Congress Catalog Card Number: 68-9113

ISBN: 012-274603-1

PRINTED IN GREAT BRITAIN BY
W. S. COWELL LTD
IPSWICH, SUFFOLK

Contributors to Volume 3

DALE E. BOCKMAN, *Department of Anatomy, Medical College of Ohio at Toledo, Toledo, Ohio 43614, U.S.A.*

NANCY B. CLARK, *Department of Zoology, The University of Connecticut, Storrs, Connecticut 06268, U.S.A.*

HERBERT C. DESSAUER, *Department of Biochemistry, Louisiana State University, School of Medicine, New Orleans, Louisiana 70112, U.S.A.*

R. DUGUY, *Muséum d'Histoire Naturelle, La Rochelle, France.*

MANFRED GABE, *Laboratoire d'Évolution des Êtres Organisés, Paris, France.*

MICHAEL D. LAGIOS, *Department of Anatomy and Pathology, University of California, School of Medicine, San Francisco, California, 94110, U.S.A.*

W. GARDNER LYNN, *Department of Biology, The Catholic University of America, Washington, D.C. 20017, U.S.A.*

MALCOLM R. MILLER, *Department of Anatomy and Pathology, University of California, School of Medicine, San Francisco, California 94110, U.S.A.*

HUBERT SAINT GIRONS, *Muséum National d'Histoire Naturelle, Écologie Générale, Brunoy, France.*

MARIE-CHARLOTTE SAINT GIRONS, *Muséum National d'Histoire Naturelle, Brunoy, France.*

The Editors would like to dedicate this volume to our friend,

WADE FOX

whose untimely death deprived us of a valued collaborator.

Preface

This, the third volume of the Biology of the Reptilia deals with aspects of the blood and of the endocrine system. As in the previous morphological volumes, most of the chapters treat only structure, with function relegated to the physiological volumes to follow.

Limited amounts of histophysiology and some general physiology are included for such topics as the parathyroid, the thyroid, and also for the adrenal; they are omitted for the hypophysis because the topic here is much more complicated and clearly requires a separate coverage under the general heading of physiology. It is hoped that the volume projected for that section will also deal with the most important effects of temperature on these systems.

The preface to the first volume of this series emphasized the editors' aim of facilitating future work. The summary statements of the contributing authors document again how much such additional work is needed. The need is threefold; we require a clear statement of interspecific variability, a characterization of the seasonal and physiological changes induced in the organ's histology, and the need to apply new techniques.

Variability is certainly quite inadequately known and the vast majority of the recorded observations have been made on less than one or two dozen species. Unfortunately the pattern of internal structure cannot be assumed to be similar among the orders of the class, among the families of an order, among the genera of a family, or among the species of a genus. The classification of organisms differs from Mendeleyev's periodic table for the chemical elements in that it is *not* predictive; the existing similarity can only be characterized *after* all of the included forms have been examined.

Many aspects here recorded are far more likely to reflect seasonal changes or those due to the animal's behavioral or physiological state than are other aspects of the animal's morphology. Many of the histological observations need to be checked for the influence of such modifying factors. The comparative studies based entirely on studies using light microscopy and histochemistry need to be reviewed with the electron microscope. A comparison of the accounts of H. Saint Girons and Gabe with the phylogenetically far more restrictive comparison of Clark, clearly points to some of the additional work that needs to be done on each of these organs.

It is the hope of the authors and of the editors that this summary of the present state of our knowledge will serve as a stimulus leading to a more accurate characterization of the similarities and differences between species and larger categories as well as to a more quantitative characterization of the dynamic structural pattern.

I wish to thank the authors, several of whom agreed to repeated and major changes in the nature of their required contributions. Drs. W. E. Adams, W. Andrew, D. Belkin, E. G. Butler, N. B. Clark, E. Cohen, W. B. Elliott, V. E. Engelbert, W. Frair, M. Gabe, J. E. Heath, E. von Herrath, V. H. Hutchison, O. P. Jones, P. Licht, W. G. Lynn, M. Miller, M. Moss, X. J. Musacchia, U de V. Pienaar, H. Rahn, H. I. Rosenberg, H. Saint Girons, M. C. Saint Girons, A. J. L. Strauss, H. Szarski, A. M. Taub, S. R. Telford, Jr., E. E. Williams, and A. Wright reviewed individual manuscripts and Mrs. Gloria Griffin and my wife provided extensive editorial assistance. My co-editor, Dr. Thomas S. Parsons shared all aspects of the work. Drs. James A. Peters and Heinz Wermuth critically read the proofs for usage and accuracy of the Latin names employed. National Science Foundation Grant GN 815 provided for some financial assistance and the Department of Biology of my University paid the considerable bills for postage and copying.

July, 1970   Carl Gans

Contents

8. The Adrenal

Manfred Gabe

9. The Pancreas

Malcolm R. Miller and Michael D. Lagios

CHAPTER 1

Blood Chemistry of Reptiles: Physiological and Evolutionary Aspects

HERBERT C. DESSAUER

Department of Biochemistry, Louisiana State University, School of Medicine, New Orleans, Louisiana, U.S.A.

I. Introduction

Active multicellular organisms require efficient circulatory systems to carry gases, nutrients, and waste materials to and from their tissues. Both volume and composition of the circulating fluids must be maintained within narrow limits (Lockwood, 1961), in spite of the changing availability of water, salts, and metabolites and their exchange with cells and extravascular fluids. In ectotherms, whose cells function or remain viable over broad ranges in temperature, mechanisms regulating blood volume and composition may be different from those characteristic of mammals (Bullock, 1955).

Homeostatic control systems and cellular requirements place far less stringent limits on the composition of the blood of reptiles than on that of endothermal animals. In a single species of turtle an osmotic pressure as low as 150 mOs/liter can occur under one circumstance and one as high as 450 mOs/liter under other conditions. Plasma of crocodilians may become virtually chloride free after feeding, with bicarbonate making up two thirds of total plasma anions. Calcium may exceed 200 mg % during estrus in snakes. Seventy per cent of the total hemoglobin of certain turtles may be nonfunctional in oxygen transport, existing as the methemoglobin derivative. Blood pH's of 6·5 and 8·1 have been observed under physiological conditions. Such values are unheard of in mammalian physiology, and probably are incompatible with endothermal life. "The maxim that life can exist only within a relatively small pH range . . . may only be true for homothermal animals" (Robin, 1962).

There is no such creature as a "typical" reptile. Chemical, physiological, and immunological findings impress upon one the differences between major groups. This chapter gathers information on the composition of the blood of reptiles and attempts to synthesize the resultant data in terms of reptilian

1

physiology and evolution. Only a bare beginning has been made in these areas. Many intriguing problems await the physiologist interested in reptiles, problems not answered by reference to concepts based upon mammalian physiology. Likewise, the biologist interested in evolution will find in blood a source of much information on speciation and on the interrelationships of living forms.

II. Blood Letting and Handling

Blood usually is obtained from unanesthetized animals, but on occasion, and especially with snakes, animals must be anesthetized. Anesthetics given by inhalation or by injection are useful (Kaplan and Taylor, 1957). As reptiles do not catabolize barbiturates rapidly, the dose of drugs such as nembutal must be chosen carefully (Karlstrom and Cook, 1955). Betz (1962) summarizes the literature on anesthesia of reptiles and describes the use of the tail and tongue reflexes for controlling the surgical plane of anesthesia in snakes. Fluothane appears to be an especially useful inhalation anesthetic (Hackenbrock and Finster, 1963).

Heparin, oxalate, citrate, ethylenediamine tetracetic acid, and ion exchange resins are effective anticoagulants (Kaplan, 1956). For direct decalcification of small samples, collect blood through a small column of resin attached to the syringe (Lund et al., 1957). Heparin is the anticoagulant of choice with turtles such as Chelydra serpentina whose red cells hemolyze in solution lacking calcium ion (Lyman, 1945).

Cardiac puncture of crocodilians, lizards and snakes is relatively easy as their hearts are located readily by the pulsations visible on the anteroventral body wall (Tiegel, 1880; Hopping, 1923; Cohen et al., 1964). Cardiac puncture is more complex with turtles (Gandal, 1958). One can approach the heart laterally by directing a long needle through the soft tissues between the plastron and carapace at the level of a front or rear leg. A more common practice is to tap the heart through a hole trephined in the anteromedial corner of the right abdominal plate of the plastron (Rapatz and Musacchia, 1957; Musacchia and Sievers, 1962). Reptiles generally survive a cardiac puncture if it is carefully done. Coulson and Hernandez (1964) have bled individual alligators as often as 10 times in a 24 hour period without causing any apparent injury. Turtles survive numerous blood lettings, living in laboratory tanks for years with the hole in their plastron sealed with a cork, wax or tape.

Other sites for blood letting are often useful in physiological experiments which require multiple sampling of blood. For crocodilians a convenient method is to cut the tip of the tail and "milk" the sample into a tube containing anticoagulant (Coulson and Hernandez, 1964). Major vessels of large lizards can be cannulated (Tucker, 1966; Moberly, 1968a). Turtle blood may be obtained from a femoral (Robin *et al.*, 1964; Haning and Thompson, 1965) or jugular vein (Lopes, 1955) or a carotid artery (Crenshaw, 1965; Berkson, 1966). Microliter samples can be obtained from the retroorbital space (Riley, 1960; Frair, 1963).

Analyses of blood constituents of reptiles date back to the late nineteenth century. Methods of analyses have undergone great changes in precision over the years. A listing of modern, simple micro-methods applicable to work on reptiles is given in the monograph on the alligator by Coulson and Hernandez (1964).

III. Composition of Blood Plasma

A. General

Plasma, making up some 60 to 80 per cent of blood volume, is a colorless or straw colored fluid in many species but is intensely pigmented in others (Brocq-Rousseu and Roussel, 1934, 1939; Putnam, 1960, 1965). In iguanid lizards and African chameleons its bright orange or yellow color reflects a high content of carotenoid pigments. Plasma of the snakes *Python*, *Bothrops* and *Mastigodryas* is greenish yellow due to a high content of carotenoids and riboflavin (Villela and Prado, 1945; Villela and Thein, 1967).

Plasma of reptiles, like that of all vertebrates, contains a great variety of different substances with most being present in trace quantities. "Representative" levels of major constituents, especially those commonly measured in blood studies, are collected in Tables I and II. When a number of laboratories have contributed data on the same species such results have been averaged. Only analyses on active animals, maintained at room temperature under fasting conditions, have been included. These averaged values represent orders of magnitude rather than fixed levels as the range of variability for most constituents is great even between individuals of a single population sample. Too little is known of reptilian physiology to define strictly basal conditions for any reptilian species.

B. Low Molecular Weight Components

1. *Electrolytes*

a. *Representative levels.* Plasma of each of the several orders of the Reptilia shows certain trends in osmotic pressure, pH, and concentration of sodium, chloride, and bicarbonate ions (Table I; Dittmer, 1961). Total osmolarity, due primarily to electrolytes in all reptiles, is relatively high in snakes, lizards, and sea turtles, but is low in fresh water turtles. Even snakes such as *Natrix*, which live close to or in fresh water, have blood with a high salt content.

TABLE I

Plasma Electrolytes

Species	Osmotic pressure mOs/liter	pH	Na+	K+	Ca++	Mg++	Cl-	HCO₃⁻	Pᵢ	SO₄=	Source[a]
			mM/liter								
TESTUDINES											
Chelydra serpentina	315	7·62	132	3·2	3·8	2·7	76	48	1·3	0·3	12, 29, 40, 47
Kinosternon subrubrum	288		121	4·2	3·5	1·0	98	30	1·7		12, 47
Sternotherus odoratus	282	7·44	126	3·8			84	25	1·8		12
Chrysemys picta		7·77	143	3·2	2·5	4·8	85	47	1·0	0·8	24, 47, 57, 60
Emydoidea blandingii			140	3·8	3·3	2·1	91	39	1·3	1·3	47, 57
Emys orbicularis	249							40	2·1		4, 37, 55
Graptemys geographica			124	2·4	3·4	0·5	87	39	1·2	0·4	47
Pseudemys scripta		7·56	121	4·1	2·8	2·2	81	40	1·1	0·2	12, 7, 24, 26, 45, 47, 50, 51, 52, 57
Terrapene carolina	345	7·68	130	4·7	1·3	3·5	108		2·4	1·2	12, 24, 34
Terrapene ornata	317			4·6	1·7	2·0	104		0·8		12
Caretta caretta	408		157	2·2	3·1	2·9	110	36	3·0		4, 5, 18, 19, 31, 44, 47
Lepidochelys olivacea			163	6·6	5·2	1·4	108	29	3·5	0·3	47
Chelonia mydas	321	7·45	158	1·5				33			3, 31
Testudo graeca	317			7·8	4·0		100				5
Testudo hermanni	274		127	4·4	2·3		95				25
Trionyx ferox			113	6·8	1·7	1·5	90				12
Trionyx spiniferus			144						2·0		22
SQUAMATA (Sauria)											
Gekko gecko			157	4·6			123				12
Anolis carolinensis		7·26	171	4·5	2·9		127	15	2·6		12, 35
Anolis			159	2·9	2·9		133	15	2·3		42
C⋯ana ⋯nthura		7·22			1·1	1·1					30

Species										References
Sceloporus occidentalis		7·50	102	4·2			127		2·5	16, 49
Amphibolurus ornatus			150		2·5					41
Agama agama			179	5·0	2·9					61
Agama impalearis	349		152	5·2	2·5					53
Uromastyx acanthinurus	307		150	7·1						59
Chamaeleo chamaeleon							114			59
Eumeces fasciatus							130			12
Trachydosaurus rugosus			151	4·7						12
Cnemidophorus sexlineatus							128			1, 46
Tupinambis nigropunctatus			136	3·5			110			12
Ophisaurus ventralis	388	7·16								12
Gerrhonotus multicarinatus	353	7·20								12
Heloderma suspectum						2·3	130	27		23
Heloderma horridum			158	4·1			114			54
Varanus griseus			181	3·5	3·1	2·5	148	31		27
SQUAMATA (Ophidia)										
Lichanura roseofusca	375		151	4·1			106			12
Coluber constrictor	384	7·63	162	4·9	3·2	1·5	101	14	2·5	12, 32
Elaphe obsoleta	313		147	5·4	3·6	2·5	131			12
Farancia abacura			155	4·4	3·3		115			12
Heterodon platyrhinos		7·53	148	4·5			126			12
Lampropeltis getulus	345	7·46	156	3·9	2·9	1·9	121	12	2·4	12, 32
Masticophis flagellum	341		176	5·9	3·4	2·1	120	10	1·1	12
Pituophis catenifer	381		164	4·1	3·6		136			12
Rhinocheilus lecontei				5·0			122			12
Natrix erythrogaster		7·22	192	6·4			146	10		12
Natrix natrix			159	4·0						42
Natrix rhombifera	359	7·32	155	4·6	3·9	1·3	139	7	2·3	12
Natrix sipedon	318	7·29	159	3·5	3·8		127	11		10, 12, 32, 38
Regina grahamiae	354		156	4·3	3·8		120			12
Thamnophis elegans	347	7·20	161	5·4	3·4	0·8	134	14	1·9	12
Thamnophis ordinoides	349	7·27	159	5·4			126	10		12
Thamnophis sauritus	324	7·19	159		2·7	2·0	125	14	1·6	12, 13

TABLE I—continued

Species	Osmotic pressure mOs/liter	pH	Na$^+$	K$^+$	Ca^{++}	Mg^{++}	Cl$^-$	HCO$_3^-$	P$_i$	SO$_4^=$	Source[a]
					mM/liter						
SQUAMATA (Ophidia)—continued											
Thamnophis sirtalis	329	7·30	152	5·9	3·0	1·5	130		0·7		12,14
Homalopsis buccata			162	4·8	4·2						2
Micrurus fulvius							134				12
Agkistrodon contortrix	361	7·32	154	5·1	3·5	2·3	138	12			12
Agkistrodon piscivorus	401		151	5·0	3·4	1·7	116	10	1·8		12,32
Crotalus atrox	345		154	3·7	3·7	1·8	131				12,39
Crotalus horridus							112				6
Crotalus viridis	325		146	3·6			123		3·5		12
Vipera aspis			170	6·5	3·5		130				36
Laticauda semifasciata	320		159								21
CROCODILIA											
Alligator mississippiensis	284	7·48	141	3·8	2·6	1·5	112	20			8,9
Crocodylus acutus			149	7·9	3·4	1·9	117	11			15

[a]Numbers designate reference source given in key below:

1. Bentley, 1959
2. Bergman, 1951
3. Berkson, 1966
4. Bottazzi, 1908
5. Burian, 1910
6. Carmichael and Petcher, 1945
7. Collip, 1921 a, b; 1920
8. Coulson and Hernandez, 1964
9. Coulson et al., 1950a
10. Dantzler, 1967
11. Dastugue and Joy, 1943

14. Dessauer et al., 1956
15. Dill and Edwards, 1931
16. Dill and Edwards, 1935
17. Dill et al., 1935
18. Drilhon and Marcoux, 1942
19. Drilhon et al., 1937
20. Dunlap, 1955
21. Dunson and Taub, 1967
22. Dunson and Weymouth, 1965
23. Edwards and Dill, 1935
24. Gaumer and Goodnight, 1957
25. Giles Baillien and Schoffeniels, 1965

28. Hailing and Thompson, 1963
29. Henderson, 1928
30. Hernandez and Coulson, 1951
31. Holmes and McBean, 1964
32. Hutton, 1958
33. Hutton, 1960
34. Hutton and Goodnight, 1957
35. Hutton and Ortman, 1957
36. Izard et al., 1961
37. Laskowski, 1936
38. LeBrie and Sutherland, 1962
39. Luck and Keeler, 1929
40. McCay, 1931
41. Mullen, 1962
42. Munday and Blane, 1961
43. Nera, 1925
44. Prosser et al., 1950

46. Shoemaker, et al., 1966
47. Smith, 1929
48. Sutton, Unpublished
49. Templeton, 1964
50. Urist and Schjeide, 1960/61
51. Williams, Unpublished
52. Wilson, 1939
53. Wright and Jones, 1957
54. Zarafonetis and Kalas, 1960
55. Verbiinskaya, 1944
56. Tucker, 1966
57. Stenroos and Bowman, 1968
58. Moberly, 1968a, b
59. Tercafs and Vassas, 1967
60. Clark, 1967
61. Bradshaw and Shoemaker, 1967

TABLE II

Packed Cell Volume and Certain Organic Constituents of Blood

Species	Packed Cell Volume %	Hemoglobin g%	Total Plasma Protein g%	Glucose mg%	Urea mg%	Uric Acid mg%	Source[a]
				TESTUDINES			
Chelydra serpentina	25	5·9*	4·7	33	96	2	6, 13, 20, 23, 35, 37, 42, 66, 76, 79, 84, 86, 102
Kinosternon subrubrum	23		5·6				20, 35
Sternotherus odoratus	33	11·2	4·5				20, 35, 39
Sternotherus minor	35	9·9	4·0				39, 79
Deirochelys reticularia	20	8·3	4·2				35, 39, 79
Chrysemys picta	23	11·2	4·4	76	37	2	35, 37, 57, 70, 75, 79, 92, 98
Clemmys guttata		4·5*	6·1				20, 71
Emys orbicularis	24	6·6*		50			2, 35, 52, 54, 74, 87, 95
Malaclemys terrapin		9·2					39
Kachuga smithii				78			97
Pseudemys dorbigni				91			15, 34, 63, 89, 99
Pseudemys floridana		8·1					82
Pseudemys scripta	26	8·0	3·6	70	22	1	20, 35, 36, 39, 44, 45, 48, 50, 55, 56, 91, 92, 98
Terrapene carolina	28	5·9*	4·5	36	30	2	3, 4, 20, 35, 37, 50
Testudo kleinmanni	27		6·6				60
Testudo hermanni					78		38
Gopherus polyphemus	30		3·5				35, 79, 102
Caretta caretta	32		4·7	60	45		12, 32, 35, 62, 85, 102
Chelonia mydas	30	6·6*	2·9		52	8	8, 35, 58, 62, 79, 102

Lissemys punctata				40			97
Pelusios			4·3				35
Chelodina longicollis			3·3				35
Phrynops geoffroanus				99			34
SQUAMATA (Sauria)							
Gekko gecko				93	4		20
Coleonyx variegatus				94	4		39, 83
Hemidactylus		10·8		54	7		39, 97
Anolis carolinensis	28	7·0*	4·1	172			20, 51, 67
Crotaphytus collaris		7·8*				8	19
Ctenosaura acanthura	35	6·0*	6·8	192	2	4	43
Iguana iguana	30	7·1*	4·5	155	1	5	43, 79, 102
Phrynosoma cornutum		7·0*	4·4	191	2		19, 93
Phrynosoma douglassii		7·7*					19
Phrynosoma modestum		9·1*					19
Sauromalus obesus	31	8·4*	4·9				26
Sceloporus clarkii		6·2*					19
Sceloporus graciosus		8·2*					19
Sceloporus jarrovii		6·1*					19
Sceloporus occidentalis		7·1*					19
Sceloporus poinsettii		7·5*					19
Sceloporus undulatus		7·2*					19, 20
Uta stansburiana	35	6·5*	3·0	141			19, 101
Cordylus cataphractus						1	20
Uromastyx		4·6		120			97, 104
Lacerta muralis		9·0					2, 74
Lacerta viridis			4·6	173			65
Chamaeleo chamaeleo					3		20
Eumeces fasciatus			3·0	107			20
Eumeces obsoletus		9·4*		112			18, 67, 68
Anguis fragilis		11·3					2, 29, 74
Cnemidophorus sexlineatus				93			20
Cnemidophorus tigris		7·2*					19
Cnemidophorus sackii		8·7*					19

Table II—continued

Packed Cell Volume and Certain Organic Constituents of Blood

Species	Packed Cell Volume %	Hemoglobin g%	Total Plasma Protein g%	Glucose mg%	Urea mg%	Uric mg%	Source[a]
SQUAMATA (Sauria)—continued							
Tupinambis nigropunctatus			7·8		2		20, 79
Tupinambis teguixin				104			72
Gerrhonotus multicarinatus		7·2*	4·5				19, 20
Ophisaurus ventralis	31	6·9	5·4				20
Heloderma horridum	30	8·0		45	3		94
Heloderma suspectum	26	8·1*	6·3	109	1		20, 31, 76
Varanus	27		6·9	106	2		20, 40, 41, 60, 97, 103
SQUAMATA (Ophidia)							
Boa constrictor	29		6·5	70			9, 102
Lichanura roseofusca				73	6	1	20, 79
Epicrates cenchria				93			9
Eryx johnii				25			97
Coluber constrictor	26		5·0	75	4	6	11, 12, 13, 20, 48
Coluber florulentus	26		6·2				60
Heterodon platyrhinos			4·5	52	5		20
Lampropeltis getulus	23		5·8	59	2	6	12, 48, 76, 77, 79
Rhinocheilus lecontei				88	2		20
Coluber viridiflavus				65			78
Xenodon merremii				55			47
Natrix cyclopion		6·5		65	5		20, 39
Natrix natrix	37		4·3	57			69, 80
Natrix tessellatus	33		6·2				59, 60
Natrix rhombifera			5·5	30	5		20
Natrix sipedon	23		5·7	49	3	6	12, 13, 17, 20, 22, 23,

Species							References
...ophis...	33	8·1	4·5		5		11, 12, 20, 22, 79
Thamnophis elegans	25		4·0				20, 22
Thamnophis sauritus	30		4·4				20, 22
Farancia abacura		7·5	4·9				20, 39, 79
Storeria dekayi		10·8	3·5				20, 39
Micrurus nigrocinctus				107			9
Naja naja			4·4	29			12, 13, 79, 97
Agkistrodon contortrix	28		5·2				20
Agkistrodon piscivorus	19		4·6	52	5	6	12, 13, 20, 23, 48, 76, 79
Bothrops atrox				60			9, 73
Crotalus atrox	45	8·6	5·2	60	1	2	20, 23, 64, 79
Crotalus horridus			3·5	60	11	3	12, 23, 79
Crotalus ruber			5·2	70			9, 12, 13, 20
Crotalus viridis			2·9	48	0	2	12, 13, 20
Vipera aspis		10·5	5·5	40	10	4	1, 28, 33
Vipera				34			88, 97
Typhlops				84	1		20
CROCODILIA							
Alligator mississippiensis	20	7·1*	5·1	74	0	3	5, 7, 16, 25, 46, 102
Caiman	26	8·6*	5·9				20, 24, 79, 102
Crocodylus niloticus	35		6·5				60
Crocodylus acutus	26	9·0*		101			9, 24, 102

*Calculated from oxygen capacity measurement: values based on oxygen capacity were given preference in tabulation.

[a]Numbers designate reference source given in key below:

1. Agid et al., 1961a
2. Alder and Huber, 1923
3. Altland and Parker, 1955
4. Altland and Thompson, 1958
5. Andersen, 1961
6. Andreen-Svedberg, 1933
7. Austin et al., 1927
8. Berkson, 1966
9. Britton and Kline, 1939
10. Carmichael and Petcher, 1945
11. Clark, 1953
12. Cohen, 1954
13. Cohen, 1955
14. Cohen and Stickler, 1958
15. Corrêa et al., 1960
16. Coulson and Hernandez, 1964
17. Dantzler, 1967
18. Dawson, 1960
19. Dawson and Poulson, 1962
20. Dessauer, Unpublished, 1952
21. Dessauer and Fox, 1959
22. Dessauer et al., 1956
23. Deutsch and McShan, 1949
24. Dill and Edwards, 1931a, 1931b

TABLE II—*continued*

25. Dill and Edwards, 1935
26. Dill et al., 1935
27. DiMaggio and Dessauer, 1963
28. Duguy, 1962
29. Duguy, 1963
30. Dunlap, 1955
31. Edwards and Dill, 1935
32. Fandard and Ranc, 1912
33. Fine et al., 1954
34. Foglia et al., 1955
35. Frair, Unpublished, 1964
36. Frankel et al., 1966
37. Gaumer and Goodnight, 1957
38. Gilles-Ballien and Schoffeniels, 1965
39. Goin and Jackson, 1965
40. Haggag et al., 1965
41. Haggag et al., 1966
42. Henderson, 1928
43. Hernandez and Coulson, 1951
44. Hirschfeld and Gordon, 1961
45. Hirschfeld and Gordon, 1965
46. Hopping, 1923
47. Houssay and Biasotti, 1933
48. Hutton, 1958
49. Hutton, 1960
50. Hutton and Goodnight, 1957
51. Hutton and Ortman, 1957

52. Issekutz and Végh, 1928
53. Izard et al., 1961
54. Kanungo, 1961
55. Kaplan, 1960b
56. Kaplan and Rueff, 1960
57. Karr and Lewis, 1916
58. Khalil, 1947
59. Khalil and Abdel-Messeih, 1962
60. Khalil and Abdel-Messeih, 1963
61. Korzhuev and Kruglova, 1957
62. Lewis, 1964
63. Lopes, 1955
64. Luck and Keeler, 1929
65. Lustig and Ernst, 1936
66. McCay, 1931
67. Miller and Wurster, 1956
68. Miller and Wurster, 1958
69. Munday and Blane, 1961
70. Musacchia and Sievers, 1962
71. Payne and Burke, 1964
72. Penhos et al., 1965
73. Prado, 1946a
74. Prosser et al., 1950
75. Rapatz and Musacchia, 1957
76. Rapoport and Guest, 1941
77. Rhaney, 1948
78. Saviano and De Francisis, 1948

79. Seal, 1964
80. Seniow, 1963
81. Sheeler and Barber, 1965
82. Southworth and Redfield, 1925/26
83. Sutton, Unpublished
84. Steggerda and Essex, 1957
85. Tercafs et al., 1963
86. Vars, 1934
87. Vlädescu, 1964, 1965b
88. Vlädescu, 1965a
89. Wagner, 1955
90. Wiley and Lewis, 1927
91. Wilson, 1939
92. Wilson et al., 1960
93. Wolfe, 1939
94. Zarafonetis and Kalas, 1960
95. Verbiinskaya, 1944
96. Tucker, 1966
97. Zain-ul-Abedin and Qazi, 1965
98. Stenroos and Bowman, 1968
99. Marques and Kraemer, 1968
100. Rao and David, 1967
101. Hadley and Burns, 1967
102. Thorson, 1968
103. Menon, 1952
104. Khalil and Yanni, 1959

Osmolarity of blood of crocodiles and fresh water turtles most commonly is equal to or slightly less than that of human blood, about 290 mOs/liter. Sodium, chloride, and bicarbonate ions account for over 85 per cent of the osmotically active components in plasma of all reptiles. Sodium, contributing about 90 per cent of the cations, is high in lizards, snakes, and marine turtles. Chloride plus bicarbonate contribute 80 to 90 per cent of the anions. Chloride levels above 115 mEq/liter typify lizards and snakes; other reptiles have lower levels. Bicarbonate is generally high in turtles, making up about a third of the total anions; it contributes only 10 to 15 per cent of the anions in other reptiles. Carbonic anhydrase is involved in renal aspects of the control of anion levels in the alligator (Hernandez and Coulson, 1954; Coulson and Hernandez, 1957). Curiously, the alligator produces an alkaline urine, conserving both sodium and chloride of plasma by excreting high concentrations of ammonium bicarbonate (Coulson and Hernandez, 1955). Blood pH of turtles is relatively alkaline, paralleling the elevated bicarbonate. A pH of 7·8 is common in control animals; blood of other reptiles is more acidic, often with a pH below 7·4. Marked changes in rate and depth of breathing are common features of reptilian behavior. These affect carbon dioxide tension and may lead to sudden changes in blood pH (Stullken et al., 1942; Andersen, 1961; Schmidt-Nielsen et al., 1966). Ionic gradients between cells and plasma are also affected (Collip, 1921b).

Plasma potassium concentration appears to be under relatively stringent control. A level of 3 to 6 mEq/liter characterizes all reptiles; higher values usually indicate analyses on hemolyzed samples. The significance of the low potassium values for the turtles *Chelonia* and *Caretta* is not known. Potassium levels undergo only minor alterations during feeding, temperature changes, osmotic stress, and other episodes in the life cycle of reptiles which drastically alter electrolyte balance. The reptilian kidney is very efficient in clearing potassium from the blood (Smith, 1951; Coulson and Hernandez, 1964; Shoemaker et al., 1966). Nasal glands play an effective role in potassium excretion in the lizards *Ctenosaura pectinata* and *Sauromalus obesus* (Templeton, 1964). The adrenal gland is involved in the control of potassium and sodium levels in the lizards *Trachydosaurus rugosus* and *Agama agama* and a snake *Natrix natrix* (Wright and Jones, 1957; Bentley, 1959).

Magnesium increases during winter torpor in the turtles *Pseudemys* and *Terrapene* (Hutton and Goodnight, 1957) and in the lizard *Varanus griseus* (Haggag et al., 1965). Total plasma calcium and magnesium attain remarkably high levels during estrus (see Sect. III C, Part 6), but levels of ionic calcium and magnesium may not undergo great change (Grollman, 1927) as most of the alkaline earths appear to be protein bound (Dessauer and Fox, 1959). Large fluctuations in ionic calcium or potassium seriously affect cell permeability (Maizels, 1956; Lockwood, 1961) and cardiac rhythms (Mullen,

1962). However, the lizard *Ctenosaura pectinata* survived an injection of potassium which tripled its usual plasma level (Templeton, 1964).

b. *Temperature and electrolytes.* Body temperature has a major role in the control of fluid and electrolyte balance in reptiles; the physical properties of electrolytes in solution and also the metabolic rate of the organisms are altered by temperature change. Carbon dioxide production and its hydration, solubility, and dissociation are all affected (Edsall and Wyman, 1958). Temperature changes can drastically affect acid base balance. In both a living turtle *Pseudemys scripta* and in an *in vitro* sample of its plasma, a rise in temperature results in an increase in carbon dioxide tension and a decrease in pH; bicarbonate remains constant in the *in vitro* system but rises in the intact animal (Robin, 1962; see also Dontcheff and Kayser, 1937; Gordon and Frankel, 1963; Frankel *et al.*, 1966). Similar responses have been observed in crocodiles (Austin *et al.*, 1927) and lizards (Edwards and Dill, 1935; Tucker, 1966). Blood pH dropped as low as 6·75 in a chuckwalla, *Sauromalus obesus*, maintained at 38°C (Dill *et al.*, 1935). Acid base changes noted in reptiles during winter torpor may result from low temperature (Grundhauser, 1960; Haggag *et al.*, 1965).

Inhibition of ion-transport at low temperatures has the overall effect of lowering plasma sodium. The emydine turtles *Chrysemys picta* and *Pseudemys scripta* often incur hemodilution during cold torpor (Musacchia and Sievers, 1956; Musacchia and Grundhauser, 1958; Hutton, 1960). The softshell turtle *Trionyx spiniferus* may lose over half of its plasma sodium during winter because active sodium transport by pharyngeal villi is suppressed by cold (Dunson and Weymouth, 1965). Short term cold exposure of the snake *Natrix* and the lizard *Anolis* leads to a decrease in both sodium and potassium (Munday and Blane, 1961). Contributing to such changes is the shift of sodium into intracellular fluids (Maizels, 1956) and probably losses of sodium through the kidney whose tubules lose their capacity for reabsorbing sodium when cooled (Hernandez and Coulson, 1957; Coulson and Hernandez, 1964). In the Greek tortoise *Testudo hermanni*, however, osmotic pressure and plasma sodium and chloride attain maximum values during the winter (Gilles-Baillien and Schoffeniels, 1965).

c. *Water and salt availability.* Reptiles tolerate marked extremes of hydration. Regulation of plasma osmolarity seems less critical than in many other vertebrates. The range of variation among 7 specimens of a tortoise (species not given), 278 to 400 mOs/liter, was three times greater than ranges observed in a frog and a number of birds and mammals (Aldred, 1940). Sea turtles *Chelonia mydas* (Holmes and McBean, 1964) and *Caretta caretta* are also able to live in fresh water. The osmotic pressure of *Caretta caretta*, accidently maintained in fresh water for three years, dropped from above 350 mOs/liter to 211 mOs/liter. The change chiefly involved a marked decrease in sodium and chloride (Tercafs *et al.*, 1963). A turtle of estuarian ecology, *Malaclemys terrapin centrata*, survived an experiment in which it was maintained for 14 days in 3·3% saline followed by 10 days in 6·6% saline – a solution of twice the osmolarity of sea water. Plasma sodium rose to about 170 mEq/liter in the hypertonic environment. The land turtle *Terrapene carolina* survived only 4 days in the 3·3% saline (Bentley *et al.*, 1967). Some regulation of salt content occurs, however, since blood osmolarity of species that survive such treatment remains very different from that of either sea or fresh water.

Some lizards and probably also snakes have high tolerance to hypernatremia. In desert dwelling agamid lizards blood osmotic pressure during dehydration may exceed 400 mOs/liter (Tercafs and Vassas, 1967). *Trachydosaurus rugosus*, a lizard of the Australian desert, usually has 150 mEq/liter of plasma sodium. During the summer water loss through the kidney is nil, but sodium rises to an average 195 mEq/liter as a result of evaporation. In their arid habitat *Trachydosaurus* apparently "conserves body water at the expense of abandoning maintenance of body fluid composition" (Bentley, 1959). Similar changes occur in *Amphibolurus ornatus* (Bradshaw and Shoemaker, 1967). During periods of water excess the lizard *Varanus griseus* stores water in its tissues (Khalil and Abdel-Messeih, 1954, 1959a and b, 1961). Subspecies of the water snake *Natrix sipedon* adapted to brackish water habitat avoid drinking salty water (Pettus, 1958). Widely different values for plasma sodium are often reported for the same species of lizard or snake, e.g. for *Lampropeltis getulus* of 124 mEq/liter (Hutton and Goodnight, 1957) and 165 mEq/liter (Dittmer, 1961).

In maintaining the osmotic pressure of the blood, the kidney is of prime importance (Smith, 1932, 1951), but specialized accessory organs contribute to the control. Fresh water turtles lack sodium ion in their environment. Their kidneys conserve sodium by excreting a dilute urine low in sodium. Specialized cells in the pharynx of *Trionyx spiniferus* contribute to salt stores by absorbing sodium from "fresh water" which contains as little as 5 mM/liter (Dunson and Weymouth, 1965). The kidney of reptiles cannot produce a urine of higher osmolarity than blood. Turtles living in marine habitats, *Caretta caretta* and *Malaclemys terrapin*, maintain the osmotic pressure of their blood lower than that of sea water by excreting concentrated salt solutions through orbital salt glands. In the marine iguana *Amblyrhynchus cristatus* a nasal salt gland performs this function (Schmidt-Nielsen and Fänge, 1958; Schmidt-Nielsen, 1962–1963). The sea snake *Laticauda semifasciata* maintains an osmotic pressure of between 290 and 350 mOs/liter by extrarenal salt excretion through a gland lying in the roof of its mouth (Dunson and Taub, 1967).

d. *Excitement and feeding.* No other group of animals is known to undergo the drastic shifts in blood pH and anion distribution that occur in reptiles during daily physiological events. Moderate excitement can lead to falls in pH which could be considered severe acidosis in a mammal. A drop in pH follows a rise in lactic acid; the lactate produced in mild excitement displaces, equivalent for equivalent, bicarbonate ions in the extracellular fluids. Periods of apnea may contribute to the fall in pH (Schmidt-Nielsen *et al.*, 1966). Handling, marked sudden changes in temperature (Austin *et al.*, 1927), and anesthesia will induce such responses. Bicarbonate levels of snakes anesthetized with ether may drop to 4 or 5 mEq/liter and blood pH may fall to 6·7 (Dessauer, unpublished). In alligators injected with epinephrine to magnify the response, lactic acid rose to 30 mEq/liter and the pH dropped as low as 6·54. Early in the experiment the rise in lactate was matched by an equivalent fall in bicarbonate; later, lactate production was buffered by the release of sodium from intracellular spaces (Hernandez and Coulson, 1956, 1958; Coulson and Hernandez, 1964). Anaerobic glycolysis, which often provides most of the energy during activity, contributes high concentrations of lactate to the blood. The return of lactate to the resting level is most rapid in lizards near their preferred body temperature (Moberly, 1968a).

All reptiles become acidemic when excited, but with alligators "the simple act of eating forces them into an equally pronounced alkalosis" (Coulson and Hernandez, 1964). Soon after a meal a shift in the anion distribution begins. Plasma chloride is slowly replaced, equivalent for equivalent, by bicarbonate. Total osmotic pressure and sodium and potassium concentration remains almost constant (Fig. 1). In one alligator plasma chloride dropped to 7 mEq/liter and bicarbonate rose to 105 mEq/liter. The maximum blood pH observed

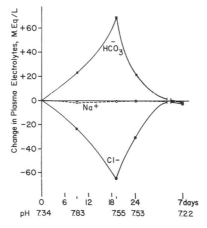

FIG. 1. Electrolyte changes in blood plasma of an alligator (*A. mississippiensis*) following feeding. Graph illustrates the reciprocal nature of the exchange of chloride for bicarbonate and the reverse exchange after the 18th hour of the experiment (from Coulson and Hernandez, 1964).

following feeding was 8·09. Bicarbonate rises for about 18 hours after which the reverse exchange commences. Ingestion of food apparently stimulates the cells of the stomach to secrete gastric juice containing copious quantities of hydrochloric acid. Chloride is transferred from the blood with hydrogen ions produced by the metabolic activities of stomach cells. Bicarbonate, another product of the cells, replaces the chloride in the blood (Coulson et al., 1950b). The lizards *Iguana iguana* and *Ctenosaura acanthura* do not exhibit such a marked "alkaline tide" (Hernandez and Coulson, 1951). Although feeding leads to the secretion of hydrochloric acid into the stomach of *Chrysemys picta* (Fox and Musacchia, 1959), the effect of feeding on blood electrolytes of turtles is not known.

e. *Diving and burrowing.* Diving and burrowing reptiles are often exposed to oxygen lack for prolonged periods (Andersen, 1966). Crocodiles, lizards, and snakes are usually able to survive without oxygen about 45 minutes at 22°C. The tolerance of turtles to anoxia is remarkable, exceeding that of all other tetrapod vertebrates. Turtles of all families except the Cheloniidae (sea turtles) commonly survive without oxygen at 22°C for about 12 hours; sea turtles are less tolerant, having an average survival time of 2 hours (Belkin, 1963, 1965). In the laboratory some *Chrysemys picta* have lived for 3 to 4 months submerged at 1·5 to 3·5°C. Many turtles probably spend the entire winter under water (Musacchia, 1959).

Blood composition changes drastically during a dive, but the patterns of changes are different in land and fresh water turtles than in other reptiles. In 1933 Johlin and Moreland found that a fresh water turtle (species not given) would survive over 24 hours in an atmosphere of pure nitrogen or carbon monoxide even though its blood pH fell to 6·8 and lactate rose to a reported 110 mEq/liter. Bellamy and Petersen (1968) have noticed similar responses in *Testudo* and *Podocnemis*. Robin and coworkers (1964) have followed the course of blood changes in such turtles during an extended submergence (Fig. 2). Soon after *Pseudemys scripta* submerge, blood oxygen tension drops to near zero where it remains throughout the dive; carbon dioxide tension increases to about 100 to 150 mm of mercury, reaching a plateau after 24 hours. Blood pH falls steadily to about 6·8 and then decreases more slowly. Lactate rises throughout submersion; increases of 50 mEq/liter occur in 24 hours. Nothing is known of the fate of other electrolytes during the dive or of the pattern of blood changes which occur after the turtle emerges from the water.

A number of adaptations make possible the remarkable diving capability of turtles. Bucco-pharyngeal and cloacal absorption contribute minor quantities of oxygen (Root, 1949; Girgis, 1961; Musacchia and Chladek 1961; Belkin, 1962; Robin et al., 1964). The heart beats more slowly (Belkin, 1964) and a functional ventricular shunt allows blood to bypass the lungs (Millen et al.,

1964). Their energy requirement under water may be less than in air, allowing glycolysis and other anaerobic pathways to meet their needs (Belkin, 1963a, 1968; Robin *et al.*, 1964). Stores of glycogen in tissues of turtles

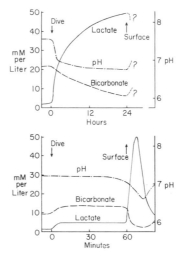

FIG. 2. Electrolyte changes in blood plasma of reptiles following a dive. Upper curves: time sequence of changes in blood of the turtle *Pseudemys scripta* (plotted from data of Robin *et al.*, 1964). Lower curves: time sequence of blood changes in *Alligator mississippiensis*; note difference in time scale from upper graph (plotted from data of Andersen, 1961).

(Issekutz and Végh, 1928; Daw *et al.*, 1967) exceed those of other reptiles (Dessauer, 1953; Agid *et al.*, 1961b; Coulson and Hernandez, 1964). Although pyruvate is a receptor for the hydrogen produced by glycolysis, other acceptors probably are involved which yield products causing less disturbance of tissue pH than lactic acid (Belkin, 1963a). The disulfide-sulfhydryl interchange involved in polymerization of turtle hemoglobins may represent such an acceptor system (see Section IV B below). Hydrogen ions generated during the dive are partially buffered by bicarbonate of plasma and probably by pools of coelomic fluids. Fresh water and land turtles store large volumes of such extravascular, extracellular fluids. These contain high concentrations of sodium bicarbonate (Smith, 1929; Thorson, 1963; Robin *et al.*, 1964).

Adaptations to diving in alligators, lizards, snakes, and, to some extent, sea turtles are similar to those of diving birds and mammals: (1) marked bradycardia with decreased cardiac output, and (2) vasoconstriction, preventing blood from circulating through muscle beds during the dive (Andersen, 1961, 1966; Murdaugh and Jackson, 1962; Murphy *et al.*, 1964; Berkson, 1966). Andersen (1961) has analyzed certain blood constituents of alligators during and after emergence from a dive (Fig. 2). In contrast to

Pseudemys scripta, blood changes are relatively slight in the alligator during submergence. The pH of the blood and levels of bicarbonate and lactate do not change as excessively. The animals apparently remain submerged only as long as some oxygen is present in circulating blood. When the animal surfaces, the vascular beds of the muscles dilate and the lactate produced during submersion diffuses into the blood. The profuse influx of lactate causes a sharp drop in pH and a marked decrease in bicarbonate. Within an hour blood levels adjust to predive values. The lizard *Iguana iguana* (Moberly, 1968b) and the water snakes, *Natrix cyclopion* and *N. sipedon*, undergo similar changes during a dive (Murdaugh and Jackson, 1962). Sea turtles *Chelonia mydas* do not exhibit large volumes of interstitial fluids (Smith, 1929; Thorson, 1963) and seem to respond to oxygen lack more like the alligator than like other turtles (Berkson, 1966). Most such experiments involve animals forced to dive. The demonstration that changes in physiological parameters may involve both submergence and withdrawal components (Gaunt and Gans, 1969) suggests the merit of partitioning as well as the observed changes in the blood.

2. *Organic Components*

Blood plasma of reptiles contains a large variety of organic compounds of low molecular weight. Some, such as glucose, are present in moderate concentration but many occur only in trace amounts. Daily events in the life of a reptile as well as seasonal metabolic cycles influence the blood levels of a number of these substances.

a. *Glucose.* Representative levels of one major metabolite, glucose, appear in Table II. The majority of these values represent total reducing substance and give somewhat high estimates of glucose. The data of Coulson and Hernandez (1964) on *Alligator mississippiensis* and that of Zain-ul-Abedin and Qazi (1965) on a variety of turtles, snakes, and lizards were obtained by means of the glucose oxidase method, a technique of high specificity. Glucose levels in lizards are consistently higher than in other reptiles. Values exceeding 150 mg% are commonly observed, especially among the Iguanidae. Among other vertebrates only birds have such elevated blood sugars (Miller, 1961). Most of the reducing substance of lizards is probably glucose; only 27 mg% of reducing substance in *Anolis carolinensis* was not fermentable (Dessauer, 1953). Analyses for glucose are commonly carried out on blood rather than plasma, but glucose is largely absent from red blood cells. Cells of the snapping turtle (McCay, 1931; Andreen-Svedberg, 1933) and the American alligator (Coulson and Hernandez, 1964) do not contain glucose.

Physiological events are accompanied by appreciable fluctuations in blood sugar in all major groups of reptiles. A rise in temperature leads to an increase in glucose in alligators (Austin *et al.*, 1927) and in the snake *Vipera aspis*

(Agid *et al.*, 1961b), but a fall in glucose in the turtle *Emys orbicularis* (Vlădescu, 1964). Glucose rises sharply in slider turtles (*Pseudemys*) subjected to sudden drops in temperature (Hutton, 1964). Crocodiles and snakes (Britton and Kline, 1939) exhibit an emotional hyperglycemia of between 10 and 25 per cent. During extended dives the fresh water turtles *Pseudemys scripta* and *Chrysemys picta* utilize anaerobic glycolysis as a source of energy and their blood glucose increases markedly (Robin *et al.*, 1964; Daw *et al.*, 1967). Similarly, after 24 hours in an atmosphere of nitrogen or carbon monoxide, glucose rises to as high as 1200 mg% (Johlin and Moreland, 1933). Neither force-feeding meat to the snake *Bothrops jararaca* (Prado, 1946b) nor fasting the adder *Vipera aspis* (Agid *et al.*, 1961a, b; Duguy, 1962) or the house snake *Natrix natrix* (Vlădescu and Baltac, 1967) will cause an appreciable change in blood sugar. Fasting the turtle *Chrysemys picta* (Rapatz and Musacchia, 1957; see also Vlădescu, 1965d) for six to eight weeks results in a drop in glucose from 79 mg% to 49 mg%.

Glucose given by mouth is rapidly absorbed, producing hyperglycemia in turtles (Corrêa *et al.*, 1960), snakes (Vlădescu, 1964), and other reptiles. Glucose apparently distributes throughout the extracellular fluid, so that the magnitude of the rise depends upon the volume of extracellular fluid as well as upon the quantity of glucose fed (Coulson and Hernandez, 1953). The rate at which glucose returns to control levels depends upon metabolic rate and thus upon temperature. Such observations, analogous to glucose tolerance studies in mammals, have been made on turtles (Lopes *et al.*, 1954; Vlădescu, 1964, 1965d), alligators (Coulson and Hernandez, 1953), lizards (DiMaggio and Dessauer, 1963; Vlădescu, 1965c; Vlădescu *et al.*, 1967),

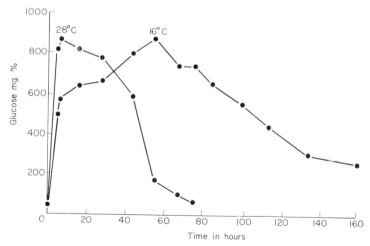

Fig. 3. Effect of temperature on blood glucose utilization in *Alligator mississippiensis* (from Coulson and Hernandez, 1964).

and snakes (Prado, 1946b; Vlădescu and Baltac, 1967). In *Alligator mississippiensis* glucose decreased three times faster at 20°C than at 16°C (Fig. 3; Coulson and Hernandez, 1953, 1964). A turtle *Emys orbicularis* utilized glucose more rapidly at its optimal temperature of 20°C than at either 10° or 32°C (Vlădescu, 1964).

The concentration of glucose in the blood varies with the season in a number of reptiles (Fig. 4). Of the species examined only the turtles *Emys*

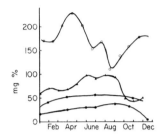

FIG. 4. Seasonal variation in blood glucose levels of fasted reptiles. Open circles = the lizard *Anolis carolinensis* (from Dessauer, 1953); closed circles = the snake *Vipera aspis* (from Agid et al., 1961a); triangles = *Alligator mississippiensis* (from Coulson and Hernandez, 1964); squares = the turtle *Emys orbicularis* (from Vlădescu, 1964).

orbicularis (Vlădescu, 1964) and *Pseudemys scripta* (Hutton, 1960) failed to exhibit a seasonal cycle in blood sugar. The most rapid fall in glucose level in the lizard *Anolis carolinensis* occurs in later summer when the species begins to store fat and glycogen in its tissues (Dessauer, 1953, 1955). In the lizard *Varanus griseus* glucose averages 95 mg% during the summer when the animals are active and 36 mg% during winter torpor (Haggag et al., 1966). The lowest blood glucose levels in alligators (Hopping, 1923; Coulson et al., 1950a; Hernandez and Coulson, 1952; Coulson and Hernandez, 1964), and in snakes (Agid et al., 1961b; Duguy, 1962) occur in autumn or early winter. Seasonal cycles in metabolic controls, rhythms inherent or related to photoperiod, are responsible in part for such differences (Bartholomew, 1959). Even when maintained at constant summer temperature, *Anolis carolinensis* (Fig. 5; DiMaggio and Dessauer, 1963) and *Alligator mississippiensis* (Coulson and Hernandez, 1964) remove glucose from the blood more rapidly in spring and summer than in winter (see Barwick and Bryant, 1966).

The control of blood sugar levels of reptiles is only poorly understood (Vlădescu, 1967), but it appears to be somewhat different in Squamata than in Testudines and Crocodilia. Small quantities of bovine insulin lead to marked decreases in glucose in alligators (Coulson and Hernandez, 1953, 1964; Stevenson et al., 1957) and turtles (Issekutz and Végh, 1928; Lopes et al., 1954). Insulin is present in the plasma of *Chrysemys* (Marques, 1967) and reaches its highest level in the turtle pancreas in winter when blood glucose is minimum (Marques and Kraemer, 1968). Bovine insulin, even in large doses, produces only small drops in blood sugar in lizards (Miller and Wurster, 1956, 1958, 1959; Miller, 1961; DiMaggio, 1961, 1961/1962; see

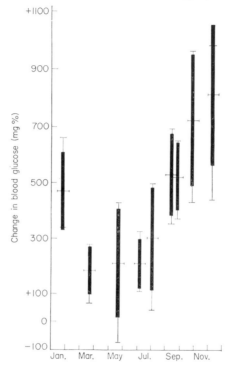

FIG. 5. Effect of season on blood glucose utilization in the lizard *Anolis carolinensis*, illustrating the presence of an annual metabolic rhythm. Each bar graph shows differences in blood glucose levels of lizards one day after receiving a standard amount of glucose. Horizontal I = mean; vertical I = range; vertical bar indicates standard deviation (from DiMaggio and Dessauer, 1963).

also Vlădescu *et al.*, 1967, and Vlădescu and Motelica, 1965) and snakes (Prado, 1947; Saviano, 1947a,b; Saviano and Francisis, 1948). Beta cells are sparse in pancreatic islets of lizards such as *Eumeces* (Miller, 1960).

Marked hyperglycemia is produced in reptiles just as in mammals by injections of glucagon (Coulson and Hernandez, 1953; Stevenson *et al.*, 1957; Miller and Wurster, 1959; Miller, 1961; DiMaggio, 1961, 1961/1962; Marques, 1967). The initial rise in glucose level commonly observed following injections of many insulin preparations into reptiles seems to be largely, but not entirely, due to glucagon contamination (Coulson and Hernandez, 1953, 1964). Epinephrine (Prado, 1947; Lopes *et al.*, 1954; Stevenson *et al.*, 1957; DiMaggio, 1961, 1961/1962), bovine somatotropin (Marques, 1955b; Stevenson *et al.*, 1957; DiMaggio, 1961, 1961/1962; Coulson and Hernandez,

1964), and hydrocortisone (Coulson and Hernandez, 1953, 1964; DiMaggio, 1961, 1961/1962; Vlădescu *et al.*, 1967) also produce hyperglycemia. Xanthine derivatives such as caffeine cause a rise in glucose and have pronounced sympathomimetic effects in alligators (Hernandez and Coulson, 1956).

Intense hyperglycemia followed pancreatectomy in the turtle *Phrynops geoffroanus hilarii* (Foglia *et al.*, 1955; Marques, 1955a) and alloxan injections in the turtle *Pseudemys d'orbigni* (Lopes, 1955). Pancreatectomy or alloxan injections caused only mild hypoglycemia in the lizard *Eumeces obsoletus* (Miller and Wurster, 1959). Hypophysectomy caused a marked decrease in the blood sugar of turtles (Houssay and Biasotti, 1933; Lopes *et al.*, 1954; Wagner, 1955; Foglia *et al.*, 1955), but led to only a mild hypoglycemia in *Eumeces obsoletus* (Miller and Wurster, 1959).

b. *Amino acids*. Plasma of reptiles contains a complex of small molecular weight, ninhydrin-positive compounds. These separate into about 35 fractions upon ion-exchange chromatography. These fractions contain the nineteen amino acids that are common constituents of proteins, ornithine, citruline, alpha-amino butyric acid and ten to fifteen unidentified compounds. The latter include cardioactive peptides in the turtles *Chelodina longicollis* and *Pseudemys scripta*, the lizard *Tiliqua scincoides*, and the crocodilian *Alligator mississippiensis*. They reach a bradykinin equivalent of 0·2 mg% in

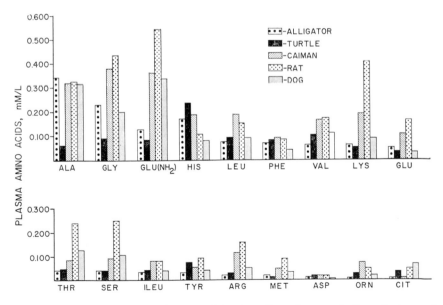

Fig. 6. Amino acid composition of plasma of fasted reptiles and mammals (from Coulson and Hernandez, 1965).

Pseudemys and 0·14 mg% in *Alligator* (Nayler *et al.*, 1965; Erdos *et al.*, 1967).

Amino acid nitrogen, a composite measurement of this complex mixture of substances, ranges from 1 to 10 mM/liter in fasted reptiles (Wiley and Lewis, 1927; Nera, 1925; Carmichael and Petcher, 1945; Khalil, 1947; Nair, 1955a; Hutton, 1958, 1960; Menon and Sathe, 1959; Coulson and Hernandez, 1959, 1961, 1962, 1964, 1965, 1966, 1968; Nair, 1960; Izard *et al.*, 1961; Hernandez and Coulson, 1961; Herbert *et al.*, 1966). Relative concentrations of specific amino acids vary over 100 fold. Some such as aspartic acid are often barely detectable, but together glycine, alanine, and glutamine make up half of total amino nitrogen. Distributions of amino acids in blood plasma of vertebrate animals show remarkable similarities (Fig. 6).

After feeding, amino nitrogen rises higher and falls more slowly in reptiles

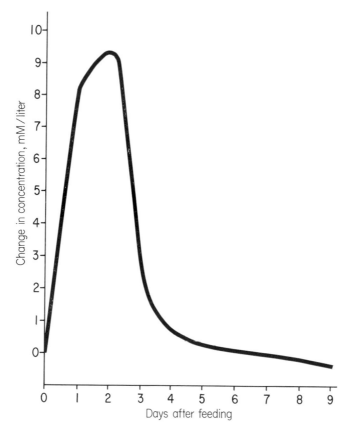

FIG. 7. Effect of feeding on total amino acid content of plasma of individual alligators. Heavy curve = average of 24 alligators (from Coulson and Hernandez, 1965).

than in endothermal animals. Coulson and Hernandez (1964, 1965) have followed the fate of absorbed amino acids in the Crocodilia and to a lesser extent in other reptiles. One to 3 days after alligators consumed 7 per cent of their body weight in fish, total amino acids reached a peak of between 8 and 15 mM/liter in the plasma and did not return to the control level for 5 or 6 days (Fig. 7). Glycine, alanine, and glutamine increased out of proportion to their content in the diet, suggesting their synthesis from other amino acids. Histidine, glutamic acid, and aspartic acid were concentrated in the extra-cellular fluid, but all other amino acids were distributed throughout body water (Hernandez and Coulson, 1967).

The rate at which each amino acid returns from an elevated to its fasting level has been followed in *Alligator* and in the turtle *Pseudemys scripta*. The concentrations of the majority of those amino acids known to be "essential" nutrients for mammals decrease slowly in the reptilian as in mammalian forms. Only lysine and histidine in the alligator and histidine in the turtle fall more rapidly than might be expected. Glycine, alanine, and glutamine are catabolized most rapidly. They appear to be the transport form of amino acid nitrogen fated for excretion, the major precursors of urinary ammonia, urea and uric acid. The plasma levels of amino acids are affected by insulin and a number of the other hormones that are involved in controlling blood glucose (Coulson and Hernandez, 1964, 1965, 1966, 1968; Hernandez and Coulson, 1961, 1968; Herbert *et al.*, 1966).

c. *Ammonia, uric acid and urea.* Representative levels of uric acid and urea, which with ammonia form the major products of protein catabolism in reptiles, appear in Table II. Ammonia is probably present in only trace amounts in the blood (Dessauer, 1952; Hutton and Goodnight, 1957; Coulson and Hernandez, 1964). The larger amounts occasionally reported in the blood (Hopping, 1923; Khalil, 1947; Coulson *et al.*, 1950a) may have originated from the decomposition of amide residues of blood proteins.

Uric acid does not normally reach a much higher blood level in reptiles than in mammals in which uric acid is a less important catabolite (Table II). Kidney tubules of reptiles are highly efficient in clearing uric acid from blood (Smith, 1951; Coulson and Hernandez, 1964; Dantzler, 1967). The de-creased tubular function at low temperatures, observed in *Alligator mississip-piensis* and *Pseudemys scripta* (Hernandez and Coulson, 1957), may explain the high uric acid level observed during winter torpor in a lizard *Varanus griseus* (Haggag *et al.*, 1966) and in the turtles *Terrapene carolina* and *Pseudemys scripta* (Hutton and Goodnight, 1957) and *Testudo hermanni* (Gilles-Baillien and Schoffeniels, 1965). Dehydration does not greatly impair uric acid excretion in alligators. The feeding of D-serine, however, causes severe renal damage leading to uric acid concentrations as high as 70 mg%. Uric acid deposits in the tissues, produce a condition resembling gout in these alligators (Coulson and Hernandez, 1961, 1964). Gout has also been described in turtles and lizards (Appleby and Siller, 1960).

Urea is present in relatively high concentrations in turtles, and low concentrations in lizards and snakes; has not been detected in the blood of crocodilians (Table II). The quantity of urea in the blood of lizards and snakes is small, generally less than 5 mg%, but this value is significant as analyses were by the highly specific urease method. Livers of Squamata lack the full complement of urea–cycle enzymes (Cohen and Brown, 1960), yet they do synthesize some urea. During pregnancy in the viviparous snake *Thamnophis sirtalis* blood urea rises to about 10 mg% due to urea produced by the embryo. Sixty per cent of the nitrogenous waste of the developing snake is urea (Clark, 1953, 1955). If carefully collected from hydrated animals, the urine of adult Squamata also contains urea (Hernandez and Coulson, 1951; Dessauer, 1952). Urea reaches an extremely high level in the spring in the turtle *Testudo hermanni* when the animal is at the end of a season of inactivity (Gilles-Baillien and Schoffeniels, 1965).

d. *Lipids*. Total lipid levels of between 300 and 1670 mg% are reported for reptilian blood (Nera, 1925; Chaikoff and Entenman, 1946; Menon, 1954; Izard *et al.*, 1961). Carotenoid pigments are present in relatively high concentrations in many squamates (see Section III C, 3 d below). Neutral fat accounts for the major share of the total. Fat levels change slowly during starvation and cold torpor in the turtle *Chrysemys picta*. Total fatty acids decreased only 89 mg% in turtles fasted 6 to 8 weeks (Rapatz and Musacchia, 1957). Total cholesterol averages 50 mg% in *Alligator mississippiensis* (Coulson and Hernandez, 1964), 100 to 172 mg% in the blood of rattlesnakes (Luck and Keeler, 1929; Carmichael and Petcher, 1945), and over 220 mg% in the snake *Vipera aspis* (Izard *et al.*, 1961). Averages as low as 69 mg% and as high as 480 mg% are reported in different species of emydine turtles (Chaikoff and Entenman, 1946; Jackson and Legendre, 1967; Stenroos and Bowman, 1968). Approximately half of the cholesterol is esterified in *Chrysemys* and *Vipera*. Total fat, cholesterol, cholesterol esters, and phospholipids are elevated in *Chrysemys* and probably in other reptiles during estrus (See Section III C, 6 below). Phospholipids are elevated in both male and female *Pseudemys* during the spring (Hutton, 1960). Atherosclerosis has been observed in reptiles (Finlayson, 1964).

C. High Molecular Weight Components

1. *General*

Three to 7 per cent of blood plasma is comprised of a complex mixture of proteins (Table II). This mixture separates into three or four molecular weight fractions with sedimentation constants in three ranges: (1) 3·3 to 4·8,

(2) 5·8 to 9·6, and (3) 12·2 to 16·2 Svedbergs. A small percentage of heavier components is occasionally present (Svedberg and Andersson, 1938; Baril *et al.*, 1961; Roberts and Seal, 1965). Molecular weights as estimated with molecular sieves (Fig. 8) include fractions (1) between 40,000 and 120,000, (2)

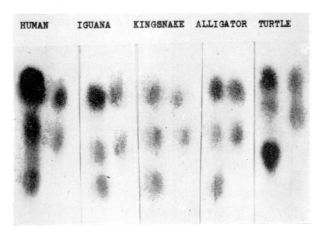

FIG. 8. Molecular weight fractions of plasma proteins of reptiles. For each species, patterns on the left are of unfractionated plasma; patterns on the right are of rivanol soluble proteins. Separation was carried out on thin layers of Sephadex G-200 (Pharmacia Co.). Uppermost spots on plasma patterns are due to proteins of lowest molecular weight, primarily albumin and transferrin; lowermost spots are due to proteins of highest molecular weight, e.g. fibrinogens; intermediate spot on human pattern contains the 7 S gamma-globulins. Uppermost spots of the rivanol soluble proteins represent transferrins; the fraction of intermediate size in the human sample is gamma-globulin; the identity of this protein in reptiles is not known.

between 120,000 and 190,000, and (3) greater than 180,000 (Masat and Dessauer, 1968).

Plasma proteins resolve into 5 to 7 major fractions of different charge density upon electrophoresis in alkaline buffers (Fig. 9). Although mobilities fall within ranges comparable to the albumin, alpha, beta, and gamma fractions of human plasma protein patterns (Seniow, 1963), one should use such designations only as reference standards of mobilities. Proteins migrating in fractions of similar mobility may often have very different structures (Dessauer and Fox, 1964). The extreme heterogeneity of plasma proteins is shown by high resolution techniques such as starch gel electrophoresis (Smithies, 1959) and immunoelectrophoresis (Lewis, 1964; Neuzil and Masseyeff, 1958). Proteins of individual reptiles resolve into as many as 30 components. Stage of development (Kaplan, 1960a), sex, season, and physiological state affect the protein complement. Individuals of a population may exhibit inherited differences in specific proteins (Dessauer and Fox, 1964; Masat and Musacchia, 1965; Dessauer, 1966). Hypophysectomy

REPTILIA

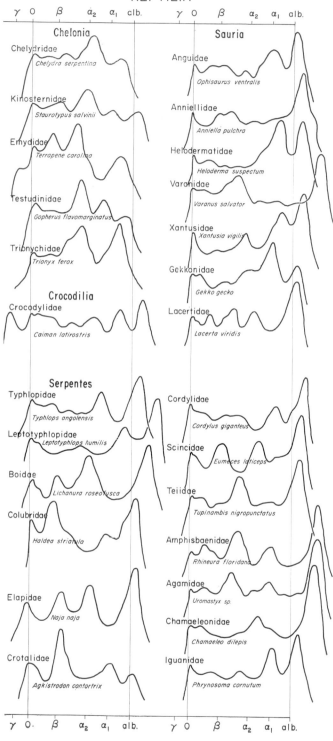

of the turtle *Clemmys caspica leprosa* leads to an increase in plasma protein and to a relative decrease in albumin (Aron *et al.*, 1959).

Some plasma proteins of reptiles have specialized transport functions; others are involved in the complex immune and coagulation functions of blood. Most are conjugated with either lipid or carbohydrate. Two or three electrophoretic fractions contain lipoproteins (Uriel *et al.*, 1957; Crenshaw, 1962; Coulson and Hernandez, 1964). Plasma proteins are conjugated to considerable carbohydrate. Lustig and Ernst (1936) found that an average of 3·0% of the protein mass was carbohydrate in *Testudo*, 3·4% in *Lacerta*, 6·4% in *Anguis*, 6·9% in *Natrix*, 4·5% in *Vipera* and 6·3% in *Elaphe*. The albumin-like component, based upon experiments with concanavalin A, appears to be the only quantitatively important plasma protein that lacks carbohydrate in its structure (Nakamura *et al.*, 1965; Masat and Dessauer, 1968). Plasma proteins of all groups of reptiles contain sialic acid as part of their structure, but those of snakes contain unusual amounts of this carbohydrate (Seal, 1964). A number of varieties of enzymes have been observed in the plasma of reptiles. Very active esterases of a number of varieties are present (Augustinson, 1959, 1961; Dessauer *et al.*, 1962b; Dessauer, 1967; Holmes *et al.*, 1968). Leucine aminopeptidase (Ehrensing, 1964; Dessauer, 1967, see also Section V, C 3 below and Fig. 14), arginase (Goodcase *et al.*, 1964), phenylenediamine oxidases (See Section 3 c below) trehalase, maltase, (Van Handel, 1968) and proteins such as haptoglobin with peroxidase activities (Liang, 1957) are present in the plasma of some reptiles.

2. *Albumin and Plasma Volume*

The volume of fluid within the circulatory system must be maintained even while water, metabolites, and electrolytes exchange with intracellular material. The delicate balance between hydrostatic and colloid osmotic pressures across capillary walls controls plasma volume (Macfarland and Robb-Smith, 1961). Colloid osmotic pressure in mammals is exerted largely by proteins of low molecular weight and high charge such as albumin which is responsible for 75 per cent of osmotic pressure of human plasma.

The identity of the principal "volume expander" of reptilian plasma has been in question (Cohen and Stickler, 1958). Plasma of reptiles of all major groups, however, contains a protein with properties analogous to human albumin: a low molecular weight, hydrophilic protein of relatively high charge. One fraction of their plasma proteins falls in the molecular weight range of albumins, 50,000 to 100,000 (Svedberg and Andersson, 1938; Roberts

---

FIG. 9. Electrophoretic patterns of plasma proteins of representative species from different families of Reptilia. Patterns were obtained under comparable conditions. Migrations of human plasma fractions form a frame of reference for comparisons (from Dessauer and Fox, 1964).

and Seal, 1965; Baril *et al.*, 1961; Masat and Dessauer, 1968). The low
molecular weight fraction of *Pseudemys*, *Alligator*, *Natrix*, and *Iguana* re-
solves into two major subfractions upon electrophoresis, with most of the
protein migrating with the subfraction of highest charge density. Protein of
this subfraction is very hydrophilic, being soluble in water, 2 M ammonium
sulfate, and alcoholic trichloracetic acid. Also like the mammalian albumins
it is insoluble in rivanol (Masat and Dessauer, 1966, 1968). Proteins of the
most highly charged electrophoretic fractions of plasma of a great variety of
turtles are soluble in 2 M ammonium sulfate (Leone and Wilson, 1961;
Frair, 1962a and b; Crenshaw, 1962). That of the turtle *Clemmys japonica*
has the same isoelectric point as human albumin (Michaelis and Nakashima,
1923).

The contribution of the albumin to plasma volume appears to vary greatly
among different reptiles. In *Alligator*, *Iguana*, and *Lampropeltis* albumin
appears to be responsible for at least 50 per cent of the colloid osmotic
pressure, whereas its contribution in emydine turtles such as *Pseudemys* is
often less than 20 per cent (Masat and Dessauer, 1966). High concentrations
of albumins with high charge densities are found in active species with high
metabolic rates and in those living in dry, hot environments, e.g. in those
lizards which generally have the highest metabolic rates among reptiles
(Benedict, 1932; Dessauer, 1953; Dawson, 1960) and high preferred body
temperatures (Dawson and Poulson, 1962). Total blood water of desert
species seems to relate directly to the amount of albumin in their plasma
(Khalil and Abdel-Messeih, 1963). At the other extreme are the fresh water
turtles which generally have low concentrations of albumins (Fig. 8) of low
charge (Fig. 9; Section V, C 2 below). Probably the "functional ascites"
noted in such turtles (Smith, 1929; Thorson, 1963) directly correlate with
the low colloid osmotic pressure of their plasma. In *Pseudemys scripta* this
was 3 to 8 mm of mercury, only 1 or 2 mm of mercury higher than the
pressure of perivisceral fluids (Campbell and Turner, 1937). Pressures were
higher for other reptiles equalling 26 mm of mercury for the sea turtle
Caretta, 23 mm for *Caiman*, 22 mm for *Iguana*, and 24 mm for *Boa constrictor*
(Scholander *et al.*, 1968).

3. Transport Proteins

a. *Albumin and anion transport*. Mammalian albumins transport fatty acids
and buffer a great variety of potentially toxic anions. Practically nothing is
known of mechanisms of such transport in reptiles, although they exhibit
marked shifts in lipid distribution during estrus (Fig. 11; Section III C, 6
below) and seasonal metabolic cycles (Dessauer, 1955; Hutton and Goodnight, 1957; Rapatz and Musacchia, 1957; Duguy, 1962; Barwick and Bryant,
1966). Albumin may be involved in fatty acid transport in the lizard *Uta*

stansburiana (Hahn, 1965, 1967). Albumins of all major groups of reptiles bind anions, but their binding affinities for dyes such as bromphenol blue are far weaker than those of the albumins of mammals (Masat and Dessauer, 1968). Alligator albumin binds indole-3- propionate and certain other indole derivatives (McMenamy and Watson, 1968).

b. *Transferrins and iron transport.* Transferrins are major constituents of blood plasma in all vertebrates. Together with albumin they make up 95 per cent of the mass of small molecular weight proteins of reptilian plasma. Their molecular weights lie between 70,000 and 90,000 and are similar in reptiles of all major groups (Fig. 8; Masat and Dessauer, 1968). In contrast, their surface charges as indicated by electrophoresis exhibit marked variability (Figs 10 and 14). Electrophoretic mobilities of turtle transferrins are

| | TRANSFERRINS | | | | | HEMOGLOBINS | | | |
	Gen. Sp.	γO Sα₂	Trans C.	ALB.		Gen. Sp.	O	S A
CHELONIA								
Chelydridae	2 2					1 1		
Kinosternidae	3 4					3 6^{ab}		
Emydidae	5 6					5 7^{cd}		
Testudinidae	1 1					1 2		
Trionychidae	1 1					1 1		
CROCODYLIA								
Crocodylidae	3 3					3 3		
SERPENTES								
Typhlopidae	1 2					1 1		
Leptotyphlopidae	1 2					1 1		
Boidae	2 2					3 3		
Colubridae	22 44					20 40		
Elapidae	1 1					2 2		
Crotalidae	2 5					4 9		
SAURIA								
Anguidae	2 4					2 4		
Anniellidae						1 1		
Helodermatidae	1 1					1 1		
Varanidae	1 2					1 1		
Xantusiidae						1 1		
Gekkonidae	3 3					2 2		
Lacertidae	1 1							
Cordylidae	1 1					1 1		
Scincidae	1 3					2 2		
Teiidae	3 7					3 4^{e}		
Amphisbaenidae						1 1		
Agamidae	1 1					1 1		
Chamaeleonidae	1 1							
Iguanidae	9 13					10 13		

FIG. 10. Relative electrophoretic migrations of transferrins and hemoglobins of species of reptiles. Migration rates of human blood proteins form the frame of reference for comparisons (from Dessauer and Fox, 1964).

as slow as human gamma-globulin, whereas those of some gekonid lizards are as fast as human albumin. Usually one but often two iron-binding proteins are present in the plasma of a single reptilian species. Marked individual variation, both within geographically limited populations and between populations from different geographic areas, occurs in a number of species (Dessauer et al., 1962a).

By complexing metal ions specialized transport proteins such as transferrin effectively remove the free ions from the blood. Heavy metal ions are generally toxic to living cells. Transferrins of reptilian plasma have considerable iron-binding capacity. Most often less than half of the transferrin molecules are saturated with iron (Dessauer et al., 1962a; Barber and Sheeler, 1961; Sheeler and Barber, 1964). Plasma iron was reduced in starved turtles (*Pseudemys scripta*) to approximately one-third the normal level (Hirschfeld and Gordon, 1965). The two transferrins of *Pseudemys scripta* have different unloading pH's and heat stabilities (Barber and Sheeler, 1963). Transferrins of reptiles are soluble in water, 2 M ammonium sulfate, and rivanol (Fig.8; Masat and Dessauer, 1966, 1968). They retain their iron-binding capability and electrophoretic mobilities after being stored at deep freeze temperatures for as long as ten years (Dessauer, personal observation).

Transferrins of *Pseudemys scripta* release iron to reticulocytes, demonstrating that they can serve as a source of iron for hemoglobin synthesis. Rat and human transferrin give up their iron readily when exposed to a pH below 6, but some iron remains in equilibrium with transferrins of turtles even at pH 5 (Barber and Sheeler, 1963; Sheeler and Barber, 1965). By binding traces of other metal ions, transferrins may also perform an antioxidant function, e.g. inhibition of lipid peroxide formation (Barber and Sheeler, 1961).

c. *Ceruloplasmin and plasma copper.* The copper binding protein of blood plasma, ceruloplasmin, has been implicated in copper transport, mechanism of iron release to the tissues, and plasma oxidase reactions (Putnam, 1965). Plasma of the Mexican beaded lizard, *Heloderma horridum*, contains 196 μg% of copper; all but 8 μg% of this is bound to protein (Zarafonetis and Kalas, 1960; see Beck, 1956). Ceruloplasmin has been assayed in reptiles of all major groups on the basis of its p-phenylene diamine oxidase activity (Seal, 1964). Activity is completely absent from plasma of some species and relatively high in others. The species distribution of activity is almost random. Protein with oxidase activity is present in the fraction with molecular weights between 120,000 and 190,000 (Masat and Dessauer, 1968). Its electrophoretic migration rate is similar in widely divergent species (Dessauer and Fox, 1964).

d. *Hormone and vitamin transport.* A number of substances which are known vitamins or hormones for mammals and birds are transported in combination with specific plasma proteins. Thyroxine binding proteins have been demonstrated in plasma of major groups of reptiles, although their capacity appears to be below that of mammalian forms (Farer et al., 1962). Protein bound iodine of alligators averages less than 0·1 μg/100 ml of plasma (Coulson and Hernandez, 1964). Transcortin, a corticosterone binding protein, varies in binding capacity with temperature. Its capacity in the alligator rises from 5 μg/100 ml of plasma at 6°C to 43 μg% at 14°C and drops to 8 μg% at 37°C. Transcortin of the garter snake has been isolated and contains hexose and sialic acid (Seal and Doe, 1963).

A lipoprotein which contains carotenoid pigments is present in plasma of iguanid lizards such as *Iguana iguana* and *Anolis carolinensis*. The protein migrates in the alpha-2 region in electrophoresis (Dessauer, personal observation). Plasma of the lizard *Varanus komodoensis* (Jensen and With, 1939) and *Uromastyx hardwickii* (Zain and Zain-ul-Abedin, 1967) and the snakes *Bothrops jararaca* and *Mastigodryas bifossatus* (Villela and Prado, 1945) contains considerable carotenoid pigment. Riboflavin, both free and protein bound, is present in the remarkably high concentrations of between 165 and 333 μg% in plasma of these snakes (Villela and Prado, 1944, 1945; Villela, 1945) and *Python molurus* (Villela and Thein, 1967). Proteins to which riboflavin is bound have L-amino acid oxidase activity and migrate as fluorescent bands in the alpha and beta regions during electrophoresis (Ribeiro *et al.*, 1955; Villela *et al.*, 1955). Vitamin B_{12} content and binding capacity of plasma varies widely among animal species. Most of the B_{12} present in blood is part of red cell structure. In 100 ml of blood of *Alligator mississippiensis* 548 millimicrograms are present in the cells but only 4mμg in the plasma; a nearly equal amount is present in plasma of a turtle. Plasma of alligators can bind an additional 94 mμg% of B_{12}. The unsaturated B_{12} binding capacity of the turtle *Pseudemys scripta* is much higher, averaging 1·8 μg% (Couch *et al.*, 1950; Rosenthal and Brown, 1954; Rosenthal and Austin, 1962).

4. *Blood Clotting*

Injury to the vascular system of reptiles is followed by a series of phenomena including vasoconstriction and blood coagulation (Brocq-Rousseu and Roussel, 1939; Engle and Woods, 1960; Macfarland and Robb-Smith, 1961; Gregoire and Taynon, 1962). Proteins involved in blood coagulation appear to be similar to those of mammals, although their concentrations may be very different. Cellular factors seem to have great importance. Plasma, if carefully collected, usually exhibits slow clotting times (Dorst and Mills, 1923; Fantl, 1961; Hackett and Hann, 1967). The addition of traces of tissue fluids, however, greatly accelerates clot formation. Clotting times of blood are often high (Hutton and Goodnight, 1957; Rabalais, 1938). Calcium is required for clot formation. Ion exchange resins (Lund *et al.*, 1957) and agents which precipitate or chelate calcium stop the clotting process (Kaplan, 1956). Heparin is also an effective anticoagulant. A related polysaccharide is present in low concentration in plasma of active *Pseudemys scripta* but rises to 4 to 6 mg% during winter torpor (Jacques and Musacchia, 1961; Jacques, 1963).

Serum expressed from blood clots of mammals and the lizard *Tupinambis nigropunctatus* retains clot promoting activity. Serum of a number of colubrid and viperid snakes, however, exhibits marked anticoagulant activity (Brazil and Vellard, 1928).

Fibrinogen is present in plasma of all major groups and will form a fibrin clot if treated with bovine thrombin. The rate of fibrin formation is slower than for mammalian plasma, presumably because of some species specificity. Fibrinogens of *Chelydra* and *Pseudemys* are less soluble than are those of amphibians but more soluble than those of mammals in plasma-ethanol mixtures (Morrison *et al.*, 1951). Fibrinogen content of plasma has been estimated in a number of forms: *Testudo graeca* = 970 mg%; *Dermochelys coriacea* = 120 mg%; *Alligator mississippiensis* = 380 mg%; *Iguana iguana* = 1200 mg% *Trachydosaurus rugosus* = 140 mg%; *Coluber constrictor* = 115 mg%; *Notechis scutatus* = 140 mg%; *Vipera aspis* = 310 mg% (Nera, 1925; Dunlap, 1955; Nair, 1958; Izard *et al.*, 1961; Fantl, 1961; Dessauer, personal observations).

Less is known of other clotting factors. Prothrombin level in the turtle *Chrysemys picta* is only 42 per cent of that of dogs (Warner *et al.*, 1939), but its synthesis by the turtle also seems to require vitamin K (Brambel, 1941). Prothrombin concentration is very low in plasma of the tiger snake *Notechis scutatus*. One can isolate prothombin by adsorption on barium sulfate (Hackett and Hann, 1967). The Hageman or surface factor is lacking in the tiger snake, but is present in the lizard *Trachydosaurus rugosus*, the turtles *Chelodina longicollis* (Fantl, 1961), *Pseudemys scripta* and *Chelydra serpentina* and in *Alligator mississippiensis* (Erdös *et al.*, 1967). Proccelerin activity (Ac-globulin) is low in plasma of turtles and chickens but high in mammals (Murphy and Seegers, 1948).

5. *Antibodies, Complements, and Cellular Antigens*

Plasma of reptiles contains proteins that are intimately involved in natural immunity, anaphylaxis, and tissue tolerance (Brocq-Rousseu and Roussel, 1939; Favour, 1958; Putnam, 1960; Hildemann, 1962; Smith *et al.*, 1966). Isoagglutinins are present in numerous turtles (Bond, 1940a; Frair, 1962a, 1962b, 1963), but have not been found in the American alligator (Bond, 1940b) nor in a number of colubrid and crotalid snakes (Bond, 1939). Heteroagglutinins have been discovered in all species examined, including turtles (Bond, 1940a; Frair, 1962a, 1962b, 1963), crocodilians (Bond, 1940b), and snakes (Bond, 1939; Dujarric de la Rivière *et al.*, 1954; Timourian and Dobson, 1962). Autoantibodies in plasma of the Gila monster, *Heloderma suspectum*, can neutralize its venom (Tyler, 1946). Similarly, a plasma anti-phosphatidase of *Vipera aspis* can neutralize the toxicity of its venom (Izard *et al.*, 1961). Plasma of the kingsnake *Lampropeltis getulus* protects mice against a dose of 7 LD_{50} of venom of the water moccasin *Agkistrodon piscivorus* (Philpot and Smith, 1950). Immune hemolytic systems involving complement occur in turtles (Frair, 1963) and are common in snakes. Plasma of numerous snakes will hemolyze mammalian red blood cells (Bond and Sherwood, 1939; Timourian and Dobson, 1962).

Reptiles of all groups respond on initial exposure to a variety of antigens with the production of antibodies (Evans *et al.*, 1965); in the light of present knowledge, earlier negative responses can be traced to technical short-comings (Hildemann, 1962). Alligators (Lerch *et al.*, 1967) have an immuno-logic memory, that is they will respond to a second exposure to an antigen with a rapid increase in circulating antibody. Circulating antibodies in the carpet snake, *Morelia argus*, react with body fluid antigens of infecting nema-todes. The presence of a specific antibody in the plasma correlates with a particular nematode infection (Timourian *et al.*, 1961). The immune res-ponse, like many other metabolic activities of reptiles, depends upon temperature (Evans and Cowles, 1959; Hildemann, 1962). The lizards *Dipso-saurus dorsalis* and *Sauromalus obesus* synthesize antibodies against *Salmonella typhosa*, bovine serum albumin, and rabbit gamma-globulin most effectively when the animals are maintained at 35°C. Synthesis is poor in lizards kept at 25°C and at 40°C. If immunized at 25°C and later transferred to 35°C, the lizards form antibodies without further immunization (Evans, 1963a, 1963b). High titers of antibodies resulted in rat snakes and slider turtles maintained at temperatures near the upper end of their temperature range (Frair, 1963). The turtles *Chrysemys* and *Chelydra* maintained at 23 to 28°C developed antibodies against bacteria (Gee, 1941). Schedules of injections must be controlled to obtain effective antibody production and to avoid anaphylaxis (Downs, 1928; Placidi and Placidi, 1960; Hildemann, 1962). Slider turtles appear to vary in their resistance to infection during different periods of the year (Kaplan and Rueff, 1960).

Proteins involved in the immune responses of reptiles have been poorly characterized. Only crocodilians and turtles have electrophoretic fractions which migrate as slowly as mammalian gamma-globulins (Dessauer and Fox, 1964; see Fig. 9). Fractions of slowest mobility in the lizards *Dipso-saurus dorsalis* and *Sauromalus obesus* (Evans, 1963a, 1963b) contain anti-bodies. Immunoelectrophoretic patterns of antisera from these lizards (Evans, 1963b), alligator, and loggerhead turtle (Lewis, 1964) exhibit precipitin arcs comparable in position and appearance to human gamma-globulin patterns. *Alligator* exhibits at least two immunoglobulins that differ in electrophoretic mobility and perhaps molecular weight (Lerch *et al.*, 1967). Plasma of reptiles of all major groups contains a fraction which, like human gamma-globulin, is soluble in rivanol and is of intermediate molecular weight (Fig. 8). Antibodies of the carpet snake *Morelia argus* (Timourian and Dobson, 1962) and autoantibodies of the Gila monster (Tyler, 1946) are insoluble in half saturated ammonium sulfate. Complement of turtles (Bond, 1940a; Frair, 1963) and of snakes (Bond and Sherwood, 1939; Timourian and Dobson, 1962) are thermolabile, being destroyed if incubated at 56° C for 5 or 6 minutes. Complement of the carpet snakes is somewhat soluble in half saturated ammonium sulfate (Timourian and Dobson, 1962).

6. Plasma Vitellin and Estrus

Striking increases in levels of alkaline earths, phosphorus and lipid fractions, and protein accompany estrus in reptiles, having been noted in turtles (Laskowski, 1936; Chaikoff and Entenman, 1946; Clark, 1967), the lizard *Uta stansburiana* (Hahn, 1965), and numerous snakes (Dessauer *et al.*, 1956; Dessauer and Fox, 1958, 1959, 1964; Izard *et al.*, 1961; Jenkins and Simkiss, 1968). Stimulation with estrogens, presumably from the developing ovary, induces the liver to enlarge and to synthesize a calcium-binding, lipo-phosphoprotein complex known as plasma vitellin. The latter moves via the blood stream to the ovary where it is involved in the synthesis of yolk (Simkiss, 1961, 1967). The rise and fall in vitellin in the plasma correlates with successive changes in follicle composition and with weight cycles of the liver and fat bodies in the ribbon snake, *Thamnophis sauritus* (Fig. 11). Vitellin appears in the blood shortly after the follicles become hydrated but before they begin to accumulate yolk. On the average each 100 ml of plasma contains about a gram of phosphoprotein and an additional 20 mg of calcium throughout the period of yolk production. About the time of ovulation extreme plasma levels occur, e.g. a total protein as high as $8·8$ g% and calcium of 360 mg%. By the time eggs attain early cleavage stages, protein, calcium, etc. return to anestrous levels (Dessauer and Fox, 1959).

Such plasma changes can be induced in turtles (Schjeide and Urist, 1960; Urist and Schjeide, 1960/61; Seal, 1964; Clark, 1967; Rao, 1968), lizards (Hahn, 1965, 1967; Suzuki and Prosser, 1968), snakes (Dessauer and Fox, 1959), and crocodiles (Prosser and Suzuki, 1968) by injections of estrogens. Natural and artificial androgens cause, at best, only slight increases in plasma protein (Rao and David, 1967). Five days after treating turtles with estrone total lipid increased 3 fold, calcium 4 fold, and protein $1·5$ times. There was an 8 fold rise in protein bound phosphorus. Lipid contained 38% trigly-ceride, 35% phospholipid, 15% sterol and 12% sterol esters (Urist and Schjeide, 1960/61). Seal (1964) induced a protein rise to 12 g% in a turtle injected daily with 100μg of 17-beta-estradiol for six weeks. Clark (1967) needed only 20 μg of estradiol to induce a significant response in *Chrysemys*. Injections of one μg/g body weight of estradiol into a lizard were followed within twenty-four hours by the appearance of plasma vitellin; after injections for 4 to 6 days vitellin made up over 60% of the plasma protein (Hahn,

1965, 1967). Rates of increase of calcium and phosphoprotein were equal and almost linear in male ribbon snakes (*Thamnophis sauritus*) injected with estradiol. Plasma and associated tissue changes occurred even though the snakes received no food for at least two weeks before or during the experi-

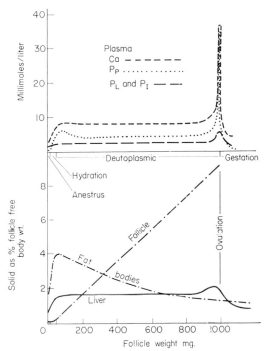

FIG. 11. Correlation of plasma vitellin levels with organ changes during the estrous cycle of the ribbon snake *Thamnophis sauritus*. P_p = protein bound phosphorus, a measure of plasma vitellin concentration; $P_L + P_I$ = lipid plus inorganic phosphorus; Ca = plasma calcium (from Dessauer and Fox, 1959).

ment (Dessauer and Fox, 1959). Reptiles may be under some stress to obtain calcium during reproduction (Simkiss, 1961, 1962). For anoles and geckos one source of calcium may be the calcareous material that fills the *saccus endolymphaticus* (Whiteside, 1922; Jenkins and Simkiss, 1968).

Plasma vitellin appears to be a complex colloidal micelle of alkaline earths and lipid stabilized by phosphoprotein. Mere ten fold dilution of plasma with water causes it to precipitate (Laskowski, 1936). Its gross composition is similar to that of yolk. Plasma vitellin of *Thamnophis elegans* contains 43% lipid and 57% protein. The protein fraction contains 1·7% phosphorus; calcium associates with the protein in equimolar quantities to its phosphorus content (Dessauer and Fox, 1959). Vitellin of *Pseudemys scripta* is of a similar gross composition; it sediments in the ultracentrifuge as a single peak with a sedimentation constant of approximately 17 S (Urist and Schjeide, 1960/61). Calcium sediments with vitellin and not as colloidal calcium phosphate (Schjeide and Urist, 1960). Electrophoretic patterns of plasma proteins of estrous females and those of male or anestrous females treated with estrogens exhibit a vitellin fraction in the alpha-2 or beta-globulin regions (Dessauer and Fox, 1958, 1959, 1964; Urist and Schjeide, 1960/61; Hahn, 1965; Suzuki and Prosser, 1968).

IV. Composition of the Red Blood Cells

A. NUMBER, SYNTHESIS AND LONGEVITY

The packed cell volume or hematocrit of reptiles generally falls between 20 and 35 per cent (Table II), although the value may vary with season (Kaplan and Rueff, 1960) and temperature (Musacchia and Sievers, 1956). Fundamental factors which control the number of circulating red cells and erythropoesis are unknown (Pienaar, 1962). Hypoxia and cobalt salts, which are effective stimulants of mammalian erythropoesis, do not induce red cell formation in the box turtle *Terrapene carolina*. Turtles kept for long periods at simulated altitudes over 45,000 feet retain the same hematocrit and hemoglobin levels (Altland and Parker, 1955; Altland and Thompson, 1958). Lizards which live at high elevations have hematocrits and hemoglobin levels similar to those of species of the same genus which live in the lowlands (note data on *Sceloporus* in Table II; Dawson and Poulson, 1962). Likewise hematocrits do not correlate with temperature tolerances of lizards (Dawson and Poulson, 1962). Anemia, whether resulting from phenylhydrazine injection (Tipton, 1933; Sheeler and Barber, 1965) or blood letting (Altland and Thompson, 1958; Hirschfeld and Gordon, 1961, 1965), is the only known stimulant of erythropoesis in turtles and alligators. Maximum reticulocytosis occurs about 3 to 5 weeks following onset of anemia. Folic acid is probably necessary for blood formation in turtles as aminopterin, a folic acid antagonist, inhibits reticulocytosis in *Terrapene carolina* (Altland and Thompson, 1958). Hirschfeld and Gordon (1964) did not find an erythropoesis stimulating factor in the blood of *Pseudemys scripta*. Hypophysectomy of a turtle, *Clemmys caspica leprosa*, did not affect its hematocrit (Aron *et al.*, 1959). Starving of this turtle caused no changes in its hematocrit or hemoglobin levels, but such starved animals appeared incapable of erythropoesis (Hirschfeld and Gordon, 1965).

Red cells of turtles and alligators have exceptionally long life spans. The mean life span of red cells of *Terrapene carolina* is 600 to 800 days (Brace and Altland, 1955; Altland and Brace, 1962). Rate of erythrocyte turnover relates directly to the low metabolic rate of the animal (Altland and Brace, 1962; Rodnan *et al.*, 1957). Mean life span of red cells of *Alligator mississippiensis* is shorter if the animal is maintained at warm rather than at cool temperatures, equaling 300 days at 31°C and exceeding 1320 days at 16 to 17°C (Cline and Waldmann, 1962). Alligator erythrocytes are also very resistant to osmotic and mechanical stress (Cohen et al., 1961; 1964). Hoffert and Fromm (1964) describe the tagging of erythrocytes of *Chrysemys picta* with hexavalent chromium.

B. HEMOGLOBIN AND OXYGEN TRANSPORT

Hemoglobin makes up the greater share of the solid content of the red blood cell. Total solids of red cells of the turtle *Testudo graeca* equal 37 per cent (Nera, 1925). The concentration of hemoglobin in erythrocytes is similar in all vertebrates (Wintrobe, 1934). Most estimates fall between 25 and 32 per cent of net weight in reptiles. Blood contains between 6 and 12 grams % of hemoglobin (Table II). The concentration is directly proportional to packed cell volume, unless large numbers of immature cells are present (Sheeler and Barber, 1965). Methemoglobin is often present in significant quantity. Prado (1946c) found 6 to 28 per cent inactive hemoglobin in the snake *Bothrops jararaca*. Methemoglobin is commonly found in turtles, ranging from 5 to 60 per cent of total heme protein in newly captured *Pseudemys scripta* (Sullivan, 1966; Sullivan and Riggs, 1964). Thus hemoglobin estimates based on measurements of total iron (Menon, 1955; Nair, 1955b) or total heme are often considerably higher than estimates based on oxygen capacity measurements (see Dawson and Poulson, 1962).

Blood of individual reptiles often contains 2 or more hemoglobins, distinguishable by molecular weight, surface charge (Fig. 10), and chemical properties. Hemoglobins with molecular weights approximately twice 68,000 are present along with those of molecular weight 68,000. Svedberg and Hedenius (1934) first discovered these "double hemoglobins" in the turtle *Chrysemys picta*, the lizard *Lacerta vivipara*, and the snake *Coluber constrictor*. Such polymerization is of common occurrence among turtles; apparently it results from sulfhydryl-disulfide exchange reactions (Riggs et al., 1964; Sullivan and Riggs, 1964, 1967a, d; Sullivan, 1966). Two or more hemoglobins of different electrophoretic mobilities are present in most turtles and in many snakes and lizards (Sydenstricker et al., 1956; Dessauer et al., 1957; Dessauer and Fox, 1964; Rodnan and Ebaugh, 1957; Nakamura, 1960; Crenshaw, 1962; Gorman and Dessauer, 1965; Sullivan and Riggs, 1967b). Both alkali stable and alkali unstable hemoglobins are present in turtles, alligators, and snakes (Ramsey, 1941) and the lizard *Heloderma horridum* (Zarafonetis and Kalas, 1960). The alkali stable and alkali unstable hemoglobins of the turtle *Pseudemys scripta* have been isolated and characterized (Ramirez and Dessauer, 1957; Manwell and Schlesinger, 1966; Sullivan and Riggs, 1967b).

The source of hemoglobin variability resides in the structure of the globin;

the iron porphyrin (heme) probably has the same structure in reptiles as in other vertebrates (Anson *et al.*, 1924; Korzhuev and Kruglova, 1957; Ramirez and Dessauer, 1957). Heme is easily separated from globin (Dozy *et al.*, 1964; Sullivan, 1966; Sullivan and Riggs, 1967b). In acid buffers globin dissociates into polypeptides which can be separated by electrophoresis. Commonly 2 or 3 but occasionally as many as 6 bands characterize globin patterns of reptiles (Dozy *et al.*, 1964; Sullivan and Riggs, 1967b; Dessauer, 1967).

In light of the remarkable degree of physiochemical variability noted among reptilian hemoglobins, it is surprising how little is known of the structural basis of these differences. Amino acid composition of acid digests

TABLE III

Amino Acid Composition of Reptilian Hemoglobins (Mole %)

Amino Acid Residue	Snapping[a] turtle	Emydid[b] turtle	American[a] alligator	Common[a] iguana	Water[a] snake
Glycine	10·0	5·5	6·3	9·3	10·8
Alanine	5·9	10·0	11·4	10·7	8·1
Serine	5·0	7·4	7·2	2·3	5·7
Threonine		6·2	0·8	6·1	3·6
Proline		3·0	0·6	0·7	0·2
Valine	8·9	9·5	9·2	9·7	8·1
Isoleucine	1·4	3·7	2·2	0·6	1·6
Leucine	13·0	12·6	10·1	12·1	13·0
Phenylalanine	6·2	5·3	7·7	6·2	5·9
Tyrosine	2·2	2·5	2·6	2·6	2·5
Methionine	0·8	0·4	1·8	1·0	0·5
Aspartic acid		7·9	7·7	11·8	9·6
Glutamic acid	12·5	9·0	9·6	7·3	8·9
Arginine	2·6	2·6	4·3	5·0	3·7
Histidine	11·6	7·4	10·8	6·6	9·8
Lysine	9·5	7·2	8·3	7·3	7·4

[a]*Macroclemys temminckii, Alligator mississippiensis, Iguana iguana* and *Natrix rhombifera.* Acid digests analyzed by ion-exchange chromatography (courtesy R. A. Coulson).

[b]*Clemmys caspica* (= *Emys caspica*). Acid digest analyzed by ion-exchange chromatography (Christomanos and Pavlopulu, 1968; see also Georgatsos, 1960).

of unfractionated hemoglobins appear in Table III. As compared to hemoglobins of fowl, lamprey, and man (Gratzer and Allison, 1960), those of these reptiles have a high content of glycine and glutamic acid and very little proline. Threonine concentration is lower in hemoglobins of *Alligator* and higher in those of *Iguana* and *Clemmys* than in hemoglobins of the other vertebrates. The presence of tryptophane is indicated by tryptophane fine structure band at 290·0 mμ of absorption spectra of hemoglobin of the garter

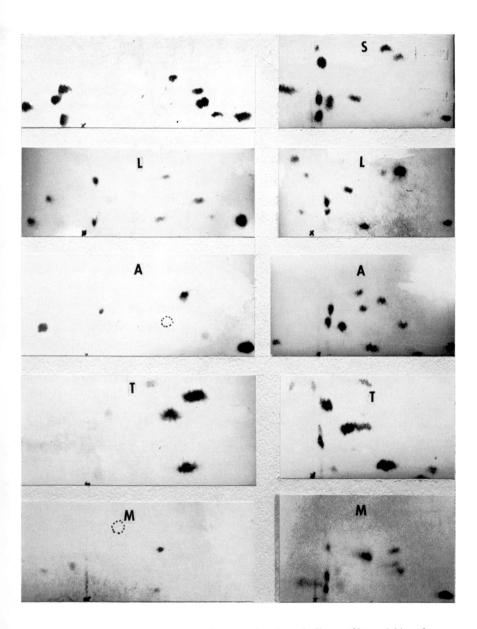

Fɪɢ. 12. Fingerprints of arginine and histidine peptides of tryptic digests of hemoglobins of representative reptiles. Peptide mixtures were applied at spots marked x, subjected to electrophoresis in the horizontal direction (pyridine-acetic acid buffer, pH 6.4), chromatography in the vertical direction (pyridine: isoamyl alcohol: water, 30:30:35), and then stained to localize peptides. Arginine fingerprints shown on the left were developed with the Sakaguchi reaction; histidine fingerprints on the right were developed with the Pauly reaction. S = the snake *Natrix taxispilota*; L = the lizard *Iguana iguana*; A = *Alligator mississippiensis*; T = the turtle *Macroclemys tem minckii*; M = *Homo sapiens* (hemoglobin A) (from Sutton and Dessauer, unpublished).

snake, *Thamnophis sirtalis* (Gratzer and Allison, 1960). "Fingerprints" of tryptic digests of hemoglobins of reptiles (Fig. 12) exhibit from one to seven tryptophane peptides, 12 to 17 histidine peptides, and 8 to 16 arginine peptides. A large percentage of insoluble "core" remains after treatment of reptilian hemoglobin with trypsin (Dessauer and Fox, 1963; Dessauer and Sutton, 1964). If the sulfhydryl groups are inactivated prior to digestion, the quantity of "core" is diminished greatly (Christomanos and Pavlopulu, 1968). Each of the two hemoglobins of *Pseudemys scripta* when isolated and digested with trypsin yields 30 peptides. The "slow" hemoglobin differs from the "fast" hemoglobin by 10 peptides (Manwell *et al.*, 1963; Manwell and Schlesinger, 1966). The N-terminal amino group of the hemoglobin of *Clemmys caspica* is threonine (Christomanos and Pavlopulu, 1968). The Val. Gly- and Val. Glu N-terminal sequences of snake hemoglobin (Ozawa and Satake, 1955) also characterize hemoglobin of a number of mammals (Gratzer and Allison, 1960).

Oxygen transport, the primary function of hemoglobins, depends upon hemoglobin's capability of combining reversibly with oxygen. Oxygen equilibrium curves describing this property are available for reptiles of all major orders (Figs 13a and b). These display the familiar S-shape typical of equilibrium curves of mammalian hemoglobins (Redfield, 1933; Prosser *et al.*, 1950; Manwell, 1960; Riggs, 1965). The sigmoid shape is caused by interactions between oxygen combining sites. Sigmoid coefficients, which measure the extent of this interaction, lie between 1 and 3 for reptilian hemoglobins (Sullivan and Riggs, 1967c; Sullivan, 1968; Dawson, 1960). Interactions between the iron porphyrin groups of turtle hemoglobins are generally lower than for human hemoglobin. The lowest yet found are for *Terrapene carolina* (Fig. 13b) and *Clemmys guttata* which have nearly hyperbolic oxygen equilibrium curves. The hemoglobins of *Clemmys*, *Phrynops*, *Malayemys*, and *Kinosternon* show little change in interaction constants with pH, but those of *Chelydra*, *Podocnemis*, *Terrapene*, *Trionyx*, *Gopherus*, and *Pseudemys* change with pH. Maximum interaction occurs at pH 7·0 in *Chelydra*, *Gopherus*, and *Trionyx*; in the others interactions are highest at pH 8 (Sullivan, 1966; Sullivan and Riggs, 1967c).

A rise in temperature (Fig. 13b) or a fall in pH (Bohr effect; Figs 13c and d) within the physiological range leads to a decrease in oxygen affinity. Considering the broad ranges of temperature and pH which the blood of reptiles experiences under physiological conditions, these influences on oxygen affinity of hemoglobin must be highly significant. Usually minimum oxygen affinity occurs near the lower limit and maximum affinity near the upper limit of the physiological pH range (Wilson, 1939; Manwell, 1960; Sullivan, 1966; Sullivan and Riggs, 1967c). Oxygen equilibrium curves vary from one reptilian species to another (Figs 13b, c, and d). The alkaline Bohr effect of hemoglobin in intact red cells (Fig. 13c) is slightly greater for *Pseudemys* than *Alligator* (Wilson, 1939); similarly the Bohr effects for *Alligator* and *Crocodylus* (Dill and Edwards, 1931a, 1931b, 1935) are greater than for the lizards *Sauromalus* (Dill *et al.*, 1935) and *Heloderma* (Dill and Edwards, 1935). Oxygen affinities of the red cells of *Uma*, *Sceloporous*, *Dipsosaurus*, and *Gerrhonotus*, though very different when tested at the same temperature, are remarkably similar when measured at the activity temperature of each species (Pough, 1969).

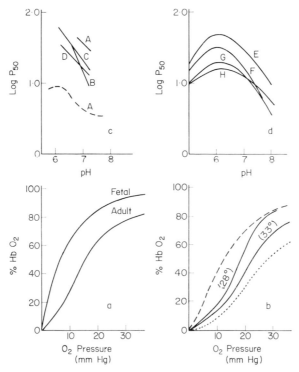

Fig. 13. Oxygen affinities of reptilian hemoglobins.

a. Affinities of fetal and adult hemoglobins of the diamondback terrapene compared at the same conditions of pH and temperature (from McCutcheon, 1947).

b. Extreme species differences and dependence on temperature. – – – the turtle *Terrapene carolina*, and . . . . . the turtle *Caretta caretta* (25·5°C., pH 7·4; from McCutcheon, 1947); ——— the lizard *Eumeces obsoletus* at two different temperatures (pH = 7·2; from Dawson, 1960).

c. Affinity of intact red blood cells under comparable conditions of temperature. For comparison, the affinity of a dilute solution of alligator hemoglobin is plotted as the dashed line. P_{50} = oxygen pressure at which 50% of active hemoglobin is oxyhemoglobin and 50% reduced hemoglobin. A = the turtle *Pseudemys scripta*; B = *Alligator mississippiensis* (from Wilson, 1939); C = *Heloderma suspectum*; D = *Sauromalus obesus* (from Edwards and Dill, 1935; Dill *et al.*, 1935).

d. Oxygen affinities of dilute solutions of turtle hemoglobins at the same temperature. E = *Terrapene carolina*; F = *Chelydra serpentina*; G = *Gopherus polyphemus*; H = human hemoglobin A (from Sullivan, 1966).

More extensive data are available for hemoglobins in dilute solutions (Fig. 13d). Hemoglobin solutions of the alligator (See Fig. 13c), the turtle *Pseudemys* (Wilson, 1939), and garter snakes *Thamnophis* (Manwell, 1960) have stronger affinities for oxygen than intact red blood cells of the same species. Hemoglobin of the *Alligator* has one of the highest oxygen affinites (Fig. 13c; Wilson, 1939) and that of the loggerhead sea turtle *Caretta caretta* (Fig. 13c) the lowest oxygen affinity at pH 7·4 of any reptile yet studied (McCutcheon, 1947; Sullivan and Riggs, 1967c). Hemoglobins of *Natrix taxispilota* and probably other snakes have very high affinities at pH 7 and are unusual in exhibiting larger acid than alkaline Bohr effects (Sullivan, 1968). Hemoglobins of numerous turtles (Figs 13b and d) have been compared (Southworth and Redfield, 1925/26; Wilson, 1939; McCutcheon, 1947; Gaumer and Goodnight, 1957; Sullivan and Riggs, 1964, 1967c; Sullivan, 1966). At the upper limit of the physiological pH range, hemoglobins of active underwater foragers and swimmers (Chelydridae, Kinosternidae, and Trionychidae) tend to bind oxygen stronger than hemoglobins of sluggish, terrestrial species. The latter have higher affinities between pH 6·5 and 6·7, as their Bohr effects are lower (Sullivan, 1966). Marine turtles, which are very active animals, have the lowest oxygen affinities (McCutcheon, 1947; Sullivan, 1966; Sullivan and Riggs, 1967c).

During development the structure of reptilian hemoglobins changes as does that of mammals. Fetal hemoglobin of man is much more resistant to solutions of high pH than adult hemoglobin. Red cells of alligators less than 2 years old contain a higher percentage of an alkali resistant hemoglobin than do those of older animals (Ramsey, 1941). Hemoglobin of embryonic diamond back terrapins has a higher oxygen affinity than hemoglobin of adult animals (Fig. 13a; McCutcheon, 1947). The fetal-maternal difference in oxygen affinity observed in viviparous garter snakes *Thamnophis sirtalis* and *Thamnophis elegans vagrans* may result from differences in the intracellular environment of the hemoglobin (Manwell, 1958, 1960).

C. Non-Hemoglobin Components

Red cells of reptiles probably have broader and more typical metabolic potentials than the highly specialized erythrocytes of mammals (Bishop, 1964). Nuclei and thus deoxyribonucleic acids (DNA) are present; from 2·8 to 3·7 per cent of cell mass in snakes, alligator, and turtle is DNA. Each red cell of the turtles *Chelonia*, *Clemmys*, and *Chelydra*, the alligator and the snake *Natrix* contains about 5×10^{-9} mg of DNA, slightly less than is present in mammalian somatic cells. The DNA content per cell of other snakes (*Elaphe* $= 4·28 \times 10^{-9}$ mg, *Coluber* $= 2·85 \times 10^{-9}$ mg) approaches levels characteristic of birds (Villela, 1947, 1949; Mirsky and Ris, 1951; Gerzeli *et al.*, 1956; Vendrely, 1958).

Presumably nucleic acid metabolism and protein synthesis occur throughout the long life span of the reptilian erythrocyte. Nucleotides occur in high concentration (Rapoport and Guest, 1941). Nucleic acid phosphatases are very active in cells of the snakes *Natrix* and *Agkistrodon*, but are of weak activity in a turtle (Rapoport *et al.*, 1942). Carbons of labeled glucose and succinate are incorporated into alanine, glutamic acid, and aspartic acid by the blood of the lizard *Egernia cunninghami* (Barwick and Bryant, 1966). All amino acids that are common constituents of proteins are present within the cell. Glycine, alanine, and glutamic acid occur in higher concentration in the red cells of *Caiman* than in its plasma. The level of 3-methyl-histidine, an amino acid of unknown function, exceeds the sum of all other amino acids in red cells of Crocodilia but is absent from erythrocytes of the turtle *Pseudemys scripta* (Herbert *et al.*, 1966).

Electrolyte gradients also exist between plasma and red cell interiors. In an African tortoise (species not given) the red cell contains only 3·5 to 4 mEq/liter of sodium; plasma sodium exceeds 100 mEq/liter. Potassium makes up the osmotic deficit of cations within the cell (Maizels, 1956). Similiar electrolyte gradients between red cells and plasma characterize blood of lizards (Dessauer, 1952), alligators (Coulson *et al.*, 1950a), and snakes (Hutton, 1958). Carbonic anhydrase, which is important in facilitating shifts of anions between plasma and the red cell, is present in erythrocytes of all major groups. That of a sea turtle *Caretta caretta* (?) has been isolated and purified 300 fold. It contains 0·2 per cent zinc and has a minimum molecular weight of 32,500. Activity is proportional to its zinc content (Leiner *et al.*, 1962). The level of carbonic anhydrase in the red cells of the alligator is less than 10 per cent of that of the dog. It is apparently inhibited by acetazolamide (Wistrand and Whitis, 1959, Coulson *et al.*, 1957). In one comparison activity was highest in red cells of *Iguana* and decreased in the order: man, kingsnake, slider turtle, and alligator (Magee and Dessauer, unpublished).

Energy is required to maintain such gradients, to preserve the structural integrity of the cell, and to keep hemoglobin in the reduced form (Bishop, 1964). Energy production by reptilian red cells is much higher than that of mammalian red cells but somewhat lower than that of birds. Oxygen consumption at 25°C varies from about 30 mm³/ml of cells/hour in *Alligator*, *Emys*, *Chelydra*, and *Pseudemys* to approximately 50 mm³/ml of cells/hour in *Terrapene*, *Natrix*, and *Thamnophis*. Rate of oxygen utilization increases in *Alligator* and *Pseudemys* directly with temperature up to 38°C; *Alligator* cells survive only briefly above 45°C. *Alligator* reticulocytes consume more oxygen than do mature red cells. Glucose and high levels of saline do not affect rates of oxygen consumption (Tipton, 1933). Energy rich phosphate compounds which result from metabolic reactions are present in higher concentration in the red cells of reptiles than in those of most mammals. The cells of lizards and snakes contain twice the level of adenosine triphosphate than those of any other animals examined (McCay, 1931; Kerr and Daoud, 1935; Rapoport and Guest, 1941).

The glycolytic pathway, tricarboxylic acid cycle, and probably the glucose-6-phosphate pathway are involved in energy production by red cells of reptiles. Tracer experiments using the lizard *Egernia cunninghami* showed that red cells oxidize glucose and acetate readily, yielding a large number of metabolic intermediates of the glycolytic and citric acid cycles. Succinic dehydrogenase, however, is probably absent from red cells of *Egernia* (Barwick and Bryant, 1966). The respiratory system of turtles furnishes the energy to maintain electrolyte gradients between red cell and plasma. In the absence of oxygen, or in cells poisoned with cyanide, gradients are maintained for short periods only because of the presence of stores of high energy phosphate (Maizels, 1956).

Stores of polysaccharides have been demonstrated histochemically in red cells of certain reptiles (Gerzeli, 1954). Diphosphoglyceric acid, an intermediate of the glycolytic cycle and of major importance in the mammalian red cell, was not found in the erythrocytes of snakes and turtles (Rapoport and Guest, 1941) but was detected in *Egernia* (Barwick and Bryant, 1966). Lactic dehydrogenase (LDH), a glycolytic enzyme, is present in reptiles (Wilson *et al.*, 1964; Kaplan, 1965). Its activity in cells of the snakes *Coluber constrictor* and *Drymarchon corais* is only slightly less than that of human red blood cells (Vesell and Bearn, 1961/1962; Vesell and Brody, 1964). Electrophoretic patterns usually exhibit five LDH isozymes for iguanid lizards (Gorman and Dessauer, 1966) and alligators and one to three for snakes (Vesell and Bearn, 1961/1962; Dessauer, unpublished). Glucose-6-phosphate dehydrogenase occurs in the red cells of *Anolis*. Active acid and alkaline phosphatases have been found in a turtle, a water snake, and a moccasin. The activity of the alkaline phosphatases is enhanced by magnesium and inhibited by oxalate and fluoride. Turtle cells contain a phytase, a phosphatase which utilizes phytic acid as substrate and does not require magnesium. Both phytic acid and phytase appear to be limited to the erythrocytes of turtles and birds (Rapoport *et al.*, 1941, 1942; see also Bishop, 1964, p. 159).

V. Blood Composition and Reptilian Systematics

A. Introduction

Blood chemistry, especially the red cell antigens and protein structure, reflects genetic affinities of the reptiles. Structures of homologous proteins exhibit hierarchies of variation that parallel degrees of divergence of different taxa (Dessauer and Fox, 1964). Homologous proteins such as the transferrins

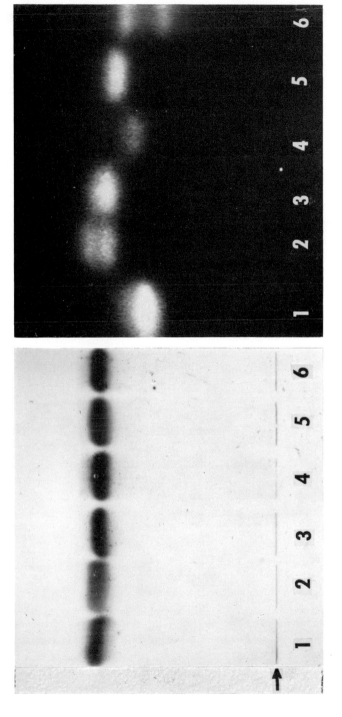

FIG. 14. Leucine naphthylamidases (Left) and transferrins (Right) of snakes of the genus *Thamnophis*, illustrating a conservative and a highly variable protein. Plasma samples to which radioactive iron was added were subjected to starch gel electrophoresis in borate buffer, pH 8.6. After electrophoresis amidases were localized by means of a histochemical method; transferrins were localized by radioautography. Arrow indicates site of sample application; anode is toward the top. (1) *T. sumichrasti*, (2) *T. eques*, (3) *T. elegans*, (4) *T. couchii hammondii*, (5) *T. sirtalis*, (6) *T. sauritus*.

(Figs 10 and 14) exhibit extensive variation. Such proteins and blood group systems demonstrate biochemical individuality and are useful in studies of population dynamics. Other proteins such as the leucine naphthylamidases (Fig. 14) are remarkably conservative structures, exhibiting little change in widely divergent species. Such molecules aid in grouping divergent forms (Dessauer, 1966).

B. Defining the Species

The presence in different individuals of cellular antigens and structural variants of homologous proteins emphasizes the population aspect of the species, the presence throughout the populations of a given species of many proteins of constant structure indicates the distinctness of the species. Variant forms of red cell antigens and of homologous proteins, probably inherited as allelomorphic genes, have been demonstrated in numerous reptiles. Systems of blood groups probably occur in all species (Section III C, 5 above). They have been examined systematically in turtles of both the Pleurodira and Cryptodira (Frair, 1963). Polymorphic forms of transferrin (Dessauer et al., 1962 a and b; Gorman and Dessauer, 1965, 1966; Fox and Dessauer, 1965), esterases (Dessauer et al., 1962b; Gorman and Dessauer, 1966), albumins (Zweig and Crenshaw, 1957; Dessauer and Fox, 1958; Crenshaw, 1965), leucine naphthylamidases (Pough and Dessauer, unpublished), and hemoglobins (Gorman and Dessauer, 1965; Manwell and Schlesinger, 1966) are known.

The number of structural variants may be extensive enough to identify individual animals. Frair (1963) was able to distinguish each of 24 tortoises *Testudo hermanni* on the basis of patterns of red cell antigens. The polymorphism of transferrins among the racer *Coluber constrictor* collected in the sand dune area of northern Indiana was great enough to identify five of a sample of six snakes (Dessauer et al., 1962a). Some variant forms occur in high frequency in a population, but others are rare and emphasize the hidden resources of variation in a species. Only one specimen out of a sample of 500 of the garter snake *Thamnophis elegans* had a variant form of leucine naphthylamidase (Dessauer, 1966).

Comparison of frequencies of individual proteins in adjacent populations shows the extent of interbreeding; comparisons of frequencies in populations throughout the range of the species may suggest clines and indicate the direction of gene flow. Frequencies of transferrins, esterases, and other variant proteins gave a measure of the extent of introgression of two subspecies of the lizard *Cnemidophorus tigris* and indicated that transferrins are inherited on allelomorphic, autosomal genes (Dessauer et al., 1962b). Crenshaw (1965), studying a hybrid population of slider turtles (*Pseudemys*), found evidence for gene exchange between species known to be isolated over most of their range and was able to suggest a possible mechanism of albumin inheritance. The distribution of transferrins among (U.S.) west coast garter snakes showed that aquatic and terrestrial populations are distinct, do not intergrade, and are different species (Dessauer et al., 1962a; Fox and Dessauer, 1965). Of two variant hemoglobins found in the turtle *Chrysemys picta* the type with a very low oxygen affinity is frequent in turtles from the warmer states, Arkansas and Louisiana. The type with a high oxygen affinity is more abundant in turtles in the colder states, Wisconsin and Minnesota (Manwell and Schlesinger, 1966). Certain populations of a species are characterized by high frequencies of an apparently unique form of a protein. In *Anolis* from the islands of the Caribbean, specific transferrins indicate the island of origin for the lizards, though they presumably belong to the same species (Gorman and Dessauer, 1965). Certain subspecies of *Pseudemys scripta* (Zweig and Crenshaw, 1957), *Natrix sipedon*, *Thamnophis sirtalis*, *Coluber constrictor*, and *Lampropeltis getulus* (Dessauer and Fox, 1958) are readily distinguished by differences in plasma albumins.

Proteins often suggest genetic affinities of species and species groups. Lactic dehydrogenase isozymes of the red cells distinguish the species of the lizard genus *Anolis* indigenous to the islands of the Lesser Antilles and tentatively assigned to the roquet-species group. Specimens of *Anolis aeneus* from three islands and the mainland of South America were classified as three named forms until study of blood proteins substantiated suspicions that populations had been recently introduced onto two of the islands and the mainland (Gorman and Dessauer, 1965, 1966). The snakes, *Regina grahami* and *R. septemvittata*, until recent years included in the genus *Natrix*, have similar plasma protein patterns, quite different from those of other species of *Natrix* (Dessauer and Fox, 1964). Numerous electrophoretic studies have demonstrated the distinctness of the protein complement of particular species (Bird, 1955; Plagnol and Vialard-Goudou, 1956; Dessauer and Fox, 1964; Latifi et al., 1965; Kmeťová and Paulov, 1966; Maldonado and Ortiz, 1966; Newcomer and Crenshaw, 1967; Voris, 1967; Rider and Bartel, 1967).

C. Relationships within Major Groups

1. *Crocodilia*

Proteins of a few members of the Crocodylidae and Alligatoridae have been compared by physicochemical and serological methods. Low serological correspondence was found between *Crocodylus niloticus* and *Alligator sinensis*; however, close correspondence was indicated for *Alligator sinensis* of China and *A. mississippiensis* of North America (Graham-Smith, 1904) and between the latter and *Caiman latirostris* (Lewis, 1964). Electrophoretic evidence is in agreement with serological findings. Plasma albumins of the Nile and American crocodile have identical electrophoretic mobilities. Mobilities of the transferrins of *Caiman* and *Alligator* are equal, but different from those of the crocodiles. Hemoglobins of the four species are electrophoretically distinguishable (Dessauer and Fox, 1964; Coulson and Hernandez, 1964).

2. *Testudines*

Immunological correspondence of serum proteins (Frair, 1964) and physicochemical properties of plasma proteins (Dessauer and Fox, 1956, 1964; Cohen and Stickler, 1958; Tondo, 1958; Leone and Wilson, 1961; Crenshaw, 1962; Frair, 1964; Lewis, 1964; Newcomer and Crenshaw, 1967) and hemoglobins (Dessauer *et al.*, 1957; Sullivan, 1966; Sullivan and Riggs, 1967a, b and c) largely support current schemes of classification and suggest affinities of living forms. Turtles of the suborder Cryptodira show low immunological correspondence to species of the suborder Pleurodira. Globins of species of the Chelidae, a family of the Pleurodira, show unique properties. Based upon blood studies the (1) marine, (2) softshell, and (3) fresh water and land turtles of the Cryptodira appear to be divergent forms. Families of sea turtles exhibit closer immunological correspondence to each other than to non-marine species. The genera *Chelonia* and *Caretta* show very high correspondence and have similar hemoglobins. Softshell turtles have unique hemoglobins. Further, antisera against *Trionyx ferox* plasma proteins interact appreciably with serum of other softshell turtles but give practically no reaction with serum of species from other families. Species of fresh water and land turtles divide into two groups on the basis of the electrophoretic behavior of plasma albumin (Fig. 9). Albumins of *Dermatemys, Staurotypus, Sternotherus* (3 species), and *Kinosternon* (5 species) have relatively fast migration rates. Plasma proteins of these genera also exhibit high immunological correspondence. The only other turtle known to have a "fast-albumin" is the pleurodire *Chelodina longicollis*. Hemoglobins of *Chelydra, Staurotypus, Claudius, Kinosternon* and *Sternotherus* show some similarities in physicochemical properties. Emydine turtles are apparently a heterogenous group; anti-*Pseudemys* sera exhibits 55% serological correspondence to *Chrysemys*, 45% to *Terrapene*, but only 7% to *Kachuga tecta*.

3. *Squamata*

Immunological evidence, although almost non-existent at the subordinal level, reveals a remote relationship between the Varanidae and lizards of the Gekkonidae, Scincidae, and Agamidae, but almost no affinity between Varanidae and snakes of the Boidae, Colubridae, Crotalinae, and Viperinae (Graham-Smith, 1904; Cohen, 1955). Electrophoretic mobilites of the albumins, transferrins and hemoglobins of a wide variety of Squamata (Dessauer and Fox, 1964) form overlapping series, not allowing differentiation of the suborders (Figs 9 and 10). Fingerprints of arginine peptides of tryptic digests of hemoglobins of iguanid lizards and of snakes have a number of common features (Fig. 12; Dessauer and Fox, 1963; Dessauer and Sutton, 1964). Blood of lizards generally contains more glucose than blood of snakes (Table II); snake plasma contains a higher concentration of sialic acid than that of other reptiles, including iguanid lizards (Seal, 1964).

Among sub-families of snakes the Boinae display high immunological correspondence with the Pythoninae; the Elapinae with the Hydrophiinae; and the Crotalinae with the Viperinae, though some authors consider members of these pairs distinct on the family level. The Colubridae show coldest and about equal affinity to the Crotalidae and Elapidae. The Typhlopidae are remote from all families tested (Boidae, Colubridae, Viperidae, and Elapidae), though they exhibit some similarity to the Boidae (Graham-Smith, 1904; Kellaway and Williams, 1931; Kuwajima, 1953; Cohen, 1955; Pearson, 1966). Leucine naphthylamidase is absent from the plasma of the Boidae, exhibits weak activity among the Crotalidae and Elapidae, but is exceptionally active in plasma of the Colubridae (Dessauer, 1967; Ehrensing, 1964). Fingerprints of tryptic peptides of hemoglobins of Boidae, Colubridae, and Crotalidae are remarkably similar (Dessauer and Sutton, 1964, and unpublished).

Recent findings may help unravel relationships of genera of snakes presently grouped in the Colubridae and Crotalidae. Within the Crotalidae, *Sistrurus* is biochemically closer to *Crotalus* than to *Agkistrodon*. Moccasins are a more divergent group of species than rattlesnakes (Cohen, 1955; Pearson, 1966). *Agkistrodon* and *Trimeresurus* on Formosa are near relatives (Kuwajima, 1953). Pearson (1966) classified 11 genera of the Colubridae into four subgroups on the basis of immunological correspondence of serum proteins. One group includes *Farancia*, *Diadophis*, and *Heterodon*. Species of the second group, including *Lampropeltis*, *Pituophis*, *Rhinocheilus*, and *Elaphe*, and the third group, including *Coluber*, *Masticophis*, and *Opheodrys*, are more closely related to each other than to species in the other groups. Pearson's fourth group, the Natricinae, also appears to be a natural category on the basis of physicochemical evidence. Plasma of natricine genera from Africa, Asia, Europe, and North America contains a unique esterase, which is absent from the plasma of other colubrid snakes. One of the polypeptide subunits of their globins is electrophoretically unique (Dessauer, 1967)

D. CHARACTERISTICS AND AFFINITIES OF MAJOR GROUPS

Both physicochemical and immunological evidence emphasize the evolutionary divergence of major groups of the Reptilia. Serology demonstrates the fairly close relationship of some lizards and snakes, indicates a very remote affinity between turtles and crocodiles, and shows the wide divergence of the Squamata from the Testudines and Crocodilia. Such conclusions find their basis in the work of Graham-Smith (1904). Utilizing antisera against serum proteins from two species of tortoise and a sea turtle, a Chinese alligator, an agamid and a varanid lizard, and a boid and a colubrid snake, he compared homologous and heterologous precipitin reactions between sera from about 40 species of reptiles. The forms sampled by him are presently classified in 4 families of turtles, 2 families of crocodilians, 6 families of lizards, and 4 families of snakes. Graham-Smith's conclusions, although obtained with the crudest of techniques, have been supported by investigators using modern methods (Wolfe, 1939; Cohen, 1955; Lewis, 1964).

Species of the three major groups of living reptiles are easily distinguished by the electrophoretic behavior of their blood proteins (Figs 9 and 10). Albumins and transferrins of the Testudines migrate at slower rates in alkaline buffers than do the albumins and transferrins of the Crocodilia and Squamata. Red cell hemolysates from turtles resolve into complex patterns of multiple hemoglobins. Hemolysates from snakes, lizards, and crocodiles resolve into simple patterns of one or two components. Hemoglobins of the Squamata have uniquely slow mobilities. Their plasma usually lacks a fraction with the mobility of mammalian gamma-globulin.

Even low molecular weight blood constituents are useful in distinguishing these forms, reflecting the many gains and losses in metabolic potential which accompanied divergent evolution. Thus, the high concentration of urea in the blood of turtles reflects the presence of active urea-cycle enzymes. The lack or low concentration of urea in blood in other reptiles is the result of the loss or suppression of the urea-cycle (Table II). Other metabolic specializations (Section IV C above) are probably responsible for the uniquely high concentration of high energy phosphates in red cells of the Squamata, the presence of phytic acid in erythrocytes of turtles, and the high levels of 3-methylhistidine in cells of the Crocodilia.

VI. Summary

The blood of reptiles is a rich source of evidence on their heritage and on the ways in which they have adapted to metabolic challenges. The composition of the blood of all major reptilian groups is typical of that of vertebrates in general. It contains most of the same components of low molecular weight. The macromolecules, though of unique and highly specific structure, include proteins analogous to and probably homologous with the volume expanders, transport proteins, clotting factors, and immune bodies of mammals. The nucleated red cells, which make up 20 to 30 per cent of their blood volume, contain approximately the same amount of hemoglobin, but have more complete systems of metabolic pathways and longer life spans than the unnucleated erythrocytes of mammals.

Concentrations of many blood constituents, however, fluctuate to a much greater extent than one would expect from a knowledge of mammalian physiology. Daily events such as feeding, diving, and changes in the temperature or availability of water in the environment often lead to drastic shifts in blood levels of salts and metabolites. Certain constituents undergo marked cyclic changes in association with reproduction. During estrus in females the yolk precursor, plasma vitellin, appears in the blood causing increased protein, calcium, and magnesium levels. Other seasonal shifts in metabolic capabilities result in dramatic cyclic changes in blood levels of metabolites such as glucose.

The wide evolutionary divergence of the three major groups of living reptiles is emphasized by blood chemistry. Major structural differences exist between the hemoglobins, albumins, transferrins, and other blood proteins of turtles, crocodiles, and squamates. Blood composition of one group of the Reptilia often responds to a physiological event quite differently from that of another group, reflecting marked differences in metabolic potentials. The pattern of changes in the blood during a dive is different in fresh water turtles than in other reptiles; the effect of insulin on blood sugar is less marked in squamates than in turtles and crocodiles; feeding leads to drastic shifts in the electrolytes of crocodiles but has little effect on salt balance of lizards. Divergence of metabolic potential is so great that one even observes differences in certain low molecular weight metabolites. Thus, only turtle blood contains phytic acid and moderate amounts of urea, and lizard blood characteristically contains a high concentration of glucose.

Homologous blood proteins exhibit hierarchies of variation that parallel degrees of divergence of taxa of close and distant relationship. Comparative evidence on proteins can clarify difficult problems of relationship. Such evidence illustrates the individuality of the organism and emphasizes that species may be composed of differing populations. It has been useful in detecting hybrids, in comparing degree of divergence of island populations, and in grouping and estimating degrees of divergence of species, genera, and higher taxonomic categories.

Presumably natural selection for mutations of adaptive value has led to the accumulation of these many differences between proteins. Variations in the structure and concentration of plasma albumin appear to correlate with the availability of water, metabolic rate and diving physiology. The structure of the hemoglobin molecule often relates to the availability of oxygen in the environment and the activity of the organism. Such meager evidence represents about all the information as yet available relating structural differences between homologous blood proteins of reptiles to physiological and ecological factors.

VII. Acknowledgements

I wish to express my sense of obligation to Carl Gans, Daniel Belkin, Wayne Frair, Bob Masat, Harvey Pough, Joe Musacchia, and Aaron Taub and to scientists unknown to me who spent much valuable time in the thankless task of reviewing the manuscript. Due to their labors I feel that my mistakes in detail and interpretation are far fewer, and I have much more confidence in passing this effort on to the scientific community. I am grateful to Mr. Caral Tate and Miss Donna Berkins for valuable assistance in preparing the manuscript and to the National Science Foundation (Grant GB-3124) for its support.

References

Agid, R., Duguy, R., Martoja, M. and Saint-Girons, H. (1961a). Influence de la température et des facteurs endocrines dans la glycorégulation chez *Vipera aspis*. Rôle de l'adrénaline. *C. r. hebd. Séanc. Acad. Sci. Paris* 252, 2007–2009.

Agid, R., Duguy, R. and Saint-Girons, H. (1961b). Variations de la glycémie du glycogène hépatique et de l'aspect histologique du pancréas, chez *Vipera aspis*, au cours du cycle annuel. *J. Physiol. Paris* 53, 807–824.

Alder, A. and Huber, E. (1923). Untersuchungen über Blutzellen und Zellbildung bei Amphibien und Reptilien. *Folia haemat. Lpz.* 29, 1–22.

Aldred, P. (1940). A note on the osmotic pressure of the blood in various animals. *J. exp. Biol.* 17, 223–226.

Altland, P. D. and Brace, K. C. (1962). Red cell life span in the turtle and toad. *Am. J. Physiol.* 203, 1188–1190.

Altland, P. D. and Parker, M. (1955). Effects of hypoxia upon the box turtle. *Am. J. Physiol.* 180, 421–427.

Altland, P. D. and Thompson, E. C. (1958). Some factors affecting blood formation in turtles. *Proc. Soc. exp. Biol. Med.* 99, 456–459.

Andersen, H. T. (1961). Physiological adjustments to prolonged diving in the American alligator, *Alligator mississippiensis*. *Acta physiol. scand.* 53, 23–45.

Andersen, H. T. (1966). Physiological adaptations in diving vertebrates. *Physiol. Rev.* 46, 212–243.

Andreen-Svedberg, A. (1933). On the distribution of sugar between plasma and corpuscles in animal and human blood. *Skand. Arch. Physiol.* 66, 113–190.

Anson, M. L., Barcroft, J., Mirsky, A. E. and Oinuma, S. (1924). On the correlation between the spectra of various haemoglobins and their relative affinities for oxygen and carbon monoxide. *Proc. R. Soc.* B 97, 61–83.

Appleby, E. C. and Siller, W. G. (1960). Some cases of gout in reptiles. *J. Path. Bact.* 80, 427–430.

Aron, E., Combescot, C., Delcroix, C., Demaret, J. and Vargues, R. (1959). Effets de l'hypophysectomie sur les éléments figurés du sange et sur l'equilibre protéique sérique chez la Tortue d'eau *Emys leprosa Schw. C. r. Séanc. Soc. Biol.* 153, 1436–1438.

Augustinsson, K. (1959). Electrophoresis studies on blood plasma esterases. *Acta chem. scand.* 13, 1081–1096.

Augustinsson, K. (1961). Multiple forms of esterase in vertebrate blood plasma. *Ann. N.Y. Acad. Sci.* **94**, 844–860.

Austin, J. H., Sunderman, F. W. and Camack, J. G. (1927). Studies in serum electrolytes. II. The electrolyte composition and the pH of serum of a poikilothermous animal at different temperatures. *J. biol. Chem.* **72**, 677–685.

Barber, A. A. and Sheeler, P. (1961). Iron binding by vertebrate blood sera. *Comp. Biochem. Physiol.* **2**, 233–240.

Barber, A. A. and Sheeler, P. (1963). A comparative study on the iron-binding proteins of vertebrate blood sera. *Comp. Biochem. Physiol.* **8**, 115–122.

Baril, E. F., Palmer, J. L. and Bartel, A. H. (1961). Electrophoretic analysis of young alligator serum. *Science N.Y.* **133**, 278–279.

Bartholomew, G. A. (1959). Photoperiodism in reptiles. *In* "Photoperiodism and Related Phenomena in Plants and Animals". American Association for the Advancement of Science, Washington, D.C. pp. 669–676.

Barwick, R. E. and Bryant, C. (1966). Physiological and biochemical aspects of hibernation in the scincid lizard *Egernia cunninghami* (Gray, 1832). *Physiol. Zool.* **39**, 1–20.

Beck, A. B. (1956). The copper content of the liver and blood of some vertebrates. *Aust. J. Zool.* **4**, 1–18.

Belkin, D. A. (1962). Anaerobiosis in diving turtles. *Physiologist, Wash.* **5**, 105.

Belkin, D. A. (1963). Anoxia: Tolerance in reptiles. *Science, N.Y.* **139**, 492–493.

Belkin, D. A. (1964). Variations in heart rate during voluntary diving in the turtle *Pseudemys concinna. Copeia.* **1964**, 321–330.

Belkin, D. A. (1965). Critical oxygen tensions in turtles. *Physiologist, Wash.* **8**, 109.

Belkin, D. A. (1968). Anaerobic brain function: Effects of stagnant and anoxic anoxia on persistence of breathing in reptiles. *Science, N.Y.* **162**, 1017–1018.

Bellamy, D. and Petersen, J. A. (1968). Anaerobiosis and the toxicity of cyanide in turtles. *Comp. Biochem. Physiol.* **24**, 543–548.

Benedict, F. G. (1932). The physiology of large reptiles. *Publs. Carnegie Inst.* 425.

Bentley, P. J. (1959). Studies on the water and electrolyte metabolism of the lizard *Trachysaurus rugosus* (Gray). *J. Physiol., Lond.* **145**, 37–47.

Bentley, P. J., Bretz, W. L. and Schmidt-Nielsen, K. (1967). Osmoregulation in the diamondback terrapin, *Malaclemys terrapin centrata. J. exp. Biol.* **46**, 161–167.

Bergman, R. A. M. (1951). The anatomy of *Homalopsis buccata. Proc. K. ned. Akad. Wet.* **54**, 511–524.

Berkson, H. (1966). Physiological adjustments to prolonged diving in the Pacific green turtle (*Chelonia mydas* Agassizii). *Comp. Biochem. Physiol.* **18**, 101–119.

Betz, T. W. (1962). Surgical anesthesia in reptiles, with special reference to the water snake, *Natrix rhombifera. Copeia* **1962**, 284–287.

Bird, G. W. G. (1955). Some serological observations on the blood of the Indian cobra *Naja tripudians. Curr. Sci.* **24**, 374.

Bishop, C. (1964). Overall red cell metabolism. *In* "The Red Blood Cell" (C. Bishop and D. M. Surgenor, eds). Academic Press, New York. pp. 147–188.

Bond, G. C. (1939). Serological studies of the Reptilia. I. Hemagglutinins and hemagglutinogens of snake blood. *J. Immun.* **36**, 1–9.

Bond, G. C. (1940a). Serological studies of the Reptilia. III. Hemagglutinins and hemagglutinogens of turtle-blood. *J. Immun.* **39**, 125–131.

Bond, G. C. (1940b). Serological studies of the Reptilia. IV. Hemagglutinins and hemagglutinogens of alligator blood. *J. Immun.* **39**, 133–136.

Bond, G. C. and Sherwood, N. P. (1939). Serological studies of the Reptilia. II. The hemolytic property of snake serum. *J. Immun.* **36**, 11–16.

Bottazzi, F. (1908). Osmotischer Druck und elektrische Leitfähigkeit der Flüssigkeiten der einzelligen, pflanzlichen und tierischen Organismen. *Ergebn. Physiol.* 7, 161–402.

Brace, K. C. and Altland, P. D. (1955). Red cell survival in the turtle. *Am. J. Physiol.* 183, 91–94.

Bradshaw, S. D. and Shoemaker, V. H. (1967). Aspects of water and electrolyte changes in a field population of *Amphibolurus* lizards. *Comp. Biochem. Physiol.* 20, 855–865.

Brambel, C. E. (1941). Prothrombin activity of turtle blood and the effect of a synthetic vitamin K derivative. *J. cell. comp. Physiol.* 18, 221–232.

Brazil, V. and Vellard, J. (1928). Action coagulante et anticoagulante des sérums coagulabilité des plasmas normaux. *Annls. Inst. Pasteur, Paris* 1928, 907–944.

Britton, S. W. and Kline, R. F. (1939). Emotional hyperglycemia and hyperthermia in tropical mammals and reptiles. *Am. J. Physiol.* 125, 730–734.

Brocq-Rousseu, D. and Roussel, G. (1934). "Le Serum Normal. Recolte et Caracteres Physiques. Masson and Cie, Paris.

Brocq-Rousseu, D. and Roussel, G. (1939). "Le Serum Normal. Proprietes physiologiques". Masson and Cie, Paris.

Bullock, T. H. (1955). Compensation for temperature in the metabolism and activity of poikilotherms. *Biol. Rev.* 30, 311–342.

Burian, R. (1910). Funktion der Nierenglomeruli und Ultrafiltration. *Pflügers Arch. ges. Physiol.* 36, 741–760.

Campbell, M. L. and Turner, A. H. (1937). Serum protein measurements in the lower vertebrates. I. The colloid osmotic pressure, nitrogen content, and refractive index of turtle serum and body fluid. *Biol. Bull. mar. biol. Lab., Woods Hole.* 73, 504–510.

Carmichael, E. B. and Petcher, P. W. (1945). Constituents of the blood of the hibernating and normal rattlesnake, *Crotalus horridus. J. biol. Chem.* 161, 693–696.

Chaikoff, I. L. and Entenman, C. (1946). The lipides of blood, liver, and egg yolk of the turtle. *J. biol. Chem.* 166, 683–689.

Christomanos, A. A. and Pavlopulu, C. (1968). Zur Konstitution der Häemoglobine der Süsswasserschildkröte *Glemys caspica rivulata* und des Aals *Anguilla anguilla. Enzymologia.* 34, 51–62.

Clark, H. (1953). Metabolism of the black snake embryo. I. Nitrogen excretion. *J. exp. Biol.* 30, 492–501.

Clark, H. (1955). Urease activity related to uric acid synthesis. *Anat. Rec.* 122, 417–418.

Clark, N. B. (1967). Influence of estrogens upon serum calcium, phosphate and protein concentrations of fresh-water turtles. *Comp. Biochem. Physiol.* 20, 823–834.

Cline, M. J. and Waldmann, T. A. (1962). Effect of temperature on red cell survival in the alligator. *Proc. Soc. exp. Biol. Med.* 111, 716–718.

Cohen, E. (1954). A comparison of the total protein and albumin content of the blood sera of some reptiles. *Science, N.Y.* 119, 98–99.

Cohen, E. (1955). Immunological studies of the serum proteins of some reptiles. *Biol. Bull. mar. biol. Lab. Woods Hole.* 109, 394–403.

Cohen, E., Hermes, P. and Miyara, A. (1964). The use of alligator erythrocytes in the anti-human globulin consumption test for the detection of S. L. E. globulins. *Proc. 9th Congr. Int. Soc. Blood Transf.* 429–433.

Cohen, E., Nisonoff, A., Hermes, P., Norcross, B. M. and Lockie, L. M. (1961). Agglutination of sensitized alligator erythrocytes by rheumatoid factor(s). *Nature, Lond.* 190, 552–553.

Cohen, E. and Stickler, G. B. (1958). Absence of albumin-like serum proteins in turtles. *Science, N.Y.* **127**, 1392.

Cohen, P. P. and Brown, G. W., Jr. (1960). Ammonia metabolism and urea biosynthesis. *In* "Comparative Biochemistry" M. Florkin and H. S. Mason, eds. Vol. II. Academic Press, New York. pp. 161–244.

Collip, J. B. (1920). The alkali reserve of marine fish and invertebrates. *J. biol. Chem.* **44**, 329–344.

Collip, J. B. (1921a). The alkali reserve of the blood of certain of the lower vertebrates. *J. biol. Chem.* **46**, 57–59.

Collip, J. B. (1921b). The acid-base exchange between the plasma and the red blood cells. *J. biol. Chem.* **46**, 61–72.

Corrêa, P. R., Marques, M. and Wagner, E. M. (1960). Hyperglycemia caused by the oral administration of glucose in turtles. *Endocrinology.* **66**, 731–734.

Couch, J. R., Olcese, O., Witten, P. W. and Colby, R. W. (1950). Vitamin B_{12} content of blood from various species. *Am. J. Physiol.* **163**, 77–80.

Coulson, R. A. and Hernandez, T. (1953). Glucose studies in Crocodilia. *Endocrinology.* **53**, 311–320.

Coulson, R. A. and Hernandez, T. (1955). Renal excretion of carbon dioxide and ammonia by the alligator. *Proc. Soc. exp. Biol. Med.* **88**, 682–687.

Coulson, R. A. and Hernandez, T. (1957). Role of carbonic anhydrase in anion excretions in the alligator. *Am. J. Physiol.* **188**, 121–124.

Coulson, R. A. and Hernandez, T. (1959). Source and function of urinary ammonia in the alligator. *Am. J. Physiol.* **197**, 873–879.

Coulson, R. A. and Hernandez, T. (1961). Renal failure in the alligator. *Am. J. Physiol.* **200**, 893–897.

Coulson, R. A. and Hernandez, T. (1962). Influence of plasma amino acid level on urine volume in the alligator. *Am. J. Physiol.* **202**, 83–87.

Coulson, R. A. and Hernandez, T. (1964). "Biochemistry of the Alligator. A Study of Metabolism in Slow Motion". Louisiana State University Press, Baton Rouge, La.

Coulson, R. A. and Hernandez, T. (1965). Amino acid metabolism in the alligator. *Fedn. Proc. Fedn. Am. Socs. exp. Biol.* **24**, 927–940.

Coulson, R. A. and Hernandez, T. (1966). Importance of glutamine, glycine and alanine in nitrogen carriage. *Fedn Proc. Fedn Am. Socs exp. Biol.* **25**, 787.

Coulson, R. A. and Hernandez, T. (1968). Amino acid metabolism in chameleons. *Comp. Biochem. Physiol.* **25**, 861–872.

Coulson, R. A., Hernandez, T. and Beebe, J. L. (1957). Effects of acetazoleamide, chlorothiazide, and dichlorphenamide on electrolyte excretion in the alligator. *Proc. Soc. exp. Biol. Med.* **96**, 606–609.

Coulson, R. A., Hernandez, T. and Brazda, F. G. (1950a). Biochemical studies on the alligator. *Proc. Soc. exp. Biol. Med.* **73**, 203–206.

Coulson, R. A., Hernandez, T. and Dessauer, H. C. (1950b). Alkaline tide of the alligator. *Proc. Soc. exp. Biol. Med.* **74**, 866–869.

Crenshaw, J. W., Jr. (1962). Variation in the serum albumins and other blood proteins of turtles of the Kinosternidae. *Physiol. Zool.* **35**, 157–165.

Crenshaw, J. W., Jr. (1965). Serum protein variation in an interspecies hybrid swarm of turtles of the genus *Pseudemys.* Evolution, *Lancaster, Pa.* **19**, 1–15.

Dantzler, W. H. (1967). Stop-flow study of renal function in conscious water snakes (*Natrix sipedon.*) *Comp. Biochem. Physiol.* **22**, 131–140.

Dastugue, G. and Joy, M. (1943). Nouvelles recherches sur la composition du sang chez *Vipera aspis.* II. Les constituants chimiques. *C. r. Soc. Phys. Biol.* **67**, 61–68.

Daw, J. C., Wenger, D. P. and Berne, R. M. (1967). Relationship between cardiac glycogen and tolerance to anoxia in the Western painted turtle, *Chrysemys picta bellii*. *Comp. Biochem. Physiol.* **22**, 69–73.

Dawson, W. R. (1960). Physiological responses to temperature in the lizard *Eumeces obsoletus*. *Physiol. Zool.* **33**, 87–103.

Dawson, W. R. and Poulson, T. L. (1962). Oxygen capacity of lizard bloods. *Am. Midl. Nat.* **68**, 154–164.

Dessauer, H. C. (1952). Biochemical studies on the lizard, *Anolis carolinensis*. *Proc. Soc. exp. Biol. Med.* **80**, 742–744.

Dessauer, H. C. (1953). Hibernation of the lizard, *Anolis carolinensis*. *Proc. Soc. exp. Biol. Med.* **82**, 351–353.

Dessauer, H. C. (1955). Seasonal changes in the gross organ composition of the lizard, *Anolis carolinensis*. *J. exp. Zool.* **128**, 1–12.

Dessauer, H. C. (1966). Taxonomic significance of electrophoretic patterns of animal sera. *Bull. serol. Mus. New Brunsw.* **34**, 4–8.

Dessauer, H. C. (1967). Molecular approach to the taxonomy of colubrid snakes. *Herpetologica* **23**, 148–155.

Dessauer, H. C. and Fox, W. (1956). Characteristic electrophoretic patterns of plasma proteins of orders of Amphibia and Reptilia. *Science, N.Y.* **124**, 225–226.

Dessauer, H. C. and Fox, W. (1958). Geographic variation in plasma protein patterns of snakes. *Proc. Soc. exp. Biol. Med.* **98**, 101–105.

Dessauer, H. C. and Fox, W. (1959). Changes in ovarian follicle composition with plasma levels of snakes during estrus. *Am. J. Physiol.* **197**, 360–366.

Dessauer, H. C. and Fox, W. (1963). Electrophoretic techniques in systematics. *XVI Int. Congr. Zool.* **4**, 128–132.

Dessauer, H. C. and Fox, W. (1964). Electrophoresis in taxonomic studies illustrated by analyses of blood proteins. *In* "Taxonomic Biochemistry and Serology". (C. A. Leone, ed.). Ronald Press, New York. pp. 625–647.

Dessauer, H. C. and Sutton, D. E. (1964). Fingerprint correspondence of enzyme digests of proteins as gauges of relationship. *Fedn Proc. Fedn Am. Socs exp. Biol.* **23**, 475.

Dessauer, H. C., Fox, W. and Gilbert, N. L. (1956). Plasma calcium, magnesium and protein of viviparous colubrid snakes during estrous cycle. *Proc. Soc. exp. Biol. Med.* **92**, 299–301.

Dessauer, H. C., Fox, W. and Hartwig, Q. L. (1962a). Comparative study of transferrins of Amphibia and Reptilia using starch-gel electrophoresis and autoradiography. *Comp. Biochem. Physiol.* **5**, 17–29.

Dessauer, H. C., Fox, W. and Pough, F. H. (1962b). Starch-gel electrophoresis of transferrins, esterases and other plasma proteins of hybrids between two subspecies of whiptail lizard. *Copeia.* **1962**, 767–774.

Dessauer, H. C., Fox, W. and Ramirez, J. R. (1957). Preliminary attempt to correlate paper-electrophoretic migration of hemoglobins and phylogeny in Amphibia and Reptilia. *Archs Biochem. Biophys.* **71**, 11–16.

Deutsch, H. F. and McShan, W. H. (1949). Biophysical studies of blood plasma proteins. XII Electrophoretic studies of the blood serum proteins of some lower animals. *J. biol. Chem.* **180**, 219–234.

Dill, D. B. and Edwards, H. T. (1931a). Respiration and metabolism of a young crocodile. (*Crocodylus acutus* Cuvier). *Copeia.* **1931**, 1–3.

Dill, D. B. and Edwards, H. T. (1931b). Physiochemical properties of crocodile blood (*Crocodilus actus*, Cuvier). *J. biol. Chem.* **90**, 515–530.

Dill, D. B. and Edwards, H. T. (1935). Properties of reptilian blood. IV. The alligator (*Alligator mississippiensis* Daudin). *J. cell. comp. Physiol.* 6, 243–254.

Dill, D. B., Edwards, H. T., Bock, A. V. and Talbott, J. H. (1935). Properties of reptilian blood. III. The chuckwalla (*Sauromalus obesus* Baird). *J. cell. comp. Physiol.* 6, 37–42.

DiMaggio, A. III (1961). Effects of glucagon and insulin on carbohydrate metabolism in a lizard. *Fedn Proc. Fedn Am. Socs exp. Biol.* 20, 175.

DiMaggio, A. III (1961/62). Hormonal regulation of growth in a lizard, *Anolis carolinensis*. *Diss. Abstr.* 22, 415.

DiMaggio, A., III and Dessauer, H. C. (1963). Seasonal changes in glucose tolerance and glycogen disposition in a lizard. *Am. J. Physiol.* 204, 677–680.

Dittmer, D. S. (ed.) (1961). "Blood and other Body Fluids". Biological Handbooks. Federation of American Society for Experimental Biology, Washington, D.C.

Dontcheff, L. and Kayser, C. (1937). Les effets des variations de la température ambiante sur le quotient respiratoire et la réserve alcaline de la tortue. *C. r. Séanc. Soc. Biol.* 124, 364–366.

Dorst, S. E. and Mills, C. A. (1923). Comparative studies on blood clotting in mammals, birds and reptiles. *Am. J. Physiol.* 64, 160–166.

Downs, C. M. (1928). Anaphylaxis. VII. Active anaphylaxis in turtles. *J. Immun.* 15, 77–81.

Dozy, A. M., Reynolds, C. A., Still, J. M. and Huisman, T. H. J. (1964). Studies on animal hemoglobins. I. Hemoglobins in turtles. *J. exp. Zool.* 155, 343–347.

Drilhon, A. and Marcoux, F. (1942). Etude biochimique du sang et de l'urine d'un chélonien: *Testudo mauritanica*. *Bull. Soc. Chim. biol.* 24, 103–107.

Drilhon, A., Fontaine, M. and Raffy, A. (1937). Recherches sur la composition chimique du milieu intérieur et sur le métabolisme respiratoire de *Thalassochelys caretta*. L. *Bull. Inst. océanogr. Monaco.* 720, 1–6.

Duguy, R. (1962). Biologie de la latence hivernale chez *Vipera aspis* L. *Vie Milieu.* 14, 311–443.

Duguy, R. (1963). Données sur le cycle annuel du sang circulant chez *Anguis fragilis* L. *Bull. Soc. zool. Fr.* 88, 99–108.

Dujarric de la Rivière, R., Eyquem, A. and Fine, J. (1954). Les hémagglutinines et hémagglutinogènes du sang de *Vipera aspis*. *Experientia.* 10, 159–165.

Dunlap, C. E. (1955). Notes on the visceral anatomy of the giant leatherback turtle (*Dermochelys Coriacea* Linnaeus). *Bull. Tulane med. Fac.* 14, 55–69.

Dunson, W. A. and Taub, A. M. (1967). Extrarenal salt excretion in sea snakes (*Laticauda*). *Am. J. Physiol.* 213, 975–982.

Dunson, W. A. and Weymouth, R. D. (1965). Active uptake of sodium by soft-shell turtles (*Trionyx spinifer*). *Science, N.Y.* 149, 67–69.

Edsall, J. T. and Wyman, J. (1958). "Biophysical Chemistry" Academic Press, New York, Vol. I, Chap. 10.

Edwards, H. T. and Dill, D. B. (1935). Properties of reptilian blood. II. The Gila monster (*Heloderma suspectum* Cope). *J. cell. comp. Physiol.* 6, 21–35.

Ehrensing, R. H. (1964). Plasma oxytocinase, cystine and leucine napthylamidases of snake, turtle and chicken. *Proc. Soc. exp. Biol. Med.* 117, 370–373.

Engle, R. L., Jr. and Woods, K. R. (1960). Comparative biochemistry and embryology. *In* "The Plasma Proteins" (F. W. Putnam, ed.). Academic Press, New York, Vol. II, pp. 183–265.

Erdös, E. G., Miwa, I. and Graham, W. J. (1967). Studies on the evolution of the plasma kinins: Reptilian and avian blood. *Life Sciences.* 6, 2433–2439.

Evans, E. E. (1963a). Antibody response in Amphibia and Reptilia. *Fedn Proc. Fedn Am. Socs exp. Biol.* 22, 1132–1137.

Evans, E. E. (1963b). Comparative immunology. Antibody response in *Dipsosaurus dorsalis* at different temperatures. *Proc. Soc. exp. Biol. Med.* 112, 531–533.

Evans, E. E. and Cowles, R. B. (1959). Effect of temperature on antibody synthesis in the reptile, *Dipsosaurus dorsalis*. *Proc. Soc. exp. Biol. Med.* 101, 482–483.

Evans, E. E., Kent, S. P., Attleberger, M. H., Sieberg, C., Bryant, R. E. and Booth, B. (1965). Antibody synthesis in poikilothermic vertebrates. *Ann. N.Y. Acad. Sci.* 126, 629–646.

Fandard, L. and Ranc, A. (1912). Sur le sucre du sang de la Tortue de mer. *C. r. Séanc. Soc. Biol.* 2, 437–438.

Fantl, P. (1961). A comparative study of blood coagulation in vertebrates. *Aust. J. exp. Biol. med. Sci.* 39, 403–412.

Farer, L. S., Robbins, J., Blumberg, B. S. and Rall, J. E. (1962). Thyroxine-serum protein complexes in various animals. *Endocrinology.* 70, 686–696.

Favour, C. B. (1958). Comparative immunology and the phylogeny of homotransplantation. *Ann. N.Y. Acad. Sci.* 73, 590–598.

Fine, J., Groulade, J. and Eyquem, A. (1954). Étude par microélectrophorèse sur papier du sérum de *Vipera aspis* et *Vipera ursini*. *Annls Inst. Pasteur, Paris* 86, 378–381.

Finlayson, R. (1964). Vascular disease in captive animals. *Symp. zool. Soc. Lond.* 11, 99–106.

Foglia, V. G., Wagner, E. M., DeBarros M. and Marques, M. (1955). La diabetes por pancreatectomia en la tortuga normal e hipofisopriva. *Rev. Soc. argent. Biol.* 31, 87–95.

Fox, W. and Dessauer, H. C. (1965). Collection of garter snakes for blood studies. *Yb Am. phil. Soc.* 1964, 263–266.

Fox, A. M. and Musacchia, X. J. (1959). Notes on the pH of the digestive tract of *Chrysemys picta*. *Copeia* 1959, 337–339.

Frair, W. (1962a). Comparative serology of turtles with systematic implications. *Diss. Abstr.* 23, 2262.

Frair, W. (1962b). Current studies of Chelonian serology. *Bull. serol. Mus. New Brunsw.* 27, 7–8.

Frair, W. (1963). Blood group studies with turtles. *Science*, 140, 1412–1414.

Frair, W. (1964). Turtle family relationships as determined by serological tests. *In* "Taxonomic Biochemistry and Serology" (C. A. Leone, ed.). Ronald Press, New York, pp. 535–544.

Frankel, H. M., Steinberg G. and Gordon, J. (1966). Effects of temperature on blood gases, lactate and pyruvate in turtles, *Pseudemys scripta elegans, in vivo*. *Comp. Biochem. Physiol.* 19, 279–283.

Gandal, C. P. (1958). A practical method of obtaining blood from anesthetized turtles by means of cardiac puncture. *Zoologica, N.Y.* 43, 93–94.

Gaumer, A. E. H. and Goodnight, C. J. (1957). Some aspects of the hematology of turtles as related to their activity. *Am. Midl. Nat.* 58, 332–340.

Gaunt, A. S. and Gans, C. (1969). Diving bradycardia and withdrawal bradycardia in *Caiman crocodilus*. *Nature, Lond.* 223 (5202), 207–208.

Gee, L. L. (1941). Defences against trout furunculosis *J. Bact.* 41, 266–267.

Georgatsos, J. G. (1960). The amino acid composition of the haemoglobin of the turtle *Emys caspica*. *Enzymologia* 22, 13–16.

Gerzeli, G. (1954). Osservazioni d'istochimica comparata: i polisaccaridi negli elementi ematici circolanti dei Vertebrati inferiori. *Arch. zool. ital.* 39, 1–14.

Gerzeli, G., Casati, C. and Gennaro, A. M. (1956). I volumi nucleari e cellulari in relazione al tenore di acido desossiribonucleico in eritrociti di alcune specie di Vertebrati. *Riv. Istochin. Norm. Path.* 110, 149–154.

Gilles-Baillien, M. and Schoffeniels, F. (1965). Variations saisonnières dans la composition du sang de la tortue grecque *Testudo hermanni* J. F. Gmelin. *Anns Soc. r. zool. Belg.* **95**, 75–79.

Girgis, S. (1961). Aquatic respiration in the common Nile turtle *Trionyx triunguis* (Forskål). *Comp. Biochem. Physiol.* **3**, 206–217.

Goin, C. J. and Jackson, C. G. (1965). Hemoglobin values of some amphibians and reptiles from Florida. *Herpetologica* **21**, 145–146.

Goodcase, G. D., Cornelius, C. E. and Freedland, R. A. (1964). Plasma and tissue arginase activities in exotic animal species. *Cornell Vet.* **54**, 50–56.

Gordon, J. and Frankel, H. M. (1963). Turtle blood gas composition at different body temperatures. *Bull. New Jers. Acad. Sci.* **8**, 23.

Gorman, G. C. and Dessauer, H. C. (1965). Hemoglobin and transferrin electrophoresis and relationships of island populations of *Anolis* lizards. *Science, N.Y.* **150**, 1454–1455.

Gorman, G. C. and Dessauer, H. C. (1966). The relationships of *Anolis* of the *roquet* species group (Sauria: Iguanidae)-I. Electrophoretic comparison of blood proteins. *Comp. Biochem. Physiol.* **19**, 845–853.

Graham-Smith, G. S. (1904). Blood relationships amongst lower vertebrata and arthropods, etc. as indicated by 2,500 tests with precipitating antisera. *In* "Blood Immunity and Blood Relationship" (G. H. F. Nuttall ed.). Cambridge Univ. Press, London, pp. 336–380.

Gratzer, W. B. and Allison, A. C. (1960). Multiple hemoglobins. *Biol. Rev.* **35**, 459–506.

Gregoire, C. and Taynon, H. J. (1962). Blood coagulation. *In* "Comparative Biochemistry" (M. Florkin and H. S. Mason, eds). Vol. IV, Academic Press, New York, pp. 435–482.

Grollman, A. (1927). The condition of the inorganic phosphorus of the blood with special reference to the calcium concentration. *J. biol. Chem.* **72**, 565–572.

Grundhauser, J. W. (1960). Water balance in the turtle in response to season and hypothermia. *Diss. Abstr.* **20**, 3803–3804.

Hackenbrock, C. R. and Finster, M. (1963). Fluothane: a rapid and safe inhalation anesthetic for poisonous snakes. *Copeia* 440–441.

Hackett, E. and Hann, C. (1967). Slow clotting of reptile blood. *J. Comp. path.* **77**, 175–180.

Hadley, N. F. and Burns, T. A. (1968). Intraspecific comparison of the blood properties of the side blotched lizard, *Uta stansburiana*. *Copeia* **1968**, 737–740.

Haggag, G., Raheem, K. A. and Khalil, F. (1965). Hibernation in reptiles. I. Changes in blood electrolytes. *Comp. Biochem. Physiol.* **16**, 457–465.

Haggag, G., Raheem, K. A. and Khalil, F. (1966). Hibernation in reptiles. II. Changes in blood glucose, haemoglobin, red blood cell count, protein and non-protein nitrogen. *Comp. Biochem. Physiol.* **17**, 335–339.

Hahn, W. E. (1965). Physiological and cytological aspects of vitellinogenesis and fat mobilization stimulated by 17β-estradiol in *Uta stansburiana*. *Diss. Abstr.* **26**, 2296–2297.

Hahn, W. E. (1967). Estradiol-induced vitellinogenesis and concomitant fat mobilization in the lizard *Uta stansburiana*. *Comp. Biochem. Physiol.* **23**, 83–93.

Haning, Q. C. and Thompson, A. M. (1965). A comparative study of tissue carbon dioxide in vertebrates. *Comp. Biochem. Physiol.* **15**, 17–26.

Henderson, L. J. (1928). "Blood: A Study in General Physiology". Yale University Press.

Herbert, J. D., Coulson, R. A. and Hernandez, T. (1966). Free amino acids in the caiman and rat. *Comp. Biochem. Physiol.* **17**, 583–598.

Hernandez, T. and Coulson, R. A. (1951). Biochemical studies on the Iguana. *Proc. Soc. exp. Biol. Med.* **76**, 175–177.

Hernandez, T. and Coulson, R. A. (1952). Hibernation in the alligator. *Proc. Soc. exp. Biol. Med.* **79**, 145–149.

Hernandez, T. and Coulson, R. A. (1954). The effect of carbonic anhydrase inhibition on the composition of urine and plasma of the alligator. *Science*, *N.Y.* **119**, 291–292.

Hernandez, T. and Coulson, R. A. (1956). Sympathomimetic action of the xanthine diuretics in the alligator. *Am. J. Physiol.* **185**, 201–204.

Hernandez, T. and Coulson, R. A. (1957). Inhibition of renal tubular function by cold. *Am. J. Physiol.* **188**, 485–489.

Hernandez, T. and Coulson, R. A. (1958). Metabolic acidosis in the alligator. *Proc. Soc. exp. Biol. Med.* **99**, 525–526.

Hernandez, T. and Coulson, R. A. (1961). The effect of insulin on amino acid metabolism *Biochem. J.* **79**, 596–605.

Hernandez, T. and Coulson, R. A. (1967). Extracellular-intracellular amino acid equilibria in caimans and turtles. *Comp. Biochem. Physiol.* **20**, 291–298.

Hernandez, T. and Coulson, R. A. (1968). Effect of insulin on free amino acids in caiman tissue and plasma. *Comp. Biochem. Physiol.* **26**, 991–996.

Hildemann, W. H. (1962). Immunogenetic studies of amphibians and reptiles. *Ann. N.Y. Acad. Sci.* **97**, 139–152.

Hirschfeld, W. J. and Gordon, A. S. (1961). Studies of erythropoiesis in turtles. *Anat. Rec.* **139**, 306.

Hirschfeld, W. J. and Gordon, A. S. (1964). Erythropoietic response of the turtle (*Pseudemys scripta elegans*) to bleeding. *Am. Zoöl.* **4**, 305

Hirschfeld, W. J. and Gordon, A. S. (1965). The effect of bleeding and starvation on blood volumes and peripheral hemogram of the turtle, *Pseudemys scripta elegans*. *Anat. Rec.* **153**, 317–324.

Hoffert, J. R. and Fromm, P. O. (1964). In vitro uptake of hexavalent chromium by erythrocytes, liver, and kidney tissue of the turtle, *Chrysemys picta*. *Physiol. Zoöl.* **37**, 224–230.

Holmes, W. N. and McBean, R. L. (1964). Some aspects of electrolyte excretion in the green turtle, *Chelonia mydas mydas*. *J. exp. Biol.* **41**, 81–90.

Holmes, R. S., Masters, C. J. and Webb, E. C. (1968). A comparative study of vertebrate esterase multiplicity. *Comp. Biochem. Physiol.* **26**, 837–852.

Hopping, A. (1923). Seasonal changes in the gases and sugar of the blood and the nitrogen distribution in the blood and urine of the alligator. *Am. J. Physiol.* **66**, 145–163.

Houssay, B. A. and Biasotti A. (1933). Hipofisis of diabetes pancreatica en los batracios y los reptiles. *Revta argent. Biol.* **9**, 29–33.

Hutton, K. E. (1958). The blood chemistry of terrestrial and aquatic snakes. *J. Cell. comp. Physiol.* **52**, 319–328.

Hutton, K. E. (1960). Seasonal physiological changes in the red-eared turtle, *Pseudemys scripta elegans*. *Copeia* **1960**, 360–362.

Hutton, K. E. (1964). Effects of hypothermia on turtle blood glucose. *Herpetologica* **20**, 129–131.

Hutton, K. E. and Goodnight, C. J. (1957). Variations in the blood chemistry of turtles under active and hibernating conditions. *Physiol. Zoöl.* **30**, 198–207.

Hutton, K. E. and Ortman, R. (1957). Blood chemistry and parietal eye of *Anolis carolinensis*. *Proc. Soc. exp. Biol. Med.* **96**, 842–844.

Issekutz, B. and Végh, F. (1928). Beiträge zur Wirkung des Insulins. III. Mitteilung: Wirkung auf den Gasstoffwechsel der Schildkröte. *Biochem. Z.* **92**, 383–389.

Izard, Y., Detrait, J. and Boquet, P. (1961). Variations saisonnières de la composition du sang de *Vipera aspis*. *Annls Inst. Pasteur, Paris* **100**, 539–545.

Jackson, C. G., Jr. and Legendre, R. C. (1967). Blood serum cholesterol levels in turtles. *Comp. Biochem. Physiol.* **20**, 311–312.

Jacques, F. A. (1963). Blood coagulation and anticoagulant mechanisms in the turtle *Pseudemys elegans. Comp. Biochem. Physiol.* **9**, 241–249.

Jacques, F. A. and Musacchia, X. J. (1961). Variations in concentrations of a metachromatic staining anti-coagulant in plasma of the turtle, *Pseudemys scripta elegans. Copeia* 222–223.

Jenkins, N. K. and Simkiss, K. (1968). The calcium and phosphate metabolism of reproducing reptiles with particular reference to the adder (*Vipera berus*). *Comp. Biochem. Physiol.* **26**, 865–876.

Jensen, H. B. and With, T. K. (1939). Vitamin A and carotenoids in the liver of mammals, birds, reptiles and man, with particular regard to the intensity of the ultraviolet absorption and the Carr-Price reaction of vitamin A. *Biochem. J.* **33**, 1771–1786.

Johlin, J. M. and Moreland, F. B. (1933). Studies of the blood picture of the turtle after complete anoxia. *J. biol. Chem.* **103**, 107–114.

Kanungo, M. S. (1961). Haemoglobin concentration in the blood of some vertebrates. *J. zool. Soc. India.* **13**, 113–115.

Kaplan, H. M. (1956). Anticoagulants isotonic with turtle blood. *Herpetologica* **12**, 269–272.

Kaplan, H. M. (1960a). Variation with age of the electrophoretic protein pattern in turtle blood. *Herpetologica* **16**, 202–206.

Kaplan, H. M. (1960b). Electrophoretic analysis of protein changes during growth of *Pseudemys* turtles. *Anat. Rec.* **138**, 359.

Kaplan, H. M. and Rueff, W. (1960). Seasonal blood changes in turtles. *Proc. Anim. Care Panel* **10**, 63–68.

Kaplan, H. M. and Taylor, R. (1957). Anesthesia in turtles. *Herpetologica* **13**, 43–45.

Kaplan, N. O. (1965). Evolution of dehydrogenases. *In* "Evolving Genes and Proteins" (V. Bryson and H. J. Vogel, eds.). Academic Press, New York, pp. 243–277.

Karlstrom, E. L. and Cook, S. F., Jr. (1955). Notes on snake anesthesia. *Copeia* 57–58.

Karr, W. G. and Lewis, H. B. (1916). A comparative study of the distribution of urea in the blood and tissues of certain vertebrates with special reference to the hen. *J. Am. chem. Soc.* **38**, 1615–1620.

Kellaway, C. H. and Williams, F. E. (1931). The serological and blood relationships of some common Australian snakes. *Aust. J. exp. Biol. med. Sci.* **8**, 123–132.

Kerr, S. E. and Daoud, L. (1935). A study of the organic acid-soluble phosphorus of the erythrocytes of various vertebrates. *J. biol. Chem.* **109**, 301–315.

Khalil, F. (1947). Excretion in reptiles. I. Non-protein nitrogen constituents of the urine of the sea-turtle *Chelone mydas* L. *J. biol. Chem.* **171**, 611–616.

Khalil, F. and Abdel-Messeih, G. (1954). Water content of tissues of some desert reptiles and mammals. *J. exp. Zool.* **125**, 407–414.

Khalil, F. and Abdel-Messeih, G. (1959a). Water, nitrogen and lipids content of tissues of *Varanus griseus* Daud. *Z. vergl. Physiol.* **42**, 403–409.

Khalil, F. and Abdel-Messeih, G. (1959b). The storage of extra water by various tissues of *Varanus griseus* Daud. *Z. vergl. Physiol.* **42**, 415–421.

Khalil, F. and Abdel-Messeih, G. (1961). Effect of water deficit and water excess on the composition of the blood of *Varanus griseus* Daud. *Z. vergl. Physiol.* **45**, 82–87.

Khalil, F. and Abdel-Messeih, G. (1962). Tissue constituents of reptiles in relation to their mode of life-I. Water content. *Comp. Biochem. Physiol.* **5**, 327–330.

Khalil, F. and Abdel-Messeih, G. (1963). Tissue constituents of reptiles in relation to their mode of life III. Nitrogen content and serum proteins. *Comp. Biochem. Physiol.* **9**, 75–79.

Khalil, F. and Yanni, M. (1959). Studies on carbohydrates in reptiles. I. Glucose in body fluids of *Uromastix aegyptia. Z. vergl. Physiol.* **42**, 192–198.

Kmeťová, S. and Paulov, Š. (1966). Protein spectra of the blood serum of colubrid snakes *Natrix natrix natrix* L. and *Natrix tessellata* Laur. *Acta. Fac. Rerum nat. Univ. comen. Bratisl. Zool.* **23**, 251–254.

Korzhuev, P. A. and Kruglova, G. V. (1957). Muscle hemoglobin of the desert tortoise. *Chem. Abstr.* **51**, 2189i.

Kuwajima, Y. (1953). Immunological researches on the main Formosan poisonous snakes, especially on the venoms. I. Classification of poisonous snakes in Formosa by means of serological methods based on employing snake blood-sera as antigens. *Jap. J. exp. Med.* **23**, 21–25.

Laskowski, M. (1936). Über das Vorkommen des Serumvitellins im Blute der Wirbeltiere. *Biochem. Z.* **284**, 318–321.

Latifi, M., Shamloo, K. D. and Amin, A. (1965). Characteristic electrophoretic patterns of serum proteins of several species of snakes of Iran. *Can. J. Biochem.* **43**, 459–461.

LeBrie, S. J. and Sutherland, I. D. W. (1962). Renal function in water snakes. *Am. J. Physiol.* **203**, 995–1000.

Leiner, M., Beck, H. and Eckert, H. (1962). Über die Kohlensäure-Dehydratase in den einzelnen Wirbeltierklassen. *Hoppe-Seyler's Z. physiol. Chem.* **327**, 144–165.

Leone, C. A. and Wilson, F. E. (1961). Studies of turtle sera. I. The nature of the fastest-moving electrophoretic component in the sera of nine species. *Physiol. Zoöl.* **34**, 297–305.

Lerch, E. G., Huggins, S. E. and Bartel, A. H. (1967). Comparative immunology. Active immunization of young alligators with hemocyanin. *Proc. Soc. exp. Biol. Med.* **124**, 448–451.

Lewis, J. H. (1964). Studies on the plasma proteins of various vertebrates. *Protides biol. Fluids* **12**, 149–154.

Liang, C. (1957). The formation of complexes between haemoglobins and plasma proteins in a variety of animals. *Biochem. J.* **66**, 552–558.

Lockwood, A. P. M. (1961). "Ringer" solutions and some notes on the physiological basis of their ionic composition. *Comp. Biochem. Physiol.* **2**, 241–289.

Lopes, N. (1955). The action of alloxan in the turtle *Pseudemys d'orbignyi* D and B. *Acta physiol. latinoam.* **5**, 39–45.

Lopes, N., Wagner, E., Barros, M. and Marques, M. (1954). Glucose, insulin and epinephrine tolerance tests in the normal and hypophysectomized turtle "*Pseudemys d'orbignyi*". *Acta physiol. latinoam.* **4**, 190–199.

Luck, J. M. and Keeler, L. (1929). The blood chemistry of two species of rattlesnakes, *Crotalus atrox* and *Crotalus oregonus*. *J. biol. Chem.* **82**, 703–707.

Lund, C., McMenamy, R. H. and Neville, G. J. (1957). A syringe attachment for decalcification of small quantities of blood. *Am. J. clin. Path.* **28**, 328–330.

Lustig, B. and Ernst, T. (1936). Über den Eiweisszucker, Eiweissgehalt und Kohlenhydratindex der Sera und Körperflüssigkeiten verschiedener Tierarten. *Biochem. Z.* **289**, 365–389.

Lyman, R. A., Jr. (1945). The anti-haemolytic function of calcium in the blood of the snapping turtle, *Chelydra serpentina*. *J. cell. comp. Physiol.* **25**, 65–73.

Macfarland, R. G. and Robb-Smith, A. H. T. (1961). "Function of the blood". Academic Press, New York.

Maizels, M. (1956). Sodium transfer in tortoise erythrocytes. *J. Physiol. Lond.* **132**, 414–441.

Maldonado, A. A. and Ortiz, E. (1966). Electrophoretic patterns of serum proteins of some West Indian *Anolis* (Sauria: Iguanidae) *Copeia* 179.

Manwell, C. P. (1958). The Repiratory Pigments. *Diss. Abstr.* **18**, 1475–1476.

Manwell, C. (1960). Comparative physiology: Blood pigments. *A. Rev. Physiol.* **22**, 191–244.

Manwell, C., Baker, C. M. A., Roslansky, J. D. and Foght, M. (1963). Molecular genetics of avian proteins, II. Control genes and structural genes for embryonic and adult hemoglobins. *Proc. nat. Acad. Sci. U.S.A.* **49**, 496–503.

Manwell, C. and Schlesinger, C. V. (1966). Polymorphism of turtle hemoglobin and geographical differences in the frequency of variants of *Chrysemys picta* "slow" hemoglobin-an example of "Temperature anti-adaptation"? *Comp. Biochem. Physiol.* **18**, 627–637.

Marques, M. (1955a). Efeitos da pancreatectomia parcial na tartaruga *Phrynops hilarii. Revta. bras. Biol.* **15**, 349–354.

Marques, M. (1955b). Accion diabetogena de la smoatotrofina en la tortuga *Phrynops hilarii. Revta. Soc. argent. Biol.* **31**, 177–183.

Marques, M. (1967). Effects of prolonged glucagon administration to turtles (*Chrysemys d'orbignyi). Gen. Comp. Endocrinol.* **9**, 102–109.

Marques, M. and Kraemer, A. (1968). Extractable insulin and glucagon from turtle's (*Chrysemys d'orbignyi*) pancreas. *Comp. Biochem. Physiol.* **27**, 439–446.

Masat, R. J. and Dessauer, H. C. (1966). Plasma albumin of reptiles. *Fedn Proc. Fedn Am. Socs exp. Biol.* **25**, 704.

Masat, R. J. and Dessauer, H. C. (1968). Plasma albumins of reptiles. *Comp. Biochem. Physiol.* **25**, 119–128.

Masat, R. J. and Musacchia, X. J. (1965). Serum protein concentration changes in the turtle, *Chrysemys picta. Comp. Biochem. Physiol.* **16**, 215–225.

McCay, C. M. (1931). Phosphorus distribution, sugar, and hemoglobin in the blood of fish, eels, and turtles. *J. biol. Chem.* **90**, 497–505.

McCutcheon, F. H. (1947). Specific oxygen affinity of hemoglobin in elasmobranchs and turtles. *J. cell. comp. Physiol.* **29**, 333–344.

McMenamy, R. H. and Watson, F. (1968). Indole-albumin association: a comparative study. *Comp. Biochem. Physiol.* **26**, 392–335.

Menon, K. R. (1952). A comparative study of the protein concentration of the blood plasma in some representative vertebrates. *J. Univ. Bombay.* **20B**, 19–23.

Menon, K. R. (1954). The glucose and fat levels in the blood of five representative vertebrates. *J. Anim. Morph. Physiol.* **1**, 65–68.

Menon, K. R. (1955). The oxyphoric capacity of the blood in five representative vertebrates. *J. Anim. Morph. Physiol.* **1**, 78–81.

Menon, K. R. and Sathe, A. M. (1959). Free amino-acids in the blood of some vertebrates. *Curr. Sci.* **28**, 401–402.

Michaelis, L. and Nakashima, T. (1923). Eine weitere Methode zur Bestimmung des isoelektrischen Punktes von Eiweisskörpern und ihre Anwendung auf die Serumalbumine verschiedener Tiere. *Biochem. Z.* **143**, 484–491.

Millen, J. E., Murdaugh, H. V., Jr., Bauer, C. B. and Robin, E. D. (1964). Circulatory adaptation to diving in the freshwater turtle. *Science, N.Y.* **145**, 591–593.

Miller, M. R. (1960). Pancreatic islet histology and carbohydrate metabolism in amphibians and reptiles. *Diabète* **9**, 318–323.

Miller, M. R. (1961). Carbohydrate metabolism in amphibians and reptiles. *In* "Comparative Physiology of Carbohydrate Metabolism in Heterothermic Animals" (A. W. Martin, ed.). Univ. Washington Press, Seattle, pp. 125–145.

Miller, M. R. and Wurster, D. H. (1956). Studies on the blood glucose and pancreatic islets of lizards. *Endocrinology* **58**, 114–120.

Miller, M. R. and Wurster, D. H. (1958). Further studies on the blood glucose and pancreatic islets of lizards. *Endocrinology* **63**, 191–200.

Miller, M. R. and Wurster, D. H. (1959). The morphology and physiology of the pancreatic islets in urodele amphibians and lizards. *In* "A Textbook of Comparative Endocrinology"(A. Gorbman, ed.). Wiley, New York, pp. 668–680.

Mirsky, A. E. and Ris, H. (1951). The desoxyribonucleic acid content of animal cells and its evolutionary significance. *J. gen. Physiol.* **34**, 451–462.

Moberly, W. R. (1968a). The metabolic responses of the common iguana, *Iguana iguana*, to activity under restraint. *Comp. Biochem. Physiol.* **27**, 1–20.

Moberly, W. R. (1968b). The metabolic responses of the common iguana, *Iguana iguana*, to walking and diving. *Comp. Biochem. Physiol.* **27**, 21–32.

Morrison, P. R., Scudder, C. and Blatt, W. (1951). The solubilities of some vertebrate fibrinogens in plasma-ethanol mixtures. *Biol. Bull. mar. biol. Lab., Woods Hole* **101**, 171–177.

Mullen, R. K. (1962). The effect of calcium on the electrocardiogram of two iguanid lizards. *Copeia* **1962**, 269–272.

Munday, K. A. and Blane, G. F. (1961). Cold stress of the mammal, bird and reptile. *Comp. Biochem. Physiol.* **2**, 8–21.

Murdaugh, H. V., Jr. and Jackson, J. E. (1962). Heart rate and blood lactic acid concentration during experimental diving of water snakes. *Am. J. Physiol.* **202**, 1163–1165.

Murphy, G. P., Sharp, J. C., Johnston, G. S. and Helms, J. B. (1964). Cross-species measurement of regional circulatory alterations during osmotic diuresis and other states. I. Observations on primate, ovine, canine, fowl and reptile. *Invest. Urol.* **2**, 82–91.

Murphy, R. C. and Seegers, W. H. (1948). Concentration of prothrombin and Ac-globulin in various species. *Am. J. Physiol.* **154**, 134–139.

Musacchia, X. J. (1959). The viability of *Chrysemys picta* submerged at various temperatures. *Physiol. Zoöl.* **32**, 47–50.

Musacchia, X. J. and Chladek, M. I. (1961). Investigations of the cloacal bladders in turtles. *Am. Zoöl.* **1**, 376.

Musacchia, X. J. and Grundhauser, J. W. (1958). Water content in turtle tissues. *Fedn Proc. Fedn Am. Socs exp. Biol.* **17**, 115.

Musacchia, X. J. and Sievers, M. L. (1956). Effects of induced cold torpor on blood of *Chrysemys picta. Am. J. Physiol.* **187**, 99–102.

Musacchia, X. J. and Sievers, M. L. (1962). Effects of cold torpor and fasting on the erythrocytes of the turtle, *Pseudemys elegans. Trans. Am. microsc. Soc.* **81**, 198–201.

Nair, S. G. (1955a). The non-protein nitrogen in the blood of some reptiles and mammals. *J. Anim. Morph. Physiol.* **2**, 96–100.

Nair, S. G. (1955b). The oxyphoric capacity of the blood of some reptiles and mammals. *J. Anim. Morph. Physiol.* **1**, 48–54.

Nair, S. G. (1958). A study of the plasma proteins of some reptiles and mammals. *J. Anim. Morph. Physiol.* **5**, 95–100.

Nair, S. G. (1960). Free amino acids in the blood of some reptiles and mammals. *J. Anim. Morph. Physiol.* **7**, 98–100.

Nakamura, E. (1960). Das mehrfache Hämoglobin. III. Amphibien and Reptilien. *Lymphatologia, Kyoto* **4**, 52–59.

Nakamura, S., Tominaga, S., Katsuno, A. and Murakawa, S. (1965). Specific reaction of concanavalin-A with sera of various animals. *Comp. Biochem. Physiol.* **15**, 435–444.

Nayler, W. G., Price, J. M. and Lowe, T. E. (1965). The presence of a substance with positive inotropic activity in blood plasma of a variety of animals. *Comp. Biochem. Physiol.* **15**, 503–507.

Nera, M. C. D. (1925). Richerche chimiche, fisico-chimiche e morfologiche sul sangue di *Testudo graeca* nell'estate e durante il sonno invernale. *Boll. 1st. Zool. R. Univ. Roma* **3**, 71–85.

Neuzil, E. and Masseyeff, R. (1958). Parénte immunochimique entre le sérum humain et celui de divers animaux: étude immunoéléctrophorétique. *C. r. Séanc. Soc. Biol.* 152, 599–603.

Newcomer, R. J. and Crenshaw, J. W. (1967). Electrophoretic comparison of blood proteins of two closely related species of South American tortoises. *Copeia* 1967, 481–483.

Ozawa, H. and Satake, K. (1955). On the species difference of N-terminal amino acid sequence in hemoglobin. *J. Biochem., Tokyo* 42, 641–648.

Payne, H. J. and Burke, J. D. (1964). Blood oxygen capacity in turtles. *Am. Midl. Nat.* 71, 460–465.

Pearson, D. D. (1966). Serological and immunoelectrophoretic comparisons among species of snakes. Dissertation, University Kansas. Lawrence, Kansas. Abstracted in: *Bull. serol. Mus., New Brunsw.* 36, 8.

Penhos, J. C., Houssay, B. A. and Lujan, M. A. (1965). Total pancreatectomy in lizards. Effects of several hormones. *Endocrinology* 76, 989–993.

Pettus, D. (1958). Water relationships in *Natrix sipedon*. *Copeia* 1958, 207–211.

Philpot, V. B. and Smith, R. G. (1950). Neutralization of pit viper venom by king snake serum. *Proc. Soc. exp. Biol. Med.* 74, 521–523.

Pienaar, U. de V. (1962). "Haematology of some South African reptiles". Witwatersrand University Press, Johannesburg.

Placidi, L. and Placidi, M. (1960). Studies on the anaphylactic shock in the lower vertebrates. Negative attempts at sensitization in tortoises and snakes. *Annls. Inst. Pasteur, Paris* 98, 463–466.

Plagnol, H. and Vialard-Goudou, A. (1956). Electrophorese sur papier du serum de différents serpents. *Annls Inst. Pasteur, Paris* 90, 276–281.

Pough, F. H. (1969). Environmental adaptations in the blood of lizards. *Comp. Biochem. Physiol.* 15, 885–901.

Prado, J. L. (1946a). A glicemia normal nos ofidios. *Mems Inst. Butantan* 19, 59–68.

Prado, J. L. (1946b). Glucose tolerance test in ophidia and the effect of feeding on their glycemia. *Revue can. Biol.* 5, 564–569.

Prado, J. L. (1946c). Inactive (non-oxygen-combining) hemoglobin in the blood of ophidia and dogs. *Science, N.Y.* 103, 406.

Prado, J. L. (1947). Effects of adrenalin and insulin on the blood sugar of ophidia (*Bothrops jararaca*). *Revue can. Biol.* 6, 255–263.

Prosser, C. L., Bishop, D. W., Brown, F. A. Jr., John, T. L. and Wulff, V. J. (1950). "Comparative Animal Physiology". Saunders, Philadelphia.

Prosser, R. L., III and Suzuki, H. K. (1968). The effects of estradiol valerate on the serum and bone of hatchling and juvenile caiman crocodiles (*Caiman sclerops*). *Comp. Biochem. Physiol.* 25, 529–534.

Putnam, F. W. (Ed.) (1960). "The Plasma Proteins" 2 Vols. Academic Press, New York.

Putnam, F. W. (1965). Structure and function of the plasma proteins. *In* "The Proteins" (H. Neurath, ed.). Vol. III, Academic Press, New York, pp. 153–267.

Rabalais, R. (1938). Observations on the blood of certain reptiles, pisces, mollusca, and one amphibian of the Grand Isle region. *Proc. La. Acad. Sci.* 4, 142–148.

Ramirez, J. R. and Dessauer, H. C. (1957). Isolation and characterization of two hemoglobins found in the turtle, *Pseudemys scripta elegans*. *Proc. Soc. exp. Biol. Med.* 96, 690–694.

Ramsey, H. J. (1941). A comparative study of hemoglobin denaturation. *J. cell. comp. Physiol.* 18, 369–377.

Rao, C. A. P. (1968). The effect of steroids on the serum protein fractions of the tortoise *Testudo elegans* Schoepff. *Comp. Biochem. Physiol.* 26, 1119–1122.

Rao, C. A. P. and David, G. F. X. (1967). The effect of certain steroids on the serum protein concentrations of the lizard, *Uromastix hardwickii* Gray. *Gen. Comp. Endocrinol.* **9**, 227–233.

Rapatz, G. L. and Musacchia, X. J. (1957). Metabolism of *Chrysemys picta* during fasting and during cold torpor. *Am. J. Physiol.* **188**, 456–460.

Rapoport, S. and Guest, G. M. (1941). Distribution of acid-soluble phosphorus in the blood cells of various vertebrates. *J. biol. Chem.* **138**, 269–282.

Rapoport, S., Leva, E. and Guest, G. M. (1941). Phytase in plasma and erythrocytes of various species of vertebrates. *J. biol. Chem.* **139**, 621–632.

Rapoport, S., Leva, E. and Guest, G. M. (1942). Acid and alkaline phosphatase and nucleophosphatase in the erythrocytes of some lower vertebrates. *J. cell. comp. Physiol.* **19**, 103–108.

Redfield, A. C. (1933). The evolution of the respiratory function of the blood. *Q. Rev. Biol.* **8**, 31–57.

Rhaney, M. C. (1948). Some aspects of the carbohydrate metabolism of the kingsnake (*Lampropeltis getulus floridana*). *Diss. Abstr.* **8**, 158–159.

Ribeiro, L. P., Mitidieri, E. and Villela, G. G. (1955). Paper electrophoretic and enzimatic studies on blood serum, venom and liver of "*Bothrops jararaca*". *Mems Inst. Oswaldo Cruz* **53**, 487–497.

Rider, J. and Bartel, A. H. (1967). Electrophoretic analysis of young caiman and crocodile serum. *Comp. Biochem. Physiol.* **20**, 1005–1008.

Riggs, A. (1965). Functional properties of hemoglobins. *Physiol. Rev.* **45**, 619–673.

Riggs, A., Sullivan, B. and Agee, J. R. (1964). Polymerization of frog and turtle hemoglobins. *Proc. natn Acad. Sci. U.S.A.* **51**, 1127–1134.

Riley, V. (1960). Adaptation of orbital bleeding technique to rapid serial blood studies. *Proc. Soc. exp. Biol. Med.* **104**, 751–754.

Roberts, R. C. and Seal, U. S. (1965). Sedimentation analysis of vertebrate serum proteins. *Comp. Biochem. Physiol.* **16**, 327–331.

Robin, E. D. (1962). Relationship between temperature and plasma pH and carbon dioxide tension in the turtle. *Nature, Lond.* **195**, 249–251.

Robin, E. D., Vester, J. W., Murdaugh, H. V., Jr., and Millen, J. E. (1964). Prolonged anaerobiosis in a vertebrate: anaerobic metabolism in the freshwater turtle. *J. cell. comp. Physiol.* **63**, 287–297.

Rodnan, G. P. and Ebaugh, F. G., Jr. (1957). Paper electrophoresis of animal hemoglobins. *Proc. Soc. exp. Biol. Med.* **95**, 397–401.

Rodnan, G. P., Ebaugh, F. G. Jr. and Fox, M. R. S. (1957). The life span of the red blood cell and the red blood cell volume in the chicken, pigeon, and duck as estimated by the use of $Na_2Cr^{51}O_4$ with observations on red cell turnover rate in the mammal, bird and reptile. *Blood* **12**, 355–366.

Root, R. W. (1949). Aquatic respiration in the musk turtle. *Physiol. Zoöl.* **22**, 172–178.

Rosenthal, H. L. and Austin, S. (1962). Vitamin B_{12} unsaturated binding capacity of sera from various animals. *Proc. Soc. exp. Biol. Med.* **109**, 179–181.

Rosenthal, H. L. and Brown, C. R., Jr. (1954). Vitamin B_{12} activity of plasma and whole blood from various animals. *Proc. Soc. exp. Biol. Med.* **86**, 117–120.

Saviano, M. (1947a). Boll. Soc. ital. Biol. sper. **23**, 1290.

Saviano, M. (1947b). Boll. Soc. ital. Biol. sper. **23**, 1300.

Saviano, M. and De Francisis, P. (1948). Ricerche sull 'azione diabetogena dell'allossana negli ofidi. *Boll. Soc. ital. Biol. sper.* **24**, 1346–1347.

Schjeide, O. A. and Urist, M. R. (1960). Proteins induced in plasma by oestrogens. *Nature, Lond.* **188**, 291–294.

Schmidt-Nielsen, K. (1962/63). Osmotic regulation in higher vertebrates. *Harvey Lect.* 182, 783–785.

Schmidt-Nielsen, K. and Fänge, R. (1958). Salt glands in marine reptiles. *Nature, Lond.* 58, pp. 53–93.

Schmidt-Nielsen, K., Crawford, E. C. and Bentley, P. J. (1966). Discontinuous respiration in the lizard, *Sauromalus obesus. Fedn Proc. Fedn Am. Socs exp. Biol.* 25, 506.

Scholander, P. F., Hargens, A. R. and Miller, S. L. (1968). Negative pressure in the interstitial fluid of animals. *Science, N.Y.* 161, 321–328.

Seal, U.S. (1964). Vertebrate distribution of serum ceruloplasmin and sialic acid and the effects of pregnancy. *Comp. Biochem. Physiol.* 13, 143–159.

Seal, U. S. and Doe, R. P. (1963). Corticosteroid-binding globulin: Species distribution and small-scale purification. *Endocrinology* 73, 371–376.

Seniów, A. (1963). Paper electrophoresis of serum proteins of the grass-snake, *Natrix natrix* (L.). *Comp. Biochem. Physiol.* 9, 137–149.

Sheeler, P. and Barber, A. A. (1964). Comparative hematology of the turtle, rabbit and rat. *Comp. Biochem. Physiol.* 11, 139–145.

Sheeler, P. and Barber, A. A. (1965). Reticulocytosis and iron incorporation in the rabbit and turtle: A comparative study. *Comp. Biochem. Physiol.* 16, 63–76.

Shoemaker, V. H., Licht, P. and Dawson, W. R. (1966). Effects of temperature on kidney function in the lizard *Tiliqua rugosa. Physiol. Zoöl.* 39, 244–252.

Simkiss, K. (1961). Calcium metabolism and avian reproductive. *Biol. Rev.* 36, 321–367.

Simkiss, K. (1962). The sources of calcium for the ossification of the embryos of the giant leathery turtle. *Comp. Biochem. Physiol.* 7, 71–79.

Simkiss, K. (1967). "Calcium in Reproduction Physiology". Reinhold, New York.

Smith, H. W. (1929). The inorganic composition of the body fluids of the Chelonia. *J. biol. Chem.* 82, 651–661.

Smith, H. W. (1932). Water regulation and its evolution in the fishes. *Q. Rev. Biol.* 7, 1–26.

Smith, H. W. (1951). "The Kidney: Its Structure and Function in Health and Disease". Oxford University Press, New York.

Smith, R. T., Meischer, P. A. and Good, R. A. (1966). "Phylogeny of Immunity". University Florida Press, Gainesville, Florida.

Smithies, O. (1959). Zone electrophoresis in starch gels and its application to studies of serum proteins. *Adv. Protein Chem.* 14, 65–113.

Southworth, F. C., Jr. and Redfield, A. C. (1925/26). The transport of gas by the blood of the turtle. *J. gen. Physiol.* 9, 387–403.

Steggerda, F. R. and Essex, H. E. (1957). Circulation and blood pressure in the great vessels and heart of the turtle (*Chelydra serpentina*). *Am. J. Physiol.* 190, 320–326.

Stenroos, O. O. and Bowman, W. M. (1968). Turtle blood I. Concentrations of various constituents. *Comp. Biochem. Physiol.* 25, 219–222.

Stevenson, O. R., Coulson, R. A. and Hernandez, T. (1957). Effects of hormones on carbohydrate metabolism in the alligator. *Am. J. Physiol.* 191, 95–102.

Stullken, D. E., Randall, W. C. and Hiestand, W. A. (1942). Respiration of the Reptilia as influenced by the composition of the inspired air. *Anat. Rec.* 84, 533.

Sullivan, B. (1966). "Structure, Function and Evolution of Turtle Hemoglobins". Dissertation, University Texas, Austin. 384 pp.

Sullivan, B. (1968). Oxygenation properties of snake hemoglobin. *Science, N.Y.* 157, 1308–1310.

Sullivan, B. and Riggs, A. (1964). Haemoglobin; Reversal of oxidation and polymerization in turtle red cells. *Nature, Lond.* 204, 1098–1099.

Sullivan, B. and Riggs, A. (1967a). Structure, function and evolution of turtle hemoglobins I. Distribution of heavy hemoglobins. *Comp. Biochem. Physiol.* 23, 437–447.

Sullivan, B. and Riggs, A. (1967b). Structure, function and evolution of turtle hemoglobins. II. Electrophoretic studies. *Comp. Biochem. Physiol.* 23, 449–458.

Sullivan, B. and Riggs, A. (1967c). Structure, function and evolution of turtle hemoglobins. III. Oxygenation properties. *Comp. Biochem. Physiol.* 23, 459–474.

Sullivan, B. and Riggs, A. (1967d). The subunit dissociation properties of turtle hemoglobins. *Biochim biophys. Acta.* 140, 274–283.

Suzuki, H. K. and Prosser, R. L., III (1968). The effects of estradiol valerate upon the serum and bone of the lizard *Sceloporus cyanogenys. Proc. Soc. exp. Biol. Med.* 127, 4–7.

Svedberg, T. and Andersson, K. (1938). Ultracentrifugal examination of serum from the lower classes of vertebrates. *Nature, Lond.* 142, 147.

Svedberg, T. and Hedenius, A. (1934). The sedimentation constants of the respiratory proteins. *Biol. Bull. mar. biol. Lab., Woods Hole* 66, 191–223.

Sydenstricker, V. P., Oliver, R., Chandler, B. M. and Sydenstricker, O. (1956). Electrophoretic behavior of some animal hemoglobins. *Proc. Soc. exp. Biol. Med.* 93, 396–397.

Templeton, J. R. (1964). Nasal salt excretion in terrestrial lizards. *Comp. Biochem. Physiol.* 11, 223–229.

Tercafs, R. R. and Vassas, J. M. (1967). Comportement osmotique des érythrocytes de lézards. *Archs int. Physiol. Biochim.* 75, 667–674.

Tercafs, R. R., Schoffeniels, E. and Goussef, G. (1963). Blood composition of a sea-turtle *Caretta caretta* L., reared in fresh water. *Archs int. Physiol. Biochim.* 71, 614–615.

Thorson, T. B. (1963). Body fluid partitioning in fresh-water, marine and terrestrial chelonians. *Am. Zool.* 3, 529.

Thorson, T. B. (1968). Body fluid partitioning in Reptilia. *Copeia* 1968, 592–601.

Tiegel, E. (1880). Notizen über Schlangenblut. *Pflügers Arch ges. Physiol.* 23, 278–282.

Timourian, H. and Dobson, C. (1962). Studies on the hemolytic and hemagglutinating activities of carpet snake serum. *J. exp. Zool.* 150, 27–32.

Timourian, H., Dobson, C. and Sprent, J. F. A. (1961). Precipitating antibodies in the carpet snake against parasitic Nematodes. *Nature, Lond,* 192, 996–997.

Tipton, S. R. (1933). Factors affecting the respiration of vertebrate red blood cells. *J. cell. comp. Physiol.* 3, 313–340.

Tondo, C. V. (1958). Paper-electrophoresis differences between turtle and human serum. *Revta. bras. Biol.* 18, 105–108.

Tucker, V. A. (1966). Oxygen transport by the circulatory system of the green iguana (*Iguana iguana*) at different body temperatures. *J. exp. Biol.* 44, 77–92.

Tyler, A. (1946). On natural auto-antibodies as evidenced by antivenin in serum and liver extract of the Gila monster. *Proc. natn. Acad. Sci. U.S.A.* 32, 195–201.

Uriel, J., Fine, J. M., Courcon, J. and Le Bourdelles, F. (1957). Contribution a l'étude des protéines et lipoprotéines des sérums animaux. *Bull. Soc. Chim. biol.* 39, 1415–1427.

Urist, M. R. and Schjeide, A. O. (1960/1961). The partition of calcium and protein in the blood of oviparous vertebrates during estrus. *J. gen. Physiol.* 44, 743–756.

Van Handel, E. (1968). Trehalase and maltase in the serum of vertebrates. *Comp. Biochem. Physiol.* 26, 561–566.

Vars, H. M. (1934). Blood studies on fish and turtles. *J. biol. Chem.* 105, 135–137.

Vendrely, R. (1958). La notion d'espèce a travers quelques données biochimiques récentes et le cycle. *Annls. Inst. Pasteur, Paris* 94, 142–166.

Verbiinskaya, N. A. (1944). Comparative study of the respiratory function of reptilian blood. *Izv. Akad. Nauk S.S.S.R.*, 1944(3), 156–171 (Russian, English summary).

Vesell, E. S. and Bearn, A. G. (1961/1962). Variations in the lactic dehydrogenase of vertebrate erythrocytes. *J. gen. Physiol.* 45, 553–565.

Vesell, E. S. and Brody, I. A. (1964). Biological application of LDH isozymes: Certain methodological considerations. *Ann. N.Y. Acad. Sci.* 121, 544–559.

Villela, G. G. (1945). Sôbre a natureza de flavina do plasma de algumas cobras. *Revta. bras. Biol.* 5, 113–115.

Villela, G. G. (1947). Isolation and properties of snake erythrocyte nuclei. *Proc. Soc. exp. Biol. Med.* 66, 398–400.

Villela, G. G. (1949). Ribosenucleic acid in snake erythrocytes. *Nature, Lond.* 164, 667.

Villela, G. G. and Prado, J. L. (1944). Flavina e outres pigmentes do plasma sanguine de cobras Brasileiras. *Revta. bras. Biol.* 4, 469–474.

Villela, G. G. and Prado, J. L. (1945). Riboflavin in blood plasma of some Brazilian snakes. *J. biol. Chem.* 157, 693–697.

Villela, G. G. and Thein, M. (1967). Riboflavin in the blood serum, the skin and the venom of some snakes of Burma. *Experientia* 23, 722.

Villela, G. G., Mitidieri, E. and Ribeiro, L. P. (1955). Flavoproteins in the blood plasma of the Brazilian snake, *Bothrops jararaca. Archs. Biochem. Biophys.* 56, 270–273.

Vlădescu, C. (1964). The influence of temperature on the glycaemia of *Emys orbicularis* L. *Rev. Roumaine Biol., Ser. Zool.* 9, 413–420.

Vlădescu, C. (1965a). Glycaemia in the *Vipera berus. Rev. Roumaine Biol., Ser. Zool.* 10, 43–46.

Vlădescu, C. (1965b). Adrenocorticotropic hormone influence on *Emys orbicularis* L. tortoise glycaemia. *Rev. Roumaine Biol., Ser. Zool.* 10, 123–128.

Vlădescu, C. (1965c). Researches on normal glycemia and induced hyperglycemia in *Lacerta agilis chersonensis. Rev. Roumaine Biol., Ser. Zool.* 10, 171–175.

Vlădescu, C. (1965d). Glycemia of *Testudo graeca ibera* turtle. *Rev. Roumaine Biol., Ser. Zool.* 10, 257–260.

Vlădescu, C. (1967). Recherches concernant les mécanismes du glycoréglage des reptiles. IVth Conf. of European Comp. Endocrinol. (In press).

Vlădescu, C. and Baltac, M. (1967). Investigations on glycoregulation in house-snake (*Natrix natrix* L.) *Rev. Roumaine Biol., Ser. Zool.* 12, 61–66.

Vlădescu, C. and Motelică, I. (1965). The influence of insulin on glycemia in *Lacerta agilis chersonensis* Andrz. *Rev. Roumaine Biol., Ser. Zool.* 10, 451–456.

Vlădescu, C., Baltac, M., Trandaburu, T. and Schmit, D. (1967). Researches on glycoregulation in *Lacerta agilis chersonensis. Rev. Bramliera Biol.* (In press).

Voris, H. K. (1967). Electrophoretic patterns of plasma proteins in the viperine snakes. *Physiol. Zoöl.* 40, 238–247.

Wagner, E. M. (1955). Effect of hypophysectomy in the turtle "*Chrysemys d'orbignyi*". *Acta physiol. latinoam.* 5, 219–228.

Warner, E. D., Brinkhous, K. M. and Smith, H. P. (1939). Plasma prothrombin levels in various vertebrates. *Am. J. Physiol.* 125, 296–300.

Whiteside, B. (1922). Remarks on the structure of the ductus and saccus endolymphaticus in the vertebrata. *Am. J. Anat.* 30, 257–266.

Wiley, F. H. and Lewis, H. B. (1927). The distribution of nitrogen in the blood and urine of the turtle *Chrysemys picta. Am. J. Physiol.* 81, 692–695.

Wilson, A. C., Kaplan, N. O., Levine, L., Pesce, A., Reichlin, M. and Allison, W. S. (1964). Evolution of lactic dehydrogenase. *Fedn Proc. Fedn Am. Socs. exp. Biol.* 23, 1258–1266.

Wilson, B., Hansard, S. L. and Cole, B. T. (1960). Total blood volume of the turtle and the frog. *Proc. La. Acad. Sci.* 23, 45–52.

Wilson, J. W. (1939). Some physiological properties of reptilian blood. *J. cell. comp. Physiol.* **13**, 315–326.

Wintrobe, M. M. (1933/1934). Variations in the size and hemoglobin content of erythrocytes in the blood of various vertebrates. *Folia haemat. Lpz.* **51**, 32–49.

Wistrand, P. and Whitis, P. (1959). Distribution of carbonic anhydrase in alligator. Effect of acetazolamide on blood and aqueous humor CO_2. *Proc. Soc. exp. Biol. Med.* **101**, 674–676.

Wolfe, M. R. (1939). Standardization of the precipitin technique and its application to studies of relationships in mammals, birds, and reptiles. *Biol. Bull. mar. biol. Lab., Woods Hole* **76**, 108–120.

Wright, A. and Jones, I. C. (1957). The adrenal gland in lizards and snakes. *J. Endocr.* **15** 83–99.

Zain, B. K. and Zain-ul-Abedin, M. (1967). Characterization of the abdominal fat pads of a lizard. *Comp. Biochem. Physiol.* **23**, 173–177.

Zain-ul-Abedin, M. and Qazi, M. H. (1965). Blood sugar levels of some reptiles found in Pakistan. *Can. J. Biochem. Physiol.* **43**, 831–833.

Zarafonetis, C. J. D. and Kalas, J. P. (1960). Some hematologic and biochemical findings in *Heloderma horridum*, the Mexican bearded lizard. *Copeia* 240–241.

Zweig, G. and Crenshaw, J. W. (1957). Differentiation of species by paper electrophoresis of serum proteins of *Pseudemys* turtles. *Science, N.Y.* **126**, 1065–1066.

CHAPTER 2

Morphology of the Circulating Blood Cells

MARIE-CHARLOTTE SAINT GIRONS

Muséum National d'Histoire Naturelle,
Brunoy, France

I. Introduction

The earliest works on the blood of reptiles described only the structure of its various elements, often comparing them with those of other vertebrates. Treatises on hematology generally contain sections on reptilian blood; unfortunately these are often based on the study of far too few, principally European species. A few recent monographs consider single species and include, besides descriptions of the different circulating blood cells, other observations on various problems – parasites of the blood, seasonal or sexual variation in the numbers of corpuscles, hematopoiesis, and the like.

The earliest published works are those of Mandl (1839) and Gulliver (1840) concerning the erythrocytes of crocodilians and turtles. Important studies of comparative morphology of the blood include those by Gulliver (1842, 1875), Milne-Edwards (1856, 1857), Hayem (1879), Pappenheim (1909), Werzberg (1910), Schulz and Krüger (1925), Loewenthal (1928, 1930), Babudieri (1930), Jordan (1938), Ryerson (1949), Altman and Dittmer (1961), and Pienaar (1962); the last work contains an important bibliography. See Efrati *et al.* (1970) for a study of hemopoiesis in a lizard.

Many questions remain unanswered, and the difficulty in determining the different cellular lineages appears to be one of the principal obstacles to a comparative study of reptilian blood. Only mature cells are considered in this chapter although various stem cells are found in the circulating blood. Pienaar (1962) gives a synonymy of the nomenclature used by the major previous authors (pp. 29–33) and attempts to standardize the names given to the cells of the circulating blood. I will use a slightly simplified version of his system of nomenclature.

The different types of mature cells in the circulating blood of reptiles are:
1. Erythrocytes (red blood cells)
2. Granulocytes (granular myeloid leucocytes)
   a. Eosinophils
   b. Basophils (mast cells)
   c. Azurophils
   d. Neutrophils
3. Lymphocytes (large, medium, or small lymphocytes)
4. Monocytes (large mononuclears)
5. Plasma cells
6. Thrombocytes.

All the cells are nucleated. The names of the different types of granulocytes do not correspond exactly with their chemical composition or with their particular staining properties.

The problems concerning the monophyletic or polyphyletic origin of the different types of cells have not been completely resolved. According to the great majority of workers, all the cells in the circulating blood derive from one multipotent type of hemoblast capable of differentiating in the bone marrow or spleen to produce erythrocytes, granulocytes (eosinophils, basophils, azurophils, and neutrophils), monocytes, and lymphocytes. The last are the scarcely modified hemocytoblasts or stem cells which retain their multiple potentialities and can give rise to all the other types of corpuscles. Thrombocytes are said to derive from small lymphocytes. Some workers postulate different origins, beginning with the hemoblasts, for the leucocytic series on the one hand and for the erythrocytes on the other. They thus do not accept all the multiple potentialities of the lymphocytes. Other hematologists believe that the cells of the circulating blood have three distinct origins: monocytes derive from a stem cell of the reticulo-endothelial system; granulocytic corpuscles, lymphocytes, and thrombocytes arise from a second type of stem cell, the myeoblast; and finally the erythrocytes arise from the erythroblasts.

The histological techniques for the study of blood and of hematopoietic organs have recently been considered by Gabe (1968).

II. Erythrocytes

The erythrocytes or red blood corpuscles of the circulating blood are nucleated, oval cells, rounded at their ends (Figs 6–13, see facing p. 82–3). Their nuclei are also oval, more or less regular, and centrally located; their long axes lie parallel to those of the cells.* In blood smears stained by the classic May-Grünwald-Giemsa technique, the yellowish cytoplasm most often appears translucent and homogeneous. The nuclei of mature erythro-

---

*In the lizard *Acanthodactylus erythrurus* the long axes of more than 50% of the nuclei deviate from those of the cells in the only specimen of this form that I have studied.

cytes are chromophilic. The masses of chromatin are more or less visible, depending on the age of the cells. The most critical staining permits the demonstration of granules within the cytoplasm (Hirschler, 1928; Ryerson, 1949) and of the Golgi apparatus (Bhattacharya and Brambell, 1924).

The circulating blood contains immature cells of the erythrocytic series (basophilic and polychromatophilic normoblasts) characterized by a rounded form, blue cytoplasm, and a large nucleus which is less chromophilic than that of a mature erythrocyte. These cells are especially common in young or moulting animals (Saint Girons, 1961) or ones heavily infected by hemoparasites (Pienaar, 1962). Mitotic figures are also present. These two phenomena reflect the process of erythropoiesis, generally in association with thyroid activity. The senile forms of the red blood cells are larger than the normal erythrocytes. Their cytoplasm stains weakly, and their nuclei are pycnotic and often irregularly shaped. In the final stage, the cytoplasm disappears, and only the nucleus is visible in a smear. These different stages have been studied in detail in one turtle (*Terrapene carolina*, Jordan and Flippen, 1913), one lizard (*Cordylus vittifer*, Pienaar, 1962), and two snakes (*Vipera russelii* and *Python regius*, Slonimski, 1934).

The presence of intracorpuscular parasites may alter the shape and size of erythrocytes considerably. With infection of the red blood cells of *Tarentola mauritanica* by the sporozoan *Pyrhemocyton tarentole*, the erythrocytes and their nuclei become more circular (Wood, 1935). In lizards from Mexico and Florida, the presence of *Plasmodium* spp. within the corpuscles affected the dimensions of the cells, causing a more or less marked increase in their size (Thomson and Huff, 1944a and b; Bergman, 1957; Reichenbach-Klinke, 1963).

A recent study (Saint Girons and Saint Girons, 1969) of 76 species of reptiles belonging to 29 families allows precise statements to be made concerning the morphology of the erythrocytes in members of the four orders of reptiles (Table I and Figs 1–5).

The cryptodiran turtles have rather large erythrocytes with regular, rounded nuclei. Their nucleo-cytoplasmic ratios (see Table I) are slightly less than the average for reptiles. Turtles of the genus *Pelomedusa* (Pleurodira) have small, almost rounded nuclei, and thus an especially low nucleo-cytoplasmic ratio (Gulliver, 1875; Taylor and Kaplan, 1961; Pienaar, 1962; Saint Girons and Duguy, 1963; Saint Girons and Saint Girons, 1969).

The erythrocytes of *Sphenodon punctatus* differ from those of all other reptiles by their great size which allows the recognition of this species, without any doubt, from a simple blood smear. Otherwise they have no striking characteristics, although their regularly shaped nuclei are slightly more rounded than in most reptiles (Saint Girons and Saint Girons, 1969).

The erythrocytes of lizards vary greatly in size depending on the family

MARIE–CHARLOTTE SAINT GIRONS

TABLE I

List of Species with Erythrocyte Dimensions.
(GD – Greatest diameter, LD – Least diameter, S – Surface
N/C – Nuclear surface/cell surface)

	Erythrocytes				Nuclei				Ratios
	GD	LD	GD/LD	S	GD	LD	GD/LD	S	N/C
	(μ)	(μ)		(μ^2)	(μ)	(μ)		(μ^2)	
TESTUDINES									
Testudinidae									
Testudo graeca	18·5	10·6	1·75	153·8	6·1	4·3	1·42	20·6	0·134
Emydidae									
Clemmys caspica leprosa	19·0	10·9	1·74	162·5	6·5	4·8	1·35	24·5	0·151
Emys orbicularis	19·9	11·7	1·70	182·8	6·0	4·5	1·33	21·2	0·116
Pelomedusidae									
Pelomedusa subrufa	19·0	10·2	1·86	150·0	5·1	4·3	1·19	12·1	0·079
RHYNCHOCEPHALIA									
Sphenodon punctatus	23·3	13·9	1·67	252·0	8·3	5·7	1·46	37·0	0·147
SAURIA									
Gekkonidae									
Coleonyx variegatus	18·9	9·6	1·97	142·5	7·3	3·7	1·97	21·5	0·151
Gehyra variegata	17·2	11·5	1·49	139·5	6·3	3·8	1·66	18·9	0·135
Heteronota binoei	21·4	10·7	2·00	179·9	8·1	3·4	2·38	21·6	0·120
Pygopodidae									
Delma fraseri	17·0	9·7	1·75	129·8	6·7	3·1	2·16	18·9	0·146
Lialis burtonis	19·9	12·5	1·59	193·5	7·7	4·3	1·79	25·9	0·134
Iguanidae									
Anolis carolinensis	15·3	8·9	1·72	106·9	6·1	3·6	1·69	17·2	0·161
Crotaphytus collaris	17·8	8·6	2·07	120·0	7·2	3·6	2·00	20·7	0·172
Dipsosaurus dorsalis	18·0	10·3	1·75	145·8	8·2	3·8	2·16	24·5	0·168
Iguana iguana	15·3	7·8	1·97	93·8	5·1	3·6	1·42	15·2	0·160
Phrynosoma maccallii	18·9	10·1	1·87	149·8	7·1	3·6	1·97	20·1	0·134
Uma inornata	17·8	9·2	1·93	128·5	7·2	3·2	2·25	18·6	0·145
Uta graciosa	14·7	9·0	1·74	103·6	6·0	3·2	1·87	15·7	0·151
Agamidae									
Agama impalearis	14·9	8·2	1·82	96·1	5·9	3·1	1·90	14·3	0·148
Amphibolurus reticulatus	14·7	7·9	1·86	92·4	6·3	2·6	1·86	12·8	0·138
Diporiphora bilineata	17·6	9·0	1·96	124·6	6·5	3·6	1·81	18·4	0·148
Chamaeleonidae									
Chamaeleo africanus	17·6	7·8	2·26	107·8	6·8	3·6	1·89	19·3	0·178
Lacertidae									
Acanthodactylus erythrurus	13·6	8·6	1·58	91·9	6·2	2·5	2·48	12·2	0·133
Lacerta agilis	14·0	8·5	1·65	93·6	5·8	2·8	2·07	12·8	0·137
Lacerta muralis	13·8	8·0	1·72	86·9	5·4	3·0	1·80	16·2	0·186
Lacerta viridis	15·5	8·3	1·86	125·0	6·0	3·1	1·94	14·6	0·117
Lacerta vivipara	14·1	8·7	1·62	96·3	5·6	3·2	1·75	14·1	0·146
Psammodromus algirus	13·8	7·8	1·77	84·3	5·4	2·8	1·93	11·9	0·141

TABLE I—*cont.*

	Erythrocytes				Nuclei				Ratios
	GD	LD	GD/ LD	S	GD	LD	GD/ LD	S	N/C
	(μ)	(μ)		(μ^2)	(μ)	(μ)		(μ^2)	
Teiidae									
Ameiva ameiva	13·8	7·6	1·82	82·3	5·8	2·7	2·15	12·3	0·149
Cnemidophorus tigris	15·8	8·3	1·90	102·8	5·9	2·4	2·46	11·1	0·108
Cordylidae									
Cordylus cordylus	17·3	9·8	1·77	133·4	6·3	4·5	1·40	22·2	0·166
Cordylus vittifer	17·2	9·5	1·81	128·0	7·1	4·6	1·54	25·6	0·200
Scincidae									
Egernia sp.	16·3	10·4	1·57	129·9	6·1	4·2	1·45	20·2	0·155
Chalcides mionecton	14·4	8·1	1·77	91·6	5·7	3·8	1·50	17·2	0·177
Eumeces algeriensis	17·8	11·1	1·61	154·8	8·4	4·0	2·10	26·4	0·170
Lygosoma									
(*Sphenomorphus*) sp.	14·6	8·2	1·78	89·7	5·7	3·1	1·84	13·4	0·149
Lygosoma taeniolatum	14·3	9·4	1·52	108·7	5·4	2·8	1·90	11·9	0·109
Scincus scincus	15·3	7·4	2·07	89·0	6·6	2·7	2·44	19·1	0·215
Tiliqua scincoides	17·3	9·6	1·80	130·7	7·5	4·3	1·74	25·2	0·193
Feyliniidae									
Feylinia currori	14·8	8·1	1·83	94·0	5·8	4·1	1·41	18·7	0·199
Anguidae									
Anguis fragilis	18·4	9·8	1·88	143·9	6·8	4·2	1·62	22·5	0·149
Gerrhonotus multicarinatus	18·8	9·1	2·07	134·5	7·7	3·4	2·26	20·5	0·152
Ophisaurus koellikeri	17·0	8·7	1·95	121·3	6·3	3·9	1·62	17·8	0·147
Anniellidae									
Anniella pulchra	19·1	9·1	2·10	136·5	6·4	3·6	1·78	18·1	0·133
Helodermatidae									
Heloderma horridum	21·4	13·5	1·58	227·0	7·9	4·6	1·72	28·5	0·125
Heloderma suspectum	17·3	10·0	1·73	134·2	6·6	4·5	1·47	27·4	0·165
Varanidae									
Varanus griseus	15·6	8·9	1·75	109·2	6·2	3·6	1·72	17·5	0·160
AMPHISBAENIA									
Amphisbaenidae									
Blanus cinereus	17·6	9·5	1·85	131·5	6·6	3·4	1·94	17·6	0·134
Trogonophidae									
Trogonophis wiegmanni	16·6	9·5	1·75	123·8	6·7	4·0	1·67	21·1	0·170
OPHIDIA									
Typhlopidae									
Typhlops punctatus	17·0	8·4	1·97	109·5	8·1	3·1	2·61	19·7	0·179
Typhlops vermicularis	15·2	8·3	1·84	98·5	7·2	3·8	1·89	21·5	0·218
Leptotyphlopidae									
Leptotyphlops dulcis	16·6	8·4	1·97	109·5	8·1	3·1	2·61	19·7	0·179
Boidae									
Eryx jaculus	16·1	9·5	1·61	120·0	7·0	3·4	2·06	18·7	0·156
Lichanura roseofusca	17·1	9·6	1·78	129·0	6·1	4·0	1·52	19·2	0·149
Morelia argus	18·0	10·2	1·76	144·1	4·9	3·4	1·44	13·1	0·091

TABLE I—*cont.*

	Erythrocytes				Nuclei				Ratios
	GD	LD	GD/ LD	S	GD	LD	GD/ LD	S	N/C
	(μ)	(μ)		(μ^2)	(μ)	(μ)		(μ^2)	
Colubridae									
Coronella austriaca	17·5	9·7	1·80	140·0	7·3	3·6	2·03	20·6	0·147
Coluber viridiflavus	16·1	9·9	1·63	124·8	8·2	3·3	2·48	21·2	0·169
Elaphe longissima	18·3	10·6	1·73	152·1	7·1	4·1	1·73	22·7	0·149
Elaphe scalaris	18·8	8·7	2·16	115·8	6·8	4·2	1·57	22·4	0·192
Lycodryas sp.	16·6	9·0	1·84	117·5	5·9	3·5	1·69	16·2	0·138
Macroprotodon cucullatus	16·4	8·7	1·88	112·4	6·0	3·7	1·73	17·5	0·156
Natrix maura	18·1	10·6	1·71	150·4	6·8	4·2	1·62	22·4	0·149
Elapidae									
Bungarus fasciatus	17·9	9·5	1·88	133·4	6·9	3·2	2·16	17·2	0·129
Denisonia suta	16·8	10·4	1·62	137·3	7·4	3·9	1·62	22·7	0·165
Naja naja	16·2	9·0	1·80	114·5	6·6	4·1	1·61	21·2	0·185
Oxyuranus scutellatus	16·6	9·1	1·82	118·7	6·5	3·7	1·76	18·9	0·159
Pseudechis australis	18·4	11·2	1·64	162·0	6·4	3·4	1·88	17·8	0·110
Pseudechis porphyriacus	17·0	11·0	1·55	146·8	7·5	3·8	1·97	22·3	0·152
Hydrophiidae									
Laticauda colubrina	19·2	11·2	1·71	169·8	7·7	3·4	2·28	20·6	0·121
Viperidae									
Atractaspis sp.	18·5	10·5	1·76	152·5	8·2	3·9	2·10	25·1	0·165
Cerastes cerastes	18·2	9·4	1·94	134·1	6·4	4·0	1·59	20·2	0·151
Vipera aspis	17·3	11·2	1·52	154·5	7·5	4·0	1·87	23·6	0·153
Vipera berus	16·1	10·5	1·53	132·8	7·3	4·2	1·74	24·1	0·181
Crotalidae									
Crotalus viridis	17·9	11·1	1·60	184·6	6·9	4·3	1·60	23·4	0·141
CROCODILIA									
Caiman crocodilus	16·9	9·9	1·71	131·5	5·7	4·2	1·36	18·8	0·135
Crocodylus niloticus	16·4	9·0	1·82	115·9	5·0	3·8	1·32	14·9	0·129

and sometimes even within one family. In the Gekkonidae and Pygopodidae’ the red blood cells are usually rather large. The nucleo-cytoplasmic ratio is quite constant and somewhat less than average. The nuclei are regular and elongated, and their ends are usually pointed rather than rounded as in most lizards. In representatives of the Iguania, the erythrocytes vary greatly in size and are usually rather elongated. This characteristic is especially marked in the Chamaeleonidae, in which the ratio of the longest diameter to the shortest diameter is very clearly greater than two in the species examined. The nuclei have a regular shape except in *Dipsosaurus dorsalis* in which most of them have more or less indented margins (Saint Girons and Saint Girons, 1969).

The Lacertidae and Teiidae form a remarkably homogeneous group; they

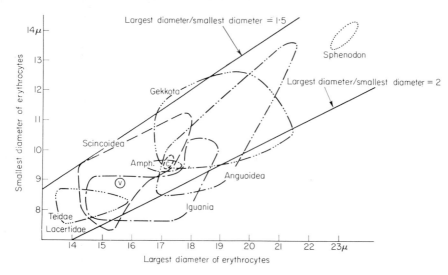

FIG. 1. Size and shape of the erythrocytes of *Sphenodon*, lizards, and amphisbaenians. Greatest versus least diameter in micra. Amph., Amphisbaenia; c, *Cordylus*; v, *Varanus griseus*. From Saint Girons and Saint Girons (1969).

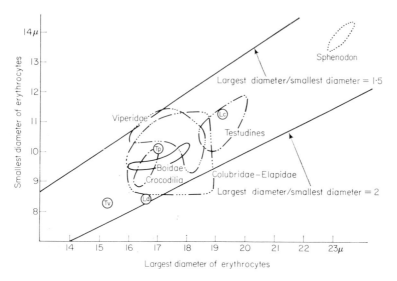

FIG. 2. Size and shape of the erythrocytes of *Sphenodon*, snakes, turtles and crocodilians. Lc, *Laticauda colubrina*; Ld, *Leptotyphlops dulcis*; Tp, *Typhlops punctatus*; Tv, *Typhlops vermicularis*. From Saint Girons and Saint Girons (1969).

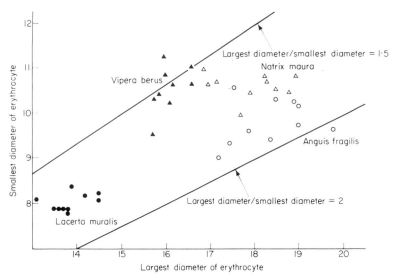

FIG. 3. Ratios of largest diameters (LD) to smallest diameters (SD) of erythrocytes of Squamata. Solid circles, *Lacerta muralis*; open circles, *Anguis fragilis*; solid triangles, *Vipera berus*; open triangles,*Natrix maura*. From Saint Girons and Saint Girons (1969).

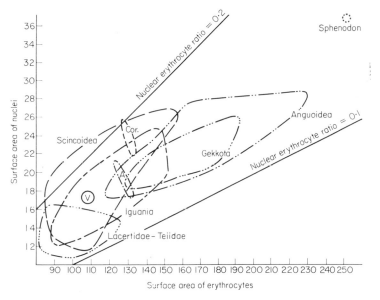

FIG. 4. Nucleo-cytoplasmic ratios of Lepidosauria. A, Amphisbaenia; Cor, Cordylidae; V Varanidae. From Saint Girons and Saint Girons (1969).

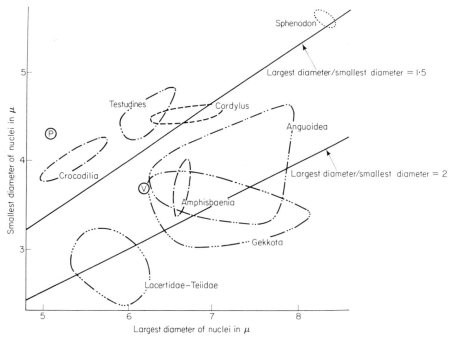

FIG. 5. Size and shape of the nuclei of erythrocytes of various reptiles. P, *Pelomedusa subrufa*; V, *Varanus griseus*. From Saint Girons and Saint Girons (1969).

have particularly small erythrocytes with regular, rather elongate nuclei. The Cordylidae differ sharply from the two preceding families. Their corpuscles are much larger, and the nucleo-cytoplasmic ratio is greatly raised by the size of their nuclei which are larger and more rounded than in most other lizards. The erythrocytes of members of the Scincoidea are more or less elongated and vary in size. They are small in *Chalcides* and *Scincus*, and reach a relatively large surface area in *Eumeces* and *Tiliqua*. The nucleo-cytoplasmic ratio is very variable, and the morphological pattern of the nuclei also changes from genus to genus; they are regular and rounded in *Egernia*, but elongated and often irregular in *Eumeces*. The red blood corpuscles of *Feylinia* are morphologically very similar to those of *Chalcides* and *Lygosoma*.

The Anguidae have large erythrocytes in which the ratio of the largest diameter to the smallest diameter is close to or greater than two. The quite large nuclei are rounded at their ends. The Helodermatidae have big erythrocytes with large nuclei. Their size is intermediate between those of the red blood corpuscles of *Sphenodon* and the Anguidae. They thus resemble *Sphenodon punctatus* more than any other lizards in erythrocyte morphology (Ryerson, 1949). Both the corpuscles and their nuclei are rounded. In the

Varanidae, the erythrocytes are the smallest found in the Diploglossa (Anguoidea plus Varanoidea). Their nuclei are regular, rather large in relation to the size of the cells, and generally rounded (Gulliver, 1842, 1875; Pienaar, 1962; Banerjee, 1966; Saint Girons and Saint Girons, 1969).

In the amphisbaenians both the erythrocytes and their nuclei are medium-sized. The latter, which are regular, are a little narrower in *Blanus* than in *Trogonophis*, so that the nucleo-cytoplasmic ratio is smaller in the former genus (Saint Girons and Saint Girons, 1969).

The snakes, except for *Typhlops vermicularis*, form a relatively homogeneous group. The two species of *Typhlops* that have been studied differ greatly. Although the erythrocytes of *Typhlops punctatus* are similar in size to those of other snakes, those of *Typhlops vermicularis* are completely different, being small and elongate. Their nuclei are relatively very large, so that the nucleo-cytoplasmic ratio is particularly high (Saint Girons and Saint Girons, 1969).

The red blood corpuscles and their nuclei appear slightly more rounded, with a little larger surface area, in the Viperidae. The nuclei are more often irregular in the Elapidae and Viperidae; this is especially marked in *Naja naja*. On the other hand, *Laticauda colubrina* is distinctive in the rather large size of its erythrocytes. Finally a boid, *Morelia argus*, has especially small, almost spherical nuclei and thus has a nucleo-cytoplasmic ratio almost as low as that of the pleurodiran turtle *Pelomedusa subrufa* (Gulliver, 1875; Jordan, 1938, Saint Girons and Saint Girons, 1969).

Although they do not reach the size of the ones in *Sphenodon punctatus*, the erythrocytes of crocodilians are large, like those of turtles. They also resemble those of turtles in having rounded nuclei (Gulliver, 1840, 1875; Reese, 1917; Wintrobe, 1933; Pienaar, 1962).

The data on erythrocytes suggest that the size of the cells is related to the systematic position of the families from which they are derived. Wintrobe (1933) postulated that the size of its erythrocytes reflects the position of a species in the evolutionary scale. The lower vertebrates and those which represent unsuccessful evolutionary experiments have large, nucleated red

---

FIGS 6–9. Photomicrographs of cells from circulating reptilian blood. Stained by May-Grünwald-Giemsa technique.

FIG. 6. *Sphenodon punctatus*. Note very large erythrocytes and a lymphocyte in the center. × 1000.

FIG. 7. *Agama impalearis*. Small erythrocytes. A large, faded eosinophilic granulocyte and a lymphocyte in the center. × 1000.

FIG. 8. *Heloderma horridum*. Large erythrocytes. A large lymphocyte at the upper right and an eosinophilic granulocyte with a clearly visible nucleus at the lower left. × 1000.

FIG. 9. *Varanus griseus*. A thrombocyte with irregularly-shaped, visible cytoplasm at the upper left, an erythrocyte in which, exceptionally, the nucleus is not oriented along the long axis of the cell at the left, and an eosinophilic granulocyte with small granules and a lymphocyte at the upper right. × 1000.

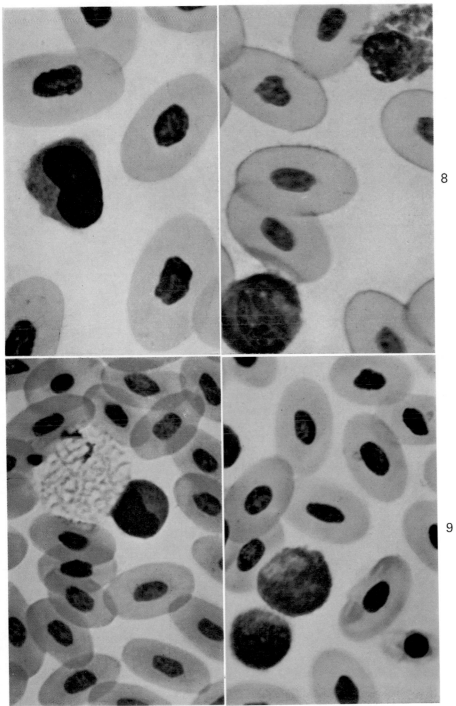

6

8

7

9

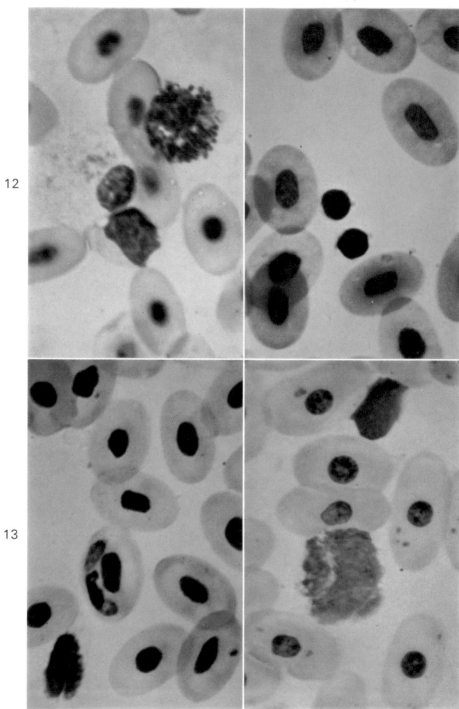

blood corpuscles; higher vertebrates, on the other hand, have small, enucleate ones. In this respect, reptiles are intermediate between amphibians and birds (Szarski and Czopek, 1966; Szarski, 1968). Within the class Reptilia, the largest erythrocytes occur in *Sphenodon punctatus*, turtles, and crocodilians, which are considered very archaic. The smallest corpuscles are found in the Lacertidae which have retained a wide evolutionary potential, as is evidenced by the populations of *Lacerta muralis* in the process of speciation on various Mediterranean islands. It is also noteworthy that the Helodermatidae, Anguidae, and Gekkota have the largest erythrocytes of any lizards (Saint Girons and Saint Girons, 1969).

III. Eosinophilic Granulocytes

The eosinophilic granulocytes of all reptiles are large, generally rounded cells in which the variably shaped nuclei lie near the periphery (Figs 7, 8, 9, and 11). The nuclei stain rather weakly with the May-Grünwald-Giemsa technique. The cytoplasm contains granules that are usually highly chromophilic and appear a more or less brilliant yellow-brown. Loewenthal (1931) reported only a weak staining reaction of the granules in *Anguis fragilis*; this is also the case in *Crocodylus niloticus* and *Caiman crocodilus*.

Two types of eosinophils may be distinguished on the basis of the shapes of the intracytoplasmic granules which may be cylindrical or, more commonly, spherical. These two types have been reported in all the orders of reptiles: Testudines (Loewenthal, 1930; Ryerson, 1943), Rhynchocephalia (Komocki, 1936), Squamata (Peña Roche, 1939, *Liolaemus*; Pienaar, 1962, *Cordylus vittifer*; Loewenthal, 1928, *Vipera aspis*), and Crocodilia (Slonimski, 1935; Ryerson, 1943). Bernstein (1938) differentiated three types of eosinophils in *Psammobates* (=*Testudo* auct.) *geometricus* based on the affinity of the cytoplasmic granules for eosin. A recent study presents histochemical and ultrastructural data on these cells in *Lacerta agilis* and *Emys orbicularis* (Kelényi and Németh, 1969).

The size of these cells is very variable, not only between species, but even in one animal and in a single blood smear. Because of this variation, the data presented in Table II, which gives the maximum, mean, and minimum lengths of the greatest diameter, can only be taken as indications, valuable

---

FIGS 10–13. Photomicrographs of cells from circulating reptilian blood. Stained by May-Grünwald-Giemsa technique. × 1000.

FIG. 10. *Vipera aspis*. Medium-sized erythrocytes with irregular, almost rectangular, nuclei. Two thrombocytes in the center.

FIG. 11. *Pelomedusa subrufa*. Erythrocytes with very small, circular nuclei. A lymphocyte at the top and an eosinophilic granulocyte with a peripheral nucleus at the right.

FIG. 12. *Caiman crocodilus*. A basophilic granulocyte with small, very chromophilic granules partly masking the peripheral nucleus and the cytoplasm to the left and, above and to the right of it, a lymphocyte and a large monocyte.

FIG. 13. *Varanus griseus*. An erythrocyte parasitized by a hemogregarine.

MARIE–CHARLOTTE SAINT GIRONS

TABLE II

Largest Diameters (in μ) of Eosinophilic Granulocytes in some Representatives
of the Different Orders of Reptiles
(after Saint Girons and Duguy, 1963, with supplements).

	Mean	Range
Sphenodon punctatus	14·78	9–23
Heteronota binoei	16·68	13–20
Lygosoma (*Sphenomorphus*) sp.	14·04	10–16
Lacerta muralis	13·58	11–16
Lacerta agilis	13·90	12–16
Lacerta vivipara	14·43	12–16
Lacerta viridis	14·25	12–17
Psammodromus algirus	10·42	9–12
Anguis fragilis	14·20	11–17
Heloderma suspectum	14·20	10–18
Coronella austriaca	18·00	16–19
Elaphe longissima	18·18	16–20
Elaphe scalaris	15·70	15–17
Coluber viridiflavus	17·88	15–20
Natrix natrix	17·59	14–20
Natrix maura	18·22	16–20
Malpolon monspessulanus	19·20	18–20
Pseudechis australis	16·73	15–19
Vipera aspis	17·70	16–20
Vipera berus	18·13	15–20
Testudo graeca	14·19	11–17
Emys orbicularis	16·55	14–19
Crocodylus niloticus	16·25	

only in that a certain number of species belonging to different orders may be compared. Surprisingly the average sizes are nearly similar in all cases. The eosinophilic granulocytes of *Sphenodon punctatus*, unlike its erythrocytes, are among the smaller ones. Lizards have small eosinophils, snakes the largest ones, and turtles and crocodilians are intermediate in this regard. The intra-cytoplasmic granules vary in size, reaching two to three micra in their largest diameter. The density of the granulation may obscure the position and form of the nucleus. The latter is often multilobate, but the number of lobes does not appear to be very high.

IV. Basophilic Granulocytes

The basophilic granulocytes are very easy to recognize. In all the species studied, they are small, circular or nearly circular corpuscles, and the cytoplasm is usually filled with extremely chromophilic granules (Fig. 12). In a blood smear, they resemble mulberries. The granulation is so dense that the weakly staining nucleus may only rarely be seen (Michels, 1923). In some species, including *Lacerta viridis* and *Typhlops punctatus*, the basophils are slightly oval.

The interspecific variation in the size of the basophilic granulocytes is less than that of the eosinophils (see Table III for their size and variability which tend to parallel those of the erythrocytes). They are smallest in the lizards, especially *Lacerta*, larger in snakes, still larger in turtles and crocodilians, and largest in *Sphenodon punctatus*. Michels (1923), who studied the basophils of a variety of reptiles, suggested the possibility that some eosinophils could, at certain periods in the annual cycle of the turtle *Clemmys caspica leprosa*, be transformed into basophils, but later work has given no support to this hypothesis (Pienaar, 1962).

TABLE III

Largest Diameters (in μ) of Basophilic Granulocytes in some Representatives of the Different Orders of Reptiles (after Saint Girons and Duguy, 1963, with supplements).

	Mean	Range
Sphenodon punctatus	14·43	12–20
Heteronota binoei	10·90	8–15
Lygosoma (*Sphenomorphus*) sp.	8·33	7–10
Lacerta muralis	10·80	9–13
Lacerta agilis	8·10	7– 9
Lacerta vivipara	10·47	9–12
Lacerta viridis	11·90	10–13
Psammodromus algirus	9·70	8–11
Anguis fragilis	11·89	9–15
Heloderma suspectum	10·92	8–16
Coronella austriaca	11·00	10–12
Elaphe longissima	12·53	9–15
Elaphe scalaris	10·10	9–11
Coluber viridiflavus	13·02	10–15
Natrix natrix	10·18	8–12
Natrix maura	11·83	9–15
Malpolon monspessulanus	11·70	11–13
Vipera aspis	12·26	9–16
Vipera berus	11·69	8–15
Testudo graeca	11·00	8–15
Emys orbicularis	14·45	13–16
Caiman crocodilus	13·50	

V. Azurophilic Granulocytes

The presence of azurophilic granulocytes in reptilian blood was first reported by Pappenheim (1909). Although they are, in most cases, difficult to differentiate by the May-Grünwald-Giemsa technique, they may be characterized by the possession of granules that stain with pure azure dyes and with the pyronin of methylgreen-pyronin mixtures (Pienaar, 1962). Hematologists have attributed them to different leucocytic series, most often to the monocytic series (Zylberszac, 1937; Ryerson, 1949) or the neutrophilic granulocytic series (Loewenthal, 1930; Slonimski, 1934; Bernstein, 1938).

These cells have relatively small, irregular, eccentric nuclei. They vary greatly in size. Azurophilic granulocytes usually contain lipid bodies in the cytoplasm, but those may be absent, as in *Cordylus* (Pienaar, 1962). Senile cells contain many vacuoles.

VI. Neutrophilic Granulocytes

The neutrophilic granulocytes are circular or oval cells that frequently form groups of two or three cells beside each other in blood smears (Pienaar, 1962). Their name refers to their staining reactions only; they are probably not homologous to the neutrophils of mammals. The small, irregular nucleus lies near the periphery of the cell. The neutrophils may be regarded as morphological variants of the azurophilic granulocytes with which they have often been confused. They have also been described as heterophils; the fact that this last name has also been applied to the eosinophilic granulocytes with cylindrical granules only adds to the nomenclatorial confusion (Ryerson, 1949).

VII. Lymphocytes

Lymphocytes form the most important class of leucocytes if, as many believe, they retain all of their potential to differentiate into the other blood cells while they are circulating in the blood. They show a large range in size, and the distinction between "large" and "small" lymphocytes is most often arbitrary. In *Cordylus vittifer*, Pienaar (1962) divided this category into large lymphocytes in which the diameter is at least 14·5 μ and small lymphocytes with diameters of 5·5 to 10 μ. Lymphocytes are characterized by transparent, moderately to weakly basophilic cytoplasm (Figs 6–11 and 12). The nuclei are circular and centrally located in small lymphocytes, but more irregular in large ones. Chromophobic vacuoles and some azurophilic granules occur in the cytoplasm.

In *Rana pipiens* there is a direct genetic relation between lymphocytes and monocytes (Jordan, 1925); all gradations occur, in morphology, physiology, and staining properties, between small lymphocytes and large monocytes. The situation is probably the same in reptiles (Pienaar, 1962).

VIII. Plasma Cells

The plasma cells, which are usually rare in the circulating blood, may arise from medium-sized or large lymphocytes. They are characterized by an eccentric nucleus, opaque basophilic cytoplasm, and a perinuclear halo of hyaloplasm.

IX. Monocytes

Monocytes have been confused with several other types of cells and may not always be distinct (Fig. 12). In *Cordylus* Pienaar (1962) considered them as a type of azurophilic granulocyte although, in his table of terms, he treats them as a distinct series. They are generally rare and have markedly irregular shapes. Their nuclei vary in shape, but are frequently polymorphous.

X. Thrombocytes

The thrombocytes are small, oval cells characterized by elongate, centrally located, highly chromophilic nuclei (Figs 9 and 10). The nucleo-cytoplasmic ratio is especially high, and the cytoplasm appears as a narrow border around the nucleus. The cytoplasm is almost colorless (faintly acidophilic) and hence difficult to see in a blood smear. It frequently contains some azurophilic granules. Pienaar (1962) described a large acidophilic granule at one pole of the nucleus in thrombocytes of the turtle *Pelomedusa subrufa*.

Thrombocytes are fragile cells, and in blood smears their very viscous cytoplasm is often lost. The nuclei are then clumped in groups which may contain ten or more elements.

XI. Parasites in the Blood of Reptiles

A. General

Although a detailed treatment of the parasites in the blood is outside the scope of this chapter, a brief mention of them may be appropriate here since they can be seen in blood smears and may affect the morphology of the different blood cells. The literature on the parasites in reptilian blood is very extensive, with papers treating hemogregarines being especially numerous. So as not to overload the text, I have cited only the most important or especially interesting works. The recent papers of Pienaar (1962) and Reichenbach-Klinke (1963) contain extensive bibliographies. (A detailed treatment of the various reptilian parasites will furthermore be included in the volumes on Ecology).

Parasites of the blood may be divided into two classes depending on whether they infect the blood without attacking the corpuscles or whether they become established within the corpuscles.

B. Extracorpuscular Parasites

Flagellates: Flagellates of the genera *Trypanosoma*, *Leptomonas*, *Leishmania*, and possibly *Proteromonas* occur in the blood of reptiles (Reichenow, 1953).

Trypanosomes are found in both terrestrial and aquatic reptiles. The first description of a trypanosome parasitizing a reptile is that of *Trypanosoma damoniae* which Laveran and Mesnil (1902) found in the Asiatic turtle *Chinemys* (=*Damonia* auct.) *reevesii*. Trypanosomes have been especially well studied in aquatic turtles. Pienaar (1962) devotes several pages to these parasites in reptiles.

Leptomonas has been reported in the blood of numerous lizards including *Anolis*, *Agama*, *Chalcides*, *Cnemidophorus*, and *Tarentola* (Hindle, 1930; Reichenow, 1953). *Leishmania* also occurs in the blood of various lizards: *Tarentola mauritanica*, *Hemidactylus brookii*, *Ceramodactylus doriae*, and *Latastia longicauda revoili* (Reichenow, 1953; Heisch, 1958).

Nematodes: Filarial worms have frequently been reported in the blood of reptiles (Chabaud and Frank, 1961; Reichenbach-Klinke, 1963; Telford, 1965).

Trematodes: Trematodes have been noted in the blood vessels of aquatic turtles (Martin and Bamberger, 1952).

C. Intracorpuscular Parasites

The blood corpuscles of reptiles are parasitized by many telosporidian species of the suborder Adeleiina belonging to the genera *Karyolysus* (*K. lacertae* is especially common in *Lacerta muralis* in France), *Hepatozoon*, and *Haemogregarina* (see Hoare, 1932, concerning these parasites in African reptiles). Hemogregarines parasitize the erythrocytes, and only rarely infect the leucocytes (Fig. 13). Telosporidians of the suborder Eimeriina also occur in the blood, but they are more commonly found in the intestine and gall bladder. Among the hemosporidians which parasitize the blood corpuscles, *Haemoproteus* and especially *Plasmodium* are the most important genera. Pienaar (1962) has studied these parasites in detail and presents a table giving the host and citing references to descriptions for 19 species of *Plasmodium*.

Pyrhemocyton have been described from lizards, snakes, and turtles (Brumpt and Lavier, 1935; du Toit, 1937; Carpano, 1939; Pienaar, 1962).

XII. Summary

The identification of the cells in smears from the circulating blood of reptiles is often difficult, since these animals have cells of all ages and showing all intermediate stages between the different types of cells. Moreover, there is still not complete agreement on the phylogeny of the various types of cells, and the differences between families or even within one family are such that it is, with our present knowledge, virtually impossible to give morphological characters for each type of cell which are valid for all species. Only the erythrocytes are becoming well known, and the study of their comparative morphology is producing data of considerable interest in relation to the phylogeny of the different families. Both the eosinophilic and basophilic granulocytes and the thrombocytes are relatively homogeneous types of cells, and their recognition in blood smears is not very difficult. It is not the same with the other cellular lineages; in them transitional forms are common and often difficult to identify without a thorough knowledge of the hematopoietic organs.

References

Altman, P. L. and Dittmer, D. S., eds. (1961). "Blood and Other Body Fluids." Federation of American Societies for Experimental Biology, Bethesda, Maryland.

Babudieri, B. (1930). Studi di ematologica comparata. Ricerche sui pesci, sugli amfibi e sui rettili. *Haematologica* 2, 199–255.

Banerjee, V. (1966). Blood of some Indian vertebrates. *Naturwissenschaften* 53(5), p. 137.

Bergman, R. A. M. (1957). The erythrocytes of snakes. *Folia haemat., Lpz.* 75, 92–111.

Bernstein, R. E. (1938). Blood cytology of the tortoise, *Testudo geometrica. S. Afr. J. Sci.* 35, 327–331.

Bhattacharya, D. R. and Brambell, R. (1924). The Golgi body in the erythrocytes of the Sauropsidae. *Q. Jl. microsc. Sci.* 69, 357–359.

Brumpt, E. and Lavier, G. (1935). Sur un hématozoaire nouveau du lézard vert, *Pirhaemocyton lacertae* n. sp. *Annls. Parasit. hum. comp.* 13, 537–543.

Carpano, M. (1939). Sui piroplasmidi dei Cheloni e sua una nuova specie rinvenuta nelle tartarughe *Nuttalia guglilmi. Riv. Parassit.* 3, 267–276.

Chabaud, A. C. and Frank, W. (1961). Nouvelle filaire parasite des artères de pythons: *Macdonaldius oschei* n. sp. (Nematodes, Onchoceroidae). *Z. ParasitKde.* 20, 434–439.

du Toit, P. J. (1937). A new piroplasm (*Sauroplasma thomasi* n. g., n. sp.) of a lizard (*Zonurus giganteus*, Smith). *Onderstepoort J. vet. Sci. Anim. Ind.* 9, 289–299.

Efrati, P., Nir, E. and Yaari, A. (1970). Morphological and cytological observations on cells of the hemopoietic system of *Agama stellio* (Linnaeus). A comparative study. *Israel J. Med. Sci.* 6(1), 23-31.

Gabe, M. (1968). "Techniques Histologiques." Masson et Cie, Paris.

Gulliver, G. (1840). On the blood corpuscles of the Crocodilia. *Proc. zool. Soc. Lond.* 8, 131–133.

Gulliver, G. (1842). On the blood corpuscles of the British ophidians, reptiles and other oviparous vertebrates. *Proc. zool. Soc. Lond.* 10, 108–111.

Gulliver, G. (1875). Observations on the sizes and shapes of the red corpuscles of the blood of vertebrates, with drawings of them to a uniform scale, and extended and revised tables of measurements. *Proc. zool. Soc. Lond.* 1875, 474–495.

Hayem, G. (1879). Recherches sur l'évolution des hématies dans le sang de l'homme et des vertébrés. II – sang des vertébrés à globules rouges nucléés. III – historique. *Arch. Physiol. Norm. Pathol.* 2(6), 201–261.

Heisch, R. B. (1958). On *Leishmania adleri* sp. nov. from lacertid lizards (*Latastia* sp.) in Kenya. *Ann. trop. Med. Parasit.* 52, 68–71.

Hindle, E. (1930). Attempts to infect hamsters with various flagellates. *Trans. R. Soc. trop. Med. Hyg.* 24, 97–104.

Hirschler, J. (1928). Studien über die Plasmakomponenten (Golgi Apparat u. a.) an vital gefärbten männlichen Geschlechtszellen einiger Tierarten. *Z. Zellforsch. mikrosk. Anat.* 7, 62–82.

Hoare, C. A. (1932). On protozoal blood parasites collected in Uganda, with an account of the life cycle of the crocodile haemogregarine. *Parasitology* 24, 210–224.

Jordan, H. E. (1925). A study of the blood of the leopard frog, by the method of supravital staining. *Am. J. Anat.* 35, 105–132.

Jordan, H. E. (1938). Comparative hematology (Reptilia) *In* "Handbook of Hematology" (Downey, H., ed.) New York, Hoeber, ed. 2, 776–788.

Jordan, H. E. and Flippen, J. (1913). Haematopoiesis in Chelonia. *Folia haemat., Lpz.* 15, 1–24.

Kelényi, G. and Németh Á. (1969). Comparative histochemistry and electron microscopy of the leosinophil leucocytes of vertebrates. I. A study of avian, reptile, amphibian and fish leucocytes. *Acta biol. Acad. Sci. Lung.* 20(4), 405–422,

Komocki, W. (1936). Nouvelles observations sur la désagrégation physiologique des leucocytes granuleux ainsi que sur les leucocytes du sang de *Sphenodon punctatus*, Gray (Hatteria). *Bull. Histol. Tech. Micr.* 13, 194–201.

Laveran, A. and Mesnil, F. (1902). Sur quelques protozoaires parasites d'une tortue d'Asie (*Damonia reevesii*). *C. r. hebd. Séanc. Acad. Sci., Paris* 135, 609.

Loewenthal, N. (1928). Etude sur les globules blancs du sang dans la série des Vertébres. Reptiles. *Arch. Anat.* 8, 255–273.

Loewenthal, N. (1930). Nouvelles observations sur les globules blancs du sang chez les animaux vertébrés. Reptiles. *Arch. Anat.* 11, 283–297.

Loewenthal, N. (1931). Des variétés de globules blancs du sang chez l'orvet et la hulotte. *Arch. Anat.* 13, 225–245.

Mandl, L. (1839). Note sur les globules sanguins du protée et des crocodiliens. *Annls. Sci. nat.* (2)12, 289–291.

Martin, W. E. and Bamberger, J. W. (1952). New blood flukes (Trematoda: Spirorchidae) from the marine turtle, *Chelonia mydas* (L.). *J. Parasit.* 38, 105–110.

Michels, N. A. (1923). The mast cell in lower vertebrates. *Cellule* 33, 339–462.

Milne-Edwards, A. (1856). Notes sur les dimensions des globules du sang chez quelques vertébrés. *Annls. Sci. nat.* 5, 165–167.

Milne-Edwards, A. (1857). "Leçons sur la Physiologie et l'Anatomie Comparée de l'Homme et des Animaux." Vol. 1. V. Masson, Paris.

Pappenheim, A. (1909). Einige interessante Tatsachen und theoretische Ergebniss der vergleichenden Leukozytenmorphologie. *Folia haemat., Lpz.* 8, 504–563.

Peña Roche, H. (1939). Contributiones à la morphologia comparada de la fauna Chilena. *Boln. Soc. Biol. Concepción* 13, 133–146.

Pienaar, U. de V. (1962). "Haematology of some South African Reptiles." Witwatersrand Univ. Press, Johannesburg.

Reese, A. M. (1917). The blood of *Alligator mississippiensis*. *Anat. Rec.* 13, 37–44.

Reichenbach-Klinke, H. H. (1963). "Krankheiten der Reptilien." G. Fischer, Stuttgart.

Reichenow, E. (1953). "Lehrbuch der Protozoenkunde." 6th edition. Begründet von F. Doflein. G. Fischer, Jena.

Ryerson, D. L. (1943). Separation of the two acidophilic granulocytes of turtle blood, with suggested phylogenetic relationships. *Anat. Rec.* 85, 25–48.

Ryerson, D. L. (1949). A preliminary survey of reptilian blood. *J. Ent. Zool.* 41, 49.

Saint Girons, M. C. (1961). Etude de l'Erythropoièse chez la Vipère berus (*Vipera berus*) en fonction de l'activité thyroïdienne et des phénomènes cycliques de la mue. *Bull. Soc. zool. Fr.* 86(1), 59–67.

Saint Girons, M. C. and Duguy, R. (1963). Notes de cytologie sanguine comparée sur les reptiles de France. *Bull. Soc. zool. Fr.* **88**(5–6), 613–624.

Saint Girons, M. C. and Saint Girons, H. (1969). Contribution à la morphologie comparée des érythrocytes chez les reptiles. *Br. J. Herpet.* **4**(4), 67–82.

Schultz, F. N. and Krüger, F. von (1925). Das Blut der Wirbeltiere. *In* "Handbuch der vergleichenden Physiologie" (H. Winterstein, ed.). I. G. Fischer, Jena.

Slonimski, P. (1934). Sur les éléments figurés du sang chez *Vipera russelli* et *Python regius*. *C. r. Ass. Anat.* (1), 25–28.

Slonimski, P. (1935a). Sur les éléments du sang chez les crocodiles, *Crocodilus rhombifer*. *C. r. Ass. Anat.* 15–17.

Slonimski, P. (1935b). Les éléments figurés du sang chez le crocodile (*Crocodilus rhombifer*). *C. r. Séanc. Soc. Biol.* **119**, 1206–1208.

Szarski, H. (1968). Evolution of cell size in lower vertebrates. *In* "Current Problems of lower Vertebrate Phylogeny." (T. Ørvig, ed.) p. 445–453. Noble Symposium No. IV. Almqvist and Wiksell, Stockholm, 445–453.

Szarski, H. and Czopek, G. 1966. Erythrocyte diameter in some amphibians and reptiles. *Bull. Acad. pol. Sci. Cl. II Sér. Sci. biol.* **14**(6), 443–437.

Taylor, K. and Kaplan, H.M. (1961). Light microscopy of the blood cells of pseudemyd turtles. *Herpetologica* **17**, 186–196.

Telford, S. R., Jr. (1965). A study of filariasis in Mexican snakes. *Jap. J. exp. Med.* **35**(6), 565–595.

Thomson, P. E. and Huff, C. G. (1944a). A saurian malarial parasite, *Plasmodium mexicanum* n. sp. with both elongatum- and gallinaceum-types of exoerythrocytic stages. *J. infect. Dis.* **74**, 48–67.

Thomson, P. E. and Huff, C. G. (1944b). Saurian malarial parasites of the United States and Mexico. *J. infect. Dis.* **74**, 68–79.

Werzberg, A. (1910). Über Blutplättchen und Thrombocyten, ihre Beziehung zu Erythrocyten und Lymphozyten, nebst einem Anhang über die Erythrogenese. *Folia. haemat.*, *Lpz.* **10**(2), 301.

Wintrobe, M. M. (1933). Variations in the size and haemoglobin concentration of erythrocytes in the blood of various vertebrates. *Folia haemat.*, *Lpz.* **51**, 32–49.

Wood, S. F. (1935). Variations in the cytology of the blood of geckos (*Tarentola mauritanica*) infected with *Haemogregarina platydactyli*, *Trypanosoma platydactyli* and *Pirhemocyton tarentolae*. *Univ. Calif. Publs Zool.* **41**(2), 9–22.

Zylberszac, S. (1937). Sur la nature des leucocytes réticulaires et spongieux du sang des reptiles. *C. r. Séanc. Soc. Biologie.* **126**, 97–98.

CHAPTER 3

Numbers of Blood Cells and Their Variation

R. DUGUY

Directeur, Muséum d'Histoire Naturelle, La Rochelle, France

I. Introduction

Studies on reptilian blood have long remained within the realm of descriptive cytology, so that the few facts relating to the physiology are of recent acquisition. Their interpretation often presents difficulties for, in most cases, the studies are fragmentary, and were carried out on a variety of reptiles, killed at different stages of their annual cycle, and belonging to very diverse systematic and faunal groups. These differences hardly allow us to ask any pertinent questions at present. The newer comparisons of blood cell counts in reptiles do suggest certain general ideas. The modifications correlated with sex, age, and taxonomic position are best shown by the erythrocytic counts. On the other hand, variations of the leucocytic formula are most informative about the annual cycle. The results from studies of the blood cells must not be considered alone: their interpretation requires as complete a knowledge as possible of the annual cycle of the species in its natural surroundings. Information obtained under these conditions and related to that supplied from studies of the endocrine glands has some value, and permits the definition of the annual cycle of a given species. Furthermore, certain interspecific comparisons can be established to permit investigation of modifications of the blood; these might reflect different physiological cycles in reptiles in which the annual cycle shows different characteristics. It is thus hoped that the new facts from investigations of the blood cells and their variations in reptiles may throw further light on our knowledge of the annual cycle.

II. Techniques

A. BLOOD SAMPLING

Many techniques may be used to take the necessary samples from the circulating blood. With large reptiles a cardiac puncture or implanted catheter may be used. On the other hand, with smaller species, particularly lizards, the simplest way is to decapitate the animal. When the same small individual or group of individuals must be sampled repeatedly, only two methods are possible: cardiac puncture or cutting pieces off the end of the tail. However, the latter method is somewhat inconvenient, for it cannot be used in all reptiles (not in lizards for example) and generally very little blood is collected. The amount is so small that, even under good conditions, erythrocyte counts can be established only for snakes over a metre long. However, when smears are prepared with these blood samples, the leucocytic formula can be determined with as much precision as with other methods.

B. Blood Cell Counts

To obtain the erythrocyte counts, the blood is mixed with a preservative (Marcano's fluid) in a hematological pipette, and then examined in a hemocytometre cell. The results are expressed as the number of erythrocytes per cubic millimetre of blood. The nuclei of reptilian erythrocytes are insoluble in the liquid (Hayem's fluid) used to study the leucocytes of mammals. The leucocyte count must be made at the same time as the erythrocyte count, utilizing certain differences of refractivity to differentiate the red and white corpuscles. The percentages of the different types of leucocytes are established after the blood smears are stained panchromatically (May-Grünwald-Giemsa's or Wright's methods).

III. Erythrocytes

A. Erythrocyte Count

Erythrocyte counts have been made for only about sixty species of reptiles (Table I). The number of erythrocytes is smaller in reptiles than in mammals

Table I

Numbers of erythrocytes per cubic millimeter of blood in reptiles

Species	Count	Authority
TESTUDINES		
Chelydra serpentina	154,166 to 530,000	Gaumer and Goodnight (1957); Hutchison and Szarski (1965)
Chrysemys picta picta	370,000 to 829,000	Hutchison and Szarski (1965)
Chrysemys picta dorsalis	240,000 to 755,000	Hutchison and Szarski (1965)

TABLE I—*cont.*

Species	Count	Authority
Chrysemys picta marginata	395,000	Gaumer and Goodnight (1957)
Clemmys guttata	475,000 to 750,000	Hutchison and Szarski (1965)
Clemmys japonica	442,000	Mori (1940)
Emydoidea blandingii	370,000 to 625,000	Hutchison and Szarski (1965)
Emys orbicularis	260,000 to 680,000	Alder and Huber (1923); Babudieri (1930); Salgues (1937a); Duguy (1967)
Gopherus agassizii	550,000	Babudieri (1930)
Malaclemys terrapin	620,000 to 770,000	Hutchison and Szarski (1965)
Psammobates geometricus	642,000	Bernstein (1938)
Pseudemys scripta	373,000	Babudieri (1930)
Pseudemys scripta elegans	257,000 to 835,000	Charipper and Davis (1932); Hutton and Goodnight (1957); Kaplan and Rueff (1960)
Pseudemys scripta troostii	495,000	Gaumer and Goodnight (1957)
Sternotherus odoratus	360,000 to 980,000	Hutchison and Szarski (1965)
Terrapene carolina	275,000 to 740,000	Wintrobe (1933); Gaumer and Goodnight (1957); Altland and Thompson (1958); Altman and Dittmer (1961)
Terrapene carolina major	235,000 to 755,000	Hutchison and Szarski (1965)
Testudo graeca ibera	362,000 to 730,000	Hayem (1879); Babudieri (1930); Salgues (1937a); Peña Roche (1939); Graziadei (1954); Girod and Lefranc (1958)
Trionyx spiniferus asper	530,000 to 960,000	Hutchison and Szarski (1965)

TABLE I—*cont.*

Species	Count	Authority
CROCODILIA		
Alligator mississippiensis	618,000 to 1,480,000	Hopping (1923); Wintrobe (1933); Coulson *et al.* (1950); Altman and Dittmer (1961)
SAURIA		
Acanthodactylus erythrurus	846,000	Salgues (1937a)
Agama atra	1,250,000	Pienaar (1962)
Anguis fragilis	466,000 to 1,615,000	Alder and Huber (1923); Salgues (1937a); Duguy (1963a)
Anolis carolinensis	610,000 to 1,210,000	Dessauer (1952)
Chalcides ocellatus	806,000	Babudieri (1930); Salgues (1937a)
Coleonyx variegatus	491,000	Ryerson (1949)
Cordylus giganteus	650,000	Pienaar (1962)
Cordylus vittifer	850,000 to 1,790,000	Pienaar (1962)
Heloderma suspectum	646,000	Ryerson (1949)
Hemidactylus turcicus	866,000	Salgues (1937a)
Lacerta agilis	945,000 to 1,420,000	Hayem (1879); Alder and Huber (1923); Salgues (1937a); Peña Roche (1939)
Lacerta lepida	1,124,000	Salgues (1937a)
Lacerta muralis	960,000 to 2,050,000	Alder and Huber (1923); Babudieri (1930); Salgues (1937a); Peña Roche (1939); Duguy (1967)
Lacerta viridis	840,000 to 1,600,000	Babudieri (1930); Salgues (1937a); Peña Roche (1939)
Lacerta vivipara	1,132,000	Salgues (1937a)
Liolaemus nigromaculatus	1,320,000 to 1,920,000	Peña Roche (1939)
Liolaemus pictus	1,488,000 to 1,800,000	Peña Roche (1939)

TABLE I—*cont.*

Species	Count	Authority
Phrynosoma solare	745,000	Ryerson (1949)
Phyllodactylus europaeus	644,000	Salgues (1937a)
Psammodromus hispanicus	756,000	Salgues (1937a)
Sceloporus magister	1,224,000	Ryerson (1949)
Tarentola mauritanica	692,000 to 842,000	Alder and Huber (1923); Salgues (1937a)
OPHIDIA *Agkistrodon piscivorus*	468,000 to 697,000	Hutton (1958)
Coluber constrictor flaviventris	730,000 to 1,075,000	Hutton (1958)
Coluber viridiflavus	908,000 to 1,608,000	Babudieri (1930); Salgues (1937a)
Coronella austriaca	580,000 to 1,406,000	Babudieri (1930); Salgues (1937a)
Coronella girondica	1,900,000	Salgues (1937a)
Crotalus horridus	1,140,000	Carmichael and Petcher (1945)
Elaphe longissima	622,000 to 1,410,000	Babudieri (1930); Salgues (1937a)
Elaphe quadrivirgata	829,750	Mori (1940)
Elaphe scalaris	1,181,000	Salgues (1937a)
Heterodon contortrix	500,000 to 690,000	Wintrobe (1933); Altman and Dittmer (1961)
Lampropeltis getulus getulus	538,000 to 1,027,000	Hutton (1958)
Malpolon monspessulanus	1,442,000	Salgues (1937a)
Natrix maura	378,000 to 1,070,000	Salgues (1937a); Duguy (1967)

TABLE I—cont.

Species	Count	Authority
Natrix natrix	668,000 to 1,302,000	Hayem (1879); Babudieri (1930); Salgues (1937a); Binyon and Twigg (1965)
Natrix sipedon pictiventris	570,000 to 885,000	Wintrobe (1933); Hutton (1958); Altman and Dittmer (1961)
Pituophis catenifer sayi	1,095,000	Ryerson (1949)
Thamnophis sirtalis	710,000 to 1,390,000	Wintrobe (1933); Altman and Dittmer (1961)
Tropidophis pardalis	501,000	Hecht *et al.* (1955)
Vipera ammodytes	667,000	Babudieri (1930)
Vipera aspis	571,000 to 1,410,000	Babudieri (1930); Dastugue and Joy (1941); Salgues (1937a); Duguy (1963b)
Vipera berus	615,000 to 1,232,000	Salgues (1937a)
Vipera ursinii	1,350,000	Salgues (1937a)

or birds. Lizards generally have more erythrocytes than snakes, and turtles have the fewest. Since lizards have the smallest erythrocytes of all reptiles, and turtles the largest, there may be an inverse correlation between the number of erythrocytes and their size; this hypothesis, advanced by Ryerson (1949), receives some support from comparisons among sixteen French reptiles (Fig. 1). *Alligator mississippiensis*, the only crocodilian studied, has a high erythrocyte count like that of lizards.

B. Variations in Erythrocyte Count

1. Sexual

Erythrocytes are more numerous in males than in females of some reptiles such as *Terrapene carolina* (Altland and Thompson, 1958), *Cordylus vittifer* (Pienaar, 1962), *Vipera aspis* (Duguy, 1963a), *Anguis fragilis* (Duguy, 1963b), and *Natrix maura* and *Emys orbicularis* (Duguy, 1967). On the other hand, this difference does not seem very apparent in other forms such as *Lacerta muralis* (Duguy, 1967).

2. With Age

The erythrocyte counts in young individuals of *Terrapene carolina*, *Coluber constrictor*, and *Heterodon contortrix* (Baker and Kline, 1932) as well

as *Vipera aspis* (Duguy, 1963a) and *Natrix maura* (Duguy, 1967) are sometimes lower than those of the adults at the same date. However without further
data this variation cannot definitely be attributed to age.

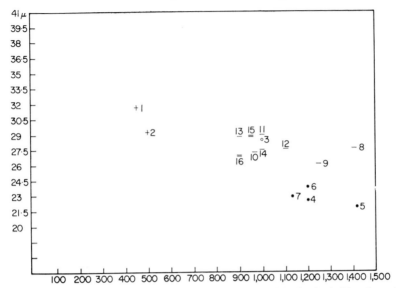

FIG. 1. Relation between the dimensions of the erythrocytes and their density in French reptiles
(After Saint Girons and Duguy, 1963). The ordinate gives the long diameter plus the small diameter
of the erythrocytes in micra, and the abscissa the number of erythrocytes in thousands per cubic
millimetre. +1, *Emys orbicularis*; +2, *Testudo graeca*; ○3, *Anguis fragilis*; ●4, *Lacerta agilis*;
●5, *Lacerta muralis*; ●6 *Lacerta viridis*; ●7, *Lacerta vivipara*; —8, *Malpolon monspessulanus*;
—9, *Coluber viridiflavus*; —10, *Coronella austriaca*; —11, *Elaphe longissima*; —12, *Elaphe
scalaris*; —13, *Natrix Maura*; —14, *Natrix natrix*; = 15, *Vipera aspis*; =16, *Vipera berus*.

3. *Annual*

Erythrocyte counts made at different times in the annual cycle show that
there are some seasonal variations. The most evident is the apparent increase
in erythrocytes just before winter, described by Carmichael and Petcher
(1945) in *Crotalus horridus*, Hutton and Goodnight (1957) in *Terrapene
carolina* and *Pseudemys scripta elegans*, Kaplan and Rueff (1960) in *Pseudemys
scripta elegans*, Pienaar (1962) in *Cordylus vittifer*, Duguy (1963a and b) in
Vipera aspis and *Anguis fragilis*, Binyon and Twigg (1965) in *Natrix natrix*,
and Duguy (1967) in *Natrix maura* and *Lacerta muralis*. However, there is
also an increase in the hematocrit at this time, and the relationship of these
two factors is uncertain.

Most of the other changes during the course of the annual cycle are correlated with the sexual cycle. For example, the decrease in the number of
erythrocytes at the end of hibernation in most of the species cited is related
partly to the use of reserves from the fat body at the end of hibernation, but
mainly to the resumption of sexual activity in the spring. In species that have

a second mating period, the number of erythrocytes also declines, presumably under the influence of the sexual activity, in autumn. These cyclical variations are particularly clearly seen in *Vipera aspis* (Duguy, 1963a) as is shown in Fig. 2. In this species there is also a decrease in the number of erythrocytes in pregnant females.

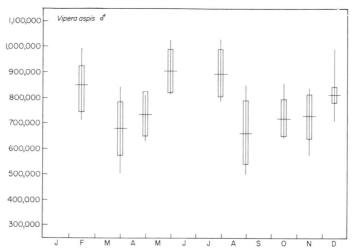

FIG. 2. Annual cycle of erythrocytes in *Vipera aspis* (After Duguy, 1963b). The ordinate shows the number of erythrocytes per cubic millimetre, and the abscissa the months during which the samples were taken.

4. *Others*

Variation can be due to pathological factors: the number of erythrocytes per cubic mm declined from 850,000 to 520,000 in a *Cordylus vittifer* infected by the intra-erythrocytic parasite *Pyrrhaemocyton* (Pienaar, 1962). The same author has also noted the influence of other factors, unfavourable climatic conditions and lack of food, on *Cordylus*. It is also possible, judging by the observations of Hutchison and Szarski (1965) on *Sternotherus odoratus*, that there is geographic variation. On the other hand, the influence of altitude does not appear to be well established. There is currently no evidence that lizards modify the number of their red blood cells, as do mammals, with altitude (Dawson, in Milstead, 1967). Simulation of an altitude of more than 45,000 feet causes no change in the numbers of erythrocytes in *Terrapene carolina* (Altland and Parker, 1955).

IV. Leucocytes

A. LEUCOCYTE COUNT

The number of leucocytes per cubic millimetre of blood appears to be particularly variable in reptiles. One cause of this apparent variation is that some authors have included the thrombocytes in their counts; Babudieri (1930) and others have specified this, but some have not done so, thus rendering their data of dubious value. Some of the variation appears to be geographical: Peña Roche (1939), who considered the Chilean fauna, and Pienaar (1962), who studied the South African fauna, mention counts of 20,000 per cubic mm, whereas in the European forms *Vipera aspis* and *Anguis fragilis* (Duguy, 1963a and b), *Natrix natrix* (Binyon and Twigg, 1965), and *Emys orbicularis*, *Lacerta muralis*, and *Natrix maura* (Duguy, 1967) the leucocyte count is generally between 1,000 and 5,000 per cubic mm. However, Pienaar (1962) noted that the number of leucocytes in *Cordylus vittifer* is clearly less in females than in males.

The counts for *Vipera aspis*, *Natrix maura*, and *Lacerta muralis* show considerable individual variation at all stages in the annual cycle. However in *Anguis fragilis* (Duguy, 1963b), the number of leucocytes varies greatly between a winter maximum and a summer minimum (Fig. 3). The regularity

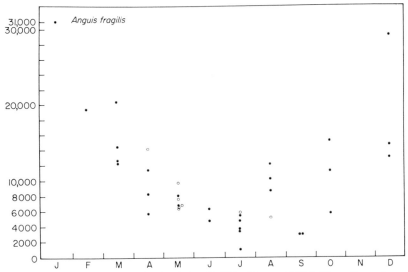

FIG. 3. Annual cycle of leucocytes in *Anguis fragilis* (After Duguy, 1963a). The ordinate shows the number of leucocytes in thousands per cubic millimetre, and the abscissa the months during which the samples were taken. ●, Males; ○, females.

of the seasonal cycle suggests that it is under the influence of an endogenous factor, but, since such a cycle has not as yet been found in other reptiles, further discussion is unprofitable.

Thrombocytes are rarely counted separately. The only precise data on them are those of Pienaar (1962): in *Cordylus vittifer* the number of thrombocytes per cubic mm varied from 10,500 to 19,500, averaging approximately 14,000.

B. Leucocyte Formula

The proportions of the different types of leucocytes in the blood are known in only a few forms, mostly from the Palaearctic fauna. The earlier observations include those of Michels (1923) on *Chrysemys picta* and *Clemmys caspica leprosa* and of Loewenthal (1930, 1931) on *Testudo graeca, Lacerta muralis, Anguis fragilis, Natrix natrix,* and *Vipera aspis.* Further contributions have been made by Babudieri (1930) on fourteen Palaearctic species, by Salgues (1937a) on twenty-six species from France, and by Mori (1940) on *Clemmys japonica, Elaphe quadrivirgata,* and *E. climacophora.* Data on South African reptiles have been provided by Bernstein (1938), who studied *Psammobates geometricus,* and Pienaar (1962), who studied twenty-four other species. Unfortunately the precise sampling dates within the annual cycle are not given; however, since he studied more forms than any other worker, his data are summarized in Table II. Other recent studies have been made by Saint Girons (1960) on *Vipera berus,* by Heady and Rogers (1963) on *Pseudemys scripta elegans, P. s. troostii, Emydoidea blandingii,* and *Chrysemys picta bellii,* and by Duguy (1963a and b, 1967) on *Emys orbicularis, Lacerta muralis, Anguis fragilis, Natrix maura,* and *Vipera aspis.* During the period of activity, the lymphocytes are the most numerous cell type in most specimens; depending on the exact phase of the annual cycle, the heterophils or eosinophils are second to the lymphocytes in abundance. The monocytes and then the basophils are the least numerous. To give a general idea of the relative numbers of these different cellular types, Table III, page 104, shows the extreme values noted in five French reptiles during the course of their annual cycle.

C. Variations in Leucocyte Counts and Formulae

1. *Sexual*

The lymphocytes are more numerous in females than in males of *Vipera berus* (Saint Girons, 1960) and *Vipera aspis* (Duguy, 1963a). This difference is less marked in *Lacerta muralis* (Duguy, 1967), and is not apparent in *Anguis fragilis* (Duguy, 1963b), *Natrix maura,* or *Emys orbicularis* (Duguy, 1967). The percentage of neutrophils appears higher in females of *Cordylus vittifer* than in males (Pienaar, 1962); males of this species have higher total leucocyte counts than females.

2. *With Age*

Although the influence of age cannot be demonstrated conclusively, the much higher percentage of basophils in very young *Vipera aspis* (Duguy, 1963a) and *Natrix maura* (Duguy, 1967) than in adults at the same date and the larger number of lymphocytes in the young of *Cordylus vittifer* (Pienear, 1962) suggest an influence of this factor.

TABLE II

Leucocytic formulae of various South African reptiles
(data slightly modified from Pienaar, 1962)

	Number of specimens	Percentages of types of leucocytes (identifiable precursors included with definitive types of cells)								
		Eosinophils	Basophils	Azurophils	Neutrophils and other granulocytes	Lymphocytes	Plasma cells	Monocytes	Primitive stem cell types	Thrombocytes per 100 leucocytes
Geochelone pardalis	1	58·0	4·6	5·2	0	29·8	0	2·0	0·4	95
Homopus areolatus	1	51·6	3·4	1·6	0	42·0	0·4	0·8	0·2	90
Pelomedusa subrufa	1	13·8	15·8	6·0	0	62·0	0	1·6	0·8	245
Pelusios sinuatus	1	35·6	3·6	4·0	0	56·0	0	0·4	0·4	190
Agama atra	3	14·3	3·7	3·1	1·4	74·3	0·6	1·6	1·0	65
Agama atricollis*	1	3·9	1·0	0·9	0·2	89·4	2·4	0·9	1·3	25
Chamaeleo d. dilepis	2	23·8	3·6	11·0	0	59·6	0	1·2	0·8	195
Cordylus giganteus	1	38·8	8·0	13·2	2·6	35·0	0	1·2	1·2	80
Cordylus jonesii	2	10·0	26·6	11·4	3·4	45·4	0	2·6	0·6	90
Cordylus vittifer	20	13·2	7·2	6·6	3·2	66·8	0·8	0·9	1·3	50
Ichnotropis squamulosa	2	51·9	4·0	19·4	0	23·3	0	0·8	0·6	300
Lygodactylus c. capensis	5	13·4	15·6	15·0	0	50·8	0	4·2	1·0	62
Mabuya capensis	1	49·4	12·2	17·8	0	17·0	0	3·2	0·4	72
Mabuya striata	2	40·8	10·8	21·3	0	24·9	0	1·2	1·0	88
Mabuya varia	3	34·4	19·0	9·0	0	36·6	0	0·6	0·4	75
Pachydactylus c. capensis	3	18·6	15·9	23·4	0	38·6	0	2·3	1·2	45
Pachydactylus bibronii	2	19·5	27·8	6·7	0	40·2	0	2·9	2·9	165
Varanus niloticus	2	11·3	0·1	10·8	0	73·7	0	3·1	1·0	130
Albabophis rufulus	2	15·6	17·6	16·0	0	49·2	0	0·8	0·8	350
Causus rhombeatus	2	12·8	9·2	49·8	8·0	17·2	0·2	2·4	0·4	175
Crotaphopeltis hotamboeia	2	11·0	11·4	22·8	0	51·8	0	2·4	0·6	155
Naja nigricollis	1	7·6	0·4	44·8	0	44·4	0	2·4	0·4	135
Psammophis s. subtaeniatus	1	5·5	26·4	28·7	0	36·6	0	1·6	1·2	200
Crocodylus niloticus	1	11·1	7·7	6·7	0	72·3	0	1·6	0·6	70

*The single specimen of *Agama atricollis* was abnormal, having lymphogenous leukaemia or some similar pathological condition.

3. *With Molting*

Only the lymphocytes vary in number during the molting cycle of snakes. There is an increase in their percentage immediately before molting, followed

TABLE III

Range of frequencies of the different types of leucocytes throughout the year in reptiles

Species	Authority	Lympho-cytes	Mono-cytes	Eosino-phils	Baso-phils	Hetero-phils
Vipera aspis	Duguy (1963a)	2%–90%	0–5%	0–75%	0–40%	2%–65%
Natrix maura	Duguy (1967)	4%–87%	0–5%	1%–68%	0–25%	5%–75%
Anguis fragilis	Duguy (1963b)	10%–77%	0–3%	3%–67%	0–28%	4%–62%
Lacerta muralis	Duguy (1967)	45%–96%	0–5%	1%–30%	0–12%	2%–23%
Emys orbicularis	Duguy (1967)	4%–76%	0–1%	12%–89%	0–25%	2%–21%

by a decrease during and immediately after the molt (Saint Girons, 1961, *Vipera berus*; Duguy, 1963a, *Vipera aspis*; Duguy, 1967, *Natrix maura*).

4. *With Pregnancy*

Pregnancy is accompanied by a leucopenia and a granulocytosis which is particularly marked in the heterophils of *Vipera aspis* (Duguy, 1963a) and *Natrix maura* (Duguy, 1967). In *Vipera aspis* the percentage of heterophils, after increasing regularly up to the time of parturition, diminishes rapidly immediately thereafter.

5. *Pathological*

The leucocyte formula may be modified by pathogenic factors. Salgues (1937a and b) mentioned the appearance of nutritional leucocytosis in captive specimens of *Vipera aspis*, *Natrix maura*, *Lacerta muralis*, and *Lacerta vivipara* held under poor conditions. Numerous authors have noted an increase in the percentage of neutrophils in parasitized animals: Babudieri (1930) in *Lacerta viridis* parasitized by hemogregarines; Wood (1938) in *Tarentola mauritanica* infected with hemogregarines, trypanosomes, and *Pyrhaemocyton*; Ryerson (1949) in *Coleonyx variegatus*, *Heloderma suspectum*, *Phrynosoma solare*, *Sceloporus magister*, and *Pituophis catenifer sayi* with heavy infections of worms in the digestive tract. Some variations in the percentage of eosinophils have been noted under the same conditions. Although Pienaar (1962) found parasitic worms in the intestine of a *Cordylus vittifer* with a high percentage of eosinophils, Wood (1938), in *Tarentola mauritanica* infected with hemogregarines, *Pyrrhaemocyton*, and *Trypanosoma*, Sabrazès and Muratet (1924), in *Lacerta muralis*, and Babudieri (1929), in *Lacerta muralis* and *L. viridis* infected with hemogregarines, report decreases in the percentages of eosinophils. Finally the leucocytic formulae of *Lacerta muralis* and *Emys orbicularis* parasitized by hemogregarines and *Vipera aspis* parasitized by worms (*Centrorhynchus*) do not differ significantly from the formulae of normal specimens at the same stage of the annual cycle (Duguy, 1967).

6. *Ecological*

The presently available data are too few to permit the precise definition of the influence of ecological factors on the leucocytic formula. Most studies have been made on the Palaearctic or other temperate faunas, but none on those from tropical regions. However, study of *Lacerta muralis* in a region in which it hardly hibernates (Duguy, 1967) as well as preliminary observations on *Vipera aspis* and *Lacerta muralis* living at altitudes of 1,500 to 2,000 metres (Duguy, unpublished) suggest that ecological factors can modify the variation in the leucocytic formula seen during the course of the annual cycle.

7. *Seasonal*

The existence of seasonal variations has only recently been noted apart from Michel's (1923) observation of a very high percentage of eosinophils in hibernating *Clemmys caspica leprosa*. Investigations of the annual cycle of *Vipera aspis* (Duguy, 1963a), *Anguis fragilis* (Duguy, 1963b), *Emys orbicularis*, *Lacerta muralis*, and *Natrix maura* (Duguy, 1967) show that each type of leucocyte follows a characteristic cycle. Comparisons between these five species suggest a common pattern, but also indicate variations between species or larger groups.

The relatively uncommon basophilic granulocytes (=mast cells) show the least seasonal variation. Although it is not possible to describe their cycle, their percentage, except in *Lacerta muralis*, is lowest during hibernation and highest during the period of activity.

The heterophilic granulocytes (=neutrophils) show a very distinct seasonal cycle in *Vipera aspis*: their percentage varies from a minimum during hibernation to a maximum in the summer. In *Emys orbicularis*, *Anguis fragilis*, and *Natrix maura*, however, individual variation completely masks any seasonal variations that may exist.

The seasonal variation in the percentage of lymphocytes is important, first for its extent and second for its similarity in *Emys orbicularis*, *Lacerta muralis*, *Anguis fragilis*, *Natrix maura*, and *Vipera aspis*. In all five the maximum percentage occurs during the summer and the minimum during hibernation. In *Lacerta muralis*, however, the percentage in winter never descends as low as in the other species; this difference may be explained by the fact that this species does not hibernate in the region from which the animals were taken.

The eosinophils (= acidophils) probably supply the best information on the annual cycle of the blood. They seem to be the least influenced by other factors, and their variations are thus essentially seasonal. These annual variations are important, and in all five species the minimum percentage occurs during the period of summer activity and the maximum during hibernation (Fig. 4). This cycle may be correlated with that of the interrenal

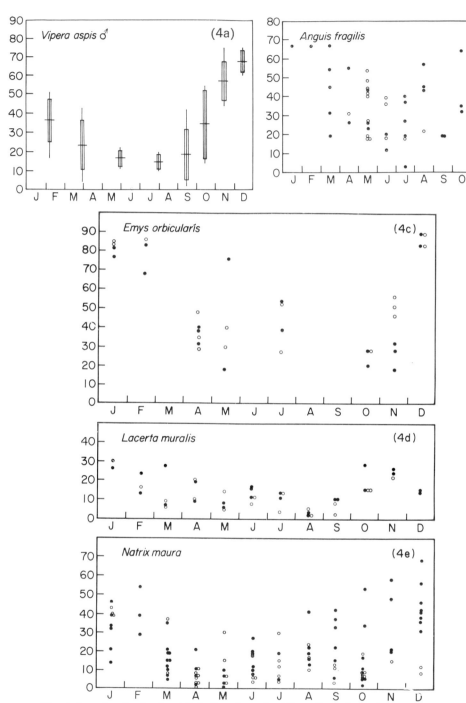

FIG. 4. Annual cycle of eosinophils in French reptiles. The ordinate shows the relative percentage of eosinophils in the blood smears, and the abscissa the months during which the samples were taken. a, *Vipera aspis* (After Duguy, 1963b); b, *Anguis fragilis* (After Duguy, 1963a); c, *Emys orbicularis* (After Duguy, 1967); d, *Lacerta muralis* (After Duguy, 1967); e, *Natrix maura* (After Duguy, 1967); ●, males; ○, females.

gland, in which the autumnal resting period could be the factor, or one of the factors, which determines the characteristic eosinophilic granulocytosis of the winter.

Thus there is an annual cycle, with particularly clear variations of the lymphocytes and the eosinophils, characterized by a winter eosinophilic granulocytosis and a summer eosinophilic granulopenia. In each species a "summer-type" leucogram and a "winter-type" leucogram can be established (Table IV). It is important that there is no abrupt transition between

TABLE IV

Seasonal changes in the leucocytic frequencies of reptiles

Species	Authority	Season	Lympho-cytes	Mono-cytes	Eosino-phils	Baso-phils	Hetero-phils
Vipera aspis	Duguy (1963a)	summer	50%	1%	13%	10%	26%
		winter	6%	1%	70%	8%	15%
Natrix maura	Duguy (1967)	summer	54%	1%	19%	3%	23%
		winter	32%	1%	39%	3%	25%
Anguis fragilis	Duguy (1963b)	summer	54%	0·5%	23%	6%	16·5%
		winter	16·5%	0	58%	2%	24%
Lacerta muralis	Duguy (1967)	summer	81%	1%	10%	1%	7%
		winter	47%	4%	28%	5%	16%
Emys orbicularis	Duguy (1967)	summer	52%	0	40%	4%	4%
		winter	11%	0	83%	0	6%

the summer and winter leucograms, and that the change in the blood formula, like that of the activity of the endocrine glands, is chronologically independent of hibernation. However, it is well established that the ecological conditions, characteristic of periods of hibernation, are necessary for the manifestation of the physiological cycle. This is proved by the persistence of a summer-type leucogram in vipers kept in heated cages during the winter. On the other hand, the slight differences between the winter-type leucograms of *Lacerta muralis* and other species suggest that the state of hibernation does influence the leucocyte formula.

These observations suggest that the annual blood cycle of reptiles is of intrinsic origin. At present the manner in which the periodicity of this cycle is determined cannot be definitely stated. However, considering the observations on *Vipera aspis* (Duguy, 1963a), which show on the one hand a correspondence between the seasonal variations of the eosinophils and the annual solar rhythm (duration of night and day) and on the other hand a complex of physiological modifications which occur in autumn, one can hypothesize a "giver of time" or "Zeitgeber" formed by a shortening of the days or temperature changes in autumn.

References

Alder, A. and Huber, E. (1923). Untersuchungen über Blutzellen und Zellbildung bei Amphibien und Reptilien. *Folia haemat.* **29**, 1–22.

Altland, P. D. and Parker, M. (1955). Effects of hypoxia upon the box turtle. *Am. J. Physiol.* **180**, 421–427.

Altland, P. D. and Thompson, E. C. (1958). Some factors affecting blood formation in turtles. *Proc. Soc. exp. Biol. Med.* **99**, 456–459.

Altman, P. L. and Dittmer, D. S. (eds) (1961). "Blood and Other Body Fluids." Fed. Am. Soc. Exp. Biol., Bethesda, Maryland.

Babudieri, B. (1929). Variazioni stagionali della formula ematica di *Lacerta muralis*. *Natura, Amst.* **20**(3), 92–102.

Babudieri, B. (1930). Studi di ematologica comparata. Ricerche sui pesci, sugli anfibi, e sui rettili. *Haematologica* **2**, 199–255.

Baker, E. G. S. and Kline, L. E. (1932). Comparative erythrocyte counts of representative vertebrates. *Proc. Indiana Acad. Sci.* **41**, 417–418.

Bernstein, R. E. (1938). Blood cytology of the tortoise, *Testudo geometrica. S. Afr. J. Sci.* **35**, 327–331.

Binyon, E. J. and Twigg, G. I. (1965). Seasonal changes in the blood and thyroid of the grass snake, *Natrix natrix. Nature, Lond.* **207**, 779–780.

Carmichael, E. B. and Petcher, P. W. (1945). Constituents of the blood of the hibernating and normal rattlesnake, *Crotalus horridus. J. biol. Chem.* **161**, 693–696.

Charipper, H. A. and Davis, D. (1932). Studies on the Arneth count. XX. A study of the blood cells of *Pseudemys elegans* with special reference to the polymorphonuclear leucocytes. *Q. Jl. exp. Physiol.* **21**, 371–382.

Coulson, R. A., Hernandez, T. and Brazda, F. G. (1950). Biochemical studies on the alligator. *Proc. Soc. exp. Biol. Med.* **73**, 203–206.

Dastugue, G. and Joy, M. (1941). Les éléments figurés du sang de vipère. *C. r. Soc. Phys. Biol.* **45**, 3.

Dessauer, H. C. (1952). Biochemical studies on the lizard *Anolis carolinensis. Proc. Soc. exp. Biol. Med.* **80**, 742–744.

Duguy, R. (1963a). Données sur le cycle annuel du sang circulant chez *Anguis fragilis* L. *Bull. Soc. zool. France* **88**, 99–108.

Duguy, R. (1963b). Biologie de la latence hivernale chez *Vipera aspis* L. *Vie Milieu* **14**, 311–443.

Duguy, R. (1967). Le cycle annuel des éléments figurés du sang chez *Emys orbicularis* L., *Lacerta muralis* Laur., et *Natrix maura* L. *Bull. Soc. zool. France* **92**, 23–37.

Gaumer, A. E. H. and Goodnight, C. J. (1957). Some aspects of the haematology of turtles as related to their activity. *Am. Midl. Nat.* **58**, 332–340.

Girod, C. and Lefranc, G. (1958). Recherches sur la cytologie sanguine des reptiles. Le sang normal de *Testudo ibera* (Pal.). *C. r. Séanc. Soc. Biol.* **152**, 490–494.

Graziadei, P. (1954). Studi sulla emopoiesi dei rettili. (1) La eritropoiesi in *Testudo graeca. Monitore zool. ital.* **62**(suppl.), 335–337.

Hayem, G. (1879). Recherches sur l'évolution des hématies dans le sang de l'homme et des vertébrés. II, Sang des vertébrés à globules rouges nucléés. III, Historique. *Arch. Physiol. norm. Path.* **6**, 201–261 and 577–613.

Heady, J. M. and Rogers, T. E. (1963). Turtle blood cell morphology. *Proc. Iowa Acad. Sci.* **69**, 587–590.

Hecht, M. K., Walters, V. and Ramm, G. (1955). Observations on the natural history of the Bahaman pigmy boa, *Tropidophis pardalis*, with notes on autohemorrhage. *Copeia* **1955**, 249–251.

Hopping, A. (1923). Seasonal changes in the gases and sugar of the blood and the nitrogen distribution in the blood and urine of the alligator. *Am. J. Physiol.* **66**, 145–163.

Hutchison, V. H. and Szarski, H. (1965). Number of erythrocytes in some amphibians and reptiles. *Copeia* **1965**, 373–375.

Hutton, K. E. (1958). The blood chemistry of terrestrial and aquatic snakes. *J. cell. comp. Physiol.* **52**, 319–328.

Hutton, K. E. and Goodnight, C. J. (1957). Variations in the blood chemistry of turtles under active and hibernating conditions. *Physiol. Zoöl.* **30**, 198–207.

Kaplan, H. M. and Rueff, W. (1960). Seasonal blood changes in turtles. *Proc. Anim. Care Panel* **10**, 63–68.

Loewenthal, N. (1930). Nouvelles observations sur les globules blancs du sang chez les animaux vertébrés. *Archs Anat. Histol. Embryol.* **11**, 245–332.

Loewenthal, N. (1931). Des variétés de globules blancs du sang chez l'orvet et la hulotte. *Arch. Anat. Histol. Embryol.* **13**, 225–245.

Michels, N. A. (1923). The mast cell in the lower vertebrates. *La Cellule* **33**, 337–462.

Milstead, W. W. (ed.) (1967). "Lizard Ecology. A Symposium." Univ. Missouri Press, Columbia.

Mori, K. (1940). Vergleichende Untersuchung des Zellbildes der Lymphe und des Blutes bei verschiedenen Wirbeltieren. *Acta. Sch. med. Univ. Kioto* **23**, 285–322.

Peña Roche, H. (1939). Contribuciones a la morfología comparada de la fauna Chilena. II. Estudios hematológicos en las especies *Liolaemus nigromaculatus* (Philippi) y *Liolaemus pictus* (Duméril y Bibron). *Boln Soc. Biol. Concepción* **13**, 133–146.

Pienaar, U. de V. (1962). "Hematology of Some South African Reptiles." Witwatersrand Univ. Press, Johannesburg.

Ryerson, D. L. (1949). A preliminary survey of reptilian blood. *J. Ent. Zool.* **41**, 49–55.

Sabrazès, J. and Muratet, L. (1924). Les globules blancs du sang de *Lacerta muralis* à l'état normal et pathologique. *C. r. Séanc Soc. Biol.* **91**, 44–46.

Saint Girons, M. C. (1960). Dimorphisme sexuel du leucogramme chez *Vipera berus* adulte. *C. r. Séanc Soc. Biol.* **154**, 342–344.

Saint Girons, M. C. (1961). Étude de l'érythropoïèse chez la vipère bérus (*Vipera berus* L.) en fonction de l'activité thyroïdienne et des phénomènes cycliques de la mue. *Bull. Soc. zool. France* **86**, 59–67.

Saint Girons, M. C. and Duguy, R. (1963). Notes de cytologie sanguine comparée sur les reptiles de France. *Bull. Soc. zool. France* **88**, 613–624.

Salgues, R. (1937a). Les éléments figurés du sang des reptiles de la faune française. *Revue gén. Sci. pur. appl.* **48**, 491–492.

Salgues, R. (1937b). Leucocytose nutriciale chez les reptiles en mauvaise condition de captivité. *C. r. hebd. Séanc. Acad. Sci. Paris* **205**, 90–92.

Wintrobe, M. M. (1933). Variations in the size and haemoglobin content of erythrocytes in the blood of various vertebrates. *Folia haemat.* **51**, 32–49.

Wood, S. F. (1938). Variations in the cytology of the blood of geckos, *Tarentola mauritanica*, infected with *Haemogregarina platydactyli*, *Trypanosoma platydactyli*, and *Pirhemocyton tarentolae*. *Univ. Calif. Publs Zool.* **41**, 9–21.

CHAPTER 4

The Thymus

DALE E. BOCKMAN*

Department of Anatomy,
The University of Tennessee Medical Units,
Memphis, Tennessee, U.S.A.

I. Introduction

The thymus is an organ unique to vertebrates. Correlated with its appearance is adaptive immunity—the ability (1) to react specifically against foreign material by cellular proliferation and antibody production and (2) to retain a "memory" of that reaction which will result in heightened response upon being challenged with the same foreign material again (Good and Papermaster, 1964; Papermaster et al., 1964). When the thymus is ablated during a critical period of the development of an individual, adaptive immunity will be but partially expressed (Archer and Pierce, 1961; Archer et al., 1962; Miller, 1961, 1962). Therefore, the thymus seems necessary for proper development of the immune response.

Reptiles, like most vertebrates, show adaptive immunity (Downs, 1928; Evans and Cowles, 1959; Papermaster et al., 1964; Maslin, 1967). Study of the reptilian thymus, however, has not progressed as far as has that of mammals and birds, and the role of the reptilian thymus in development and maintenance of adaptive immunity must, for the present, be based on inference, approached through careful comparison with other vertebrates.

The immunological deficiencies caused by neonatal thymectomy of mice may be corrected by implantation of thymus fragments contained within cell-impermeable diffusion chambers (Osoba and Miller, 1963). It seems reasonable, therefore, to consider the thymus a gland capable of producing some humoral factor important for immunological maturation.

Several excellent reviews (Bargmann, 1943; Hammar, 1909; Pischinger, 1937) summarize the older investigations of reptilian thymus. The present discussion is not meant to recapitulate these. Rather, I present generalizations on the morphology typical of the various reptilian groups and point out

*Present address: Department of Anatomy, Medical College of Ohio at Toledo, Toledo, Ohio, U.S.A.

deviations from that pattern. Light microscopic anatomy is correlated with recent ultrastructural observations of the reptilian thymus as well as with the fine structure of the thymus in other vertebrates. It is hoped that this approach will establish a reasonable basis for subsequent extension of knowledge of the thymus, both in reptiles and in other animals.

II. General Morphology

A. GENERAL

Reptilian thymus glands typically are bilateral organs which occupy a variable area of the neck in close relationship with the large vessels and nerves. The thymus of each side frequently consists of two small white or yellowish lobes which are completely separate from each other. These lobes may be termed anterior and posterior according to their disposition along the longitudinal axis of the body, or they may be given the number of the pharyngeal pouch from which they are derived. There are differences in the number and shape of thymic lobes within the major reptilian groups, but a characteristic anatomical situation may be described for each group.

B. LEPIDOSAURIA

A "typical" thymic morphology for the tuatara and lizards may be derived from studies of *Sphenodon punctatus* (Van Bemmelen, 1888; Adams, 1939), *Lacerta* sp. (Maurer, 1899; Adams, 1939), *Chalcides ocellatus*, and *Scincus scincus* (Sidky, 1967).

Two apparently non-lobulated lobes, a cephalic thymus 2 and a caudal thymus 3 (Fig. 1), lie lateral to the pharyngeal wall on each side. The lobes may lie within richly pigmented connective tissue chambers which are dis-

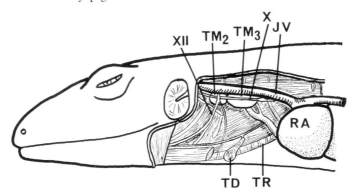

FIG. 1. Location of the thymus in the lizard, *Lacerta agilis*. The two thymic lobes (TM2 and TM3) lie in close relationship to the vagus nerve (X) and jugular vein (JV). The anterior lobe (TM2) is crossed by the hypoglossal nerve (XII). TD, Thyroid; TR, trachea; RA, right atrium. (Redrawn after Maurer, 1899.)

tinct from the thymic capsule proper (Salkind, 1915; Sidky, 1967). Thymus 3 is larger and reaches the carotid arch posteriorly. Thymus 2 is situated close to the base of the skull, dorsal to the laterally projecting recessus piriformis, and thus is not evident in ventral view (Adams, 1939; Sidky, 1967). The hypoglossal nerve crosses thymus 2 superficially (Fig. 1).

Both lobes lie ventral to the internal carotid artery and medial to the internal jugular vein and vagus nerve; the nodose ganglion of the latter is located close to the posterior margin of thymus 3.

The relative size of the two lobes varies between individuals as well as between species. The lobes may overlap each other slightly at their opposed extremities or be separated by a considerable distance. They may be elongate and flattened, oval, or cone-shaped. Except for such minor variations, however, a "typical" saurian thymus has been described, in addition to the examples cited above, in *Iguana iguana*, *Ophisaurus aspodus*, and *Gekko gecko* (Van Bemmelen, 1888); *Uromastyx*, *Agama*, and *Acanthodactylus* (Salkind, 1915); and *Varanus* (Pischinger, 1937).

Greater variation may occur in specific cases. Some specimens of *Uromastyx*, *Agama*, and *Acanthodactylus* have only one lobe on each side (Salkind, 1915). The thymus of *Psammodromus* (*op. cit.*) consists of six or seven small lobes which are distributed over almost the total length of the neck; the lobes are completely isolated except for a tract connecting the units with one another. The thymus of *Psammodromus* is thus more similar to that of birds than to that of a "typical" lizard. A Y-shaped thymus occurs in *Amphisbaena*, the unpaired posterior portion presumably resulting from a fusion of right and left sides.

Salkind (1915) described one small, whitish thymic lobe just posterior to the mandible on each side of the neck in *Chamaeleo* sp. However, Pischinger (1937) found only a thin, undivided, roundish strand stretching along the great vessels from the base of the skull to the thoracic aperture and compared his findings with a similar condition described by Simon (1845) for the Lacertidae and Gekkonidae. Since Simon does not state what species he studied, it is impossible to tell whether this represents species differences or some other variation.

The unlobulated thymus of snakes is located immediately anterior to the heart (Fig. 2). Two lobes lie between the median thyroid gland and the lateral fat body of each side in *Natrix natrix* and *Coronella austriaca* (Van Bemmelen, 1888). The lobes are closely associated with the common carotid artery, jugular vein, and vagus nerve; the nodose ganglion is situated near their posterior ends. The thymus may be asymmetrical, with the lobes of one side larger than those of the other (Simon, 1845; van Bemmelen, 1888).

The number and disposition of lobes varies as in lizards. Only a single elongate lobe on each side is found in some specimens of *Boa*, *Python*,

Coluber, Hydrus, and *Crotalus* (Simon, 1845). In *Malpolon,* the thymus is composed of confluent lobes that may be enclosed in fat, simulating a single median organ (Salkind, 1915).

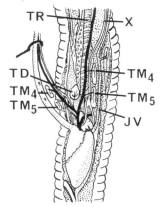

FIG. 2. Location of the thymus in the grass snake, *Natrix natrix.* The two thymic lobes (TM4 and TM5) of each side lie close to the vagus nerve (X) and jugular vein (JV) immediately anterior to the heart. TD, Thyroid; TR, trachea. (Modified from Van Bemmelen, 1888.)

C. TESTUDINES

The thymus of turtles appears lobulated. A fairly constant thymus 3 lies, on each side, in the angle formed by the division of the subclavian and common carotid arteries (Fig. 3). Thymus 4, which is always smaller and variable

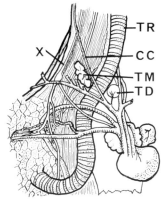

FIG. 3. Location of the thymus in the tortoise, *Geochelone denticulata.* The thymus (TM) lies in the angle formed by the division of the subclavian and common carotid (CC) arteries. TR, Trachea; X, vagus nerve. (Redrawn after Van Bemmelen, 1888.)

in development (Shaner, 1921), may not be evident. The vagus nerve lies lateral to the thymus lobe. The nodose ganglion, like that of lizards and snakes, is located at the posterior end of the gland.

Except for minor variations in lobe structure, the above description applies to relatively mature examples of *Emys orbicularis* (Afanassiew, 1877; Van Bemmelen, 1888) and several species of *Testudo* (Van Bemmelen, 1888; Dustin, 1909). In young *Chelonia mydas*, however, Van Bemmelen (1888) described the thymus as a larger mass stretched out over the posterior third of the neck, covering the carotid artery, and broadened at its posterior end. This situation is like that normally encountered in adult Crocodilia.

D. CROCODILIA

Crocodiles and alligators have a thymus more like that of birds than that typical of other reptilian groups. Figure 4 depicts the elongate left thymus of

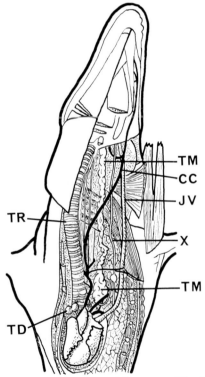

FIG. 4. Location of the thymus in a young *Crocodylus porosus*. The thymus (TM) is broadened posteriorly and is stretched along the full extent of the neck in relation to the carotid artery (CC), jugular vein (JV), and vagus nerve (X). TD, Thyroid; TR, trachea. (Redrawn after Van Bemmelen, 1888.)

young *Crocodylus porosus* (Van Bemmelen, 1888). A broadened posterior extremity lies immediately anterior to the heart, and a narrower portion traverses the neck region to approach the base of the skull. The common carotid artery is ventromedial and the jugular vein and vagus nerve ventro-lateral to the extensive gland on each side of the body.

The reviews by Hammar (1909) and Pischinger (1937) indicate that this basic scheme, with minor variations, is found in all species of crocodiles and alligators which have been investigated. Young animals are more apt to have a thymus which occupies the total length of the neck. The prismatic posterior enlargements of the right and left thymus may meet in the midline, covering the thyroid gland (Simon, 1845). In adult *Caiman crocodilus* and *Caiman latirostris* the anterior end of the thymus may reach only the anterior end of the chest cavity (Rathke, 1866). The latter species may have additional, rounded, cervical lobes.

III. Embryonic Development

The reptilian thymus originates from the pharyngeal pouches. Like those of fish, Amphibia, and birds, reptilian thymic primordia are dorsal outgrowths of the pharyngeal walls (Fig. 5) in distinction to the ventral outgrowths

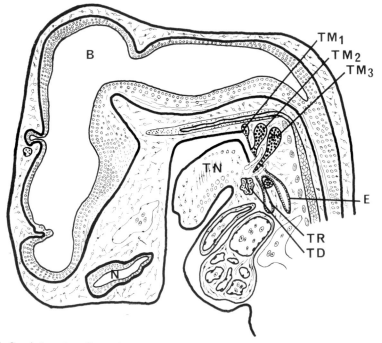

FIG. 5. Saggital section of an embryonic lizard (*Lacerta agilis*) showing dorsal thymic outgrowths (TM1, TM2, and TM3) from the first three pharyngeal pouches. The posterior two are retained in the adult. B, Brain; E, esophagus; TD, thyroid; TN, tongue; TR, trachea. (Redrawn after Maurer, 1899.)

which produce the thymus of mammals (see reviews by Saint-Remy and Prenant, 1904; Dustin, 1909; Shaner, 1921).

The thymus of lizards, snakes, and turtles develops from different pairs of the five pharyngeal pouches (Fig. 6). To my knowledge, there have been no comparable studies of Amphisbaenia or Crocodilia.

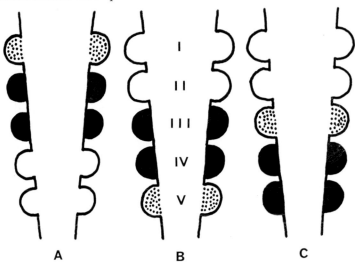

FIG. 6. Diagrammatic representation of pharyngeal pouches (I–V) which give rise to transitory (stippled) and definitive adult thymus (solid). A, Lizard (Maurer, 1899); B, turtle (Shaner, 1921); C, snake (Saint-Remy and Prenant, 1904).

The definitive anterior and posterior thymic lobes in lizards originate as dorsal outgrowths of the second and third pharyngeal pouches. In addition, a transient thymus rudiment associated with the first pouch (Figs 5 and 6A) has been described in *Lacerta agilis* and *L. muralis* (Maurer, 1899). Saint-Remy and Prenant (1904) corroborated that the thymus of *Anguis fragilis*, *Chalcides ocellatus*, *Lacerta viridis*, and *L. agilis* developed from the second and third pouches, but denied the existence of a rudimentary thymus 1 in any of these species. They also noted that some thymic tissue develops from the ventral portion of the third pouch and is incorporated in the posterior lobe (thymus 3).

A constant thymus 3 originates from the corresponding pharyngeal pouch in turtles (*Chelonia mydas*, Van Bemmelen, 1893; *Chrysemys picta*, Shaner, 1921). A variable thymus 4 and a transitory bud develop from the fourth and fifth pouches respectively (Fig. 6B).

A further caudal shift is seen in snakes (Fig. 6C). The definitive thymic lobes originate from pharyngeal pouches 4 and 5 (*Natrix natrix*, Van Bemmelen, 1886; *Elaphe longissima* and *Natrix natrix*, Saint-Remy and Prenant,

1904). A transitory thymus 3 may appear as a dorsal outgrowth of the third pouch.

Thymic development begins as a slight crescentic invagination of pharyngeal epithelium just medial to the branchial placode. Epithelial proliferation forms a hollow, lobulated, fingerlike projection. Connection with the pharyngeal pouch is broken and the intermediate pouch tissue disappears, so the thymus lies free in surrounding mesenchyme. Progressive cellular proliferation obliterates the central cavity. The cells take on a typical lymphoid appearance. Thymic lobules become subdivided into distinct cortical and medullary areas, and thymic corpuscles appear in the medulla (Saint-Remy and Prenant, 1904; Shaner, 1921).

Aberrant collections of thymic tissue may occur at locations distinctly separated from major thymus lobes. Adams (1939), for instance, found a microscopic thymus 4 posterior to thymus 3 (the definitive posterior thymus) in histologic sections of *Lacerta*. Thymic tissue has also been noted within the postbrachial body of the turtle *Pseudemys scripta* (Thompson, 1910).

The thymus and parathyroid glands originate very close to each other in the branchial pouches. It is not surprising that this intimate association is sometimes maintained throughout development. Follicles of flattened, spindle-shaped cells have been described within the thymus of the tortoise and alligator (Watney, 1882). These follicles were almost certainly the same as the parathyroid with cells "arranged in a whorl" described in the thymus of *Natrix sipedon fasciata* by Thompson (1910). Parathyroid glands are sometimes embedded in the thymus of embryonic and adult turtles (*Chrysemys*, Shaner, 1921) and young rattlesnakes (*Crotalus atrox*, Bockman and Winborn, 1967).

The cells from which thymic lymphoid cells, or thymocytes, differentiate during organogenesis have not been clearly established. Maurer (1899) concluded from histological evidence that lizard thymocytes derived from endodermal epithelial cells. Experimental studies of developing thymus have recently led Auerbach (1961) to conclude that epithelial cells are the progenitors of thymocytes in mice, and these results were corroborated by electron microscopic investigation of thymic development in the chick (Ackerman and Knouff, 1964). Thus it is likely that reptilian thymocytes arise from epithelial cells but strong supporting evidence is still lacking.

IV. Histology

The thymus of reptiles is surrounded by a well defined capsule of dense connective tissue. Septal extensions from the capsule subdivide the thymus of turtles into distinct lobules (Afanassiew, 1877). Lepidosaurians and crocodilians characteristically lack such lobulation, although small connective tissue trabeculae are associated with penetrating blood vessels.

Kohnen and Weiss (1964) have pointed out the wide variety of structures which have been described in the literature as thymic corpuscles. The relatively solid, lamellar arrangement of epithelial cells typical of thymic corpuscles in humans is rare or non-existent in reptiles. Rather, cyst-like structures are present. Reptilian thymic cysts range from minute intracellular structures through formations well over 0·1 mm in diameter (Fig. 7). Epithelial cells comprise the boundary of the cysts. The central portion of

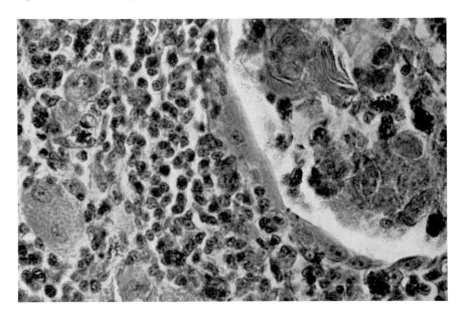

FIG. 7. Photomicrograph of a portion of thymus from the Gila monster, *Heloderma suspectum*. Dense thymocyte nuclei are most numerous. A large thymic cyst is seen on the right. It contains homogeneous material, cellular debris, and granulocytes. Epithelial cells border the cyst and are recognizable in other locations by their lighter nuclei and prominent nucleoli. A large, binucleated myoid cell is located in the lower left corner of the micrograph.

large cysts is frequently occupied by cellular elements in varying stages of degeneration. Granulocytes and myoid cells (see below) may be recognized within some. Such formations probably represent foci of cellular degradation segregated from surrounding thymic parenchyma by a continuous layer of epithelial cells.

The predominant cell type, particularly in young animals, is a lymphoid cell, the thymocyte (Fig. 7). Large, medium, and small thymocytes are present, the latter in greatest quantity. At the periphery of the thymic lobes or lobules, in the thymic cortex, they tend to be so numerous that they mask the details of other cells. The more central tissue, the medulla, appears less dense because of a reduced concentration of thymocytes and a concommitant higher proportion of other, lighter-staining cells.

Epithelial cells constitute the second principal cell type. They are easily identified in the medulla by their large, relatively clear nuclei, prominent nucleoli, and abundant cytoplasm (Fig. 7). Epithelial cells are distributed throughout the cortical area as well, but their cytoplasmic processes are there attenuated between intervening lymphocytes, making identification more difficult. Epithelial cells may occur singly, in aggregates (nests), or in relationship with thymic corpuscles.

Myoid cells are many times the diameter of thymocytes and have long been recognized in the reptilian thymus (Hammar, 1905, 1909). They have also been referred to as granular cells (Watney, 1882), as myoepithelioid cells (Dustin, 1909), as unicellular thymic corpuscles (Jordan and Looper, 1928), and perhaps also as enlarged blood corpuscles (Afanassiew, 1877). Although a concentric patterning is sometimes seen within their cytoplasm, they are clearly not thymic corpuscles, but a distinct type of cell.

Myoid cells are most numerous in the medulla, but do occur in the cortex. They have one, occasionally two, pale-staining nuclei each with one or two prominent nucleoli (Fig. 7). The nuclear diameter of a myoid cell usually greatly exceeds the total diameter of a thymocyte. Round or oval cell profiles (Bockman and Winborn, 1967) and elongate forms are found (cf. Dustin, 1909; Strauss et al., 1966; Van de Velde and Friedman, 1966a, and b). Cross striations similar to those of skeletal muscle are evident in some myoid cells. The ultrastructural basis for cytoplasmic lamellation and crossbanding will be discussed in another section.

Granulocytes are sometimes prominent in reptilian thymuses. Cells with rounded or slightly lobulated nuclei and eosinophilic granules frequently are numerous in the connective tissue, thymic parenchyma, and cysts (Fig. 7). These granules are PAS positive, a condition described for avian eosinophils (Sommer et al., 1962). Cells with basophilic granules (mast cells) occur in smaller numbers. The latter are found in relation with connective tissue and to a lesser extent in the parenchyma (Dustin, 1909). There is no consensus of opinion as to whether these granulocytes originate within the thymus or penetrate from the blood stream after forming at another site (see discussion by Bargmann, 1943). Jordan and Looper (1928) described, in the thymus of the box turtle (Terrapene carolina), cells which contained both basophilic and eosinophilic granules and concluded that cells with basophilic granules develop from thymocytes and that the granules subsequently "ripen into acidophilic conditions". Partial corroboration of this interpretation has been presented recently by Ginsburg and Sachs (1963) who described transformation of mouse thymic cells into mast cells in tissue culture.

Numerous reticular fibers may be shown in the capsule and septa by silver techniques (Jordan and Looper, 1928; Bargmann, 1943) and the periodic acid-Schiff reaction. Such reticular fibers are particularly prominent in association with blood vessels, but may be interposed between elements of the thymic parenchyma as well. They tend to be sparse in areas replete with small thymocytes.

There probably are neither arborizations of nerves nor lymphatic vessels within the thymic parenchyma (Salkind, 1915).

V. Fine Structure

A. GENERAL

The fine structure of reptilian thymus is similar in many respects to that described for mammals (Clark, 1963; Hoshino, 1963; Weiss, 1963; Weakley et al., 1964; Lundin and Schelin, 1965; Murray et al., 1965; Izard, 1966; Törö and Oláh, 1966), embryonic chicks (Ackerman and Knouff, 1964), the axolotl (Klug, 1967), and frogs (Canaday, 1968). Figure 8 diagramatic-ally summarizes some of the salient ultrastructural features of the reptilian thymus based on electron microscopic studies (Bockman and Winborn, 1967, 1969; Bockman, 1968a) of snakes (Crotalus, Lampropeltis), lizards (Eumeces, Heloderma), and a turtle (Trionyx).

B. CELL TYPES

1. Thymocytes

Most reptilian thymocytes have a diameter of approximately 4 to 6 μ. Although they tend to be spherical, considerable deformation may be produced by surrounding cells. Especially for smaller cells the amount of cytoplasm is small in relation to the area occupied by the nucleus of each thymocyte.

The nucleus may be circular in outline or may mirror the deformation of the cell membrane. The nuclear membrane is frequently indented. Clumps of chromatin are prominent at the periphery of the nucleus, while one or more clumps usually occur centrally, either isolated or continuous with the peripheral chromatin.

The cytoplasm of thymocytes contains an abundance of ribosomes ar-ranged singly or in groups. Rough endoplasmic reticulum is very sparse. A few relatively large mitochondria are usually present. A small Golgi ap-paratus and centrioles may be seen in some cells.

2. Epithelial Cells

Thymic cells are identified as epithelial primarily by the presence of cyto-plasmic tonofilaments and/or desmosomes. The latter two elements are abundant in some cells. In others, they may be so sparse that they are not observed in a particular section. Such cells are considered to be epithelial because of their similarity with other epithelial cells. The major variations in morphology of thymic epithelial cells are represented in Figure 8.

One type of thymic cell (E1, Fig. 8) has a large, electron lucid nucleus which contains one or two prominent nucleoli. Chromatin is relatively evenly distributed throughout the nucleus with some concentration at the periphery. The cytoplasm contains scattered ribosomes, small mitochrondria and short elements of rough endoplasmic reticulum. Tonofilaments may appear as isolated bundles in the cytoplasm or in association with desmosomes. A basement membrane occurs at the boundary between epithelial cells and connective tissue.

A much more irregular and dense nucleus characterizes a second type of thymic cell (E3, Fig. 8). Coarse, angular blocks of chromatin are scattered throughout its nucleus. The cytoplasm is dense and may contain phagocytic inclusions of varying size, structure, and contents. Slender processes of these cells extend between other elements of the thymic parenchyma. In some sections connections of processes with the cell body are not evident, giving the appearance of isolated fragments of cytoplasm interspersed between thymocytes. Few desmosomes are present.

Small, moderately dense granules approximately $0 \cdot 2 \mu$ in diameter occupy the cytoplasm of a third cell type (E2, Fig. 8) whose cytoplasm contains a well-developed Golgi apparatus. The nature of the small granules is unknown. The nucleus is fairly regular in outline and intermediate in density between the two types of epithelial cells (E1 and E3) described above. There is a morphological similarity between these cells and the beta cells of pancreatic islets. Recent evidence suggests that an insulin-like factor is produced by the "beta" cells of the mouse thymus (Pansky and House, 1965; Pansky et al., 1965), and the techniques used to determine this (aldehyde-fuchsin staining, bioassay of thymic extract, immunoassay, immunofluoresence) should, when applied in conjunction with ultrastructural studies, be useful in determining the presence or absence of similar cells or factors in the reptilian thymus.

Another variant of epithelial cell is characterized by a very irregular nucleus with thin, highly elongate nuclear extensions which may exceed 13 μ in length but be only $0 \cdot 3 \mu$ in diameter (E4, Fig. 8). The chromatin is dense and concentrated at the margins of the nuclear extensions. Cytoplasmic organelles are similar to those of other epithelial cells. This cell type tends to

FIG. 8. Diagrammatic representation of the ultrastructural features of the reptilian thymus. Numerous thymocytes (L) are interposed between epithelial cells (E1–E4). A basement membrane, or basal lamina (BM), is present at the junction of a connective tissue space (CT) with epithelial cells and a myoid cell (MY). Cross-striated myofibrils run in various directions in the myoid cell. Tonofilaments occur in isolated bundles in cytoplasm of epithelial cells and in relation with desmosomes (D). They are especially numerous in epithelial cells bordering a cyst. Microvilli and cilia (C) project into the cyst. Portions of a plasma cell (PL) and a mucous cell (MU) are shown. A granulocyte (G) with heterogeneous granules is represented in the centre. See text for discussion.

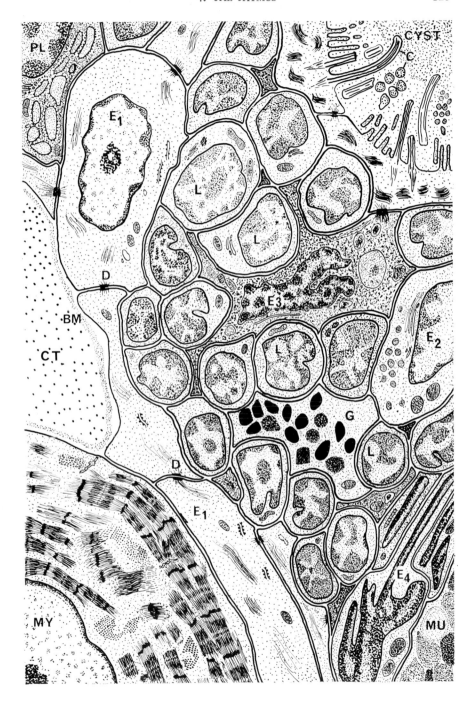

occur in groups, with the filamentous nuclear extensions and surrounding cytoplasm running parallel for some distance.

3. Myoid Cells

The fine structure of thymic myoid cells has been studied recently in many species of reptiles, birds, amphibians, and mammals (Raviola and Raviola, 1966, 1967; Van de Velde and Friedman, 1966a, 1966b, 1967; Strauss et al., 1966, 1967; Bockman and Winborn, 1967, 1969; Bockman, 1968a, 1968b; Canaday, 1968). Table I lists the reptilian species which were specified.

TABLE I

Reptiles in which the Fine Structure of Thymic Myoid Cells has been described

Group	Species	Study
LIZARDS	Eumeces laticeps Heloderma suspectum	Bockman, 1968a; Bockman and Winborn, 1969
SNAKES	Thamnophis eques megalops	Van de Velde and Friedman, 1966b
	Crotalus atrox Lampropeltis getulus	Bockman and Winborn, 1967, 1969
	Natrix rhombifera	Raviola and Raviola, 1967
TURTLES	Pseudemys scripta elegans	Strauss et al., 1966, 1967; Raviola and Raviola, 1967
	Gopherus berlandieri	Van de Velde and Friedman, 1966b
	Trionyx spiniferus	Bockman, 1968a; Bockman and Winborn, 1969

Myoid cells in the reptilian thymus may be rounded to highly elongate. Spherical myoid cells (Fig. 8) are very large, frequently 20 to 30 μ in diameter with a centrally placed nucleus 4 to 8 μ in diameter. Myofibrils are disposed circumferentially around the nucleus in various planes, so that longitudinal, transverse, and oblique profiles are observed in a single section. The myofibrils of elongate cells tend to lie parallel to the longitudinal axis of the cell.

The myofibrils usually are composed of thick and thin myofilaments like those of skeletal muscle. Raviola and Raviola (1967) have shown myofibrils which lack thick filaments. The cross-banding patterns also resemble those of skeletal muscle; A, I, H, and M bands, and Z lines are evident in most complete fibrils when sectioned in a proper plane. Corresponding bands of adjacent myofibrils are positioned directly opposite each other in some cases, but this alignment "in register" is never as complete as that typical of skeletal muscle. The absence of fiber alignment keeps the cross-striations from being obvious when myoid cells are viewed with the light microscope, even though many myofibrils are present. This is particularly true for rounded myoid cells.

Not all myoid cells contain fully developed myofibrils. Some cells, even in adult reptiles, resemble some of the earliest stages of development of the skeletal muscle fibers. Scattered primitive Z lines with associated myofilaments occupy the perinuclear cytoplasm of these myoblast-like cells (Fig. 9).

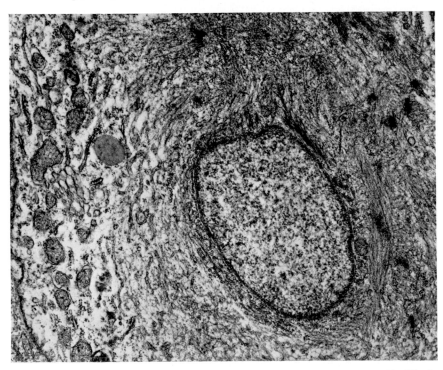

FIG. 9. Electron micrograph of part of the nucleus and cytoplasm of an immature myoid cell in the thymus of an adult king snake, *Lampropeltis getulus*. The perinuclear area is filled with myofilaments associated with dense condensations (primitive Z bands). On the right are elements of rough and smooth endoplasmic reticulum, free ribosomes and mitochondria. ×25,000. (From Bockman and Winborn, 1967, Fig. 11.)

Accumulations of rough and smooth endoplasmic reticulum, as well as mitochondria, are concentrated peripherally in these immature myoid cells.

Immature and mature myoid cells are often directly apposed to epithelial cells. Desmosomes occasionally connect epithelial and myoid cells (Raviola and Raviola, 1966, 1967; Bockman and Winborn, 1969). Mature myoid cells may also border on connective tissue spaces; in such cases a basement membrane (BM, Fig. 8) is found. Elements of sarcoplasmic reticulum, ribosomes, and glycogen granules are irregularly scattered between myofibrils. Although myoid cells probably are not innervated, they contract upon direct stimulation (Van de Velde and Friedman, 1966a). Myoid cells degenerate *in situ*.

There is a progressive loss of cellular detail which results in a large mass of more or less homogeneous, electron dense material.

The presence of immature myoid cells in the adult reptilian thymus suggests myogenesis may occur there (Bockman and Winborn, 1967, 1969; Raviola and Raviola, 1967). An alternate, but apparently less likely, explanation for their presence would be the persistence of arrested developmental stages. The question of the origin of myoid cells remains unsettled. Immature myoid cells resemble epithelial cells more than any other type of thymic cell. As was noted above, desmosomal connections with epithelial cells do occur. There is no direct evidence, however, that myoid cells are derived from epithelial cells, and myoblasts may have simply been included secondarily (Van de Velde and Friedman, 1967; Wassjutotschkin, 1913).

Serum gamma globulins in some patients with the disease myasthenia gravis react *in vitro* like an antibody against antigens of mammalian skeletal and cardiac muscle and thymic myoid cells (Strauss and Kemp, 1967). These human globulins also react with reptilian myoid cells (Strauss *et al.*, 1966). The large population of myoid cells characteristic of reptiles should make them useful as an experimental model for studying the origin, development, and alteration of thymic muscle antigen; an important step toward understanding the relationships of this antibody to the disease process.

C. THYMIC CYSTS

The ultrastructure of thymic cysts in reptiles does not differ significantly from that described in mammals (Hoshino, 1962; Clark, 1963; Kohnen and Weiss, 1964; Izard, 1966; Törö and Oláh, 1966). Cysts always are associated with epithelial cells; they vary from small, intracellular pockets to intercellular cysts, large structures involving many cells (Fig. 8). Intracellular cysts frequently contain amorphous material interspersed between microvillous projections from the surrounding cytoplasm. They may contain cellular debris. Cilia may also project into both intracellular and intercellular cysts, although they are more common in the latter. These cilia (C, Fig. 8) exhibit the typical (9 peripheral plus 2 central) arrangement of filaments and associated basal bodies in the epithelial cells from which they project.

The epithelial cells surrounding intercellular cysts characteristically show a marked accumulation of tonofilaments, which are arranged in groups or clumps, and dense granular structures as well as numerous small vesicles are frequently found in their cytoplasm. Numerous desmosomal connections occur between adjoining epithelial cells.

Epithelial cysts appear to be associated with degenerative processes. Whether the amorphous, PAS-positive material which they contain is a "necrohormone" (Törö and Oláh, 1966) or a sulphated acid mucopolysaccharide manufactured and secreted by epithelial cells (Clark, 1966) and capable of stimulating lymphopoiesis remains to be determined. Shier (1963) has suggested that cystic formations are manifestations of the original endodermal epithelial tubules from which the thymus develops.

D. OTHER CELLS

Most electron microscopic investigations of eosinophils have concentrated on mammalian species (Watanabe, 1957; Low and Freeman, 1958; Florey, 1962; Archer, 1963; Hirsch, 1965). These show considerable interspecific variation in size and number of granules. In addition, there is heterogeneity of granular structure within each eosinophil. Eosinophils have generally been identified by single or multiple bars or plates of a crystalline-like material which occupies part of each granule. Lamellated specific granules occur in eosinophils of the common goldfish, *Carassius auratus* (Weinreb, 1963). However, the eosinophilic granules of the paddlefish, *Polyodon spathula*, lack central nucleoid crystals (Clawson *et al.*, 1966), while immature granules of the eosinophils of rabbit (Wetzel *et al.*, 1967) and mouse (Fawcett, 1966) may appear quite homogeneous before the crystalline core develops.

The ultrastructural appearance of granulocytes in the reptilian thymus is difficult to correlate with their appearance in light microscopy. Although the thymus of some reptiles has a high population of cells with eosinophilic granules, few cells have elements with ultrastructural features characteristic of the mature eosinophilic granules seen in other species. Angular granules with denser, block-like central portions are occasionally observed. Other cells show dense, angular, or ellipsoidal granules with narrow, curved lighter areas resembling the granules of paddlefish eosinophils (Clawson *et al.*, 1966). One also finds granules identical in size, shape, and electron density to the latter, but lacking the narrow light areas.

The ultrastructural features of most granulocytes of the reptilian thymus are more consistent with those described for mammalian mast cells and basophils (Low and Freeman, 1958; Winqvist, 1963; Smith, 1963; Wetzel *et al.*, 1967). Each cell contains a heterogeneous population of granules. Most are dense and homogeneous, but some are more electron lucent, with a filamentous or flocculent substructure. Most have a circular profile but some are irregular or angular. The dense, homogeneous, spherical granules resemble, in many respects, both mature basophilic granules and immature eosinophilic granules. It is interesting to note that Low and Freeman (1958) described dense, homogeneous "basophilic bodies" within human eosinophils. A correlated ultrastructural and cytochemical study of reptilian blood, marrow, and thymus should add much interesting information useful for positive identification and phylogenetic comparison of granulocytes.

Plasma cells (PL, Fig. 8) occur with some regularity in the connective tissue and in the thymic parenchyma. Rough endoplasmic reticulum is abundant throughout their cytoplasm. The cisternae of the rough endo-plasmic reticulum are sometimes relatively flat in profile and sometimes markedly dilated by a light, homogeneous material.

Mucous cells and macrophages are few in number. The cytoplasm of mucous cells (MU, Fig. 8) is filled with flocculent oval inclusions which resemble the mucous droplets of intestinal goblet cells. Phagocytosed material and lipid droplets are found in varying amounts in macrophage cytoplasm.

VI. Thymic Involution

The thymus of young reptiles has distinct cortical and medullary areas. The cortex is distinguished primarily by its very high density of thymocytes, whose relative proportions decrease with increasing age leading to reduced distinction between the cortex and medulla. The weight and size of the organ also decrease with age and blood vessels and connective tissue occupy a progressively larger portion of the gland. Watney (1882) described three parts in the involuting thymus of a tortoise (*Testudo*): an outer cortical part consisting of flattened cells and intervening reticulum, a medullary portion containing most of the concentric corpuscles, and a zone of tissue between the first two parts which contained a ring of vessels and a large number of thymocytes. The involuted thymus contains hardly any lymphoid cells.

Factors other than age may cause thymic involution in reptiles. Starvation causes reversible changes similar to those described above (Dustin, 1909; Salkind, 1915). Dustin (1909) distinguished between definitive and seasonal involution. The former included involution with age and accidental involu-tion resulting from factors such as disease and starvation. Seasonal involution was considered transitory, and its variation was superimposed on the decrease in size due to definitive involution. Figure 10 represents this idea schematically.

Steroid hormones have a marked effect upon thymic size in mammals (Dougherty, 1952; Kaplan *et al.*, 1954) and it might be inferred that similar mechanisms exist in reptiles. However, no definitive experiments to deter-mine the presence and extent of hormonal control of the thymus have yet been carried out.

VII. Conclusion

This chapter has summarized the knowledge gained from approximately a century of work on the reptilian thymus. Of necessity, it has been primarily descriptive in nature, rather than analytical. With the relatively recent development of new techniques such as electron microscopy and auto-radiography, and improvements in tissue culture, histochemistry, and cyto-chemistry, there exists the potential for a tremendous expansion of this

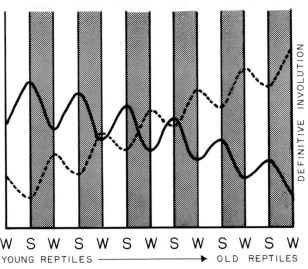

DEFINITIVE INVOLUTION

W S W S W S W S W S W S W
YOUNG REPTILES ————————→ OLD REPTILES

FIG. 10. Schematic representation of the periodic seasonal variation in the number of thymocytes (solid line) and the inverse proportion of blood vessels and connective tissue (dotted line) in reptiles. This variation is superimposed on the definitive involution due to age. W, Winter; S, spring. (Modified from Dustin, 1909.)

knowledge. Utilizing the available techniques within the framework of planned experimental procedures, it should be possible to contribute significantly in at least four areas:

(1) understanding of the variation of the organ in different species and group of reptiles;

(2) expansion of the fundamental understanding of the origin, development and function of the components of the reptilian thymus *per se*;

(3) comparison of the thymus of reptiles with that of other vertebrate classes, thus adding to the understanding of the phylogenetic development and relationships of the thymus, and

(4) use of the reptilian thymus as an experimental model for study of pathological alterations observed in humans.

Many other questions about the reptilian thymus remain unanswered. Is the reptilian thymus necessary during ontogenetic development of adaptive immunity? If so, when does this take place? Does the reptilian thymus participate in the immune response? Does it produce antibodies? From which cells do thymocytes originate? Are thymocytes different from other lymphoid cells? How do myoid cells originate? Do myoid cells differentiate within the adult thymus? Do they serve as an antigen against which antibodies are produced under certain conditions? Do hormone-producing cells occur in the thymus?

Some of these questions have been answered for other animals. Some have not. Complete understanding of thymic function can be approached, however, only through consideration of its varying role in all the classes of animals in which it is found.

VIII. Acknowledgements

Part of the work reported in this chapter was supported by grants GB–4159 and GB–6984 from the National Science Foundation and grant FR–05423 from the National Institutes of Health. The technical assistance of Miss Peggy Stephenson is gratefully acknowledged.

References

Ackerman, G. A. and Knouff, R. A. (1964). Lymphocyte formation in the thymus of the embryonic chick. *Anat. Rec.* 149, 191–216.

Adams, W. E. (1939). The cervical region of Lacertilia. A critical review of certain aspects of its anatomy. *J. Anat.* 74, 57–71.

Afanassiew, B. (1877). Weitere Untersuchungen über den Bau und die Entwickelung der Thymus und der Winterschlafdrüse der Säugethiere. *Arch. mikrosk. Anat. EntwMech.* 14, 343–390.

Archer, O. K. (1963). "The Eosinophil Leucocytes." F. A. Davis, Philadelphia.

Archer, O. K. and Pierce, J. C. (1961). Role of the thymus in development of the immune response. *Fedn Proc. Fedn Am. Socs exp. Biol.* 20, 26 (Abstract).

Archer, O. K., Pierce, J. C., Papermaster, B. W. and Good, R. A. (1962). Reduced antibody response in thymectomized rabbits. *Nature, Lond.* 195, 191–193.

Auerbach, R. (1961). Experimental analysis of the origin of cell types in the development of the mouse thymus. *Devl. Biol.* 3, 336–354.

Bargmann, W. (1943). Der Thymus. *In* "Handbuch der Mikroskopischen Anatomie" (W. von Möllerdorf, ed.). Springer, Berlin, 6(2), 1–172.

Bockman, D. E. (1968a). Fine structure of myoid cells in human and reptilian thymus. *Anat. Rec.* 160, 319 (Abstract).

Bockman, D. E. (1968b). Myoid cells in adult human thymus. *Nature, Lond.* 218, 286–287.

Bockman, D. E. and Winborn, W. B. (1967). Electron microscopy of the thymus in two species of snakes, *Crotalus atrox* and *Lampropeltis getulus. J. Morph.* 121, 277–294.

Bockman, D. E. and Winborn, W. B. (1969). Ultrastructure of thymic myoid cells. *J. Morph.* 129, 210–260.

Canaday, S. D. (1968). Light and electron microscopy of the thymus in adult *Rana pipiens. Anat. Rec.* 160, 326 (Abstract).

Clark, S. L., Jr. (1963). The thymus in mice of strain 129/J, studied with the electron microscope. *Am. J. Anat.* 112, 1–33.

Clark, S. L., Jr. (1966). Cytological evidences of secretion in the thymus. *In* "The Thymus" (G. E. W. Wolstenholme and R. Porter, eds), pp. 1–30. Little, Brown and Company, Boston.

Clawson, C. C., Finstad, J. and Good, R. A. (1966). Evolution of the immune response. V. Electron microscopy of plasma cells and lymphoid tissue of the paddlefish. *Lab. Invest.* 15, 1830–1847.

Dougherty, T. F. (1952). Effect of hormones on lymphatic tissue. *Phys. Rev.* 32, 379–421.

Downs, C. M. (1928). Anaphylaxis VII. Active anaphylaxis in turtles. *J. Immun.* 15, 77–81.

Dustin, A. P. (1909). Contribution á l'étude du thymus des reptiles. Cellules épitheliodes, cellules myoides et corps de Hassall. *Archs Zool. exp. gén.* 2, 43–227.

Evans, E. E. and Cowles, E. B. (1959). Effect of temperature on antibody synthesis in the reptile, *Dipsosaurus dorsalis*. *Proc. Soc. exp. Biol. Med.* **107**, 482–483.

Fawcett, D. W. (1966). "The Cell." Saunders, Philadelphia, pp. 206–207.

Florey, H. W. (1962). Inflammation. *In* "General Pathology, 3rd Edition" (H. W. Florey, ed.), pp. 40–127. Saunders, Philadelphia.

Ginsburg, H. and Sachs, L. (1963). Formation of pure suspensions of mast cells in tissue culture by differentiation. *J. natn. Cancer Inst.* **31**, 1–39.

Good, R. A. and Papermaster, B. W. (1964). Ontogeny and phylogeny of adaptive immunity. *Adv. Immunol.* **4**, 1–115.

Hammar, J. A. (1905). Zur Histogenese und Involution der Thymusdrüse. *Anat. Anz.* **27**, 23–30 and 41–89.

Hammar, J. A. (1909). Fünfzig Jahre Thymusforschung. *Ergebn. Anat. EntwGesch.* **19**, 1–274.

Hirsch, J. G. (1965). Neutrophil and eosinophil leucocytes. *In* "The Inflammatory Response" (B. W. Zweifach, L. Grant and R. T. McCluskey, eds), pp. 245–280. Academic Press, New York.

Hoshino, T. (1962). The fine structure of ciliated vesicle-containing reticular cells in the mouse thymus. *Expl. Cell Res.* **27**, 615–616.

Hoshino, T. (1963). Electron microscopic studies of the epithelial reticular cells of the mouse thymus. *Z. Zellforsch. mikrosk. Anat.* **59**, 513–529.

Izard, J. (1966). Ultrastructure of the thymic reticulum in guinea pig. *Anat. Rec.* **155**, 117–132.

Jordan, H. E. and Looper, J. B. (1928). The histology of the thymus gland of the box-turtle, *Terrapene carolina*, with special reference to the concentric corpuscles of Hassall and the eosinophilic granulocytes. *Anat. Rec.* **40**, 309–337.

Kaplan, H. G., Nagareda, C. S. and Brown, M. B. (1954). Endocrine factors and radiation-induced lymphoid tumors of mice. *Recent Prog. Horm. Res.* **10**, 293–333.

Klug, H. (1967). Submikroskopische Zytologie des Thymus von *Ambystoma mexicanum*. *Z. Zellforsch. mikrosk. Anat.* **78**, 388–401.

Kohnen, P. and Weiss, L. (1964). An electron microscopic study of thymic corpuscles in the guinea pig and the mouse. *Anat. Rec.* **148**, 29–58.

Low, F. N. and Freeman, J. A. (1958). "Electron Microscopic Atlas of Normal and Leukemic Human Blood." McGraw-Hill, New York.

Lundin, P. M. and Schelin, U. (1965). Ultrastructure of the rat thymus. *Acta path. microbiol. scand.* **65**, 379–394.

Maslin, T. P. (1967). Skin grafting in the bisexual teiid lizard *Cnemidophorus sexlineatus* and in the unisexual *C. tesselatus*. *J. exp. Zool.* **166**, 137–150.

Maurer, F. (1899). Die Schilddrüse, Thymus und andere Schlundspaltenderivate bei der Eidechse. *Morph. Jb.* **27**, 119–172.

Miller, J. F. A. P. (1961). Immunological function of the thymus. *Lancet* **2**, 748–749.

Miller, J. F. A. P. (1962). Immunological significance of the thymus of the adult mouse. *Nature, Lond.* **195**, 1318–1319.

Murray, R. G., Murray, A. and Pizzo, A. (1965). The fine structure of the thymocytes of young rats. *Anat. Rec.* **151**, 17–40.

Osoba, D. and Miller, J. F. A. P. (1963). Evidence for a humoral thymus factor responsible for the maturation of immunological competence. *Nature, Lond.* **199**, 653–654.

Pansky, B. and House, E. L. (1965). The granular reticular cells of the thymus in the AKR/JAX mouse. *Anat. Rec.* **152**, 451–458.

Pansky, B., House, E. L. and Cone, L. A. (1965). An insulin-like thymic factor. *Diabetes* 14, 325–332.

Papermaster, B. W., Condie, R. M., Finstad, J. and Good, R. A. (1964). Significance of the thymus in the evolution of the lymphoid tissue and acquired immunity. *In* "The Thymus in Immunobiology" (R. A. Good and A. E. Gabrielson, eds), pp. 551.259– Harper and Row, New York.

Pischinger, A. (1937). Kiemenanlagen und ihre Schicksale bei Amnioten—Schilddrüse und epitheliale Organe der Pharynxwand bei Tetrapoden. *In* "Handbuch der vergleichenden Anatomie der Wirbeltiere" (L. Bolk, E. Göppert, E. Kallius, W. Lubosch, eds), 3, 279–348. Urban und Schwarzenberg, Berlin and Wien.

Rathke, H. (1866). "Untersuchungen über die Entwicklung und den Körperbau der Krokodile" (Wilhelm von Wittich, ed.). Friedrich Vieweg und Sohn, Braunschweig.

Raviola, E. and Raviola, G. (1966). Fine structure of the myoid cells in reptilian and avian thymus. *Anat. Rec.* 154, 483 (Abstract).

Raviola, E. and Raviola, G. (1967). Striated muscle cells in the thymus of reptiles and birds: An electron microscopic study. *Am. J. Anat.* 121, 623–646.

Saint-Remy, G. and Prenant, A. (1904). Recherches sur le développment des derivés branchiaux chez les sauriens et les ophidiens. *Archs Biol., Paris* 20, 145–216.

Salkind, J. (1915). Contributions histologiques a la biologie comparée du thymus. *Archs Zool. exp. gén.* 55, 81–322.

Shaner, R. F. (1921). The development of the pharynx and aortic arches of the turtle, with a note on the fifth and pulmonary arches of mammals. *Am. J. Anat.* 29, 407–429.

Shier, K. J. (1963). The morphology of the epithelial thymus. Observations on lymphocyte-depleted and fetal thymus. *Lab. Invest.* 12, 316–326.

Sidky, Y. A. (1967). The carotid sinus in lizards with an anatomical survey of the ventral neck region. *J. Morph.* 121, 311–322.

Simon, J. (1845). "A Physiological Essay on the Thymus Gland." H. Renshaw, London.

Smith, D. E. (1963). Electron microscopy of normal mast cells under various experimental conditions. *Ann. N. Y. Acad. Sci.* 103, 40–52.

Sommer, J. R., Weinstein, D., Becker, C., Beaudreau, G. S., Beard, D. and Beard, J. W. (1962). Virus of avian myeloblastosis. XIX. Protein, polysaccharide, lipide, and nucleic acid of myeloblasts and cytidine uptake *in vitro. J. natn. Cancer Inst.* 28, 75–97.

Strauss, A. J. L. and Kemp, P. G., Jr. (1967). Serum auto-antibodies in myasthenia gravis and thymoma: selective affinity for I-bands of striated muscle as a guide to identification of antigen(s). *J. Immun.* 99, 945–953.

Strauss, A. J. L., Kemp, P. G., Jr. and Douglas, S. D. (1966). Myasthenia gravis. *Lancet* 1, 772–773.

Strauss, A. J. L., Kemp, P. G., Jr. and Douglas, S. D. (1967). An immunohistological delineation of striated muscle cells in the thymus. *In* "Ontogeny of Immunity" (R. T. Smith, R. A. Good, and P. A. Miescher, eds), pp. 180–185. University of Florida Press, Gainesville.

Thompson, F. (1910). The thyreoid and parathyreoids throughout vertebrates, with observations on some other closely related structures. *Phil. Trans. R. Soc.* (B) 201, 91–132.

Törö, I. and Oláh, I. (1966). Electron microscopic study of guinea-pig thymus. *Acta morph. hung.* 14, 275–290.

Van Bemmelen, J. F. (1886). Die Visceraltaschen und Aortenbogen bei Reptilien und Vögeln. *Zool. Anz.* 9, 543–546.

Van Bemmelen, J. F. (1888). Anatomische Untersuchungen in der Halsgegend der Reptilien. *Bijdr. Dierk.* 16, 102–146.

Van Bemmelen, J. F. (1893). Ueber die Entwickelung der Kiementaschen und der Aorta-bogen bei den Seeschildkröten, untersucht an Embryonen von *Chelonia viridis*. *Anat. Anz.* 8, 801–803.

Van de Velde, R. L. and Friedman, N. B. (1966a). Muscular elements of the thymus. *Fedn Proc. Fedn Am. Socs exp. Biol.* 25, 661 (Abstract).

Van de Velde, R. L. and Friedman, N. B. (1966b). The thymic "Myoidzellen" and myasthenia gravis. *J. Am. med. Ass.* 198, 287–288.

Van de Velde, R. L. and Friedman, N. B. (1967). Muscular elements in the thymus. *Anat. Rec.* 157, 392 (Abstract).

Wassjutotschkin, A. (1913). Untersuchungen über die Histogenese der Thymus. I. Über den Ursprung der myoiden Elemente der Thymus des Hühnerembryos. *Anat. Anz.* 43, 349–366.

Watanabe, Y. (1957). Observations of white blood cells with electron microscope. *J. Electron. microsc., Chiba Cy* 5, 46–57.

Watney, H. (1882). The minute anatomy of the thymus. *Phil. Trans. R. Soc.* (B) 173, 1099–1123.

Weakley, B. S., Patt, D. I. and Shepro, D. (1964). Ultra-structure of fetal thymus in the golden hamster. *J. Morph.* 115, 319–354.

Weinreb, E. L. (1963). Studies on the fine structure of teleost blood cells. I. Peripheral blood. *Anat. Rec.* 147, 219–238.

Weiss, L. (1963). Electron microscopic observations on the vascular barrier in the cortex of the thymus of the mouse. *Anat. Rec.* 145, 413–438.

Wetzel, B. K., Horn, R. G. and Spicer, S. S. (1967). Fine structural studies on the development of heterophil, eosinophil, and basophil granulocytes in rabbits. *Lab. Invest.* 16, 349–382.

Winqvist, G. (1963). Electron microscopy of the basophilic granulocyte. *Ann. N. Y. Acad. Sci.* 103, 352–375.

CHAPTER 5

The Pituitary Gland

HUBERT SAINT GIRONS

Muséum National d'Histoire Naturelle, Écologie Générale,
Brunoy, France

I. Introduction

The important role of the pituitary as an endocrine gland became progressively more obvious at the end of the last and beginning of the century. More recently the discovery of the adenohypophyseal mechanism controlling the hypothalamic neurosecretory products has caused a renewal of interest in the whole of that region, and now numerous publications appear on it each year. However, as in many other studies, our knowledge of comparative morphology and physiology lags behind that concerning the laboratory mammals, and the reptiles are, of all the vertebrates, those which have been studied least. This is clearly demonstrated by the recent three volume treatise on the pituitary edited by Harris and Donovan (1966), despite the original work in the chapter by Wingstrand (1966a).

Since Rathke's publications (1838, 1839) it has been known that the morphology of the pituitary in snakes is basically similar to that of the other tetrapod vertebrates. Numerous later works, of which the oldest generally deal with embrology, have discussed the pituitary in other snakes (Siler, 1936; Hartmann, 1944; Cieslak, 1945), in lizards (Gaupp, 1893; Haller, 1896; Staderini, 1903; Sterzi, 1904; Gentes, 1907; Woederman, 1914; Poris and Charipper, 1938; Altland, 1939; Miller, 1948; Romieu, 1949; Panigel, 1956), in *Sphenodon* (Dendy, 1899; Wyeth and Row, 1923; Gabe and Saint Girons, 1964b), in turtles (Müller, 1871; Woederman, 1914; Combescot, 1955; Herlant and Grignon, 1961; Yamada *et al.*, 1960), and in crocodilians (Reese, 1910; Gabe and Rancurel, 1958).

Particular attention should be called to the important works on embryology or comparative morphology dealing with representatives of several orders of reptiles (Baumgartner, 1916; Wingstrand, 1951, 1966a and b; Green, 1951, 1966; and Nemee, 1952). Finally, I have recently described numerous additional species (Saint Girons, 1961a, 1968; Saint Girons *et al.*, 1964).

Table I indicates that the morphology of the reptilian pituitary is known in representatives of all the suborders and many families. It is therefore possible

TABLE I

List giving the number of species in each family in which the morphology (anatomy and histology) of the hypophysis is known.
Forms known only from older or purely embryological studies are not included.

RHYNCHOCEPHALIA		OPHIDIA	
Sphenodontidae	1	*Typhlopoidea*	
SAURIA		Typhlopidae	3
Gekkota		*Leptotyphlopoidea*	
Gekkonidae	10	Leptotyphlopidae	1
Pygopodidae	2	*Booidea*	
Xantusiidae	2	Boidae	5
Iguania		*Colubroidea*	
Iguanidae	15	Colubridae	13
Agamidae	9	Elapidae	9
Chamaeleonidae	3	Hydrophiidae	3
Scincomorpha		Viperidae (including	
Scincidae	12	Crotalinae)	7
Feyliniidae	1	TESTUDINES	
Lacertidae	9	*Cryptodira*	
Cordylidae (including		Testudinidae (including	
Gerrhosaurinae)	3	Emydinae)	6
Anguimorpha		*Pleurodira*	
Anguidae	3	Pelomedusidae	1
Anniellidae	1	CROCODILIA	
Helodermatidae	2	Crocodylidae	4
Varanidae	2		
AMPHISBAENIA			
Amphisbaenidae	1		
Trogonophidae	1		

and desirable to give a general description rather than to analyze in sequence the numerous publications which have been devoted to it.

The terminology used to designate the different parts of the hypophysis and hypothalamic–neurohypophyseal complex varies considerably with different authors. Table II, which includes only terms used in comparative morphology, will help to clarify these.

II. The Hypothalamic–Neurohypophyseal Complex

A. GENERAL

Although the anatomy of the neural lobe of the hypophysis of reptiles has long been known, the idea of neurosecretion is much more recent, and their hypothalamic–neurohypophyseal relations have been the object of only a few

TABLE II

Terminology used to designate the various parts of the hypothalamic-hypophyseal complex

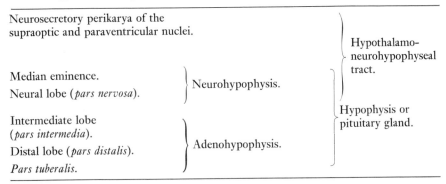

studies (Bargmann, 1949, 1955; Drager, 1950; Bargmann *et al.*, 1950, 1957; Hild, 1951; Scharrer, 1951; Ghiara, 1954, 1956, 1957; Gabe and Rancurel, 1958; Oota, 1963; Gabe and Saint Girons, 1964a; Nayar and Pandalai, 1964; Green, 1966). The neurosecretory phenomena in reptiles have most recently been dealt with by Gabe (1966).

B. THE NEUROSECRETORY PERIKARYA

The neurosecretory perikarya of the hypothalamic-hypophyseal tract in reptiles are generally small, few in number, and gathered together in the supraoptic and paraventricular nuclei. The supraoptic nuclei form two distinct groups of cells lying dorsal to the optic tract at the point where it joins the diencephalon. The crescentic paraventricular nucleus is situated anterodorsal to the supraoptic nuclei. In most reptiles, the supraoptic nuclei are small and rich in neurosecretory cells; the paraventricular nucleus is often more extensive, but, except among the Testudines (Bargmann, 1955), has few neurosecretory elements.

The size and appearance of the neurosecretory perikarya vary greatly, perhaps from one species to another, but chiefly according to the functional phase of their secretory cycle. The only nearly constant characteristic is the presence of a large, spherical, basal nucleus, averaging 6 μ in diameter, with a very low chromatin content and a distinct nucleolus (Figs 1 and 2). The perikayra may be reduced to a thin border of cytoplasm in which some granules can be distinguished. More generally, they are ovoid and reach a size of 13 by 6 μ. Little or very little secretion is discernible with chromic hematoxylin, paraldehyde fuchsin, or alcian blue after permanganate oxidation. There are one or more small peripheral vacuoles. Finally, in some individuals, most neurosecretory cells are of an average size and completely filled with granules of variable size. Of course all the neurosecretory perikarya from one individual are never at the same stage, but usually the majority fall into one of the patterns which have just been described.

The descending axons from the neurosecretory perikarya of the paraventricular and supraoptic nuclei converge towards the floor of the third

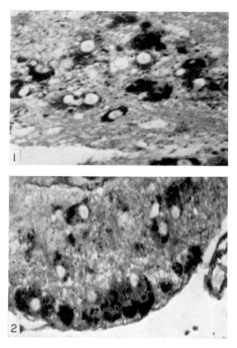

Figs 1 and 2. Neurosecretory perikarya of the supraoptic nucleus in the lizard *Agama impalearis* (Agamidae). Stained with alcian blue and PAS, and photographed through an orange filter; × 400. The neurosecretory material is condensed and abundant in September (Fig. 1); the perikarya are tall and more or less degranulated in April, the period of sexual activity (Fig. 2).

ventricle and attach themselves along the ventral wall of the infundibular recess. Their pathways are marked by an irregular string of small spherical granulations, occasionally intersected by pools of colloidal material; these are often numerous among the perikarya.

C. The Median Eminence

Just anterior or dorsal to the anterior end of the pars distalis, the ventral wall of the infundibular recess forms a distinct swelling, the median eminence. A transverse section shows, from dorsal to ventral (Fig. 4): (1) a layer of ependymal cells; (2) a layer mainly composed of pituicytes, but containing a certain number of horizontal neurosecretory fibres; (3) a thicker layer than the preceding ones, formed mostly by rectilinear and vertical neurosecretory

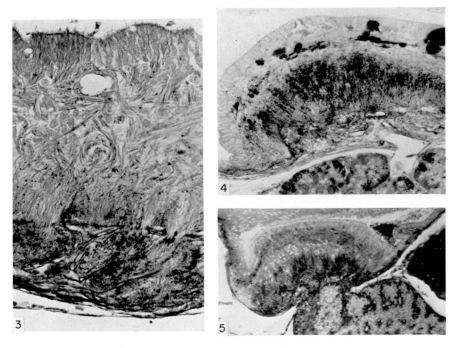

FIGS 3 to 5. Sagittal sections through the median eminence of lepidosaurs.

FIG. 3. *Sphenodon punctatus* (Sphenodontidae). Stained with paraldehyde fuchsin-trichrome, and photographed through an orange filter; × 250. The different layers described in the text are clearly shown at the top of the figure. Note the groups of neurosecretory fibres that traverse the ventral glial limiting membrane and approach the capillaries. In all the figured examples, the trichrome, whether used alone or in combination with paraldehyde fuchsin, is the trichrome in a single solution of Gabe and Martoja-Pierson (1957).

FIG. 4. *Egernia* sp. (Scincidae). Same technique and magnification as in Fig. 3. Note the abundance of neurosecretory material along the course of the horizontal fibres. The neurosecretory fibres do not cross the ventral glial limiting membrane. The anterodorsal region of the pars distalis appears at the bottom of the photograph.

FIG. 5. *Demansia* sp. (Elapidae). Stained with alcian blue and PAS, and photographed through an orange filter; × 100. A thick connective tract joins the base of the median eminence to the anterior end of the pars distalis.

fibres, as well as by some extensions from the basal poles of the ependymal cells, and also by some pituicytes; and (4) an external limiting layer of glia. Above this there is a mass containing much connective tissue and many capillaries. In most reptiles, these capillaries lift the limiting glia locally, without crossing it, and are thus in direct contact with the original fibres of the neurosecretory perikarya. In *Sphenodon punctatus*, on the contrary, the neurosecretory fibres cross over the ventral limiting glia and pass in front of the primary capillary network of the median eminence (Fig. 3).

In the Rhynchocephalia, Testudines, and Crocodilia, the base of the median eminence and a fairly large portion of the infundibular floor are overlapped by the cellular cords of the pars tuberalis. These are vestigial or absent in the Squamata.

In the Colubroidea, the median eminence is joined to the anterior end of the pars distalis by a distinct connecting tract (Fig. 5), sometimes called the pars terminalis (Siler, 1936). In most other squamates and in *Sphenodon* the median eminence is situated nearer the neural lobe, immediately dorsal to the anterior third of the pars distalis. Its contact with the latter is generally fairly diffuse. In the Testudines and Crocodilia the position is the same as in the Sauria, but a thick pars tuberalis, especially in turtles, forms a large connecting area containing the vessels of the hypophyseal portal system.

In the Leptotyphlopidae, the median eminence is clearly hypertrophic and larger than the pars nervosa (Fig. 68). As in all the limbless burrowing Squamata, it is closely applied to the diencephalic floor.

D. The Neural Lobe

The spherical or ovoid, more or less lobulated pars nervosa forms a simple extended cul-de-sac of the infundibular recess, situated dorsal to the pars distalis in the majority of reptiles. However, the neural lobe is dorsolateral to the distal lobe in snakes, and in a distinctly lateral or posterior position in certain limbless, burrowing squamates.

In the Rhynchocephalia, Sauria, Testudines, and Crocodilia, the infundibular recess penetrates deeply into the pars nervosa, where it often forms very extensive hollow lobules laterally (Figs 5, 6, 7 and 9). In snakes the neural lobe is massive, solid, and incompletely divided into lobules by connective tissue septa (Fig. 8). In the first case, the structure of the pars ner-

---

FIGS 6 to 9. Sagittal sections through the neural and intermediate lobes of reptiles. The anterior end is toward the top and ventral to the left in all four figures.

FIG. 6. *Hoplodactylus pacificus* (Gekkonidae). Stained with paraldehyde fuchsin-trichrome, and photographed through an orange filter; × 100. The infundibular recess penetrates deeply into the neural lobe which contains much neurosecretory material (black in the photograph). The intermediate lobe, with a thick internal layer and a very thin external layer separated from each other by a large hypophysial cleft, nearly surrounds the neural lobe.

FIG. 7. *Sceloporus occidentalis* (Iguanidae). Same technique and magnification as in Fig. 6. The infundibular recess forms hollow lobules in the neural lobe. The moderately developed intermediate lobe is composed of irregular cords.

FIG. 8. *Demansia* sp. (Elapidae). Stained with PAS, hematoxylin, and orange G, and photographed through a green filter; × 100. The neural lobe is massive and lobulated, but solid. The intermediate lobe, formed of irregular cords, lies mainly posterior to the neural lobe.

FIG. 9. *Crocodylus niloticus* (Crocodylidae). Stained with paraldehyde fuchsin-trichrome, and photographed through an orange filter; × 63. The infundibular recess penetrates deeply into the neural lobe, but its lumen is very narrow. The well-developed intermediate lobe consists of numerous cords formed mainly of chromophobic cells.

vosa is reminiscent of the median eminence; two layers can be distinguished between the opening in the infundibular recess and the external limiting membrane, first a layer of ependymal cells and then a fairly thick mass formed by a combination of pituicytes, fibres arising from the neurosecretory perikarya, and extensions from the basal poles of the ependymal cells. The

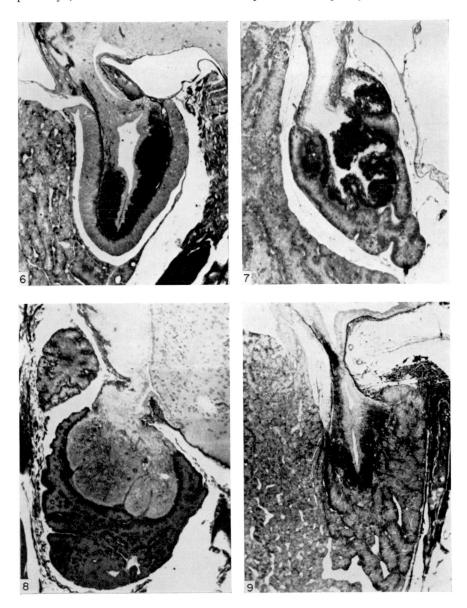

pituicytes are more abundant in the central region and the neurosecretory fibres in the peripheral region. In snakes the ependymal cells are present only at the anterior extremity of the pars nervosa which is composed almost entirely of a large mass of clustered neurosecretory fibres with occasional pituicytes. The neural lobe tends to become massive in the limbless burrowing lizards and amphisbaenians as in the Ophidia. The infundibular recess penetrates the lobe more deeply, but its opening is generally very flattened, and the principal mass of the organ is formed by a thick layer of clustered neurosecretory fibres (Figs 62 and 64).

In the neural lobe, the neurosecretory products are visible as granules and particles of a colloidal appearance. Their abundance varies greatly among individuals, but they are generally much more distinct in lizards than in snakes.

The ultrastructural characters of the different parts of the hypothalamo-neurohypophyseal tract have been studied in only a few reptiles: *Natrix natrix* (Bargmann *et al.*, 1957), *Gekko japonicus* (Murakami, 1961, 1963), and *Clemmys japonica* (Oota, 1963). They do not appear to have any notable differences from those in other amniotes (see Harris and Donovan, 1966).

III.   The Adenohypophysis

A.   GENERAL

The adenohypophysis is not an anatomical entity; the intermediate lobe is closely associated with the neural lobe, and is joined to the distal lobe only by an often narrow isthmus. However, embryological studies show that the pars intermedia and the pars distalis have a common origin, and the histological structure confirms the relationship of these two lobes; both of them are composed of classic glandular cells.

B.   THE INTERMEDIATE LOBE

The intermediate lobe, which may be thought of as composed of two layers of cells separated by the hypophyseal cleft, encloses the posteroventral half of the neural lobe, from which it is separated by a double membrane of connective tissue. The internal layer, which is in contact with the pars nervosa, is always well developed and is simple or pseudostratified. The external layer is fairly flat, even endothelial in appearance. In a narrow area at the posterior or posteroventral part of the intermediate lobe, the external layer continues without a break in continuity into the distal lobe, and some cells originally from the latter may invade it, particularly towards the ventral area. Numerous capillaries lie between the connective tissue membranes which separate the pars intermidia from the pars nervosa.

This basic arrangement is subject to numerous variations. In the Gekkonidae (Figs 6 and 38) the intermediate lobe almost completely surrounds the neural lobe and extends forward to the connection of the pituitary stalk; on the other hand, in some Iguanidae and Lacertoidea, as well as in the Testudines, it surrounds only the posteroventral third of the pars nervosa. Finally, in larger species, the internal layer is more or less festooned with and sometimes composed of cellular cords of irregular size and shape. This phenomenon is particularly marked in the Varanidae, which form a transition to the second arrangement described below.

In chamaeleonids, iguanids of the genus *Anolis*, agamids, at least one lacertid, and one crocodilian, the intermediate lobe is distinctly hypertrophied compared with the rest of the hypophysis (Figs 10, 12, 44 and 49). In these

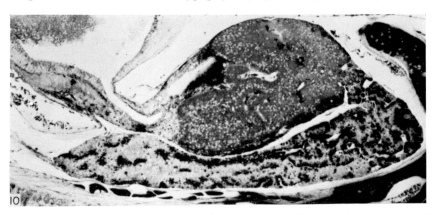

FIG. 10. Sagittal section through the pituitary of *Anolis carolinensis* (Iguanidae) in situ. Stained with paraldehyde fuchsin-trichrome, and photographed through a green filter. Note the weak development of the neural lobe, the marked hypertrophy of the intermediate lobe, and the elongation of the distal lobe. In the last, the alpha cells (posteriorly, to the right of the figure) and the X cells (anteriorly, to the left) appear black. Note also the blood vessel that joins the ventral part of the median eminence to the anterodorsal zone of the pars distalis.

cases the two cellular layers described above cannot be distinguished, and the entire organ is formed of fairly regular, thick cords; the reduced hypophyseal cleft is restricted to the posteroventral part of the lobe. There are a fair number of capillaries between the cellular cords of the pars intermedia. Anatomically, the intermediate lobe of *Crocodylus niloticus* is of this type, but the cellular cords are much thinner and more irregular (Figs 9 and 13).

Morphologically the intermediate lobe of snakes is fairly distinctive and constant. It encloses the posterior half of the neural lobe with a fairly thin layer of cells which sends digitations between the lobules of the latter; its principal mass, formed from irregular cellular cords, is situated between the pars nervosa and the pars distalis and communicates extensively with the latter (Fig. 8). Numerous isolated cells of the intermediate lobe are found throughout the posterodorsal region of the distal lobe.

Finally, in fossorial reptiles the intermediate lobe is more or less atrophied (Fig. 14). During the first stages of reduction in the Boidae, burrowing Viperidae, and Anniellidae there is a simple decrease in size, and the general form characteristic of the family or superfamily is retained. In the Feyliniidae and the Amphisbaenia the intermediate lobe is reduced to a thin strip joining the neural lobe to the posterior end of the distal lobe (Fig. 63). In the Typhlopidae and Leptotyphlopidae, the pars intermedia has completely disappeared.

When the internal layer is formed by a simple epithelium, the cells of the intermediate lobe are regularly prismatic, with large basal nuclei which are generally spherical and poor in chromatin (Fig. 11). The shapes of the cells and the positions of the nuclei obviously vary when the epithelium is

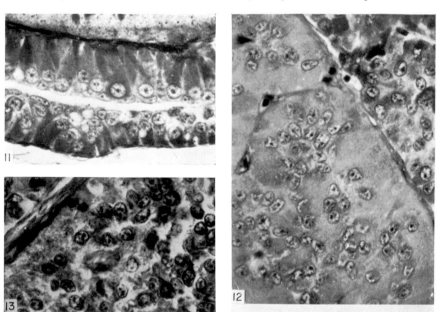

FIGS 11 to 13. Cells of the intermediate lobe of reptiles. Stained with PAS, hematoxylin and orange G, and photographed through a green filter; ×650.

FIG. 11. *Anguis fragilis* (Anguidae). The neural lobe is above; below note the two concentric layers of the intermediate lobe separated by the hypophysial cleft. Note the great development of the internal layer and the palisade arrangement of the large prismatic cells which contain many PAS-positive secretory granules.

FIG. 12. *Chamaeleo lateralis* (Chamaeleonidae). The distal lobe appears in the upper right. The hypertrophied intermediate lobe consists of thick, irregular cords which contain extremely fine, only slightly chromophilic secretory granules.

FIG. 13. *Crocodylus niloticus* (Crocodylidae). The distal lobe appears in the upper left. Despite its large size, the intermediate lobe consists of small cells which are often involuted and always contain but little secretory material.

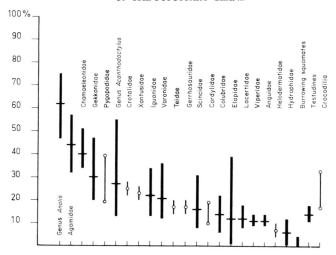

FIG. 14. Size of the intermediate lobe, expressed as a percentage of the entire hypophysis, in different families of reptiles. The circles indicate values found in a single species.

pseudostratified. When the intermediate lobe is formed by cellular cords, the cells are more or less ovoid, with large, spherical, transparent nuclei (Fig. 12); depending on the species, a variable number of small involuted cells lie at the centre of these cords. The cells of the intermediate lobe are always as large as or larger than any in the distal lobe, and this greater size is even more marked at the nuclear level. Apart from the special case of the burrowing reptiles, the only exception to this rule is *Crocodylus niloticus*, in which the intermediate lobe is large, but the cells appear poor in cytoplasm and show little chromophilia (Fig. 13).

In the fossorial Boidae that have been studied and in *Trogonophis wiegmanni*, most of the cells of the intermediate lobe are involuted and lack secretory products, but a small number of them appear normal and well developed. In the Anniellidae all the intermediate cells are small, but still have chromophilic granules. In the other burrowing reptiles examined there are no functional cells in the intermediate lobe.

In most other cases, the entire supranuclear region of the cells of the pars intermedia is filled with fine granules; these are not very dense and are cyanophilic or somewhat amphophilic. They stain lightly with periodic acid Schiff (PAS) and retain a little paraldehyde fuchsin, alcian blue, or lakes of hematoxylin after permanganate oxidation (Table III). In *Anolis*, the Boidae, and the Colubroidea, the numerous secretory granules are large, very chromophilic, and stain strongly with paraldehyde fuchsin and alcian blue; in *Anolis*, the Colubridae, Elapidae, and Hydrophiidae, they are peculiar in being exceedingly erythrophilic.

TABLE III

Histochemical reaction and staining properties of the
intermediate and gonadotrophic LH cells

	Intermediate Cells					Gonadotrophic LH Cells					
	PAS	AB–PF	E	A	C	PAS	AB–PF	H	E	A	C
Sphenodontidae	±	±	0	+	0	++	+	+	0	+	0
Gekkonidae	++	±	0	±	±	+++	±	+	0	+	0
Xantusiidae	++	+	0	±	±	+++	0	+	0	+	0
Delma fraseri	++	+	0	±	±	+++	±	+	0	+	0
Lialis burtonis	++	0	0	0	+	+++	0	0	+	0	0
Iguanidae	+	++	0	+	0	±	±	±	0	+	0
Anolis	0	+++	+	0	0	±	±	±	0	+	0
Agamidae	+	+	0	+	0	+	+	+	0	+	0
Chamaeleonidae	++	++	0	+	0	+	+	+	0	+	0
Lacertidae	+	±	0	±	±	++	±	+	0	+	0
Teiidae	±	±	0	±	±	++	0	+	0	+	0
Gerrhosaurinae	++	0	±	±	0	+++	0	±	0	+	0
Cordylinae	+	±	0	±	±	+++	0	±	0	+	0
Scincidae	+	+	0	0	+	+++	0	+	0	+	0
Feyliniidae						++	0	+	0	+	0
Anguidae	+	+	0	0	+	+++	+	+	0	+	0
Anniellidae						+++	±	±	0	+	0
Helodermatidae	±	±	0	0	+	+++	+	+	0	+	0
Varanidae	0	0	0	±	±	0	0	+	0	0	+
Trogonophidae	+	+	0	±	±	+++	+	0	0	0	+
Amphisbaenidae						+++	++	+	0	+	0
Typhlopidae						++	+	+	0	+	0
Leptotyphlopidae						++	++	+	0	0	+
Boidae	++	++	0	0	+	++	++	+	0	+	0
Colubridae	+	++	+	0	0	+	++	+	+	0	0
Elapidae	+	++	+	0	0	+	++	+	+	0	0
Hydrophiidae	+	++	+	0	0	+	++	+	+	0	0
Viperinae	+	++	0	0	+	+++	+++	+	0	+	0
Crotalinae	+	++	0	0	+	+++	+++	+	0	+	0
Testudines	±	0	0	±	0	+++	±	+	0	+	0
Crocodilia	+	+	+	0	0	+++	0	0	+	0	0

A.　　　Amphophily: the secretory granules are both erythrophilic and cyanophilic; they stain violet with azan (Romeis method).

AB–PF.　Cells stain, other permanganate oxidation, with alcian blue at pH3 and with paraldehyde fuchsin.

C.　　　Cyanophily: an affinity for acid stains with low coefficients of diffusion, such as aniline blue and light green.

E.　　　Erythrophily: an affinity for acid stains with high coefficients of diffusion, such as erythrosin, azocarmin, orange G, and azorubin S.

H.　　　Cells stain with lakes of hematoxylin.

PAS.　　Cells give positive reaction with periodic acid-Schiff reagent.

　　　　+++, strong reaction; ++, moderate reaction; +, slight reaction; ±, variable reaction; 0, no reaction.

C. THE DISTAL LOBE

The general form of the distal lobe is that of an anteroposteriorly elongated and more or less dorsoventrally flattened strip. As already noted, the pars distalis generally lies ventral to the pars nervosa and posteroventral to the median eminence; the hypophysis is bilaterally symmetrical. In the non-burrowing snakes, the distal lobe is situated ventrolateral to the neural lobe, which distinctly depresses its left dorsal region. In the Amphisbaenia and the Typhlopidae (Fig. 15), the anterior part of the pars nervosa and the

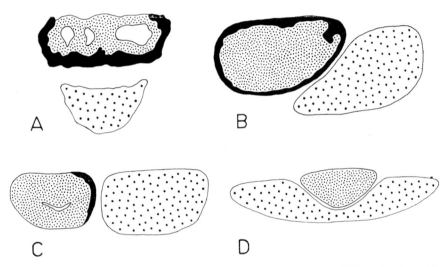

FIG. 15. Transverse sections through the hypophysis of Squamata. The neural lobe and regions with many neurosecretory fibres are indicated by fine stippling, the distal lobe by coarse stippling, and the intermediate lobe by black.

A. *Sceloporus graciosus* (Iguanidae), a lizard of the classic type. The hypophysis is bilaterally symmetrical.

B. *Elaphe longissima* (Colubridae), a snake of the classic type. The distal lobe lies ventrolateral to the neural lobe.

C. *Anniella pulchra* (Anniellidae), a fossorial lizard. The distal lobe lies lateral to the neural lobe, and the intermediate lobe is atrophied.

D. *Typhlops punctatus* (Typhlopidae). The hypophysis is bilaterally symmetrical, but the neural lobe is embedded in the distal lobe, and, as in amphisbaenians, extends posterior to the latter. There is no intermediate lobe.

pituitary stalk occupy a longitudinal median depression in the pars distalis, the lateral regions of which form two flanges. In the Gekkota the morphology of the distal lobe is quite distinctive, with a well-developed anterior region and a flattened posterior region which becomes thickened again posterior to the intermediate lobe (Fig. 38). In the Varanidae the distal lobe, which is lodged in the deep sella turcica, is massive and particularly thick (Fig. 58). In the Boidae, Viperidae (including the Crotalinae), and *Acanthophis antarcticus*, the distal lobe is ovoid with a swollen posterior region (Figs 70 and 77). In *Anolis*, on the other hand, it is particularly elongate and small relative to the rest of the hypophysis (Fig. 10). The distal lobe is very flat dorsoventrally in the Testudines, and has a regular ovoid form in the Crocodilia.

The pars distalis is composed of fairly regular and thick cellular cords, which are surrounded by a thin connective tissue membrane; these cords contain many chromophilic cells peripherally and many apparently involuted or undifferentiated chromophobic cells centrally. The proportion of these two cell types evidently varies during the functional cycle, but it is also an extremely constant specific characteristic. There are numerous capillaries, as well as vascular sinuses of varying size and form, between the cellular cords, but the capillaries are always much larger and more abundant in the posterior region. The vascular sinuses are almost absent in the Varanidae, but are consistently very large and numerous in the Anguidae, Helodermatidae, and Testudines.

The recognition and functional significance of the different types of cells within the pars distalis raise critical problems and thus require discussion. For a long time, aside from the chromophobic cells, only acidophilic cells and so-called "basophilic" cells* were recognized. Then Siler (1936), Poris and Charipper (1938), Poris (1941), Hartmann (1944), Cieslak (1945), Miller (1948), and Wingstrand (1951) recognized two different types of erythrophilic cells in numerous squamates. Some, in the posterior region, generally contain fairly fine granules which colour orange with azan; others, in the anterior region, have large carminophilic granules. The former are one particular type of cell termed the alpha cell, but the latter, in most species, represent at least two types of cells.

At the present time the use of simple histochemical reactions and of some specific stains (Gabe, 1962) permits the recognition, in the pars distalis of reptiles, of five different and well characterized cellular types, or even six if the chromophobic or principal cells are included (see especially Gabe and Rancurel, 1958, for the Crocodilia; Herlant and Grignon, 1961, for the Testudines; Saint Girons, 1961a and 1968, for the Squamata). In a few species (*Testudo graeca*, Herlant and Grignon, 1961; *Vipera aspis*, Saint Girons and Duguy, 1962; *Cerastes cerastes*, *Anguis fragilis*, and *Agama impalearis*, Saint Girons, 1962, 1963 and 1967), study of the changes in these different types of cells during the annual cycle and under certain

---

* The term "basophilic" is incorrect since aniline blue is an acid stain like eosin, azocarmin, or erythrosin. In this work I will use the terms erythrophilic (with the variants carminophilic and orangophilic) for acidophilic and cyanophilic for basophilic.

experimental conditions provides quite precise information on the roles of three of the types. Rather strict and constant localization of each of these types permits their easy recognition in different species despite some variation in their histochemical characteristics and staining properties. However, attributing the same functional significance to them is clearly only a working hypothesis. In any case, the respective roles of the different types of adenohypophyseal cells need not be discussed in a morphological study. Moreover, in considering such topics, reptiles cannot be treated by themselves, and I refer to the recent reviews by Herlant (1964) and Purves (1966) for a discussion of this problem in vertebrates generally. However, to avoid further complication of an already confused subject, I shall, wherever possible, use a functional nomenclature to define different types of cells in the pars distalis.

In the few cases which have been studied, the appearance of the different types of adenohypophyseal cells shows important variations during the course of the annual, and especially the reproductive, cycle mainly in females. This is clearly taken into account in the comparisons between species and families, comparisons which are based, as much as possible, on males.

The gonadotrophic LH (or gamma) cells are always localized in the anterior part of the pars distalis. Generally fairly numerous, these cells are prismatic or sometimes ovoid, and are often arranged in palisades along the capillaries (Figs 16 and 18); they have spherical basal nuclei. The secretory granules, of varying size and number, are amphophilic; that is, they stain simultaneously with aniline blue and the erythrosin dyes and thus appear violet in azan. The granules show a marked affinity for the lakes of hematoxylin and, to a varying degree, for alcian blue and paraldehyde fuchsin; they are generally strongly PAS-positive (Table III). In the Gekkonidae, the gonadotrophic LH cells are ovoid and scattered (Fig. 39). In the Iguania and Lacertoidea they are small and rare; on the other hand, they are particularly large and numerous in the Anguidae, Helodermatidae, Colubridae, Elapidae, Hydrophiidae, and Crocodilia (Figs 21, 71 and 82). In the latter four groups, they are clearly carminophilic, but they stain very lightly with PAS in the Colubroidea and their allies. Their constant location, amphophilia, and affinity to the lakes of hematoxylin permit the easy recognition of the gonadotrophic LH cells.

The gonadotrophic FSH (or beta) cells, less numerous than the preceding type, generally lie in the medial and lateral parts of the distal lobe, where they frequently form easily visible groups (Fig. 42). However, they can also be dispersed throughout the anterior two-thirds of the pars distalis. They are generally ovoid cells, with small, spherical, central nuclei (Fig. 16) or, sometimes, with flat basal ones. The secretory product forms fine cyanophilic granules which stain to a variable degree with alcian blue and paraldehyde fuchsin and are PAS-positive (Fig. 17 and Table IV). In some species,

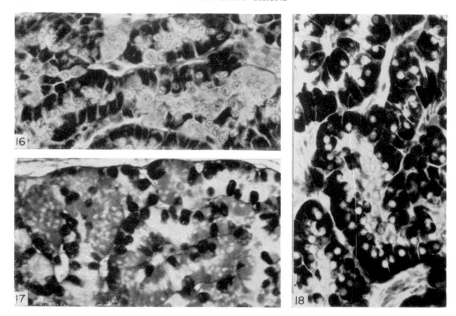

FIGS 16 to 18. Gonadotrophic cells of reptiles. × 400.

FIG. 16. *Eumeces algeriensis* (Scincidae). Stained with PAS, hematoxylin, and orange G, and photographed through a green filter. The gonadotrophic LH cells, in black, form a palisade along the capillaries. Some spherical gonadotrophic FSH cells with central nuclei appear a very light gray.

FIG. 17. *Agama impalearis* (Agamidae). Stained with alcian blue and PAS, and photographed through an orange filter. The gonadotrophic FSH cells are black and the gonadotrophic LH cells gray. The clear zones are formed by involuted elements and X cells.

FIG. 18. *Pseudechis australis* (Elapidae). Stained with PAS, hematoxylin, and orange G, and photographed through a green filter. The large ovoid gonadotrophic LH cells, which fill the anterior part of the pars distalis, appear black.

there are also large erythrophilic secretory granules or small erythrophilic lumps which stain strongly with alcian blue and paraldehyde fuchsin; in these cases the gonadotrophic FSH cells may be confused with thyrotrophic cells. In the Testudines, the numerous gonadotrophic FSH cells are distinctly fusiform. They are particularly large and easily recognized in some Elapidae and Viperidae (including Crotalinae) (Fig. 72).

The thyrotrophic (or delta) cells vary less among reptiles than do the other types of cells. They are rarely numerous, and may be scattered throughout the pars distalis or lie only in its posterior half. They are conical and often lie near the centres of the cellular cords, with long apical extensions towards the capillaries. They have spherical, basal nuclei. Their large or very large secretory granules may be either cyanophilic or erythrophilic; they always stain deeply with alcian blue and paraldehyde fuchsin, and are PAS-positive

TABLE IV

Histochemical reactions and staining properties of the
gonadotrophic FSH and thyrotrophic cells

	Gonadotrophic FSH Cells				Thyrotrophic Cells			
	PAS	AB–PF	E	C	PAS	AB–PF	E	C
Sphenodondidae	±	±	0	+	++	+++	+	+
Gekkonidae	+	+	0	+	++	+++	0	+
Xantusiidae	+	0	0	+	+	+++	0	+
Pygopodidae	+	+	0	+	++	+++	0	+
Iguanidae	+	+	0	+	++	+++	0	+
Agamidae	++	++	0	+	+++	+++	0	+
Chamaeleonidae	++	±	0	+	+++	+++	0	+
Lacertidae	+	+	0	+	++	+++	+	+
Teiidae	+	+++	0	+	+	+++	+	+
Gerrhosaurinae	+	+	0	+	+++	+++	0	+
Cordylinae	++	++	0	+	+++	+++	0	+
Scincidae	+	+++	+	+	++	+++	+	+
Feyliniidae	++	+++	0	+	++	+++	0	+
Anguidae	+	+++	+	+	+	+++	+	+
Anniellidae	+	+++	0	+	+	+++	0	+
Helodermatidae	+	+++	+	+	+	+++	+	+
Varanidae	+++	+	+	+	0	±	0	+
Trogonophidae	+++	+	0	+	++	+++	0	+
Amphisbaenidae	+	++	0	+	++	+++	0	+
Typhlopidae	+++	++	0	+	+++	+++	+	+
Leptotyphlopidae	+	+	0	+	++	+++	0	+
Boidae	++	+++	+	+	++	+++	+	+
Colubridae	++	±	0	+	+++	+++	+	±
Elapidae	++	±	0	+	+++	+++	+	±
Hydrophiidae	++	±	0	+	+++	+++	+	±
Viperinae	+++	+	+	+	+++	+++	+	+
Crotalinae	+++	+	+	+	+++	+++	+	+
Testudines	+++	++	0	+	+++	+++	0	+
Crocodilia	+	+	±	+	+++	+++	0	+

AB–PF. Cells stain, after permanganate oxidation, with alcian blue at pH3 and with paraldehyde fuchsin.

C. Cyanophily: an affinity for acid stains with low coefficients of diffusion, such as aniline blue and light green.

E. Erythrophily: an affinity for acid stains with high coefficients of diffusion, such as erythrosin, azocarmin, orange G, and azorubin S.

PAS. Cells give positive reaction with periodic acid-Schiff reagent.
In columns C and E, a + may refer either to large secretory granules or to small erythrophilic spots on a cyanophilic ground.
+++, strong reaction; ++, moderate reaction; +, slight reaction; ±, variable reaction; 0, no reaction.

(Fig. 19 and Table IV). In the Scincidae, Anguidae, and Helodermatidae, the thyrotropic cells are more or less cuboidal with irregular basal nuclei, and are arranged along the blood sinuses of the posterior part of the distal lobe (Fig. 20). In the Colubridae, Elapidae, and Hydrophiidae, these cells are

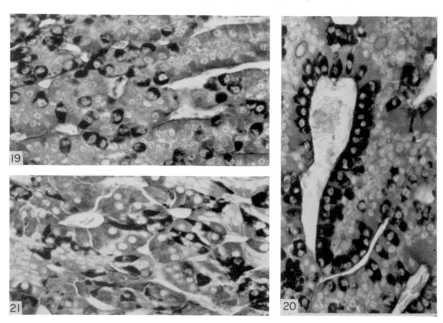

FIGS 19 to 21. Thyrotrophic cells of reptiles. Stained with paraldehyde fuchsin-trichrome, and photographed through an orange filter; × 400.

FIG. 19. *Hoplodactylus pacificus* (Gekkonidae). The rather numerous thyrotrophic cells, in black, are scattered throughout the pars distalis. This section is from the anteromedial region.

FIG. 20. *Anguis fragilis* (Anguidae). The large, prismatic or cuboid thyrotrophic cells, in black, form palisades along the blood sinuses of the posterior region. The alpha cells appear gray.

FIG. 21. *Pseudechis porphyriacus* (Elapidae). The conical or elongated thyrotrophic cells, in black, are scattered throughout the distal lobe in the cords. In this section through the anteromedial region, the gonadotrophic LH cells appear gray.

particularly large and numerous (Figs 21 and 74); they all appear to be erythrophilic, whereas in other forms having large granules of this type, the granules are separated from a cyanophilic substratum. In turtles, the thyrotrophic cells are larger than the gonadotrophic FSH cells.

The alpha cells, the function of which is unknown, are always numerous and restricted to the posterior half of the pars distalis. However, their form and size vary greatly from one family to another (Figs 22 to 25). They are generally prismatic or cuboidal with hemispherical or irregular basal nuclei, but may be lanceolate with ovoid central nuclei. The large, fairly regular

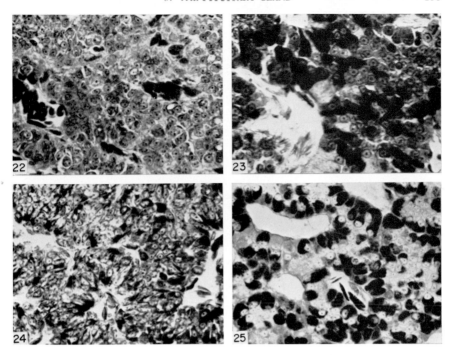

Figs 22 to 25. Alpha cells of reptiles. Stained with trichrome, and photographed through a green filter; × 400.

Fig. 22. *Acanthodactylus scutellatus* (Lacertidae). As in many of the Lacertoidea and Iguania, the alpha cells, which fill the posterior part of the distal lobe, are small and contain very few secretory granules.

Fig. 23. *Anguis fragilis* (Anguidae). The rather large, variably shaped alpha cells, in black, contain many secretory granules. The thyrotrophic cells appear very light gray.

Fig. 24. *Elaphe longissima* (Colubridae). The small, conical or lanceolate alpha cells, in black, are characteristic of the Colubridae, Elapidae, and Hydrophiidae.

Fig. 25. *Cerastes cerastes* (Viperidae). The prismatic or cuboid alpha cells, in black, have basal and often hemispherical nuclei characteristic of the Viperidae (including the Crotalinae).

secretory granules are coloured orange by azan, but are not stained by alcian blue or paraldehyde fuchsin; they are PAS-negative (Table V). The amount of granulation varies greatly both from one family to another and from one individual to another. When the alpha cells lack granules completely, they may appear mauve in azan.

The X cells, generally less numerous than the preceding ones, occur only in the medial or anteromedial parts of the pars distalis, where they often form small homogeneous cellular cords (Fig. 26). In most reptiles they are large, prismatic or elongate ovoid cells, with ovoid basal nuclei. The fairly

TABLE V

Histochemical reactions and staining properties of the alpha and X cells

	Alpha cells AR	X cells AR	PAS
Sphenodontidae	orange–red	orange–red	+
Gekkonidae	yellow or purple	red	0
Xantusiidae	yellow	orange	0
Pygopodidae	yellow	orange	0
Iguanidae	yellow or purple	red	0
Agamidae	yellow or purple	red	0
Chaemaeleonidae	orange	red	+
Lacertidae	yellow or purple	red	±
Teiidae	orange	red	0
Gerrhosaurinae	orange	red	0
Cordylinae	orange	red	0
Scincidae	yellow	red	0
Feyliniidae	red	red	0
Anguidae	orange–red	pink	0
Anniellidae	red	red	0
Helodermatidae	orange–red	rose	0
Varanidae	orange	red	0
Trogonophidae	yellow	red	0
Amphisbaenidae	red	red	0
Typhlopidae	orange	orange	0
Leptotyphlopidae	yellow	pink	0
Boidae	orange–red	orange–red	±
Elapidae	orange–red	orange–red	±
Colubridae	orange–red	orange–red	±
Hydrophiidae	orange–red	orange–red	±
Viperinae	orange–red	pink	±
Crotalinae	orange–red	pink	±
Testudines	orange	red	0
Crocodilia	yellow	red	0

AR.   Staining reaction with azan (Romeis method).
PAS.   Reaction of cells with periodic acid-Schiff reagent: +, positive; ±, variable; 0, negative.

large, abundant secretory granules are distinctly carminophilic in azan and are not stained by alcian blue or paraldehyde fuchsin. In *Sphenodon punctatus*, the Chamaeleonidae, and the Colubroidea, these granules react slightly with PAS. In the Anguidae, Helodermatidae, and Ophidia, the fairly small X cells are greatly reduced in number (Figs 27 and 55); moreover, their staining properties are very similar to those of the alpha cells (Table V). The X cells often tend to be clustered around small pseudofollicles composed of lanceolate cells with elongated central nuclei. Granules are restricted to the supranuclear region.

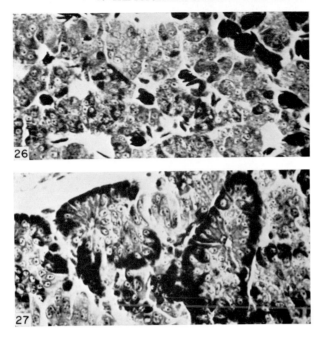

Figs 26 and 27. X cells of reptiles. Stained with trichrome, and photographed through a green filter; × 400.

Fig. 26. *Cerastes cerastes* (Viperidae). The rare and very small X cells appear black.

Fig. 27. *Acanthodactylus erythrurus* (Lacertidae). The X cells, in black, are grouped in small homogeneous cords in the posteromedial region.

The so-called chromophobic or principal cells, small cells lying in the centre of the cellular cords, do not represent a separate category. In most cases, close examination reveals some secretory granules which relate the cells to one or another of the different chromophilic types; the chromophobic types simply represent a stage in their involution. Others are apparently undifferentiated, but the massive hyperplasia of many types of cells, particularly of the gonadotrophic cells at certain stages of their cycle, suggests that the chromophobic cells may become functional. Whether they can be transformed into any cellular type is still being discussed, but the strict localization of the different types of cells in the pars distalis in reptiles does not support this hypothesis. The abundance of involuted or apparently undifferentiated cells varies with the stage of the secretory cycle, and is also a very constant specific character. These cells are particularly rare in the Anguidae, Helodermatidae, and, to a lesser degree, Scincidae (Fig. 29). On the other hand, they are very numerous in the Iguania and Lacertoidea (Fig. 28).

Histochemical studies in a strict sense have only rarely been carried out on reptilian adenohypophyses (Gabe, 1958; Saint Girons, 1959; Herlant and Grignon, 1961). The intracellular secretory granules are always rich in proteins, but the amount of sulphydrylated protein varies with the species and type of cell. A positive reaction with PAS indicates the presence of mucoproteins and is characteristic of the so-called "mucoid" cells, that is the gonadotrophic and thyrotrophic elements; acid mucopolysaccharides are apparently lacking. The few data on reptiles do not permit a useful discussion of the histochemical characteristics of the different types of adenohypophyseal cells. This problem has been treated, for vertebrates in general,

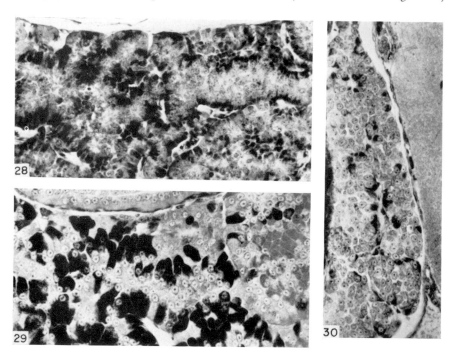

FIGS 28 to 30. Photographs showing the comparative sizes of adenohypophysial cells of reptiles, all × 340.

FIG. 28. *Cnemidophorus tigris* (Teiidae). Stained with paraldehyde fuchsin-trichrome, and photographed through a green filter. The X cells (to the left) and alpha cells (to the right), which are red on the slide, appear black here. Note the small size of the cells and the many involuted or undifferentiated elements at the centre of the cords.

FIG. 29. *Ophisaurus koellikeri* (Anguidae). Stained with PAS, hematoxylin, and orange G, and photographed through a green filter. The gonadotrophic LH cells appear black, and the alpha cells, to the right of the photograph, appear gray. Note the large size of the cells, the regular spheric shape of the nuclei, and the rarity of undifferentiated elements at the centre of the cords.

FIG. 30. *Leptotyphlops dulcis* (Leptotyphlopidae). Stained with trichrome, and photographed through a green filter. The secretory granules of the X and alpha cells appear black. Although the nuclei are relatively large, the cells have extraordinarily little cytoplasm.

in several reviews, notably that of Herlant (1962) which contains an extensive bibliography.

The size of the different cells in the pars distalis evidently varies according to their type and to their stage in the functional cycle, but, taking these factors into account, it is also a specific character (Figs 28, 29 and 30). They are particularly large, with surface areas of about 100 μ^2, in *Sphenodon punctatus*, the Anguidae, the Helodermatidae, *Tiliqua scincoides*, and, to a lesser degree, the Scincidae, Boidae, and Colubroidea. On the other hand, they are relatively small in the Iguania and Lacertoidea, where their average surface area is less than 50 μ^2. In the burrowing reptiles, the adenohypophyseal cells are much smaller than those in related families, but the relative differences between the different systematic groups persist. The cells of the Leptotyphlopidae are particularly small and have a very sparse cytoplasm.

The form of the cells of the pars distalis depends more on their type than on the systematic position of the animal. However, in the Testudines all the cells tend to be characteristically elongated and fusiform (Fig. 80).

The proportion of the different types of chromophilic cells in the distal lobe, without considering some undifferentiated cells, varies with the species studied and the stage of the functional cycle. There are no systematic numerations,* but the following very approximate proportions can be recognized: alpha cells, 25 to 40% (perhaps 50% in the Agamidae); gonadotrophic LH cells, 20 to 35%; gonadotrophic FSH cells and thyrotrophic cells 10 to 20% each; X cells, 5 to 25%.

The relative volume occupied by each cellular type, irrespective of their numbers and aside from seasonal variation, may differ greatly from one family to another. In the Colubridae, Elapidae, Hydrophiidae, Anguidae, and Helodermatidae, the gonadotrophic LH cells fill most of the anterior two-thirds of the pars distalis, and can occupy almost half its total volume (Fig. 71). In contrast, the alpha cells dominate in the Agamidae and Varanidae.

In some mammals, a sixth type of cell, which appears to secrete corticotrophic hormone (ACTH), can be demonstrated after preliminary treatment of the animal. They probably also occur in reptiles in which such cells could easily be confused with more or less degranulated alpha cells.

D. The Pars Tuberalis

In the Rhynchocephalia and Crocodilia, the pars tuberalis consists of small groups of cells forming pseudo-follicles along the ventral surface of the infundibular recess, especially in the vicinity of the median eminence

---

* See, however, Hartmann (1944) and Cieslak (1945) concerning various snakes of the genus *Thamnophis*.

(Fig. 31). These cells, which are slightly larger in the Crocodilia than in *Sphenodon punctatus*, have spherical central nuclei and chromophobic or slightly erythrophilic cytoplasm.

In the Testudines (Fig. 32) the pars tuberalis is continuous with the anterodorsal part of the pars distalis. Besides the numerous small chromophobic cells, there are some large ovoid cells filled with large granules which are moderately PAS-positive and stain strongly with alcian blue and paralde-

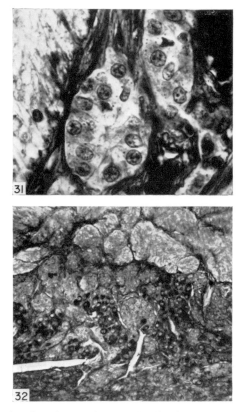

FIGS 31 and 32. Sagittal sections through the pars tuberalis of reptiles.

FIG. 31. *Crocodylus niloticus* (Crocodylidae). Stained with PAS, hematoxylin, and orange G, and photographed through a green filter; × 650. The pars tuberalis is formed by small groups of weakly chromophilic but not involuted cells.

FIG. 32. *Clemmys caspica leprosa* (Testudinidae, Emydinae). Stained with paraldehyde fuchsin-trichrome and photographed through an orange filter; × 100. The pars tuberalis (in the centre) is crossed by the portal vessels and forms a connection between the median eminence (at the top) and the distal lobe (at the bottom). Note the presence of large elements (black in the photograph) which retain strongly the paraldehyde fuchsin and are surrounded by many small, chromophobic cells.

hyde fuchsin. These cells, which resemble slightly the thyrotrophic cells, are also found in very small numbers in the pars tuberalis of *Sphenodon punctatus*.

The Squamata generally lack a pars tuberalis, but sometimes traces of it may be found beside the median eminence in the form of a thin layer of visibly involuted, small chromophobic cells.

IV. Embryonic Development and Vascularization

A. MORPHOGENESIS

Numerous works describe the development of the reptilian hypophysis, which is essentially similar to that in other amniotes; it involves the simultaneous participation of an oral ectodermal bud and of a primordium from the diencephalon (Rathke, 1838 and 1839).

In the Sauria (Hoffmann, 1886; Gaupp, 1893; Zeleny, 1901; Woederman, 1914; Bruni, 1914; Baumgartner, 1916; de Beer, 1926; Wingstrand, 1951; Herlant and Pasteels, 1955; Enemar, 1960; Miller, 1963), a depression appears in the roof of the mouth at the 22–27 somite stage. This primordium of Rathke's pouch deepens rapidly, and its blind, aboral extremity comes into contact with the floor of the diencephalon. A little later, a cavity extends posteriorly within the infundibulum at the level of contact with Rathke's pouch, gradually bending the latter posteriorly. The walls of Rathke's pouch thicken, and the pouch develops a stalk by the contraction from its oral connection. The aboral extremity of the pouch becomes slightly more posterior, and widens out at its contact with the diencephalon. At the same time a diverticulum is formed anteriorly, and two cellular cords, the Anlagen of the pars tuberalis, extend laterally. These three structures extend progressively towards the diencephalon and become connected to it, the first at the level of the future median eminence and the other two slightly more dorsolaterally.

Next, the hypophyseal canal closes completely, and the lumen of Rathke's pouch is gradually filled by the formation of cellular cords. Thus the adenohypophysis consists of an anterior (oral) lobe formed from two narrow, elongate lateral expansions and of a posterior (aboral) lobe, which is enlarged at its posterior end. This enlarged area becomes the intermediate lobe, which is more or less distinct depending on the species; the anterior lobe and the anterior part of the posterior lobe fuse to form the pars distalis. However, as Wingstrand (1951) has demonstrated in both birds and reptiles, the adenohypophyseal cytology, even in the adult, shows traces of this initial separation. The infundibular recess, originally elongated posteriorly, swells at its posterior end, but the pituitary stalk remains largely open. It is at this stage that the hypophyseal portal system, which will provide most or all of the blood supply to the distal lobe of the adult, is established.

During the second half of embryonic development, the hypophysis slowly assumes its definitive form. The neural lobe enlarges and differentiates, the intermediate lobe becomes even further separated from the anterior part of the original posterior lobe, and the pars distalis completes its differentiation. The hypophyseal cleft is reduced and may disappear completely within the distal lobe, but it persists within the intermediate lobe where it extends around the neural lobe to a variable degree. Finally, the pars tuberalis atrophies and loses its contact with the distal lobe; at birth it is represented only by two cellular islets attached to the floor of the diencephalon on either side of the median eminence.

The hypophyseal development in other reptiles hardly differs from that which has just been described. However, in the Ophidia (Rathke, 1839; Sasse, 1886; Hoffmann, 1886; Baumgartner, 1916; Wingstrand, 1951; Enemar, 1960), the distal lobe takes up, well after birth, a position lateral to the mass formed by the complex of the neural and intermediate lobes. The atrophy of the pars tuberalis seems more marked than in lizards; on the other hand, the pars nervosa continues to thicken during the last weeks of embryonic development and only in the adult assumes the large and full form already described (Fig. 33). In *Sphenodon* (Gisi, 1908; Wyeth and Row, 1923), the Crocodilia (Reese, 1910; Baumgartner, 1916), and especially the Testudines (Zeleny, 1901; Woederman, 1914; Baumgartner, 1916; Sprankel, 1956), there is no involution of the pars tuberalis; even when the latter loses its lateral contact with the distal lobe, well-developed cellular cords are retained on the infundibular floor.

All recent workers agree that the diencephalic floor plays an inductive role in the differentiation of the intermediate lobe. In *Chamaeleo bitaeniatus*, a species with a marked ability of changing colour and a hypertrophied intermediate lobe, the area of attachment of the base of Rathke's pouch to the infundibular floor is more extensive in the earliest stages than in the Scincidae and Lacertidae (Herlant and Pasteels, 1955); this characteristic persists throughout life.

At birth, the morphology of the hypophysis is quite similar to that of the adult, except that the posterior part of the pars distalis is proportionally smaller. In *Vipera aspis*, the only species in which this phenomenon has been studied in detail, the development of this region occurs during the first weeks of life, rather than at the time of sexual maturity.

B. CYTOGENESIS

Although the morphology of the hypophysis of numerous reptiles of all orders and most suborders has long been studied, the differentiation of the various glandular cells during embryonic growth is still very poorly known, having been described in only two works, one on a snake and one on a lizard.

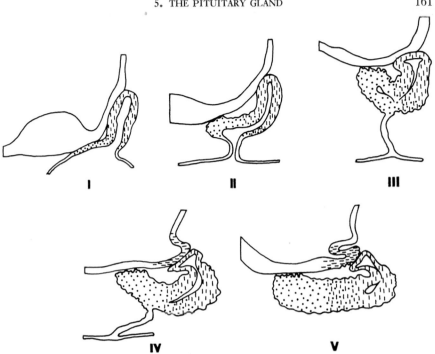

FIG. 33. Embryonic stages in the development of the hypophysis of *Natrix natrix* (Colubridae), after Enemar (1960). The aboral or posterior lobe of Rathke's pouch is indicated by vertical dashes, the oral or anterior lobe of Rathke's pouch by stipples, and the infundibular recess by horizontal dashes.

In *Vipera aspis* (Saint Girons, 1961b), secretory granules first appear in the adenohypophysis at about the middle of gestation, shortly after the establishment of a vascular connection between the median eminence and the anterior end of the pars distalis (Figs 34 and 35). Both thyrotrophic cells posteriorly and gonadotrophic FSH cells medially and laterally can be recognized in the well formed distal lobe, which already has a hypophyseal cleft. A little later, the gonadotrophic LH cells differentiate in the anterior part of the pars distalis. In the second third of gestation some erythrophilic cells, the X cells, are recognizable in the anteromedial region; 8 to 15 days later secretory products appear in the cells of the intermediate lobe. Only at the end of embryonic development, or sometimes even after birth, do cells of the last adenohypophyseal type, the alpha cells, differentiate in the posterior region which is then developing rapidly. The secretory granules of the adenohypophyseal cells have, from their first appearance, the same staining properties and histochemical characteristics as in the adult.

At birth, most of the differentiated adenohypophyseal cells show signs of

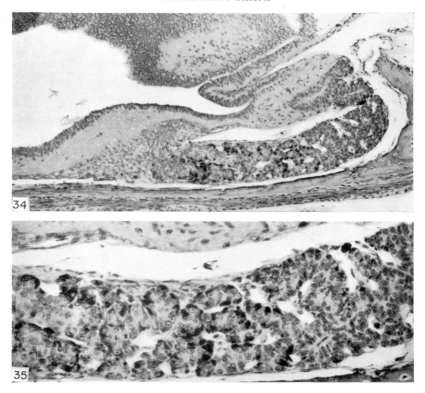

FIG. 34. Hypophysis of a two-thirds developed embryo of *Vipera aspis* (Viperidae). Stained with PAS, hematoxylin, and orange G, and photographed through a green filter. Note the development of the pars terminalis, the already clear differentiation of the intermediate lobe near the massive neural lobe, and the presence of secretory granules in certain cells of the distal lobe.

FIG. 35. Detail of the section shown in Fig. 34. Gonadotrophic LH cells appear black and X cells gray in the anterior region of the pars distalis (left side of the photograph). Gonadotrophic FSH cells occur in the centre. The rare chromophilic elements in the posterior region (right side of the photograph) represent the thyrotrophic cells.

functional activity and are more or less non-granular and vacuolated. This pattern is retained until the onset of hibernation; then many cells, which had been chromophobic, differentiate. The numbers of alpha cells and, to a lesser degree, thyrotrophic cells increase the most. For two to three years, until the approach of sexual maturity, the histology of the distal lobe changes very little; the gonadotrophic FSH cells are quiescent, the gonadotrophic LH cells are clearly involuted, the numerous large X cells are apparently active, and, as in the adults, the alpha cells are first large and filled with secretory granules and later become more or less non-granular and of variable size.

In *Xantusia vigilis* (Miller, 1963), which has an embryonic period of about

13 weeks, the first secretory granules, partially PAS-positive, appear in the adenohypophysis of 8mm (about 5 week old) embryos. By the middle of the gestation period, in 9 to 10mm embryos, the gonadotrophic LH (gamma) cells anteriorly, the gonadotrophic FSH (beta) and thyrotrophic (delta) cells posteriorly and medially, and the cells of the intermediate lobe are clearly differentiated. However, although PAS-positive products are fairly abundant, no secretory granules stain with paraldehyde fuchsin. Later the different types of cells come to resemble those of the adult. The alpha cells differentiate only about two weeks before birth; as in some Gekkonidae, X cells and alpha cells cannot be distinguished even in adults.

The results obtained in this lizard and the snake *Vipera* are therefore very similar; however, definitive secretory granules tend to appear at slightly earlier stages in *Xantusia vigilis*.

The cytogenesis of the hypothalamo-neurohypophyseal tract is even less well known than that of the adenohypophysis. In *Vipera aspis*, neurosecretory products detectable by paraldehyde fuchsin, alcian blue, or chromic hematoxylin, after permanganic oxidation first appear in very small quantities in the median eminence, and their appearance is noted in the neural lobe at the end of the second third of gestation, at about the same time as secretion appears in the gonadotrophic LH cells and the X cells. Secretory products only become abundant in the pars nervosa during the first hibernation.

In *Xantusia vigilis* (Miller, 1963), neurosecretory products appear in the median eminence and in the neural lobe in 9 to 10mm embryos (near the middle of the gestation period), and their quantity increases noticeably until birth. *Xantusia* and *Vipera aspis* thus differ considerably, but it should be remembered that neurosecretory products are generally much more abundant in lizards than in snakes.

C. VASCULARIZATION

The physiological importance of the blood supply to the hypophysis has provoked numerous anatomical studies; those of Green (1951), Wingstrand (1951), and Diepen (1952) deal with reptiles. More recently, Enemar (1960) has studied the development of the vascular system in some squamates. This last work contains an extensive bibliography.

In the Reptilia, the blood supply to the hypophysis is fundamentally the same as in the other amniotes. Its essential characteristic is the presence of a portal system which supplies the distal lobe with venous blood from the capillaries of the primary plexus in the median eminence.

In lizards (*Anolis carolinensis*, Green, 1951; various lacertids and *Anguis fragilis*, Wingstrand, 1951, Diepen, 1952, Enemar, 1960), the hypophysis appears to receive all its blood from the infundibular arteries, which arise

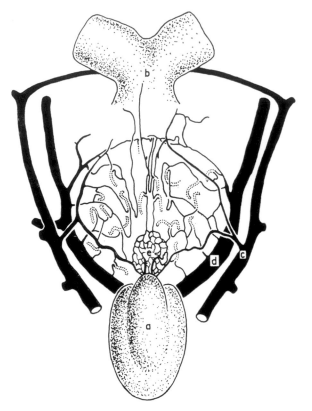

FIG. 36. *Lacerta agilis* (Lacertidae). Ventral view of the blood vessels of the hypothalamus between the optic chiasma and the hypophysis, after Enemar (1960). Ink rejection followed by clearing in benzyl benzoate. The course of the capillary loops penetrating the cerebral wall (dotted lines) are somewhat simplified in the drawing. a, Hypophysis; b, optic chiasma; c, anterior ramus of the internal carotid branching off the infundibular artery; d, vein draining the hypophysis; e, primary plexus on the median eminence. Two portal vessels are visible.

from the anterior ramus of the internal carotid (Fig. 36). The infundibular artery divides into an anterior branch, which extends to the vicinity of the optic chiasma, and a posterior branch, which is nearer the hypophysis and provides its major blood supply. At the level of the median eminence, the capillaries covering the infundibular floor form a very dense primary plexus which does not penetrate deeply into the neural tissue. The capillaries unite to form four to six rather elongate portal vessels, thus providing the connection with the anterodorsal part of the pars distalis. There they form a secondary plexus which supplies the entire distal lobe. Capillaries from the primary network of the median eminence vascularize the pars nervosa and the pars intermedia; these capillaries do not penetrate the neural lobe, but, in *Anolis carolinensis*, lie between the cellular cords of the hypertrophied intermediate lobe. The retrohypophyseal vein receives all the blood from the hypophysis.

In snakes (*Thamnophis sirtalis*, Green, 1951; *Natrix natrix*, Wingstrand, 1951, Enemar, 1960; *Vipera berus*, Wingstrand, 1951; Diepen, 1952), the primary plexus of the medium eminence is particularly well developed, and the portal vessels are often more numerous (6–8) and larger than in lizards. The neural lobe receives a few capillaries from the median eminence, but most of its blood supply is from arterioles originating directly from the infundibular arteries. The capillaries do not penetrate the neural tissue, but accompany the connective tissue septa which divide it into many lobules; they also surround the intermediate lobe. Because of the large area of contact between them, the pars intermedia undoubtedly receives, especially postero-ventrally, some blood from the pars distalis. Most of the blood supply to the distal lobe is provided by the important hypophyseal portal system which joins the anterior end of the distal lobe to the median eminence; however, the pars distalis also receives some arterioles directly from the internal carotids.

The vascularization of the hypophysis of turtles (*Chrysemys picta*, Green, 1951, Taylor, 1952; *Testudo graeca*, Diepen, 1952, Grignon and Grignon, 1962) and crocodilians (*Alligator mississippiensis*, Green, 1951) resembles closely that of snakes. However, in turtles and crocodilians, the portal must cross the cellular cords of the pars tuberalis before reaching the anterodorsal surface of the pars distalis.

Inter-carotid anastomoses, which are characteristic of birds (Wingstrand, 1951), occur in the Testudines and the Crocodilia. They are absent in the Lepidosauria and mammals. Posterior to the distal lobes, the cavernous sinuses of turtles and crocodilians are replaced by a simple enlarged transverse vein in the Lepidosauria.

The positions and courses of the larger vessels have been little studied in reptiles, but the essential point—that the pars distalis is supplied with venous blood originating from the median eminence—has been well demonstrated in all the orders.

V. Comparative Morphology of the Reptilian Hypophysis

A. General

It is impossible to consider the detailed anatomy and cytology of the hypophyses of all the reptiles that have been studied. A brief summary is given for each family, paying particular attention to characteristic points and to differences from the general descriptions given in the previous sections.

B. Rhynchocephalia

The neurohypophysis of *Sphenodon punctatus* is of the saurian type, and the infundibular recess penetrates it deeply (Fig. 37). The median eminence

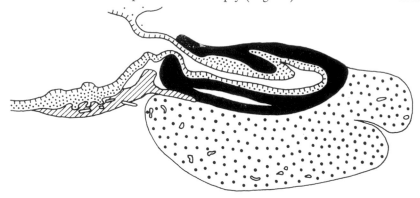

Fig. 37. Sagittal section through the hypophysis of *Sphenodon punctatus* (Sphenodontidae). The neural lobe and regions with many neurosecretory fibres are indicated by fine stippling, the distal lobe by coarse stippling, the intermediate lobe by black, and the pars tuberalis by diagonal lines.

is characterized by the neurosecretory fibres passing through the ventral limiting glia towards the capillaries.

The intermediate lobe surrounds the posterior two-thirds of the distal lobe. It is made up of the two typical layers; as in all large reptiles, the internal layer is festooned and largely formed by true cellular cords. The tall, prismatic intermediate cells contain fine, barely chromophilic granules.

The massive distal lobe is connected to the intermediate lobe only by a very narrow bridge. The gonadotrophic LH cells show no special peculiarities. The gonadotrophic FSH cells, scattered throughout the distal lobe, are particularly rare and weakly chromophilic. The thyrotrophic cells, which are more numerous than the former, are also scattered throughout or sometimes clustered in small groups; they contain large granules or a few small erythrophilic particles on a cyanophilic base. The very numerous alpha cells lack granules in the posterior third of the pars distalis, but contain many fairly large ones in the central third. The X cells show the same staining properties as the alpha cells, but are easily distinguished by their elongate ovoid form, their location in small homogeneous cellular cords at the anterior end of the pars distalis, and their positive reaction to PAS.

C. Sauria

1. *Gekkonidae*

The median eminence and the neural lobe show no peculiarities. The large intermediate lobe almost completely surrounds the pars nervosa, and its two layers are separated by a continuous hypophyseal cleft. The epithelium of the internal layer is simple and formed by high columnar cells; the external layer is squamous (Figs 6 and 38).

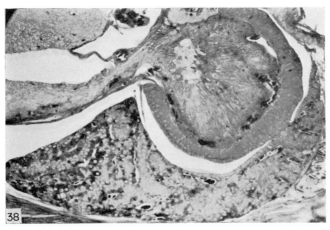

FIG. 38. Sagittal section through the hypophysis of *Hemidactylus turcicus* (Gekkonidae). Stained with paraldehyde fuchsin-trichrome and photographed through a green filter. Note the form of the distal lobe which is characteristic of the Gekkota, as well as the hypertrophy of the internal layer of the intermediate lobe and the atrophy of the almost endotheliform external layer of the latter lobe.

The distal lobe, which is attached to the posteroventral side of the intermediate lobe, has a characteristic form with a well-developed anterior region and a flattened posterior region. The relatively few gonadotrophic LH cells are ovoid and scattered throughout the anterior half (Fig. 39). The gonadotrophic FSH cells, often prismatic, are more numerous in the central region

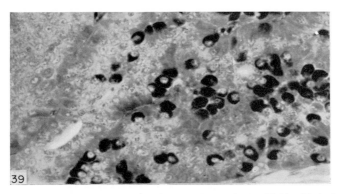

FIG. 39. Anterior region of the pars distalis of *Tarentola mauritanica* (Gekkonidae). Stained with PAS, hematoxylin, and orange G, and photographed through a green filter; ×400. The gonadotrophic LH cells, in black, are rather scattered and more or less ovoid in the Gekkota. The X cells, in gray, are often elongated.

and contain fine cyanophilic granules. The few thyrotrophic cells are scattered throughout the lobe and are prismatic or conical with numerous large granules (Fig. 19). The alpha cells, localized in the flat posterior region, are particularly small and few in number; they are generally only slightly granular. The larger X cells, which are fairly numerous in the anterior region, contain numerous, medium-sized secretory granules.

2. Pygopodidae

The hypophysis of *Delma fraseri* (Fig. 40) is entirely like those of the Gekkonidae, but that of *Lialis burtonis* shows a number of peculiarities. The sella turcica of the latter is shallower, and the complex of neural and inter-

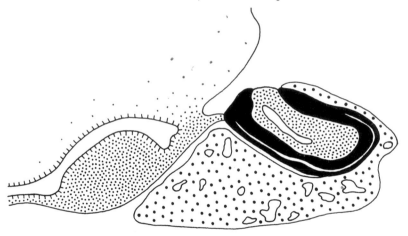

FIG. 40. Sagittal section through the hypophysis of *Delma fraseri* (Pygopodidae). The neural lobe and regions with many neurosecretory fibres are indicated by the fine stippling, the distal lobe by coarse stippling, and the intermediate lobe by black.

mediate lobes tends to lie posterior to the distal lobe and on almost the same horizontal plane, although the posterior part of the pars nervosa is completely flat. Moreover, the median eminence has a narrow attachment to the diencephalon. The intermediate lobe is well developed, and its festooned internal layer tends to form cellular cords. Except in this last character, the hypophysis of *Lialis burtonis* suggests the condition in fossorial lizards. The gonadotrophic LH cells are large and numerous, do not retain hematoxylin lakes, and are strongly erythrophilic. However, the hypophysis of *Lialis* basically resembles that of the gekkonids.

3. Xantusiidae

The hypophyses of *Xantusia vigilis* and *X. henshawi* closely resemble those of the Gekkonidae and *Delma fraseri*. However, the intermediate lobe is a little less developed and slightly less flat posteriorly, and the alpha cells, which are larger and contain many secretory granules, hardly differ from the X cells.

4. Iguanidae

The neural lobe is fairly large, irregularly shaped, and deeply penetrated by the infundibular recess. The small intermediate lobe caps the posterior third or half of the pars nervosa; it is formed by small, irregular cellular cords containing numerous involuted cells (Fig. 7).

The form of the rather small distal lobe varies. The often parallel cellular cords are separated by numerous, elongate, very small vascular sinuses and contain many undifferentiated cells. The few gonadotrophic LH cells are restricted to the anterior end; they are small and weakly chromophilic. The more numerous gonadotrophic FSH cells are concentrated ventromedially; they contain fine secretory granules and sometimes some small, regular particles (Figs 42 and 43). The fairly numerous thyrotrophic cells are scattered throughout the gland and always have large dense granules. The moderate-sized alpha cells contain fairly fine and rather weakly orangophilic granules, and are abundant posteriorly (Figs 10 and 41). The X cells, which are a little larger than the preceding ones and may also be numerous, are restricted to the anterior half of the lobe; their secretory granules are fairly large, strongly staining, and carminophilic. Generally the adenohypophyseal cells are small; the nuclei, which are often irregular but poor in chromatin, are also small.

The hypophysis of *Anolis* is characterized by a considerable hypertrophy of the intermediate lobe (Fig. 10). The latter, which represents more than two-thirds of the hypophyseal volume, is made up of thick cords formed of large, regularly arranged prismatic cells; their very abundant secretory product appears as large erythrophilic granules which are PAS-negative, but stain strongly with alcian blue and paraldehyde fuchsin. The distal lobe is reduced to a long, thin strip lying ventral to the intermediate lobe.

5. Agamidae

The neural lobe is quite small and narrow. The well-developed inter-mediate lobe, formed from numerous, fairly thick cellular cords, almost completely encloses it (Fig. 44). The tall, prismatic intermediate cells contain fine, weakly chromophilic granules.

The rather elongate and narrow distal lobe is slightly enlarged anteriorly and is formed from thick, irregular cellular cords with many undifferentiated cells. The rare gonadotrophic LH cells are restricted to the anterior end and contain many, rather large, weakly chromophilic granules. The gonadotrophic FSH cells are common in the anterior and anteromedial regions and have

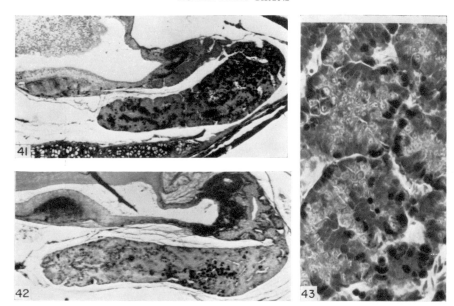

FIG. 41. Sagittal section through the hypophysis of *Sceloporus graciosus* (Iguanidae). Stained with paraldehyde fuchsin-trichrome and photographed through a green filter. The alpha cells in the posterior region of the pars distalis (to the right of the photograph) and X cells in the anterior region (to the left) appear black.

FIG. 42. Sagittal section through the hypophysis of *Uma inornata* (Iguanidae). Stained with alcian blue and PAS and photographed through an orange filter. The small, scattered thyrotrophic cells in the distal lobe appear black as do the larger gonadotrophic FSH cells which are concentrated in a characteristic way in the posteromedial zone. Note also the chromophily of the cells at the periphery of the cords in the intermediate lobe and the abundance of neurosecretory product in the neural lobe and median eminence.

FIG. 43. Median region of the pars distalis of *Uta stansburiana* (Iguanidae). Stained with PAS, hematoxylin, and orange G, and photographed through a green filter; ×400. The gonadotrophic FSH cells, in black, are small as in many Iguanidae. Both alpha and X cells occur in this zone and appear gray.

fine, weakly chromophilic granules (Figs 45 and 46). The conical thyrotrophic cells are scattered throughout the gland and contain fairly large cyanophilic granules. The alpha cells are generally non-granular and small; they occupy most of the posterior two-thirds of the pars distalis. The X cells are larger and much less numerous than the preceding ones; they have fairly large carminophilic granules and form rare, almost homogeneous cellular cords in the anterior region. The nuclei of the adenohypophyseal cells are generally small and irregular.

6. *Chamaeleonidae*

The morphology of the hypophysis is extremely homogeneous in the known representatives of this family; there is a moderate-sized, slightly

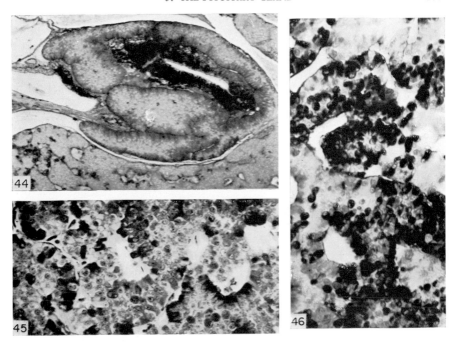

FIG. 44. Sagittal section through the neural lobe and hypertrophied intermediate lobe of *Agama impalearis* (Agamidae). Stained with alcian blue and PAS, and photographed through an orange filter; × 100. Note the many chromophobic cells in the large cords of the intermediate lobe. The scattered, small thyrotrophic and some of the clustered gonadotrophic cells in the distal lobe (bottom of the figure) appear black.

FIG. 45. Anterior region of the pars distalis of *Agama impalearis* (Agamidae). Stained with trichrome and photographed through a green filter; × 250. The X cells appear black, the gonadotrophic LH cells gray, and the gonadotrophic FSH cells and rare thyrotrophic cells very light gray.

FIG. 46. Section adjacent to that in Fig. 45. Stained with alcian blue and PAS, and photographed through an orange filter; × 250. The gonadotrophic FSH cells, as well as some small thyrotrophic cells, appear black. The gonadotrophic LH cells are light gray, and the X cells colourless.

flattened neural lobe, a well-developed intermediate lobe which extends mainly lateral and posterior to the neural lobe, and a massive distal lobe (Fig. 47). The cords of the intermediate lobe are regular, with large prismatic cells containing fine weakly chromophilic granules.

As in the two preceding families, the few gonadotrophic LH cells are weakly chromophilic and restricted to the anterior end of the pars distalis. The numerous gonadotrophic FSH cells are scattered throughout the anterior two-thirds, but are distinctly commoner ventrally; they contain fine granules. The few scattered thyrotrophic cells are small and have large cyanophilic granules. The rather large alpha cells are common posteriorly and contain a variable number of large orangophilic secretory granules. The

X cells, concentrated in the medial and anteromedial regions, have large carminophilic granules which are peculiar in being strongly PAS-positive. The undifferentiated cells at the centre of the cellular cords, while numerous,

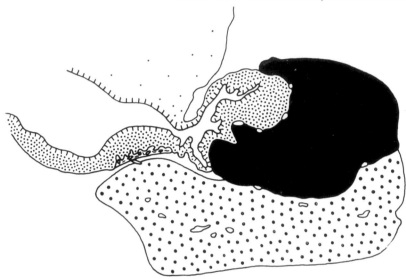

FIG. 47. Sagittal section through the hypophysis of *Chamaeleo lateralis* (Chamaeleonidae.) The neural lobe and regions with many neurosecretory fibres are indicated by fine stippling, the distal lobe by coarse stippling, and the intermediate lobe by black.

are slightly less common than in the two preceding families. The nuclei of the adenohypophyseal cells are large and poor in chromatin, but are very irregular and often divided.

7. *Lacertidae*

The small neural lobe is ovoid with an extended longitudinal axis. The poorly developed intermediate lobe surrounds the posteroventral half of the pars nervosa. It is made up of two or three rows of cells, variable in form, some being involuted while others contain rather weakly staining granules of moderate size. The hypophyseal cleft is often reduced.

The massive distal lobe is formed by thick cellular cords with many undifferentiated cells. There are hardly any blood sinuses. The few, highly chromophilic gonadotrophic LH cells are restricted to the anterior end of the lobe (Fig. 48). The equally rare gonadotrophic FSH cells have rather weakly staining, very fine granules and generally occur in the ventromedial region. The thyrotrophic cells are smaller than the preceding ones and are scattered throughout the distal lobe; they contain a variable number of large cyanophilic granules. The alpha cells, which are very numerous posteriorly, are small and usually non-granular (Fig. 22). On the other hand, the X cells, which are collected in homogeneous cords or sometimes in small, regular pseudo-follicles in the anteromedial region, are always filled with carminophilic secretory granules (Fig. 26). The nuclei of the adenohypophyseal cells are generally small and irregular; although not really abundant, the chromatin is less scanty in lacertids, and indeed in most lacertoids, than in most other reptiles.

In *Acanthodactylus scutellatus* (but not in some other members of this genus) the distinctly hypertrophied intermediate lobe is formed by large,

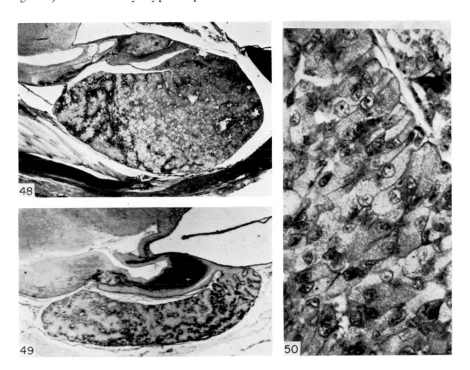

FIG. 48. Sagittal section through the hypophysis of *Psammodromus algirus* (Lacertidae). Stained with PAS, hematoxylin, and orange G, and photographed through a green filter. Note the small size of the neural and intermediate lobes, and the massive form of the distal lobe. The gonadotrophic LH cells, in black, are restricted to the anterior quarter of the pars distalis.

FIG. 49. Sagittal section through the hypophysis of *Cnemidophorus tigris* (Teiidae). Stained with alcian blue and PAS, and photographed through an orange filter. The general shape of the hypophysis resembles that seen in numerous Iguanidae, but the intermediate lobe is clearly of the lacertoidean type. The gonadotrophic FSH and thyrotrophic cells appear black in the pars distalis.

FIG. 50. Intermediate lobe of *Acanthodactylus scutellatus* (Lacertidae). Stained with PAS, hematoxylin, and orange G, and photographed through a green filter; × 650. The hypertrophied intermediate lobe of this species is formed of large cells which are more or less filled with weakly chromophilic secretory granules.

irregular cellular cords like those of other lacertids, but made up of much larger cells with more secretory products (Fig. 50).

8. *Teiidae*

The neural and intermediate lobes are similar to those of the Lacertidae. However, the hypophyseal cleft is more distinct and, in the posteroventral part of the intermediate lobe, delimits the two characteristic layers.

The distal lobe is long and narrow (Fig. 49). The irregular cellular cords contain many undifferentiated cells. There are fairly numerous, elongate vascular sinuses, particularly in the posterior region. The different types of cells of the pars distalis do not differ significantly from those of the Lacertidae. The gonadotrophic FSH cells resemble closely the thyrotrophic cells.

9. *Cordylidae* (*including the Gerrhosaurinae*)

The hypophyses of the few studied representatives of this family generally resemble those of the Lacertidae and the Teiidae. They differ in the greater number of gonadotrophic LH and FSH cells. The latter contain large granules similar to those of the thyrotrophic cells.

10. *Scincidae*

The hypophyses of the Scincidae differ markedly from all those that have already been described. The pyriform neural lobe is quite deeply penetrated by the infundibular recess. The intermediate lobe, which covers the postero-ventral half and the lateral parts of the neural lobe, is made up of a high columnar internal layer of cells and a squamous external layer, except postero-medially where it is invaded by numerous alpha cells (Fig. 51).

The elongate pars distalis has a fairly constant thickness and is formed by distinct cellular cords, which are rather thin and contain few undifferentiated cells. There are some small, elongate vascular sinuses. Gonadotrophic LH cells are numerous in the anterior half; they are large with moderate-sized granules and are arranged regularly along the cords (Fig. 16). The ovoid or spherical gonadotrophic FSH cells are scattered throughout the anterior two-thirds of the lobe and contain both large cyanophilic granules and small erythrophilic particles. The cuboidal thyrotrophic cells, which are restricted to the posterior third or half of the pars distalis, are smaller than the preceding ones, but have an apparently identical secretory product. The orangophilic alpha cells are numerous in the posterior half; they are generally small and non-granular (Fig. 52). The X cells, which form small homogeneous cords anteriorly, are always larger and densely filled with moderate-sized, carminophilic granules. In all species, the nuclei are rather small and often irregular and very poor in chromatin. In *Tiliqua scincoides* the adenohypophyseal cells are particularly large.

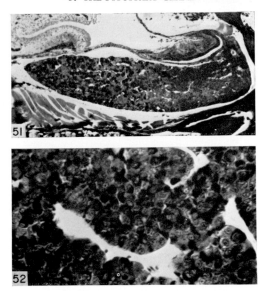

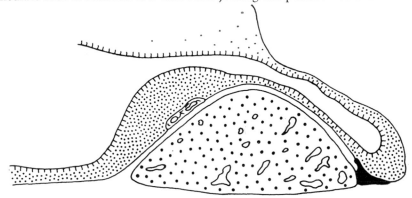

FIG. 51. Sagittal section through the hypophysis of *Egernia* sp. (Scincidae). Stained with PAS, hematoxylin, and orange G, and photographed through a green filter. Note the form of the intermediate lobe, formed by two regular layers separated by a continuous hypophysial cleft, and the abundance of gonadotrophic LH cells (black in the photograph) in the anterior region of the pars distalis.

FIG. 52. *Ablepharus boutonii* (Scincidae). Stained with trichrome, and photographed through a green filter; × 400. The numerous alpha cells in the posterior region appear black, but are small and, as in many Lacertoidea, have few secretory granules.

11. *Feyliniidae*

The wide neural lobe lies posterior to the distal lobe (Fig. 53). The intermediate lobe is reduced to a thin band joining the posteromedial end of the

FIG. 53. Sagittal section through the hypophysis of *Feylinia currori* (Feyliniidae). The neural lobe and regions with many neurosecretory fibres are indicated by fine stippling, the distal lobe by coarse stippling, and the intermediate lobe by black.

neural lobe to the posterior end of the pars distalis; it has layers of small, apparently non-functional, cuboidal chromophobic cells. The distal lobe is enclosed between the median eminence and the pars nervosa. As in all limbless burrowing reptiles, the sella turcica is poorly developed and the hypophysis is extremely flattened dorsoventrally.

The cellular cords of the pars distalis are narrow and contain few undifferentiated cells. The different types of cells are poorly localized and difficult to recognize; the gonadotrophic FSH and thyrotrophic cells, and the alpha and X cells cannot be distinguished. The gonadotrophic LH cells are concentrated anterodorsally.

12. *Anguidae*

The neural and intermediate lobes resemble those of the Scincidae. The part of the large distal lobe posterior to the intermediate lobe is slightly incurved dorsally. Its cellular cords are distinct and almost completely devoid of undifferentiated cells. The numerous, very large vascular sinuses give a characteristic appearance to the posterior part of this lobe (Fig. 54).

The many, very large gonadotrophic LH cells occupy much of the anterior half of the pars distalis and contain fairly fine but very densely staining granules (Fig. 55). The gonadotrophic FSH cells, which are scattered throughout the anterior half, resemble those of the Scincidae (Fig. 56). The same is true of the cuboidal thyrotrophic cells which are regularly arranged along the large blood sinuses of the posterior region (Fig. 57). On the other hand, the more or less carminophilic alpha cells are large, prismatic, and almost always filled with moderate-sized granules. The rather few X cells are concentrated in small groups anteromedially; their granules resemble those of the alpha cells, but are distinctly less abundant. Most adenohypophyseal cells of the Anguidae are particularly large, as are the nuclei which are poor in chromatin and have very distinct nucleoli.

13. *Anniellidae*

The hypophysis of *Anniella* clearly shows adaptations to a fossorial life, but a little less than that of some other reptiles. The spherical neural lobe lies lateral to the distal lobe; the infundibular recess penetrates it deeply, but it is very flat and its lumen is almost completely closed. The poorly developed intermediate lobe is of the usual lacertilian form, and the cells of its internal layer appear functional. The ovoid distal lobe is formed from distinct cellular cords which are almost devoid of undifferentiated cells. There are numerous, very large blood sinuses in the posterior part of this lobe.

As in the Feyliniidae, only three types of chromophilic cells can be distinguished in the pars distalis, and they are not well localized. The nuclei are often more irregular than in the Anguidae, but the presence of large

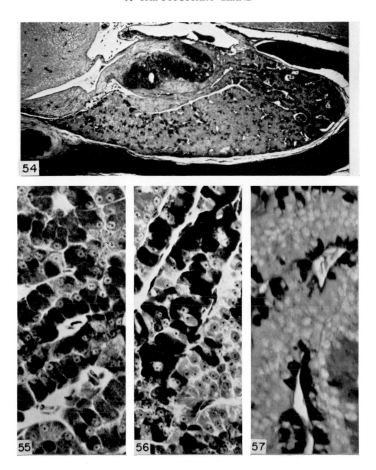

FIG. 54. Sagittal section through the hypophysis of *Anguis fragilis* (Anguidae). Stained with paralde-hyde fuchsin-trichrome, and photographed through an orange filter. Note the massive form of the hypophysis and the development of the posterior region of the pars distalis and of the vascular sinuses which occur there. The gonadotrophic FSH cells, scattered through the anterior two-thirds of the pars distalis, and the thyrotrophic cells, numerous in the posterior third, appear black.

FIGS 55 to 57. Different types of cells in the pars distalis of *Ophisaurus koellikeri* (Anguidae). × 400.

FIG. 55. Anterior region. Stained with trichrome, and photographed through a green filter. Some small, black X cells may be recognized among the numerous, large, dark gray gonadotrophic LH cells.

FIG. 56. Middle region. Stained with erythrosin, aniline blue, and orange G, and photographed through a green filter. Some gonadotrophic FSH cells, involuted in this specimen, appear lighter than the surrounding alpha cells.

FIG. 57. Posterior region. Stained with alcian blue and PAS, and photographed through an orange filter. The thyrotrophic cells appear black along the vascular sinuses.

vascular sinuses in the distal lobe, the relatively large size of the cells, the scarcity of undifferentiated elements, and the histochemical characteristics of the gonadotrophic LH cells demonstrate the close relationship between the Anguidae and the Anniellidae.

14. *Helodermatidae*

The hypophyses of *Heloderma suspectum* and *H. horridum* are almost identical to those of the Anguidae, the only difference being that the intermediate lobe is a little smaller in *Heloderma*.

15. *Varanidae*

In contrast, the hypophyses of the Varanidae are completely different from those of the preceding families (Fig. 58). The quite large neural lobe has

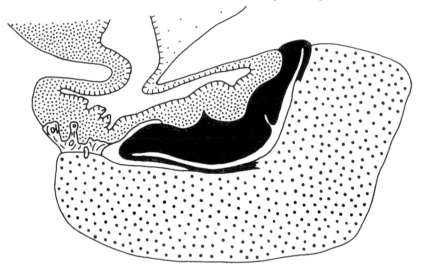

FIG. 58. Sagittal section through the hypophysis of *Varanus niloticus* (Varanidae). The neural lobe and regions with many neurosecretory fibres are indicated by fine stippling, the distal lobe by coarse stippling, and the intermediate lobe by black.

many neurosecretory fibres and is largely surrounded by the voluminous intermediate lobe. The latter is made of thick cellular cords separated by connective tissue septa. The cords contain both weakly chromophilic polyhedric cells and distinctly involuted cells (Fig. 61).

The thick, massive distal lobe is lodged in a very deep sella turcica. It is almost completely devoid of vascular sinuses. The gonadotrophic LH cells, which are restricted to the anterior third, are weakly chromophilic and PAS-negative. One type of cell is difficult to identify: rare, very chromophilic ovoid cells restricted to the ventromedial region. Other, slightly smaller cells

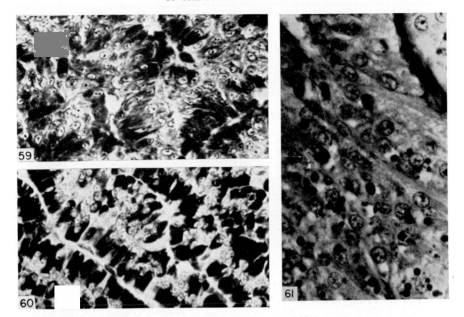

FIGS 59 to 61. Adenohypophysial cells of *Varanus griseus* (Varanidae).

FIG. 59. Middle region of the pars distalis. Stained with erythrosin, aniline blue, and orange G, and photographed through a green filter; × 400. The long, sinous X cells appear dark gray or black. Some prismatic alpha cells, especially near the top of the photograph, also appear black.

FIG. 60. Posterior region of the pars distalis. Stained with trichrome, and photographed through a green filter; × 400. The numerous alpha cells appear black, and the rare gonadotrophic FSH or thyrotrophic cells are lighter.

FIG. 61. Intermediate lobe. Stained with PAS, hematoxylin, and orange G, and photographed through a green filter; × 650. The intermediate lobe of varanids is very well developed, but formed of cells of variable size and shape. There are frequently small erythrophilic vacuoles that appear black in the photograph.

are fairly numerous and scattered throughout the pars distalis; they contain few granules. The very numerous alpha cells are filled with orangophilic secretory granules and occupy much of the posterior and medial regions (Fig. 60). The abundant X cells, which are restricted to the anterior third, are often very elongate and contain dense carminophilic secretory granules (Fig. 59). Most of the nuclei are fairly small, irregular, and poor in chromatin.

D. AMPHISBAENIA

1. *Amphisbaenidae*

The ovoid, elongate neural lobe lies posterodorsal to the distal lobe into which it is strongly pressed along a median groove; the extremely flat infundibular recess does not penetrate it very deeply (Fig. 64). The well-developed median eminence lies near the distal lobe. The intermediate lobe is reduced to a long thin band ventral to the pars nervosa and appears to lack functional cells.

The large, columnar gonadotrophic LH cells are common in the anterior half of the pars distalis (Fig. 65). The gonadotrophic FSH cells are scattered throughout the lobe and contain rather lightly staining, moderate-sized granules. The conical thyrotrophic cells are also scattered throughout the lobe and have more abundant secretory granules. The few small or very

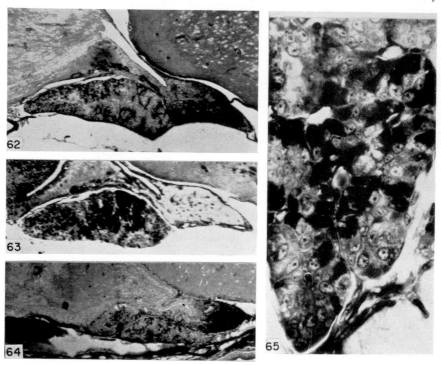

FIG. 62. Sagittal section through the hypophysis of *Trogonophis wiegmanni* (Trogonophidae). Stained with alcian blue and PAS, and photographed through an orange filter. Note the position of the neural lobe, anterior to and almost in the same horizontal plane as the distal lobe. The median eminence thus lies ventral to the pars distalis. The gonadotrophic FSH and thyrotrophic cells appear black.

FIG. 63. Section adjacent to that in Fig. 62. Stained with trichrome, and photographed through a green filter. Note ventral to the neural lobe, the small strip of tissue representing the intermediate lobe. In the pars distalis, the X cells and the rare alpha cells appear black.

FIG. 64. Sagittal section through the hypophysis of *Blanus cinereus* (Amphisbaenidae). Stained with alcian blue and PAS, and photographed through an orange filter. The neural lobe is almost encased in the distal lobe, which is thus poorly shown in a sagittal section. The gonadotrophic FSH and thyrotrophic cells appear black and the gonadotrophic LH cells, in the anterior region, gray.

FIG. 65. Anterior region of the pars distalis of *Blanus cinereus* (Amphisbaenidae). Stained with PAS, hematoxylin, and orange G, and photographed through a green filter; ×650. The gonadotrophic LH cells, which retain strongly the hematoxylin lakes, appear black.

small alpha cells are found only at the posterior end of the lobe. The fairly large X cells are often elongate and filled with carminophilic granules; they occur medially and anteriorly. The nuclei generally contain more chromatin than those of most other reptiles.

2. *Trogonophidae*

The hypophysis of *Trogonophis wiegmanni* resembles that of the Amphisbaenidae, but its neural lobe is larger and more posteriorly situated in relation to the distal lobe which the pituitary stalk hardly depresses (Figs 62 and 63). The intermediate lobe is slightly less atrophied than in *Blanus cinereus* and contains some cells having secretory granules.

The quite rare gonadotrophic LH cells are restricted to the anterior third of the pars distalis; their many, moderate-sized secretory granules do not stain with hematoxylin lakes. The ovoid gonadotrophic FSH cells contain fairly fine, dense granules and are scattered throughout the lobe but are most numerous dorsomedially. The few thyrotrophic cells are scattered in the posterior and ventromedial regions; they contain large, dense granules. The alpha and X cells resemble those of *Blanus cinereus*. They also have similar nuclei.

E. OPHIDIA

1. *Typhlopidae*

The large, elongate neural lobe lies posterior to the distal lobe (Fig. 66). The infundibular recess hardly penetrates it. The intermediate lobe seems to have disappeared completely. As in the Amphisbaenidae, the flat distal lobe is markedly depressed in the midline by the pituitary stalk and the entire anterior part of the neural lobe. The irregular and indistinct cellular cords contain only a few undifferentiated cells. There are no vascular sinuses.

The rather uncommon gonadotrophic LH cells are restricted to the anterior end of the pars distalis. The gonadotrophic FSH cells, which are particularly abundant medially and ventromedially, generally contain numerous secretory granules, but may sometimes be hypertrophied, more or less non-granular, and vacuolate (Fig. 67). The numerous thyrotrophic cells are scattered throughout the gland and have large erythrophilic granules. The very small alpha cells occur only at the posterior end of the lobe. The X cells are distinctly larger than the alpha cells and are scattered in small groups throughout the distal lobe; they contain many large orangophilic granules. The nuclei of the adenohypophyseal cells of the Typhlopidae are a little larger and distinctly poorer in chromatin than those of the Amphisbaenidae.

2. *Leptotyphlopidae*

Aside from the flatness of the sella turcica and the absence of an intermediate lobe, the hypophysis of the *Leptotyphlops dulcis* shows no resemblance to that of the Typhlopidae. The neural lobe is reduced to a small

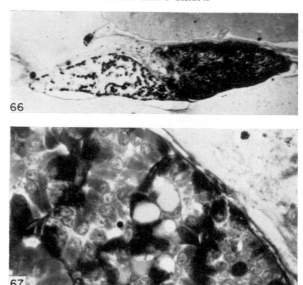

FIG. 66. Sagittal section through the hypophysis of *Typhlops punctatus* (Typhlopidae). Stained with alcian blue alone, and photographed through an orange filter. Note the large size and elongated form of the neural lobe. As in *Blanus*, a sagittal section gives only an imperfect idea of the size of the distal lobe which extends laterally on either side of the neural lobe. The gonadotrophic FSH and thyrotrophic cells appear black.

FIG. 67. The dorsal region of the pars distalis of the same animal as shown in Fig. 66. Stained with PAS, hematoxylin, and orange G, and photographed through a green filter; ×650. The gonadotrophic FSH cells, many appearing hypertrophied and vacuolated, contain black secretory granules. Some small thyrotrophic cells appear equally black, and the X cells are gray.

spherical mass lateral to the distal lobe. The well developed or even hypertrophied median eminence is broadly attached to the enlarged anterior end of the pars distalis (Fig. 68).

The distal lobe forms a thick band, truncated anteriorly and flattened posteriorly. It is characterized cytologically by the small size of the cells, all of which have very few secretory granules and are nearly filled by the large, turgid, transparent nuclei (Fig. 69). The few gonadotrophic LH cells lie at the periphery of the cellular cords in the anterior region. Most of the gonadotrophic FSH cells, which are slightly larger than the preceding ones, are medially located. The thyrotrophic cells are uncommon, very elongate, and scattered throughout the lobe. The alpha cells contain few large orangophilic granules and are dispersed throughout the distal lobe. The carminophilic X cells are restricted to the medial region.

3. *Boidae*

The massive, spherical neural lobe lies dorsolateral to the distal lobe in

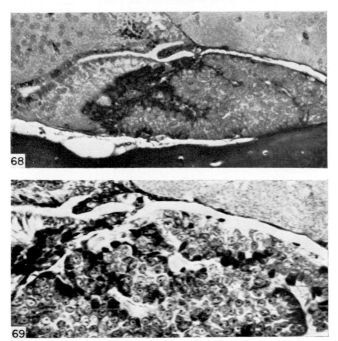

FIG. 68. Sagittal section through the hypophysis of *Leptotyphlops dulcis* (Leptotyphlopidae). Stained with PAS, hematoxylin, and orange G, and photographed through a green filter. The very reduced neural lobe cannot be seen in a sagittal section, but the transversely oriented pituitary stalk is clearly recognizable. Note especially the hypertrophied median eminence which is joined with the anterior part of the pars distalis.

FIG. 69. Section adjacent to that shown in Fig. 68. Stained with trichrome, and photographed through a green filter; × 400. Some alpha cells in the dorsal region of the pars distalis appear black. Note the characteristic appearance of the adenohypophysial cells which are especially poor in cytoplasm in the Leptotyphlopidae.

which it is partially enclosed. The infundibular recess does not penetrate it, but connective tissue septa incompletely divide it into lobules. The median eminence lies just dorsal to the anterior end of the pars distalis, and the pars tuberalis is less developed than in the Colubroidea. The quite irregularly shaped intermediate lobe encloses the posterior part of the neural lobe and rejoins the posterodorsal region of the right extremity of the pars distalis. It is made up of irregular cellular cords, in which the larger cells are filled with large very chromophilic granules.

The massive, ovoid distal lobe has irregular thick cords containing some undifferentiated cells. Small vascular sinuses occur posteriorly. The numerous, very chromophilic gonadotrophic LH cells are restricted to the anterior third of the pars distalis. The gonadotrophic FSH cells, which are more common ventrally, contain large erythrophilic granules. The conical thyrotrophic cells are smaller and scattered throughout the gland. The alpha and X cells are indistinguishable from each other and are abundant posteriorly and medially; they are small cells with scanty cytoplasm and many moderate-sized erythrophilic granules. The size and shape of the nuclei of the various types of cells differ characteristically, but all are poor or very poor in chromatin.

In *Eryx jaculus* (Fig. 70) and *Lichanura roseofusca*, two semi-fossorial boids, the intermediate lobe is distinctly reduced and contains few chromophilic cells. The median eminence lies nearer the neural lobe and more dorsal to the anterior region of the pars distalis than in other boids.

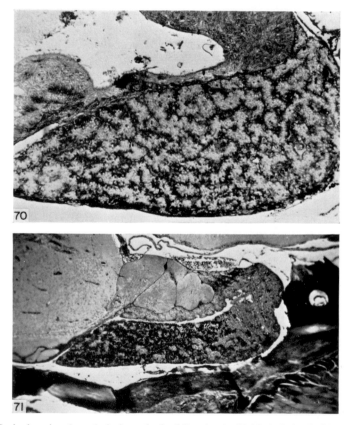

FIG. 70. Sagittal section through the hypophysis of *Eryx jaculus* (Boidae). Stained with paraldehyde fuchsin-trichrome, and photographed through an orange filter. Note the massive form of the distal lobe and the large cavity of the infundibular recess. The many small thyrotrophic cells, in black, are scattered throughout the pars distalis.

FIG. 71. Sagittal section through the hypophysis of *Natrix maura* (Colubridae). Stained with PAS, hematoxylin, and orange G, and photographed through a green filter. The hypophysis is asymmetrical, with both the neural and distal lobes cut off laterally. Note the abundance of gonadotrophic LH cells, in black, which fill the anterior two-thirds of the pars distalis.

4. *Colubridae, Elapidae and Hydrophiidae*

In members of these three families, the hypophysis is very similar to that of the non-burrowing Boidae, except that the median eminence lies farther anterior to the distal lobe to which it is joined by a thick connective tract and the pars tuberalis is better developed. Moreover, the pars distalis is slightly more elongate anteroposteriorly (Fig. 71).

Cytologically, the distal lobe is characterized by the large size and extreme abundance of the gonadotrophic LH cells, which occupy most of the anterior two-thirds of the lobe and are filled with large, carminophilic, barely PAS-positive granules (Figs 18 and 71). The much less numerous gonadotrophic FSH cells are almost entirely restricted to the ventromedial and lateral regions and contain fine cyanophilic granules (Figs 72 and 73). The thyrotrophic cells, which are very abundant and scattered throughout the lobe, are also characteristic, being regularly conical with very large erythrophilic granules (Figs 21 and 74). The alpha cells are generally small and have few large secretory granules; they are numerous in the posterior third of the pars distalis (Figs 24 and 76). The slightly larger X cells are rare and restricted to the medial region; their granules are similar to those of the alpha cells, having most of the same staining properties but also reacting slightly to PAS (Fig. 75).

In the Hydrophiidae, the hypophysis tends to be bilaterally symmetrical. The neural lobe, which is often richer in neurosecretory products than in the other families, lies dorsal or a little posterior to the distal lobe.

Aside from these very slight differences and a few small specific variations, the homogeneity of these three families is remarkable. However, in two colubrids from Madagascar (*Mimophis mahafalensis* and *Lycodryas* sp.) the morphology of the distal lobe and of its different types of cells is very similar to that in the Viperidae.

5. *Viperidae*

Anatomically, the hypophyses of the Viperidae (including the Crotalinae) differ from those of the preceding families only in the more massive form of the distal lobe, which is ovoid with a well-developed posterior region (Fig. 77). This difference is greatly magnified by the relatively large size of the heads of viperids. Since a similar phenomenon occurs in the elapid *Acanthophis antarcticus*, it has no systematic value.

In contrast, the cytological characteristics of the different types of cells in the distal lobe are entirely distinct from those of the other Colubroidea, although their locations are identical. The less numerous gonadotrophic LH cells are amphophilic, strongly PAS-positive, and stain particularly deeply with alcian blue and paraldehyde fuchsin. The ovoid gonadotrophic FSH cells contain large secretory granules or small erythrophilic particles on

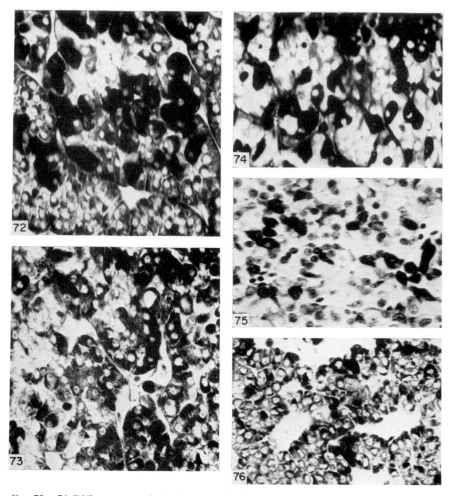

FIGS 72 to 76. Different types of cells in the pars distalis of *Oxyuranus scutellatus* (Elapidae). × 400.

FIG. 72. Ventromedian region. Stained with erythrosin, aniline blue, and orange G, and photographed through an orange filter. The large gonadotrophic FSH cells, which are blue but appear black in the photograph, are clustered within this zone. The gonadotrophic LH cells, especially in the lower part of the photograph, appear gray.

FIG. 73. Ventromedian region. Stained with PAS, hematoxylin, and orange G, and photographed through a green filter. The gonadotrophic LH cells fill the anterior part of the pars distalis and appear black. The gonadotrophic FSH cells appear gray and clearly contain irregular granules.

FIG. 74. Ventromedian region. Stained with alcian blue and PAS, and photographed through an orange filter. The thyrotrophic cells, in black, are clearly differentiated from the other types of cells.

FIG. 75. Ventromedian region. Stained with Romeis's azan, and photographed through a green filter. Some small X cells, in black, are scattered among the gonadotrophic FSH and thyrotrophic cells only the nuclei of which can be seen in this photograph.

FIG. 76. Posterior region. Stained with trichrome, and photographed through a green filter. Three large thyrotrophic cells, which are highly erythrophilic and appear black in the photograph, lie among the numerous alpha cells.

a cyanophilic base. The thyrotrophic cells, which are fairly small and rather uncommon, are unusual in possessing many, quite large erythrophilic granules. The large, often cuboid alpha cells have large and generally very abundant secretory granules and hemispherical or flat basal nuclei; they occupy much of the enlarged posterior region (Fig. 25). The X cells are much less numerous than the alpha cells (Fig. 27) and often form small

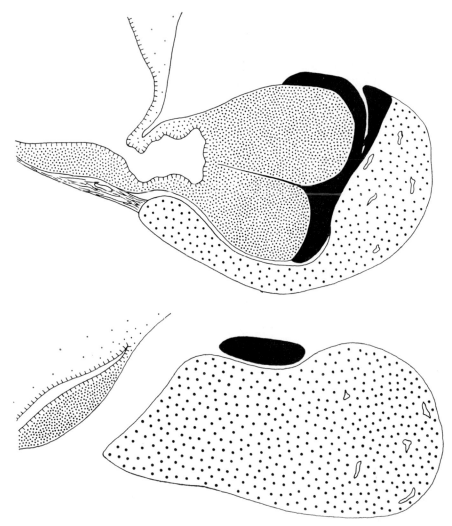

FIG. 77. Parasagittal sections through the hypophysis of *Cerastes cerastes* (Viperidae) passing (above) through the middle of the neural lobe and (below) through the centre of the distal lobe. The neural lobe and regions with many neurosecretory fibres are indicated by fine stippling, the distal lobe by coarse stippling, and the intermediate lobe by black.

homogeneous cords anteromedially. Their granules are distinctly less abundant than those of the alpha cells and slightly PAS-positive.

In the burrowing viper *Atractaspis* sp. the neural lobe lies distinctly lateral to the distal lobe. Moreover, the intermediate lobe is very reduced and formed entirely by involuted chromophobic cells. However, neither the form of the distal lobe nor its cytological characteristics are modified.

F. TESTUDINES

1. *Testudinidae*

The ovoid neural lobe does not extend very far laterally and is more or less divided into hollow lobules. The infundibular recess penetrates it deeply, therefore the volume occupied by neurosecretory fibres is small. The median eminence is slightly swollen and lies anterodorsal to the anterior end of the distal lobe. The intermediate lobe is situated between the posterior half of the pars distalis and the neural lobe, which it surrounds laterally (Fig. 78); it is little developed and thin medially where there may be a hypophyseal cleft, but is thicker laterally and is made up of irregular cords of small, weakly chromophilic cells.

The rather flat distal lobe overlaps the complex of neural and intermediate lobes, especially anteriorly. It is formed by irregular cellular cords, which often delimit a kind of thick cortical region in the anterior half ot the lobe. There are very large vascular sinuses posteriorly, and all the cells show a distinct tendency towards an elongate ovoid form. The fairly numerous gonadotrophic LH cells are concentrated in the anterior region (Fig. 79). The gonadotrophic FSH cells are abundant in the anterior half or two-thirds, particularly in the cortex. The thyrotrophic cells are often difficult to differentiate from the preceding ones and have the same distribution; however, their granules are often slightly larger and distinctly cyanophilic, whereas those of the gonadotrophic FSH cells are slightly amphophilic. The alpha cells are often grouped around homogenous pseudo-follicles and are abundant in the posterior region of the pars distalis, although they occur throughout all the lobe except its anterior end. They contain fine, very densely staining, orangophilic granules. The X cells, which are less numerous than the preceding ones, are especially concentrated in the anterior half (Fig. 80); their fine granules are less dense than those of the alpha cells and are somewhat carminophilic.

The pars tuberalis, which is especially well developed in turtles, has already been described.

2. *Pelomedusidae*

In one specimen of *Pelomedusa subrufa*, the neural lobe appears much larger than in members of the preceding family. The infundibular recess hardly penetrates it, and the pars nervosa, which is somewhat similar to that of snakes, consists largely of solid, more or less spherical lobules between which pass the cellular cords of the intermediate lobe. The latter is distinctly

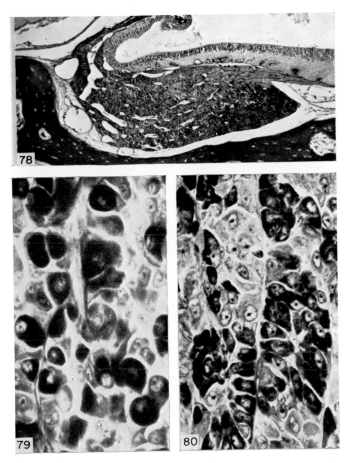

FIG. 78. Sagittal section through the hypophysis of a young *Clemmys caspica leprosa* (Testudinidae, Emydinae). Stained with PAS, hematoxylin, and orange G, and photographed through a green filter. Unlike the other figures, the anterior end is towards the right. Note the thinness of the "Glandular tissue" in the neural lobe, the small size of the intermediate lobe which is, moreover, poorly differentiated, the importance of the blood sinuses in the pars distalis, and the presence of a pars tuberalis between the median eminence and the distal lobe.

FIG. 79. *Testudo graeca* (Testudinidae, Testudininae). Stained with PAS, hematoxylin, and orange G, and photographed through a green filter; ×650. The gonadotrophic LH cells in the anterior region appear black. Some gonadotrophic FSH and thyrotrophic cells appear gray.

FIG. 80. *Clemmys caspica leprosa* (Testudinidae, Emydinae). Stained with trichrome, and photographed through a green filter; ×650. X cells lie in the anteromedial region of the pars distalis. Note the lanceolate form of many of the cells.

better developed than in other turtles (18% of the hypophyseal volume, instead of 11–14%).

In contrast, the form of the distal lobe and the adenohypophyseal cytology show nothing remarkable. It is possible that the morphological characters described in *Pelomedusa* distinguish the pleurodires from the cryptodires; however, the examination of many other species would be necessary to confirm this.

G. Crocodilia

In *Crocodylus porosus*, *C. niloticus*, and *Alligator mississippiensis*, the neural lobe is small but rather massive; the flattened infundibular recess penetrates it deeply (Fig. 81). The intermediate lobe is well developed and almost

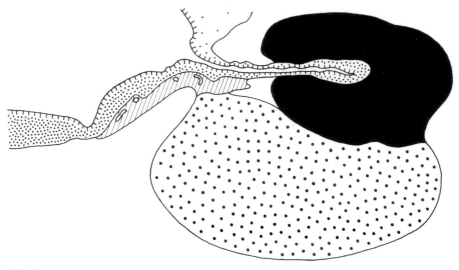

Fig. 81. Sagittal section through the hypophysis of *Crocodylus niloticus* (Crocodylidae). The neural lobe and regions with many neurosecretory fibres are indicated by fine stippling, the distal lobe by coarse stippling, the intermediate lobe by black, and the pars tuberalis by diagonal lines.

completely surrounds the neural lobe; however, the cellular cords are made up only of small, weakly chromophilic cells and some involuted cells (Fig. 13). The distal lobe is massive and more or less ovoid. There are some small vascular sinuses posteriorly and a few undifferentiated cells in the thick cellular cords.

The adenohypophyseal cytology is only known in *Crocodylus niloticus*. The very numerous gonadotrophic LH cells are restricted to the anteroventral and lateral regions (Fig. 82). Their very dense granules are erythrophilic and do not stain with hematoxylin lakes. The slightly larger gonadotrophic FSH cells are concentrated in the anteromedial region (Fig. 84); they contain

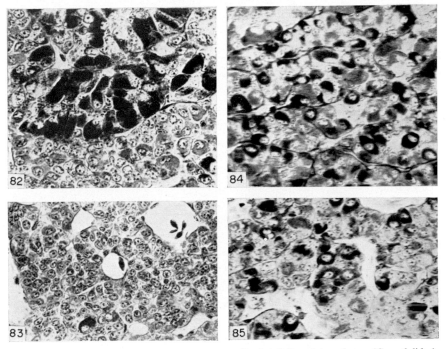

FIGS 82 to 85. Different types of cells in the pars distalis of *Crocodylus niloticus* (Crocodylidae). ×400.

FIG. 82. Middle region. Stained with PAS, hematoxylin, and orange G, and photographed through a green filter. The large gonadotrophic LH cells appear black.

FIG. 83. Posterior region. Same preparation as in Fig. 82. One gonadotrophic LH cell (in black) and some thyrotrophic cells (in gray) appear among the numerous small alpha cells which are almost entirely devoid of sensory granules.

FIG. 84. Ventromedial region. Stained with paraldehyde fuchsin-trichrome, and photographed through an orange filter. The more or less spherical gonadotrophic FSH cells and the smaller, often conical thyrotrophic cells appear black, and the gonadotrophic LH cells gray.

FIG. 85. Dorsomedial region. Same preparation as in Fig. 84, photographed through a green filter. The X cells appear black, and the gonadotrophic FSH and thyrotrophic cells gray.

fairly fine, mostly amphophilic granules. The small, conical thyrotrophic cells are scattered throughout the distal lobe; they have much larger and distinctly basophilic secretory granules. The alpha cells are very small and have few orangophilic granules (Fig. 83). They are restricted to the posterior third of the lobe. The numerous X cells are carminophilic like the gonadotrophic LH cells, but have less dense secretory granules (Fig. 85); they are most abundant in the dorsomedial part of the pars distalis.

In *Caiman crocodilus* the infundibular recess remains largely open, and the walls of the neural lobe are thinner than in the other Crocodilia studied. Moreover, the intermediate lobe is distinctly less developed (17% of the hypophyseal volume instead of 33%). In two very young specimens, the adenohypophyseal cytology differs markedly from that of *Crocodylus niloticus* of the same age, but only comparisons between adults could be used.

VI. Conclusions

The morphology of the hypophysis is clearly modified in fossorial species. In all the very specialized families in which the representatives are limbless and more or less blind the sella turcica is only a slight depression, the hypophysis is distinctly flattened dorsoventrally with the neural lobe being lateral or posterior to the distal lobe, and the intermediate lobe is atrophied or absent. These characteristics are much less marked in burrowing snakes of relatively unspecialized families; first, there is a reduction in the size of the intermediate lobe as in Erycinae, and then that lobe atrophies as the neural lobe becomes clearly lateral (*Atractaspis*). These tendencies are not present in snake-like but non-burrowing lizards, such as *Anguis*, *Ophisaurus*, *Delma*, and certain *Chalcides*, nor in the arenicolous species that "swim" in the sand, such as *Scincus scincus* and *Uma inornata*. The families with the most specialized hypophyses are the Typhlopidae and Leptotyphlopidae, and then the Amphisbaenidae and Feyliniidae. The Trogonophidae and Anniellidae are distinctly less specialized.

Other modes of life do not seem to influence the morphology of the hypophysis. However, the posterodorsal (not dorsolateral) position of the neural lobe of the Hydrophiidae and the larger amount of neurosecretory products in this family should be noted. There are no significant differences between the terrestrial turtles (Testudininae) and those of fresh water (Emydinae). The intermediate lobe is well developed, even hypertrophied, in the lizards that change colour rapidly (Chamaeleonidae, *Anolis*, *Calotes*, *Phelsuma*). However, this lobe may be just as important in species in which the chromatophores undergo only slow and rather slight changes, such as many Agamidae, most Gekkonidae, and certain *Acanthodactylus*. In several groups, for example the Scincidae and Amphisbaenia, there is usually a positive correlation between the duration of daily exposure to the sun and the size of the intermediate lobe. However, there are numerous exceptions to this rule; in the Gekkonidae, for example, the intermediate lobe of diurnal species is no more developed than that of nocturnal ones (Fig. 14).

Within broad limits, the morphology of the hypophysis can be correlated with the systematic position, and the complex of anatomical and cytological characters of this organ permits the recognition of several different structural types, which are homogeneous and well defined.

The chelonian type, studied in only a few species, is characterized principally by an elongated hypophysis, a very hollow pars nervosa (except in the only pleurodire examined), an intermediate lobe formed from irregular cellular cords, the presence of a well-developed pars tuberalis and of large vascular sinuses in the posterior region of the pars distalis, and finally the frequently lanceolate form of the adenohypophyseal cells.

The crocodilian type, also studied in only a few species, shows a massive, high hypophysis, a poorly developed neural lobe, and a large intermediate lobe made up of small, weakly chromophilic cells and rather specialized gonadotrophic LH cells.

The ophidian type (not found in typhlopids and leptotyphlopids) is far more distinctive than the chelonian and crocodilian types. The solid, spherical neural lobe lies dorsolateral to the pars distalis, so that the hypophysis is bilaterally symmetrical, as in all other non-burrowing reptiles. The pars terminalis is well developed, and the intermediate lobe is of a special type and is broadly united to the distal lobe. Three homogeneous groups may easily be recognized: (1) the Boidae, (2) the Colubridae, Elapidae, and Hydrophiidae, and (3) the Viperidae.

There appears to be a rhynchocephalian-saurian pattern characterized by a well-developed neural lobe which is deeply penetrated by the infundibular recess, a poorly differentiated pars terminalis, and an intermediate lobe which is always filled with large chromophilic cells, often arranged in two regular layers and separated by a distinct hypophyseal cleft. However, this group is not homogeneous, and contains several very distinct types.

The rhynchocephalian type has a poorly developed but distinct pars tuberalis and a massive pars distalis with very few, weakly chromophilic FSH gonadotrophic cells. The mode of contact between the neurosecretory fibres and the primary capillaries of the median eminence is especially characteristic and, indeed, unique among the studied vertebrates.

The gekkonid type, found also in the Pygopodidae and Xantusiidae, is very characteristic; the distal lobe has a well-developed anterior region and a flat posterior region with some scattered gonadotrophic LH cells. The intermediate lobe largely surrounds the neural lobe and possesses an internal layer formed from a single layer of large, regular prismatic cells.

The varanid type occurs in only one family. It differs from all the others in the general form of the massive and erect hypophysis and in the very special characteristics of most of the types of cells in the distal lobe.

The anguid and helodermatid type is easily recognized by the presence of very large vascular sinuses in the posterior region of the pars distalis and by the scarcity of undifferentiated cells. All the cells of the adenohypophysis are large, particularly the very numerous gonadotrophic LH cells; in contrast, and exceptionally in the Sauria, the X cells are rare and smaller than the alpha cells, and have the same staining properties as the latter. The numerous cuboid thyrotrophic cells are regularly arranged along the vascular sinuses. The nuclei are particularly large, spherical, and clear.

The scincid type is very homogeneous and is represented in a single family. It shows some common points with the preceding types: the small number of undifferentiated cells, the abundance and large size of the gonado-trophic LH cells, and the form and distribution of thyrotrophic cells. It also resembles the lacertid type in having numerous, small, non-granular alpha cells and large carminophilic X cells.

The iguanid-lacertid type is, unlike those just reviewed, not very homo-geneous. The anatomy is characteristic, with the internal layer of the inter-mediate lobe being formed of stratified or irregular, pseudo-stratified cells, the small alpha cells being abundant and more or less nongranular, the X cells being large and carminophilic, and the gonadotrophic LH cells being rare and, in the Iguania, weakly chromophilic. The intermediate lobe is always hypertrophied in the Chamaeleonidae, the Agamidae, and Iguanidae of the genus *Anolis*.

It is clear that the limbless and blind fossorial squamates of different families are not closely related despite their numerous convergent characteris-tics. The cytological characteristics of the pars distalis, which do not re-semble modifications of a particular type for subterranean life except for a distinct tendency to the reduction in size of the cells, differ greatly even between the Amphisbaenidae and the Trogonophidae. On the other hand, these characteristics clearly link the Anniellidae with the Anguidae and Helodermatidae, and, to a lesser extent, the Feyliniidae with the Scincidae. The anatomical resemblance of the hypophyses of the Typhlopidae and Amphisbaenidae is evidently the result of convergence. The Leptotyphlo-pidae, which have reduced neural lobe, a hypertrophied median eminence, and some very small cells with little secretory product, are quite different.

In most respects, the study of the hypophysis is consistent with the classification adopted by Romer (1956). However, some points require further discussion. The morphology of the hypophysis suggests a very isolated position for the Varanidae and, on the other hand, close relationships between the Anguidae and Helodermatidae and among the Gekkonidae, Xantusiidae, and Pygopodidae. The homogeneity of the Colubridae, Elapi-dae, and Hydrophiidae and of the Viperinae and Crotalinae is noteworthy.

No single criterion suffices to establish or modify a classification. If the observations on the comparative morphology of the hypophysis are confirmed on additional characters, they would suggest the following modifications of Romer's classification:

(1) Inclusion of the Xantusiidae in the Gekkota.

(2) Recognition of the Feyliniidae as a distinct family, closely related to but not included in the Scincidae.

(3) Differentiation of the Scincoidea from the Lacertoidea if the infra-order Scincomorpha is to be retained as a unit. As noted before, the hypo-

physis shows some resemblances among the Scincidae, Anguidae, and Helodermatidae on one hand and between the Lacertoidea and Iguanidae on the other.

(4) Placement of the Helodermatidae in the super-family Anguoidea rather than the Varanoidea.

(5) Recognition of the Trogonophidae as a family, related to but distinct from the Amphisbaenidae.

(6) Elevation of the Typhlopidae and the Leptotyphlopidae to the rank of distinct infra-orders.

(7) Placement of the Booidea and the Colubroidea in the same infra-order.

(8) Recognition within the Colubroidea of two distinct lineages, one including the Colubridae, Elapidae, and Hydrophiidae, and the other the Viperidae (including the Crotalinae). If it were not for the taxonomic problems caused by the large number of colubrids, one would reduce these four families to two.

These suggestions have been made only to summarize the results that can be derived from the various studies of the reptilian hypophysis. It must again be emphasized that these observations, based on one organ, have only limited weight. It would be just as regrettable to have a classification based solely on this character as to ignore it completely.

The study of the comparative morphology of the reptilian hypophysis is not complete. This organ has not been examined in numerous families, such as the Gavialidae, many Testudines, some limbless burrowing lizards of doubtful affinities (Dibamidae, Anelytropsidae), the Xenosauridae (including *Shinisaurus* of unclear systematic position), the Lanthanotidae, and all the more or less fossorial familes related to the Boidae. It would also be interesting to study the hypophysis in some already fairly specialized burrowing lizards which belong to families, such as the Scincidae and Teiidae, members of which live above ground; this has been done in the case of certain groups of snakes. Finally, the significant differences which exist between the two main lines of the Colubroidea might allow the recognition, if they still exist, of some colubrids which have retained certain primitive characteristics and which might have given rise to the Viperidae.

It is thus clear that the morphology of the reptilian hypophysis shows important variation between the different families or orders and also sometimes depending on the mode of life. However, if the latter factor and several exceptions are ignored, it is possible to separate the essential characters and to compare them with those of other tetrapods (see especially Wingstrand, 1966a). The presence of a well-developed pars tuberalis (except in the Squamata; however, in this case, regression appears to be secondary) and the markedly pediculate structure of the neural lobe, which is separated from the infundibulum by a well differentiated pituitary stalk, distinguish reptiles from amphibians and show a closer resemblance to conditions in birds and mammals. The very clear zonation of the pars distalis is a common characteristic of reptiles and birds, but the latter, like certain mammals, lack an intermediate lobe. It should be noted that no other vertebrates show as marked hypertrophy of the intermediate lobe as do many reptiles. Finally, the morphology and histochemical characteristics of the different types of reptilian adenohypophyseal cells resemble more closely those of birds and mammals than those of amphibians.

References

Altland, P. D. (1939). Cytology of the hypophysis of the fence lizard. *Anat. Rec.* 74, 109–127.

Bargmann, W. (1949). Über die neurosekretorische Verknüpfung von Hypothalamus und Hypophyse. *Z. Zellforsch. mikrosk. Anat.* 34, 610–634.

Bargmann, W. (1955). Weitere Untersuchungen am neurosekretorischen Zwischenhirn-Hypophysensystem. *Z. Zellforsch. mikrok. Anat.* 42, 247–272.

Bargmann, W., Hild, W., Ortman, R. and Schiebler, T. H. (1950). Morphologische und experimentelle Untersuchungen über das hypothalamisch-hypophysäre System. *Acta neuroveg.* 1, 233–275.

Bargmann, W., Knoop, A. and Thiel, A. (1957). Elektronenmikroskopische Studie an der Neurohypophyse von *Tropidonotus natrix* (mit Berücksichtigung der Pars intermedia). *Z. Zellforsch. mikrosk. Anat.* 47, 114–126.

Baumgartner, E. A. (1916). The development of the hypophysis in reptiles. *J. Morph.* 28, 209–275.

Beer, G. R. de (1926). "The Comparative Anatomy, Histology and Development of the Pituitary Body." Oliver and Boyd, Edinburgh.

Bruni, A. C. (1914). Sullo sviluppo del lobo ghiandolare dell'ipofisi negli amnioti. *Int. Monat. Anat. Physiol.* 31, 129–237.

Cieslak, E. S. (1945). Relation between the reproductive cycle and the pituitary gland in the snake *Thamnophis radix. Physiol. Zoöl.* 18, 299–329.

Combescot, C. (1955). L'hypophyse, la thyroïde et la surrénale de la tortue d'eau algérienne. *C. r. Séanc. Soc. Biol.* 149, 1969–1971.

Dendy, H. (1899). Outlines of the development of the tuatara, *Sphenodon (Hatteria) punctatus. Quart. Jl. microsc. Sci.* 42, 1–87.

Diepen, R. (1952). Vergleichend-anatomische Untersuchungen über das Hypophysen-Hypothalamus-System bei Amphibien und Reptilien. *Verh. anat. Ges., Jena* 50, 79–89.

Drager, G. A. (1950). Neurosecretion following hypophysectomy. *Proc. Soc. exp. Biol. Med.* 75, 712–713.

Enemar, A. (1960). The development of the hypophysial vascular system in the lizards *Lacerta a. agilis* Linnaeus and *Anguis fragilis* Linnaeus and in the snake *Natrix n. natrix* (Linnaeus), with comparative remarks on the Amniota. *Acta zool. Stockh.* 41, 142–237.

Gabe, M. (1958). Répartition des protides sulfhydrilés dans l'adéno-hypophyse de quelques Vertébrés poïkilothermes. *C. r. hebd. Séanc. Acad. Sci., Paris* 247, 2457–2459.

Gabe, M. (1962). Techniques cytologiques et histochimiques appliquées à l'étude de l'adénohypophyse. *Biol. Med.* 51, 158–165.

Gabe, M. (1966). "Neurosecretion." Pergamon Press, Oxford.

Gabe, M. and Martoja-Pierson, M. (1957). Sur une coloration trichrome en un temps sans différenciation. *Bull. Microsc. appl.* 7, 80–83.

Gabe, M. and Rancurel, P. (1958). Particularités histologiques du complexe hypothalamo-hypophysaire chez *Crocodilus niloticus* Laurenti. *C. r. hebd. Séanc. Acad. Sci., Paris* 247, 522–524.

Gabe, M. and Saint Girons, H. (1964a). Le troisiéme type de contact hypothalamo-hypophysaire proximal: l'éminence médiane de *Sphenodon punctatus*. *C. r. hebd. Séanc. Acad. Sci., Paris* 259, 2136–2139.

Gabe, M. and Saint Girons, H. (1964b). "Contribution à l'Histologie de *Sphenodon punctatus* Gray." Centre National de la Recherche Scientifique, Paris.

Gaupp, E. (1893). Über die Anlage der Hypophyse bei Sauriern. *Arch. mikrosk. Anat. EntwMech.* 42, 569–580.

Gentes, L. (1907). Recherches sur l'hypophyse et le sac vasculaire des vertébrés. *Soc. Sci. Arcachon* 10, 129–281.

Ghiara, G. (1954). Neurosecrezione nel maschio di *Lacerta s. sicula* Raf. *Rc. Accad. naz. Lincei* (8) 17, 132–136.

Ghiara, G. (1956). La struttura dell'eminenza mediana dell'ipothalamo di *Lacerta s. siculus* Raf. *Boll. Zool.* 23, 255–261.

Ghiara, G. (1957). Il sistema diencefalo-ipofisario nel maschio di *Lacerta s. siculus* Raf. I. Rapporti tra lobo nervoso e lobo intermedio dell'ipofisi (Nota preliminare). *Boll. Zool.* 24, 77–86.

Gisi, J. (1908). Das Gehirn von *Hatteria punctata. Zool. Jb., Abt. Anat.* 25, 71–236.

Green, J. D. (1951). The comparative anatomy of the hypophysis, with special reference to its blood supply and innervation. *Am. J. Anat.* 88, 225–311.

Green, J. D. (1966). The comparative anatomy of the portal vascular system and of the innervation of the hypophyses. *In* "The Pituitary Gland" (G. W. Harris and B. T. Donovan, eds), p. 1, 127–146. Butterworths, London.

Grignon, G. and Grignon, M. (1962). La vascularisation de l'hypophyse chez la tortue terrestre (*Testudo mauritanica*). *Anat. Anz.* 109, 492–506.

Haller, B. (1896). Untersuchungen über die Hypophyse und die Infundibular-Organe. *Morph. Jb.* 25, 31–114.

Harris, G. W. and Donovan, B. T., eds. (1966). "The Pituitary Gland." 3 vols. Butterworths, London.

Hartmann, J. F. (1944). Seasonal cytological changes in the anterior hypophysis of the garter. snake. *Am. J. Anat.* 75, 121–148.

Herlant, M. (1962). Cytochimie du lobe antérieur de l'hypophyse. *Anat. Anz.* 109, 562–596.

Herlant, M. (1964). The cells of the adenophypophysis and their functional significance. *Int. Rev. Cytol.* 17, 299–382.

Herlant, M. and Grignon, G. (1961). Le lobe glandulaire de l'hypophyse chez la tortue terrestre (*Testudo mauritanica* Dumer.). Etude histochimique et histophysiologique. *Arch. Biol., Stockh.* 72, 97–151.

Herlant, M. and Pasteels, J. (1955). Etude comparée du développement de l'hypophyse chez deux lacertiliens africains: *Mabuia megalura* (Peters) et *Chamaeleo bitaeniatus ellioti* (Gunther). *Arch. Biol., Stockh.* 66, 167–193.

Hild, W. (1951). Vergleichende Untersuchungen über Neurosekretion im Zwischenhirn von Amphibien und Reptilien. *Z. Anat. EntwGesch.* 115, 459–479.

Hoffmann, C. K. (1886). Weitere Untersuchungen zur Entwicklungsgeschichte der Reptilien. *Morph. Jb.* 11, 176–219.

Miller, M. R. (1948). The gross and microscopic anatomy of the pituitary and the seasonal histological changes occurring in the pars anterior of the viviparous lizard, *Xantusia vigilis. Univ. Calif. Publs Zool.* 47, 225–246.

Miller, M. R. (1963). The histogenesis of the endocrine organs of the viviparous lizard, *Xantusia vigilis. Gen. comp. Endocrinol.* 3, 579–605.

Müller, W. (1871). Über Entwicklung und Bau der Hypophysis und des Processus infundibuli cerebri. *Jena. Z. Naturw.* 6, 354–425.

Murakami, M. (1961). Elektronenmikroskopische Untersuchungen über die neurosekretorischen Zellen im Hypothalamus von *Gecko japonicus. Archvm. histol. jap.* 21, 323–327.

Murakami, M. (1963). Weitere Untersuchungen über die Feinstruktur der neurosekretorischen Zellen im Nucleus supraopticus von *Gecko japonicus. Z. Zellforsch. mikrosk. Anat.* 59, 684–699.

Nayar, S. and Pandalai, K. R. (1964). Neurohypophysial structure and the problem of neurosecretion in the garden lizard, *Calotes versicolor. Anat. Anz.* 114, 270–278.

Nemee, H. (1952). Zur mikroskopischen Anatomie und Topographie der Reptilienhypophyse. *Z. mikrosk.-anat. Forsch.* 59, 254–285.

Oota, Y. (1963). Fine structure of the median eminence and the pars nervosa of the turtle *Clemmys japonica. J. Fac. Sci. Tokyo Univ. (Zool.)* 10, 169–179.

Panigel, M. (1956). Contribution à l'étude de l'ovoviviparité chez les Reptiles: Gestation et parturition chez le lézard vivipare *Zootoca vivipara. Annls. Sci. nat. (Zool.)* (11) 18, 569–668.

Poris, E. G. (1941). Studies on the endocrines of reptiles. II. Variations in the histology of the hypophysis of *Anolis carolinensis*, with a note on the Golgi configuration in cells of the pars anterior and pars intermedia. *Anat. Rec.* 80, 99–121.

Poris, E. G. and Charipper, H. A. (1938). Studies on the endocrines of reptiles. The morphology of the pituitary gland of the lizard (*Anolis carolinensis*) with special reference to certain cell types. *Anat. Rec.* 72, 473–489.

Purves, H. D. (1966). Cytology of the adenohypophysis. *In* "The Pituitary Gland" (G. W. Harris and B. T. Donovan, eds), p. 1, 147–232. Butterworths, London.

Rathke, H. (1838). Über die Entstehung der Glandula pituitaria. *Arch. Anat. Physiol.* 1838, 482–485.

Rathke, H. (1839). Entwickelungsgeschichte der Natter (*Coluber natrix*). Gebrüder Bornträger, Königsberg.

Reese, A. M. (1910). Development of the brain of the American alligator: The paraphysis and hypophysis. *Smithson. misc. Collns.* 54 (1922), 1–20.

Romer, A. S. (1956). "Osteology of the Reptiles." Univ. Chicago Press, Chicago.

Romieu, M. (1949). L'hypophyse du gecko (*Tarentola mauritanica*). *C. r. Ass. Anat.* 55, 334–341.

Saint Girons, H. (1959). Données histochimiques sur l'hypophyse de *Chamaeleo lateralis* Gray, 1831. *Ann. Histochim.* 41, 115–122.

Saint Girons, H. (1961a). Particularités anatomiques et histologiques de l'hypophyse chez les Squamata. *Arch. Biol., Stockh.*, 72, 211–299.

Saint Girons, H. (1961b). Evolution des différentes catégories cellulaires de l'adénohypophyse, chez *Vipera aspis* (L.), au cours de la croissance embryonnaire et post-embryonnaire. *C. r. Séanc. Soc. Biol.* 155, 1207–1210.

Saint Girons, H. (1962). Le cycle reproducteur de la Vipére à cornes, *Cerastes cerastes* (L.), dans la nature et en captivité. *Bull. Soc. zool. Fr.* 87, 41–51.

Saint Girons, H. (1963). Données histophysiologiques sur le cycle annuel des glandes endocrines et de leurs éffecteurs chez l'Orvet, *Anguis fragilis* (L.). *Arch. Anat. microsc.* 52, 1–51.

Saint Girons, H. (1967). Le cycle sexuel et les corrélations hypophyso-génitales des mâles chez *Agama bibroni* Duméril au Maroc. *Bull. Biol., Stockh.* 101, 321–344.

Saint Girons, H. (1968). La morphologie comparée des glandes endocrines et la phylogénie des reptiles. *Bijdr. Dierk.* 37, 61–79.

Saint Girons, H., Bassot, J. M., and Pfeffer, P. (1964). Données anatomiques et histologiques sur l'hypophyse de quelques Hydrophidae et Elapidae. *Cah. Pacif.* 6, 133–141.

Saint Girons, H. and Duguy, R. (1962). Données histophysiologiques sur le cycle annuel de l'hypophyse chez *Vipera aspis* (L.). *Z. Zellforsch. mikrosk. Anat.* 56, 819–853.

Sasse, H. F. A. (1886). "Bijdrage tot de kentnis van de ontwikkeling en beteekenis der hypophysis cerebri." Thesis, Univ. Utrecht.

Scharrer, E. (1951). Neurosecretion. A relationship between the paraphysis and the paraventricular nucleus in the garter snake (*Thamnophis* sp.). *Biol. Bull., Stockh.* 101, 106–113.

Siler, K. A. (1936). The cytological changes in the hypophysis cerebri of the garter snake (*Thamnophis radix*) following thyroidectomy. *J. Morph.* 59, 603–622.

Sprankel, H. (1956). Beiträge zur Ontogenese der Hypophyse von *Testudo graeca* L. und *Emys orbicularis* L. mit besonderer Berücksichtigung ihrer Beziehungen zu Praechordalplatte, Chorda und Darmdach. *Z. mikrosk.-anat. Forsch.* 62, 587–660.

Staderini, R. (1903). La sviluppo dei lobi dell'ipofisi nel *Gongylus ocellatus*. *Archo. ital. Anat. Embriol.* 2, 50–163.

Sterzi, G. (1904). Intorno alla struttura dell'ipofisi nei Vertebrati. *Atti Accad. scient. veneto-trent.-istriana* 1, 70–141.

Taylor, S. J. (1952). Vascularity of the hypophysis of lower vertebrates. The painted turtle, *Chrysemys picta marginata* Agassiz. *Can. J. Zool.* 30, 134–143.

Wingstrand, K. G. (1951). "The Structure and Development of the Avian Pituitary from a Comparative and Functional Viewpoint," C. W. K. Gleerup, Lund.

Wingstrand, K. G. (1966a). Comparative anatomy and evolution of the hypophysis. *In* "The Pituitary Gland" (G. W. Harris and B. T. Donovan, eds), p. 1, 58–126. Butterworths, London.

Wingstrand, K. G. (1966b). Microscopic anatomy, nerve supply and blood supply of the pars intermedia. *In* "The Pituitary Gland" (G. W. Harris and B. T. Donovan, eds), p. 3, 1–27. Butterworths, London.

Woerdeman, M. W. (1914). Vergleichende Ontogenie der Hypophysis. *Arch. mikrosk. Anat. EntwMech.* 86, 198–291.

Wyeth, F. J. and Row, R. W. H. (1923). The structure and development of the pituitary body in *Sphenodon punctatus*. *Acta zool., Stockh.* 4, 1–63.

Yamada, K., Sano, M., Nonomura, K. and Ieda, M. (1960). Histological studies of the anterior pituitary of the turtle, *Clemmys japonica*. *Okajimas Folia. anat. jap.* 35, 133–143.

Zeleny, C. (1901). The early development of the hypophysis in Chelonia. *Biol. Bull., Stockh.* 2, 267–281.

CHAPTER 6

The Thyroid

W. GARDNER LYNN

*Department of Biology,
The Catholic University of America,
Washington, D.C., U.S.A.*

I. Introduction

Studies on a wide variety of vertebrates have clearly demonstrated that both the morphology of the functional unit of the thyroid gland and the mechanism of production of the thyroid secretion are essentially identical throughout the group. In all vertebrates the gland is composed of more or less spherical follicles, each made up of epithelial cells arranged in a single layer around a lumen filled with secreted material, the thyroid "colloid". In most vertebrates the follicles are closely associated to form a well-defined compact gland in which the individual units are bound together with loose connective tissue, the whole enclosed in a connective tissue capsule. However, cyclostomes and most teleost fishes have the follicles diffusely spread throughout the tissue beneath the pharynx. The gland is always well vascularized, usually with extensive networks of capillaries around the follicles. The height of the follicular epithelium, the amount of colloid present, the staining reaction of the colloid, and the extent of vascularization all vary with the degree of functional activity of the gland. It is therefore possible to utilize histological criteria as one, largely qualitative, indication of the level of secretory activity of the thyroid.

The outstanding physiological feature of the thyroid is its ability to concentrate iodine from the circulation. The biochemical mechanisms by which this is accomplished have been studied intensively (see reviews by: Desmarais and Laham, 1960; Gross, 1957; Halmi, 1961; Kurosumi, 1961; Leloup and Fontaine, 1960; Pitt-Rivers, 1961). Briefly, the following steps, most of them enzymatically controlled, are involved. Iodine, in the form of iodide, enters the blood stream from the food and also, in the case of fishes and amphibians, from the surrounding water. Iodide is concentrated from the blood by the cells of the thyroid follicles ("iodide pump" of the thyroid). It is then oxidized and organically bound. The latter involves the formation of monoiodotyrosine (MIT), diiodotyrosine (DIT), tetraiodothyronine (thyroxine, T_4), and triiodothyronine (T_3). All these compounds are present in bound form in the thyroid protein, thyroglobulin, which accumulates in the colloid. The biosynthesis of thyroglobulin probably occurs in the intra-follicular colloid rather than in the cells themselves. The binding of iodine in this way makes possible the concentration of this element in the thyroid even when the rate of intake into the body is extremely low. Thyroglobulin may be stored indefinitely in the colloid or it may at any time undergo hydrolysis to yield free MIT, DIT, T_3, and T_4. The latter two compounds, which are regarded as the active hormones of the thyroid, are then able to pass into the blood stream and reach the general body tissues. Most of the thyroid hormone found in the circulating blood is in the form of T_4 which does not enter the red blood cells in any significant concentration but is bound to plasma proteins. Free MIT and DIT undergo deiodination in the colloid, and the iodide may then return to the circulation to be again picked up by the thyroid cells or to be eliminated from the body. These various steps may occur rapidly or slowly depending upon environmental conditions and upon the physiological state of the animal. Therefore, some of the most useful indices of thyroid activity are measurements of the rate and amount of iodide uptake, the rate of iodide turnover, and the rate of incorporation of iodine into the various compounds involved in synthesis of the hormone. Such measurements have been made feasible primarily through the use of radioisotopic techniques and chromatographic analysis.

The thyroid is one of the endocrine glands whose functioning is controlled by a specific hormone of the pituitary. The thyrotrophic or thyroid-stimulating hormone (TSH) is a glycoprotein secreted by certain basophilic cells of the anterior lobe of the pituitary. Administration of TSH causes an increase in thyroid activity that may easily be demonstrated by both histological and biochemical methods. Absence of TSH, which can be achieved by hypophysectomy, results in cessation of thyroid activity and atrophy of the gland. In a normal animal the thyroid and pituitary exert reciprocal effects upon each other by means of a feed-back mechanism that results in maintenance of the normal balance of hormone production.

Several reviews concerning thyroid morphology and physiology have dealt with reptiles in greater or less detail (Eggert, 1938a; Goldsmith, 1949; Lynn and Wachowski, 1951; Berg et al., 1959; Gorbman, 1959; Lynn, 1960; Leloup and Fontaine, 1960; Gorbman and Bern, 1962; Bern and Nandi, 1964; Rall et al., 1964). For this reason much of the earlier work will be only briefly summarized in the present account.

II. Gross Morphology

In turtles and in snakes the thyroid is an unpaired, roughly spherical gland, lying ventral to the trachea and just anterior to the heart. In *Sphenodon* it is a single narrow body, transversely elongate, in the same general position.

Members of the Crocodilia have a thyroid with well-defined lobes on the two sides of the trachea connected by a narrow isthmus. Lizards exhibit a wide variety of thyroid forms with unpaired, bilobed, and completely paired glands found even in different members of the same family.

Detailed descriptions of the anatomical relations of the thyroid are available for only a small number of reptiles. In the turtle *Emys orbicularis* (Naccarati, 1922) the gland is a spheroidal structure lying in the cavity of the arch of the innominate trunk, just anterior to the heart and ventral to the point where the trachea divides into the two bronchi. Its blood supply is through two pairs of arteries. The superior thyroid arteries are branches of the carotids. They are rather thin, variable in position, and sometimes absent. The inferior thyroid arteries are larger, short, vessels that emerge directly from the innominate trunk just below the point where it gives rise to the right and left carotid and subclavian arteries. The thyroid veins join the accessory pectoral veins and empty into the subclavians at the junction of the jugular and axillary veins. A lymphatic network is found around the external surface of the thyroid and this connects with the lymphatics of the neck. Innervation is derived from the laryngeal branches of the vagus and from fine branches of the cervical sympathetics which accompany the arterial supply into the gland. In this species the thyroid may be exposed by trepanning if one applies the instrument one-half centimetre anterior to the point where hyoplastral and hypoplastral plates join. If the bone is removed and the forelimbs are drawn apart so as to put tension on the scapuloclavicular ligaments the gland can be visualized by extending the animal's neck. *Testudo graeca* shows essentially the same features (Naccarati, 1922).

Published accounts of thyroid morphology in snakes are limited to brief descriptions for *Natrix*, *Coluber*, and *Malpolon*. *Natrix sipedon fasciata* was reported by Thompson (1910) to have a median, spherical gland, and Bragdon (1953) stated that *Natrix sipedon sipedon* possesses an ovoid or globular thyroid, measuring 3·0 by 4·0 mm in a large female, and located at the level of the twenty-first to twenty-fourth ventral scute. Francescon (1929) referred briefly to the thyroid in *Coluber viridiflavus* and *Malpolon monspessulanus* in connection with his observations on the ultimobranchial body, but gave neither figures nor detailed descriptions.

The thyroid of *Sphenodon punctatus* was described by van Bemmelen (1887) as a single transversely elongate body lying across the trachea anterior to the heart. O'Donoghue's (1920) account of the blood vascular system of *Sphenodon* includes a figure showing these features and a description of the superior thyroid and inferior thyroid arteries which branch respectively, from the external carotid artery and the pulmonary arch. The paired thyroid veins reach the precaval by way of the tracheal veins. The description given by Adams (1939) agrees closely with these accounts.

The lizard and amphisbaenian thyroid is of special interest. As early as

1844, Simon pointed out that the general form of the gland differs widely in representatives of different families of lizards so that, whereas the members of some families have an unpaired median thyroid, other lizards have completely paired lateral thyroids, and still others have a bilobed gland with a narrow connecting isthmus. It is now clear that in only a few families are all members of the family uniform with respect to thyroid morphology and, in fact, several of the larger families have representatives showing each of the three types mentioned. On the other hand, a particular thyroid form is always characteristic for a given species and usually for the genus as well. Thyroid morphology may, therefore, be of some significance in indicating systematic relationships in lizards. The accompanying table (Table I) summarizes presently available data, some of it not previously published, on the form of the thyroid gland in the various lacertilian and amphisbaenian families. Earlier references on this subject may be found in the review paper of Lynn (1960). Some of the more recent studies concerning the gross morphology of the lizard and amphisbaenian thyroid are as follows: Lynn and Walsh, 1957; Lynn and Komorowski, 1957; Yamamoto, 1960; Soetjipto, 1960; Chakrabarty, 1962; Gans and Lynn, 1965; Lynn and Colorigh, 1967; Lynn and Zmich, 1967; Lynn, 1967; Lynn et al., 1966a and b.

It may be noted that, if one considers all lizards but not the members of the Amphisbaenia, the most common thyroid form is like that of mammals, a bilobed gland with a connecting isthmus beneath the trachea. A single broad thyroid stretching across the trachea is found almost as frequently however, and these two types often occur in different genera of the same family. Single, rounded thyroids are rare and appear to be characteristic of only two small families, Pygopodidae and the monogeneric Anniellidae. It is noteworthy that completely paired thyroids, aside from their occurrence in two closely related monogeneric groups (Helodermatidae and Varanidae), are found in only four other families all of which also have representatives with bilobed and single broad glands. Among these four families two (Iguanidae and Agamidae) belong to the Ascalabota and the other two (Teiidae and Anguidae) belong to the Autarchoglossa. These facts may be taken to indicate that the paired condition has evolved independently at least twice in lizards and that pairing of the thyroid may be regarded as derived from the unpaired condition, probably with bilobing as an intermediate step.

The amphisbaenians prove to be aberrant in thyroid form as they are in so may other features. A bilobed thyroid is rare in this group. Paired glands are common but are of two diverse types. Although it is not indicated in the table, some species have paired thyroids of the usual spherical or ovoid shape, but others have extremely elongated, attenuated, thread-like glands which, though less than 1·0 mm wide, stretch alongside the trachea for as much as

TABLE I

Form of the Thyroid in Lizard and Amphisbaenian Families

	Approx. No. of genera known	No. of genera studied	No. of species studied	Number with										Source of data
				Paired		Bilobed		Single, broad		Single, round		Single, long		
				Gen.	Sp.	Gen.	Sp.	Gen.	Sp.	Gen.	Sp.	Gen.	Sp.	
Ascalabota														
Gekkota														
Eublepharidae	5	5	7			2	2	4	5					Lynn, 1967
Sphaerodactylidae	5	3	5			3	5							Lynn, 1967
Gekkonidae	69	49	56			46	50	2	4	1	2			Lynn, 1967
Pygopodidae	8	4	5							2	5			Lynn and Komorowski, 1957; Lynn unpubl.
Dibamidae	1													
Anelytropsidae	1													
Iguania														
Iguanidae	55	43	73	6	21	24	33	14	19					Lynn et al., 1966b
Agamidae	35	26	53	19	33	7	16	1	4					Lynn et al., 1966b
Chamaeleonidae	6	4	7					4	7					Lynn and Colorigh, 1967
Xantusiidae	4	3	5					3	5					Lynn, unpubl.
Autarchoglossa														
Scincomorpha														
Scincidae	46	25	56					24	49	5	7			Lynn and Zmich, 1967
Feyliniidae	3	3	3			1	1			2	2			Lynn, unpubl.
Cordylidae	9	5	9					5	9					Lynn and Colorigh, 1967
Lacertidae	20	16	66			16	66							Lynn et al., 1966a
Teiidae	40	30	52	3	8	17	32	10	12					Lynn et al., 1966b

TABLE I—*cont.*

	Approx. No. of genera known	No. of genera studied	No. of species studied	Paired		Bilobed		Single, broad		Single, round		Single, long		Source of data
				Gen.	Sp.	Gen.	Sp.	Gen.	Sp.	Gen.	Sp.	Gen.	Sp.	
Anguinoidea														
Anguidae	7	7	22	3	13	3	6	1	3					Lynn and Colorigh, 1966
Anniellidae	1	1	1				1	1	1	1				Lynn and Walsh, 1957
Xenosauridae	2	2	2			1	1	1	1		1			Lynn and Walsh, 1957
Varanoidea														
Helodermatidae	1	1	1	1	1									Lynn and Walsh, 1957
Varanidae	1	1	4	1	4									Lynn, unpubl.
Lanthanotidae	1													
Amphisbaenia														
Amphisbaenidae + Trogonophidae	20	16	27	11	19	3	4					3	4	Lynn and Komorowski, 1957; Lynn, unpubl.; Gans and Lynn, 1965

several centimetres. Such thin elongate thyroids are not known to occur in other reptiles or, indeed, in any other group of vertebrates. In the family Trogonophidae most genera have single thyroids of elongate form and these are sometimes found to one side of the trachea rather than in the midline. In this family only the genus *Trogonophis* has paired thyroids, but these are elongate and are also connected by an isthmus at the posterior end. Finally, the position of the thyroid is unusual in amphisbaenians. In all cases the gland lies much further forward than in other reptiles. It is, therefore, not situated near the heart but lies either midway along the trachea or near its anterior end. Thyroid morphology does not support any concept of a close relationship between the Amphisbaenia and the snakes; in no amphisbaenian does the form or position of the thyroid resemble that of snakes.

III. Histology and Cytology

The reptilian thyroid is always enclosed in a capsule of connective tissue containing argyrophilic fibers and, in some cases, a few elastic fibers. Scattered melanophores may also be found in the capsule. Connective tissue septa can sometimes be traced from the capsule into the gland dividing it into ill-defined lobules, and a delicate areolar connective tissue network containing argyrophilic fibers always surrounds the follicles. The follicles vary in diameter from 50 μ to 300 μ and may reach much larger sizes in large turtles (Yamamoto, 1960). They are commonly rounded but may be of quite irregular shape, particularly in glands that are in phases of intense secretory activity. The simple epithelium lining the follicles varies in height from flat to columnar depending upon the functional state of the follicles and the amount of colloid present in its lumen. Mitotic figures may be seen in the epithelium during periods of increased thyroid activity (Miller, 1955). The colloid masses within follicles are eosinophilic. They may have a uniform homogeneous appearance or may exhibit large numbers of chromophobe droplets, especially at their peripheries. The epithelial cells have basally situated nuclei, usually with rather indistinct nucleoli. The cytoplasm may contain well-defined fuchsinophilic granules which are taken to be droplets of secretion. Photomicrographs illustrating some of these features are shown in Figs 1 through 4.

Early studies of the normal histology of the thyroid in a variety of reptiles are cited by Lynn (1960). They include Viguier's (1909a, b, 1911c) brief descriptions for several lizards (*Tarentola mauritanica*, *Lacerta lepida*, *Psammodromus algirus*, and *Chalcides ocellatus*), Naccarati's (1922) accounts for *Emys orbicularis* and *Testudo graeca*, and Hellbaum's (1936) study on *Thamnophis radix* and *T. sirtalis*. Normal thyroid histology is also discussed in a number of papers that are primarily concerned with the effects of various experimental treatments. The earliest of these is the study of

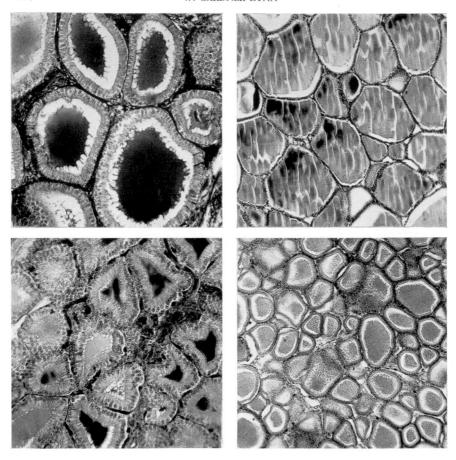

FIGS 1 and 2. Sections of thyroids of untreated control specimens of *Pseudemys scripta elegans* to show normal variation in follicle size, epithelial height, and nature of colloid. × 100.

FIG. 3. Section of thyroid of *Pseudemys scripta elegans* after administration of thiourea over a period of ten days. Note increased epithelial height and area of chromophobe colloid at peripheries of colloid masses. × 100.

FIG. 4. Section of thyroid of *Pseudemys scripta elegans* after administration of TSH over a period of ten days. Note marked increase in epithelial height, decrease in follicle size and colloid content, increased vascularization, and appearance of chromophobe droplets. × 100.

Galeotti (1897) concerning changes in the follicular epithelium of the thyroid in turtles treated with certain toxic substances. Barchiesi's (1928) observations on the effects of prolonged starvation on the thyroid of *Emys orbicularis* are noteworthy in that they emphasize the high degree of individual variation in histological appearance of the gland in normal turtles. An important source of information on the histology of the reptilian thyroid is to be found in the numerous studies of seasonal variation in the gland and in studies on the relation between thyroid activity and molting. These subjects will be considered in detail in later sections of this chapter.

Several recent studies deserve special mention. Yamamoto (1960) has provided further histological data for the following species: *Clemmys japonica, Lepidochelys olivacea, Gekko japonicus, Eumeces l. latiscutatus, Elaphe climacophora, E. quadrivirgata, E. conspicillata, Natrix v. vibikari, N. t. tigrina,* and *Agkistrodon halys blomhoffii.* The general histological features in these reptiles are in accord with those summarized above. In addition Yamamoto found a sparse scattering of epithelial cells which show the characteristics of the "colloid cells" of earlier authors. They stain red-purple with PAS and have small, sometimes pycnotic, nuclei. They are interpreted as either degenerating or resting cells. He also reported that some of the snakes he examined had funnel-shaped sphincter apparatuses at the branching points of arteries in the thyroid which resemble such sphincters found in mammals. Certain spherical or ovoid cysts consisting of a stratified epithelium enclosing degenerating cells, cellular detritus, and a crystalloid material were sometimes found in the thyroids of *Clemmys japonica* and *Elaphe climacophora.* Yamamoto considers that these represent similar enigmatic structures of mammals which may be of branchiogenous origin.

Large ovoid cells known as "macrothyreocytes" or "parafollicular cells" have been found in the thyroids of mammals (Kroon, 1958), and these also occur in reptiles (Gabe, 1961; Saint Girons and Duguy, 1962a). They are usually intra- or sub-epithelial rather than truly parafollicular and they enclose a secretory product in the form of PAS-positive granules or large droplets. The secretion is reported to contain muco- or glyco-proteins as well as amino acids and protein-bound sulfhydryl groups. In snakes (*Python, Vipera, Cerastes*) the secretory granules coalesce to form large homogeneous masses which may occupy the greater part of the cell. Macrothyreocytes increase in number during thyroid activation and intermediate forms between follicle cells and macrothyreocytes are not uncommon (Gabe, 1961). Kroon suggests that the macrothyreocyte may represent a phase in the development of ordinary cells of the follicular epithelium and that their morphological features may be interpreted as evidence of intracellular colloidogenesis.

Blood cells are occasionally found in the colloid. Intrafollicular granulocytes have been reported in *Lacerta* (Eggert, 1935) and *Chelydra* (Dimond, 1954). Miller (1955) found that both eosinophilic granulocytes and erythrocytes occur in the colloid of *Xantusia* following any period of thyroid hyperactivity when there is a sudden thinning of the epithelium.

There are relatively few studies of the ultrastructure of the reptilian thyroid. Kurosumi (1961) presents a photomicrograph of an electron microscope preparation of part of a thyroid cell of the snake *Elaphe quadrivirgata* which shows a well developed endoplasmic reticulum with unusually large cisternae. Secretory granules of highly variable size and density are present, and the smallest of these are said to resemble Golgi vesicles. The nuclear envelope has well-defined pores.

With advancing age the histology of the lizard thyroid is altered by gradual invasion of lymphocytes which spread throughout the tissue or may form large nodules. Some follicles undergo involution and fatty tissue appears in the resulting spaces (Eggert, 1935). Brown pigment granules in the supra-nuclear zone in some snakes have also been interpreted as characteristic of advanced age (Yamamoto, 1960).

IV. Embryology

There is no indication that reptiles are in any way unusual in the mode of origin and development of the thyroid. Studies have been made on representatives of all the major groups of living reptiles except the Rhynchocephalia. In all of these the gland has been shown to arise as a midventra outpocketing of the embryonic digestive tract at the level of the first pair of pharyngeal pouches. A connection with the pharynx (thyreoglossal duct) persists only briefly and the tissue mass elongates posteriorly in the form of solid strands or cords. These then break into groups of cells that begin to form primary follicles. The lumina of newly organized follicles usually contain only small amounts of a non-stainable colloid, but the typical staining reaction appears within a short time. Meanwhile the follicles gradually migrate posteriorly to their definitive position and become encapsulated to form a compact gland. This sequence of events is illustrated for the lizard *Sphaerodactylus argus argus* in Figs 5 through 10. References to earlier work have been cited previously (Lynn, 1960).

Raynaud and Raynaud (1961) and Raynaud *et al.* (1963) report that a number of endocrine organs (thyroid, gonads, suprarenals, hypophysis)

FIG. 5. Section through pharyngeal region of 3·0 mm embryo of *Sphaerodactylus a. argus*. Thyroid Anlage is a compact mass at centre of figure. × 230.

FIG. 6. Section through thyroid Anlage at same stage as that shown in Fig. 5. Cells still essentially like those of pharyngeal wall. × 950.

FIG. 7. Section through pharyngeal region of a 4·5 mm embryo of *Sphaerodactylus a. argus*. The thyroid now extends laterally beneath the trachea. × 230.

FIG. 8. Detail of portion of thyroid shown in Fig. 7. Thyroid cells now organized into follicles but without any accumulation of colloid. × 950.

FIG. 9. Section through pharyngeal region of a 5·0 mm embryo of *Sphaerodactylus a. argus*. Note well developed follicles, prominent capillaries, and connective tissue capsule. × 230.

FIG. 10. Detail of portion of thyroid shown in Fig. 9. Note follicles with cuboidal epithelium and mostly chromophobic colloid. Interfollicular capillaries are abundant. × 950.

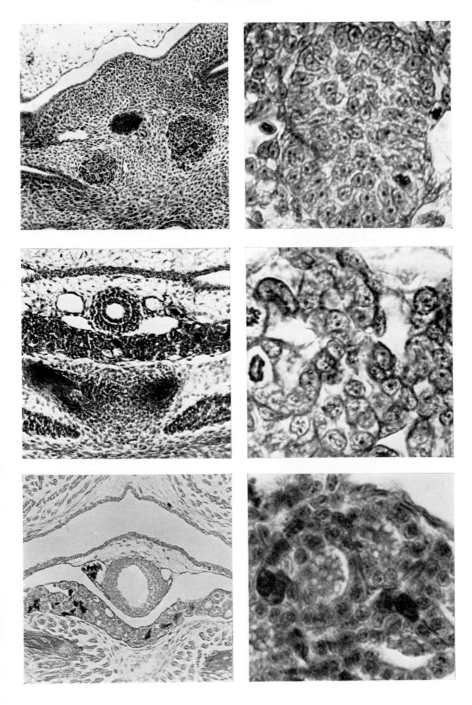

exhibit indications of precocious secretory activity in *Anguis fragilis*. Cells of the thyroid Anlage are found to contain fine PAS-positive granules in their cytoplasm at early stages before the appearance of organized cell cords or follicles. This material is later seen in intercellular spaces and still later (embryos of 21 or 22 mm crown-cloaca length) can be found at the centres of cell cords. In the viviparous lizard *Xantusia vigilis*, organized follicles containing thin colloid are present at the 7 to 8 mm stage which is about one week before the basophil cells of the anterior pituitary are differentiated. The embryonic thyroid shows histological evidence of high activity during the last third of the gestation period (Miller, 1963).

Dimond's (1963) investigation of thyroid embryology in four species of turtles shows that organized follicles are present during the second quarter of development and are capable of binding iodine. Thyroid hypertrophy and hyperplasia results when potassium perchlorate or thiourea are administered to embryos shortly after the mid-stage in development, and this is taken to indicate that pituitary stimulation of the thyroid has begun by this time. Pituitary beta cells, the presumed source of TSH, are also demonstrable at this stage.

V. Thyroid-pituitary Relations

A. EFFECTS OF THYROIDECTOMY, HYPOPHYSECTOMY, T_4 ADMINISTRATION, OR TSH ADMINISTRATION

The reptilian thyroid, like that of other vertebrates, is under pituitary control. Evidence for a relationship between thyroid and pituitary function was first obtained by studies of histological changes in the pituitary in thyroidectomized animals. Viguier (1911b) reported an increase in basophil cells of the anterior pituitary in lizards (*Uromastyx*) killed 8 to 10 weeks after having been thyroidectomized and similar results have been obtained for *Thamnophis radix* (Siler, 1936) and *Testudo graeca* (Herlant and Grignon, 1961). Recent interest in the histology and cytology of the pituitary gland and in neurosecretory activity in the hypothalamus has led to histochemical characterization of pituitary cell types in a number of reptiles and to some definition of neurosecretory pathways in reptiles (Gabe and Rancurel, 1958; Grignon and Herlant, 1959; Herlant and Grignon, 1961; Legait and Legait, 1957; Saint Girons, 1959, 1960, 1961, 1963a; Saint Girons and Duguy, 1962b). It is to be expected that these studies will be followed by observations on thyroidectomized animals which will lead to a more precise identification of the cells of the anterior pituitary which are responsible for the secretion of the thyroid-stimulating hormone (TSH) in reptiles and to a better understanding of the mechanism of action of the thyroid-pituitary axis.

Histological observations concerning seasonal changes in the pituitary which can be correlated with the thyroid cycle also indicate dependence of one upon the other. Some observations of this kind have been made on *Xantusia vigilis* (Miller, 1948, 1955) and on *Clemmys caspica leprosa* (Combescot, 1955).

Removal of the hypophysis results in regressive changes in the thyroid characterized by flattening of the follicular epithelium and failure of release of the colloid (Hellbaum, 1936, *Thamnophis*; Combescot, 1956, *Clemmys*; Eakin *et al.*, 1959, *Sceloporus*). Hellbaum found that daily administration of anterior pituitary extract to snakes which had been hypophysectomized earlier caused a rapid return to normal thyroid histology. Hypophysectomy also brings about a marked reduction in the per cent uptake of radioiodine by the thyroid (Nussbaum, 1963, *Anolis*; Chiu and Phillips, 1969, *Gekko*; Chiu *et al.*, 1970, *Sceloporus*).

Administration of pituitary extracts or of purified TSH preparations to unoperated animals results in histological evidence of increased activity in the thyroid although the degree of response shows much individual variation (Eggert, 1936c, *Lacerta*). Eggert was unable to demonstrate any thyroid response to TSH in lizards treated during hibernation. Turtles (*Chrysemys*) given 36 daily injections of pituitary extract showed a thyroid response that persisted as long as 136 days after the first injection (Evans and Hegre, 1940). *Natrix* (= *Tropidonotus* auct.) *natrix* gives a well defined and very constant histological response to TSH even at temperatures as low as 13°C (Mason, 1938).

As would be expected, administration of exogenous T_4 to an animal results in a reduction of the activity of its own thyroid since a high level of thyroxin in the blood causes a decrease in production of TSH by the pituitary. This has been demonstrated for two lizards (Eggert, 1936c *Lacerta*; Chiu *et al.*, 1967, *Gekko*) and one snake (Chiu and Lynn, 1970, *Chionactis*).

B. EFFECTS OF GOITROGENIC DRUGS

There are various drugs that inhibit the production of thyroid hormone either by interfering with the uptake of iodide or by inhibiting the formation of iodinated protein. Administration of these substances can thus cause a functional thyroid deficiency which may be severe enough to correspond closely to that resulting from surgical thyroidectomy. Animals so treated show a thyroid response characterized by hyperemia and by hyperplasia and hypertrophy of the follicular epithelium. If treatment is long-continued the whole gland may enlarge strikingly to form a definite goitre. These responses are attributable to a high output of TSH by the pituitary which has been stimulated to excessive thyrotrophic activity because of the low level of thyroxin in the blood. The use of goitrogens thus provides a less radical method than thyroidectomy for studying the pituitary's response to thyroid deficiency. Various turtles, both embryonic and adult, have been subjected to such treatment. The changes in thyroid histology are always clear-cut although there is much individual variability in the degree of responsiveness. The thyroids of most lizards studied show a well-marked histological response to goitrogen administration, but *Lacerta* is reported to be very unreactive (Lynn, 1960; Lynn *et al.*, 1965).

The effects of goitrogens upon the uptake of radioiodine by the thyroid have been investigated in *Chrysemys* (Bileau, 1956), *Pseudemys* (Waterman, 1961b), *Anolis* (Lynn *et al.*, 1965), *Xantusia* (Buckingham, 1970), and *Alligator* (Waterman, 1961a). The results of these studies will be discussed in the next section.

VI. Biosynthesis of Thyroid Hormones

The basic similarity in thyroid physiology in reptiles and other vertebrates was indicated by early studies showing that the reptilian thyroid has a high iodine content, a certain proportion of which is present in thyroxin, and that feeding of reptilian thyroid is effective in inducing precocious metamorphosis in amphibians or in raising the basic metabolic rate in rabbits (Lynn, 1960).

Recent work using radioiodine and chromtatographic analysis serves to elucidate some of the details of biosynthesis of thyroid hormones in reptiles. In both *Terrapene carolina*, a terrestrial turtle, and *Pseudemys floridana*, an aquatic species, the thyroid is capable of accumulating I^{131} and synthesizing T_4, and it responds to TSH injection by an increased rate of I^{131} accumulation (Shellabarger *et al.*, 1956). Turtles kept under wet conditions show less I^{131} accumulation in the thyroid and more I^{131} excretion in the urine than do those kept under dry conditions. Under dry conditions as much as 80% of the administered radioiodine is present in the thyroid by 8 days after administration. There is almost no excretion of I^{131} in the urine under these conditions, and it is postulated that, due to urinary retention, the urinary bladder acts as a reservoir for radioiodine which is slowly returned to the circulation by way of the cloaca. There is also a seasonal difference in thyroid function in these turtles. *Pseudemys* studied in March at one to four days after I^{131} administration showed incorporation in MIT and DIT only. Similar experiments in September revealed the presence of labelled T_4, as well as MIT and DIT, within three days. The amount of labelled T_4 then increased throughout the 27-day period of study. T_3 was also found, although in very small amounts.

The pattern of uptake and release of I^{131} by the thyroid in *Anolis carolinensis* and *Sceloporus occidentalis* has also been studied for both normal and dehydrated animals (Kobayashi and Gorbman, 1959). In these animals the uptake of I^{131} by the gland did not differ in the two groups. The maximum uptake did not occur until 24 to 48 hours after administration, but thereafter there was no decrease in level for as long as eight days. This plateau level was about 10% of the injected dose in *Anolis* and 15% in *Sceloporus*. These observations suggest a rather slow thyroidal accumulation of I^{131} from the blood and reservoir tissues and a low rate of turnover. Synthesis of thyroid hormone also occurred slowly. MIT and DIT were found at highest levels at 24 to 48 hours after I^{131} administration and these decreased progressively while the levels of T_3 and T_4 (plus two unidentified radioiodinated compounds) gradually increased. In contrast to the results of the experiments on turtles, these studies show no well-defined effect of dehydration on the metabolism of radioiodine.

The uptake and release of I^{131} by the thyroids of lizards (*Anolis carolinensis*) acclimated at two widely differing temperatures (15° and 35°C) show marked differences (Lynn *et al.*, 1965). At 15° the highest levels of radio-activity are found during the first 24 hours after I^{131} administration and there is then a gradual decline throughout the next five days. At 35° there is a rapid increase in I^{131} accumulation to reach a peak which is much higher than is ever attained at 15°. This peak occurs at 48 hours and is followed by a fairly rapid decrease in activity so that by six days after injection the level is the same as that found in the lizards kept at 15°. Thiourea administration to animals maintained at these two temperatures strongly depresses the initial uptake of I^{131} in the thyroid, but specimens kept at 15° show a slower rate of turnover than do those kept at 35°.

Xantusia, a nocturnal lizard, kept at 26°C, shows the expected responses to thiourea or TSH treatment with respect to radioiodine uptake and release, but also gives some evidence of diurnal fluctuations in thyroid activity that may be correlated with its nocturnal habits (Buckingham, 1970).

In young alligators I^{131} uptake by the thyroid rises steadily to reach a peak of 19·6% of the injected dose at five days, and this declines to 7·8% by seven days. TSH administration causes only a slight loss of radioactivity; propylthiouracil or KI injection reduces the uptake sharply (Waterman, 1961a). Young turtles (*Pseudemys scripta*) reach peak uptakes earlier and at somewhat higher levels and also show a marked response to propylthiouracil, KI, or T_4 injection. Late embryos show relatively lower levels of uptake but also respond to propylthiouracil (Waterman, 1961b).

Differences in the rate of accumulation of I^{131} by the thyroid of *Lacerta* as compared with that of the dogfish have been interpreted as indicating differences between the active agents of the thyroid in these two animals (Sembrat, 1963).

VII. Seasonal Changes in the Thyroid

A. SEASONAL CHANGES RELATED TO TEMPERATURE

Seasonal changes in the histological appearance of the thyroid in temperate zone lizards were reported by Weigmann (1932) for *Lacerta*. These changes, as might be expected, indicate a higher functional activity in summer than in winter. Eggert's (1935) study for three different species of *Lacerta* confirms and extends Weigmann's observations. Moreover, his investigation of thyroid histology in lizards kept in the laboratory under controlled temperature conditions leads to the conclusion that the seasonal changes seen in animals collected in the field are mainly dependent upon environmental temperature (Eggert, 1936c). Gravid females of *Lacerta vivipara* have thyroid levels slightly higher than those of non-gravid animals, but Eggert considers that this is also a temperature effect related to the fact that pregnant lizards expose themselves to the sun for longer periods than usual.

Sceloporus undulatus shows a similar seasonal variation in thyroid histology (Wilhoft, 1958; Eakin *et al.*, 1959), but in addition to temperature-dependent changes there are alterations in the thyroid connected with breeding activity. Wilhoft's work also clearly emphasizes the fact that observations on thyroid histology in lizards collected in the field may be quite misleading in indicating a direct relation between air temperature and thyroid activity. Because of the well-known basking habit of reptiles, records of average daily air temperature may differ widely from the temperatures to which the animals are actually exposed. When the air temperature is low most reptiles spend a large proportion of the daylight hours basking in direct sunlight, but periods of extremely high air temperature may be spent entirely in shaded areas at significantly lower temperatures. Wilhoft found that thyroid activity, as judged by histological criteria, in *Sceloporus* fell steadily from July into September despite the fact that air temperatures in the collecting area were steadily rising during that time. Field observations showed that the animals were less active during this period and some could be said to be aestivating. Experimental exposure of *Sceloporus* to continuous high temperatures (34°–35°C) for periods up to thirteen weeks caused marked increases in thyroid epithelial height beginning within three weeks. A high mortality occurred in animals given the high temperature treatment for longer than six weeks.

Lizards that inhabit warmer climates and do not have a hibernating period give histological signs of highest thyroid activity during the cool winter months, possibly in relation to the maintenance of feeding activity in the winter, and a decrease in physical activity in the summer (Evans and Hegre, 1938, *Anolis carolinensis*; Miller, 1955, *Xantusia vigilis*). *Leiolopisma rhomboidalis* of tropical Australia shows less seasonal variation in thyroid epithelial height than do either *Sceloporus* or *Xantusia*, but, in general, the lowest activity occurs during the cold season (May to August) (Wilhoft, 1963, 1964). In this species there are also variations in thyroid activity in both males and females that are related to the reproductive cycle. In *Agama agama savattieri* a marked increase in thyroid activity is found in March and

April as compared with January and February (Charnier and Dutarte, 1956). This apparently corresponds with a notable change in humidity rather than an increase in environmental temperature. It is probably also related to an increase in physical activity at this time and to the onset of the breeding season. Young *Anguis fragilis* are reported to show the highest thyroid activity in April and May (Raynaud *et al.*, 1963).

Few studies of seasonal variations in the thyroid are available for snakes. Both *Vipera aspis* and *V. berus* exhibit low levels of thyroid activity during hibernation and higher levels in the summer, but the differences are more marked in *V. berus*, specimens of which were collected in the Alps at altitudes of 3,300 to 5,600 feet, than in *V. aspis*, a lowland species. In both, however, the highest levels of thyroid activity are associated with reproductive events (Saint Girons and Duguy, 1962a and b). A similar situation is reported for *Natrix maura* (Saint Girons and Duguy, 1966).

Turtles (*Chrysemys picta bellii*) exhibit evidence of very low thyroid activity during hibernation (Evans and Hegre, 1940). There is a direct relation between environmental temperature and the per cent uptake of radioiodine by the thyroid of *Pseudemys* and *Terrapene* (Shellabarger *et al.*, 1956). Moreover, injection of TSH is unable to influence the rate of thyroidal accumulation of I^{131} at very low temperatures ($2°–3°C$).

The thyroids of lizards (*Anolis carolinensis*) maintained in the laboratory at $35°C$ show histological evidence of slightly higher activity and much less variability than do those of animals kept at $15°C$, but the effect of this temperature difference upon the functioning of the gland, as indicated by its uptake and release of radioiodine, is very great (Lynn *et al.*, 1965). We have obtained similar results for *Phrynosoma cornutum*.

The length of day may also influence thyroid activity. Exposure of turtles (*Testudo horsfieldii*) to continuous illumination causes a stimulation of the thyroid which reaches a peak within five days but then gradually declines so that the gland becomes inactive by the thirty-fifth day (Voitkewitsch, 1944).

B. SEASONAL CHANGES RELATED TO REPRODUCTIVE CYCLES

Eggert (1936c) reported that he could find no evidence of histological changes in the thyroid correlated with the breeding season in *Lacerta*. However, he found that thyroidectomy results in striking effects on both gonadal structure and breeding behaviour (Eggert, 1937). The gonads show degenerative changes which ultimately result in loss of reproductive ability. Males fail to get the spring nuptial coat and do not mate. Eggert postulated that the effect of thyroidectomy in the gonads may be indirect, partly due to a decrease in general metabolism and partly to some interference with anterior pituitary function. Wilhoft's (1958) measurements of the height of the thyroid epithelium in adult *Sceloporus occidentalis* collected throughout the period of activity (March through November) shows a gradual increase in epithelial height in both sexes through the period of mating in April or May until June. Thereafter there is a rapid decrease in females immediately after egg-laying. Males show a more gradual decrease beginning in July, and, as has been noted above, these decreases continue into September despite the fact that environmental temperatures are increasing during this period. Study of the gonads indicates that spermatogenesis occurs during or shortly after emergence from hibernation and thus takes place during a time of relatively low thyroid activity. There is also a period of increase in testis size in September when thyroid epithelial height is again decreasing. In the females there seems to be a definite peak in thyroid activity associated with yolk deposition and ovulation. In *Anolis carolinensis* there is an increase in thyroid epithelial height in ovulating females, and experiments indicate that an increased level of ovarian hormones may be responsible for the thyroid response (Evans and Hegre, 1938).

The Japanese lacertid lizard *Takydromus* exhibits characteristic changes in the Golgi apparatus of the cells of the thyroid epithelium during the breeding season, and these changes can be induced in castrated animals by the injection of sex hormones (Hatta, 1944). The thyroid also shows a cycle that is related to the reproductive system in *Anguis fragilis* (Saint Girons, 1963b). *Xantusia vigilis*, a viviparous lizard, has a gestation period of three months. The thyroid of the female is hyperactive during the period of yolk deposition, ovulation, and the early part of gestation, declines in activity during the latter half of gestation, and is relatively inactive by the time of parturition (Miller, 1955). The male thyroid, though less markedly hyperactive than that of the female, shows increased activity correlated with spermatogenesis, development of sex accessories, and copulatory behaviour in the spring and another peak of activity in the fall when a new cycle of spermatogenesis begins. Wilhoft's (1963, 1964) findings for *Leiolopisma rhomboidalis* also show high thyroid activity in females during yolk deposition and in males during spring and fall periods of spermatogeneis and increased reproductive activity.

The sexual cycle of *Vipera aspis* is characterized by two periods of mating activity each year (Saint Girons, 1957; Duguy, 1958). Copulation occurs shortly after emergence from hibernation (March–April) and again in the fall (late September). Females have a two-year cycle. The first year, following the spring mating, yolk deposition and ovulation occur and gestation begins. The second year there is no spring mating but copulation does occur in the fall. Males show a slight rise in thyroid activity during the two mating periods, but no change that can be correlated directly with spermatogenesis. Females show similar increases in spring and fall, but the thyroid epithelium is at a low level during both yolk deposition and gestation (Saint Girons and Duguy, 1962a).

In the cobra (*Naja naja*) there is a peak of thyroid activity in males just after emergence from hibernation in the spring which corresponds with the time of active spermiogenesis and mating. Moreover, a secondary secretory peak occurs during the period of testicular recrudescense in September (Chiu *et al.*, 1969). It has been shown that the cobra also exhibits two peaks of testosterone production at these same times (Tam *et al.*, 1967). In *Natrix maura* males show peaks of thyroid stimulation in spring and autumn, and females have peaks that correspond to periods of mating and ovulation. The thyroid is not in a resting stage at the beginning of hibernation but colloid accumulation becomes marked during the winter (Saint Girons and Duguy, 1966).

Increased activity of the thyroid during sexual activity is found in both males and females of *Clemmys caspica leprosa*, and administration of either male or female hormones to immature specimens is reported to cause activation of the thyroid as well as of the sexual system (Combescot, 1956).

It is difficult to assess the degree to which seasonal changes in thyroid histology or physiology can be taken to demonstrate a direct association between the thyroid secretions and reproductive events. Miller (1959) has pointed out that the period of breeding corresponds with a time of greatest bodily activity (feeding, fighting, etc.) in reptiles, and the thyroid secretions may increase in association with this rather than with any specific reproductive event. Unfortunately experimental studies that would serve to elucidate this matter are still scanty. Mellish and Meyer (1937) found that thyroxin injection causes ovarian atrophy in the horned lizard (*Phrynosoma*), and Evans and Hegre (1938) reported evidence for increased thyroid activity after theelin administration in *Anolis*.

There is no clear evidence for increased thyroid function during pregnancy in live-bearing reptiles. No appreciable changes in thyroid histology occur during gestation in *Vipera* (Saint Girons and Duguy, 1962a). Eggert (1935) reported that thyroid activity is high throughout gestation in *Lacerta* but attributed this to the tendency of the pregnant females to bask in the sunlight. In *Xantusia* thyroid activity declines after the second or third week of pregnancy and remains relatively low thereafter (Miller, 1955).

VIII. The Thyroid and Metabolism

Whether the thyroid plays a role in the control of metabolic rate in reptiles, or indeed in any poikilotherm, has long been open to question. Several early investigators maintained, on the basis of indirect evidence, that some of the features that seem related to changes in thyroid function in reptiles could be interpreted as accompaniments of thyroid-caused alterations in metabolic rate (Weigmann, 1932; Eggert, 1933, 1936a; Krockert, 1941; Rivera Commers, 1955). However, until recently, attempts to demonstrate direct effects of T_4 administration or thyroidectomy upon oxidative metabolism were unsuccessful (Lynn, 1960). The explanation for these failures now seems clear. It has been shown that in *Anolis carolinensis*, although thyroidectomy or administration of T_4 or TSH cause no change in oxygen consumption in animals maintained at 21° to 24°C, all of these treatments have striking effects in lizards kept at 30°C. This suggests that the tissues may be more responsive to thyroid hormone at 30°C (which is near the optimal temperature for *A. carolinensis*) than they are at lower temperatures (Maher and Levedahl, 1959). This seems to be the case for, in *Eumeces obsoletus* maintained at 30°C and given daily injections of T_4 for three weeks, determinations of oxygen consumption of individual tissues (liver, brain, heart, lung) show significantly higher levels as compared with those for controls. Only skeletal muscle failed to show a response, possibly because the technique used resulted in a low survival of the muscle tissue (Maher, 1964). The relation between environmental temperature and the metabolic response to thyroid hormone has been convincingly demonstrated in *Lacerta muralis* by maintaining groups of T_4-injected and control animals at 30°C for two weeks, by which time a striking difference in oxygen consumption was demonstrable, and then reducing the temperature to 20° while still continuing the T_4 injections. Within nine days the oxygen consumption in the two groups was at the same level. Returning the lizards to 30°C resulted in re-establishment of a marked difference within a week (Maher, 1961). In *Eumeces fasciatus* similar results are obtained with T_4 administration, and thyroidectomy causes a corresponding lowering of oxygen consumption at 30°C but not at 20°C. *Eumeces* given daily T_4 injections and subjected to 10 hours at 33°C and 14 hours at 20° each day show a rise in oxygen consumption after one or two weeks (Maher, 1965). Some of the above work has been reviewed by Jankowsky (1964).

IX. The Thyroid and Ecdysis

A relation between thyroid function and moulting of the outer layer of the skin is well established for *Lacerta*. This was first indicated by the work of Drzewicki (1926, 1927, 1929) which showed that thyroidectomy causes cessation of moulting. In thyroidless animals the horny layer is formed continuously and the differentiation of a border sheet (*stratum terminativum*) fails to occur. Eggert's (1933, 1936a) extensive investigation of this phenomenon in *Lacerta agilis*, *L. muralis*, and *L. vivipara* showed that the thyroid is relatively inactive during the phase of rapid formation and cornification of new epidermis. During the brief period of actual moulting, however, the height of the thyroid epithelium increases, chromophobe droplets become numerous in the colloid, and colloid release occurs. This activity continues for several days after ecdysis but gradually decreases to reach a low point again during the period preceding the next moult. Eggert confirmed the fact that thyroidectomy causes cessation of ecdysis and also found that implantation of thyroid tissue into the musculature of thyroidectomized lizards enables them to carry out several successful moults. Other studies on *Lacerta* confirm these findings (Sembrat and Drzewicki, 1935, 1936; Adams and Craig, 1950). Recent histological studies on the moulting cycle and its relation to thyroid activity in the lizard *Gekko gecko* (Maderson, 1965b, 1966) also agree with this general picture.

Later investigations concerning other lizards gave less clear-cut results. Noble and Bradley (1933) reported that neither thyroidectomy nor hypophysectomy causes cessation of moulting in *Hemidactylus brookii*, although either operation does result in a lengthening of the period between moults, an effect which can be eliminated by thyroxin administration. Ratzersdorfer *et al.* (1949) found that thiourea administration to *Anolis carolinensis* has no detectable effect on ecdysis, even though the thyroid shows definite histological indications that effective inhibition of thyroid function has been achieved. On the other hand, in Wilhoft's (1958) experiments with *Sceloporus occidentalis* kept continuously at 34·0° to 35·0°C it was observed that shedding, in the form of gradual flaking off of the skin, occurred more frequently in the experimental animals than in controls and was correlated with the time of greatest increase in height of the thyroid epithelium. Recent findings by Chiu *et al.* (1967) show that thyroidectomy decreases the frequency of moulting in the Tokay (*Gekko gecko*) whereas thyroxine injection into unoperated animals increases the frequency. The effects of thyroidectomy may be eliminated by administration of exogenous thyroxine. Hypophysectomy is similarly effective in decreasing the frequency of ecdysis, and this effect can be eliminated by injection of either TSH or prolactin. In this lizard it appears that the thyroid secretion affects only the resting phase of the sloughing cycle and has no effect upon the keratinization phase. Thus no hyperkeratosis occurs after thyroidectomy.

For snakes the evidence thus far indicates that the thyroid influence on ecdysis is the reverse of that in lizards. Schaefer (1933) found that either hypophysectomy or thyroidectomy results in a significant increase in molting activity in *Thamnophis*, while thyroid administration causes a cessation of shedding. Results leading to a similar conclusion were reported by Krockert (1941) for *Python*, by Halberkann (1953, 1954a, and b) and Goslar (1958a and b, 1964) for *Natrix*, by Maderson *et al.* (1969) for *Ptyas*, and by Chiu and Lynn (1970) for *Chionactis*. Saint Girons and Duguy (1962a) note some indication of brief periods of increased thyroid activity corresponding to moulting in *Vipera aspis* but do not feel that their studies are decisive on this point. Details of the histological changes in the skin of snakes during the moulting cycle are given by Maderson (1965a).

Ecdysis in squamates is also reported to be influenced by various other substances, notably thymus extract, growth hormone, ACTH, various sex hormones (Goslar, 1958b and c), and prolactin (Chiu et al., 1967; Licht and Jones, 1967; Maderson and Licht, 1967). Whether these act directly upon the sloughing cycle or through some influence on the thyroid gland remains to be investigated.

X. The Thyroid and Growth and Differentiation

There are no reports of comprehensive experiments concerning the effect of thyroidectomy, of thyroid inhibition, or of T_4 or TSH administration upon growth rate in young reptiles. Drzewicki (1929) gave some incidental observations indicating that thyroidectomy causes growth inhibition in the young of *Lacerta agilis*, and Giusti (1931), on the basis of a single specimen of *Clemmys caspica leprosa* thyroidectomized at the age of three months, reported a marked retardation in growth rate in this animal as compared with a control of the same initial age and size. Wilhoft (1958) found that juveniles of *Sceloporus occidentalis* show a higher thyroid epithelium throughout most of the summer than do adults which may indicate a relation to their high growth rate. Krockert (1941), however, observed that a young python fed regularly on pig thyroid gland showed an inhibition in growth rate as compared with a control fed on pig pineal or one fed on rodents.

Inhibition of thyroid function during embryonic stages has been studied in *Chelydra serpentina* (Dimond, 1954). Developing eggs were treated with thiourea solutions either by injection into the albumen or by raising them on cotton moistened with the solutions. Thyroids of these embryos showed the typical response to goitrogens indicating that the concentrations used were effective in inhibiting production of thyroid hormone. The embryos had a decreased growth rate, abnormalities of the carapace were common, hatching was delayed, and normal retraction of the yolk sac into the body did not occur.

Thyroidectomy of pregnant females of *Lacerta* six to eight weeks before the end of term often results in premature discharge of the eggs which, however, contain normal embryos. If the eggs are retained, some embryos degenerate and others survive but are unable to hatch. Thyroidectomy at later stages in pregnancy is followed by more normal development and hatching (Eggert, 1933).

XI. The Thyroid and Other Endocrine Organs

In addition to the direct control of thyroid function by pituitary-produced TSH and the relations between the thyroid and gonadal activity which have been discussed above, there are also correlations between thyroid function and various other endocrine mechanisms.

Early studies showed that histological changes occur in the parathyroid glands of lizards after thyroidectomy (Viguier, 1911a, *Uromastyx acanthinurus*; Drzewicki, 1927, *Lacerta agilis*). These changes involve disappearance of some cellular elements and formation of colloid-filled epithelial vesicles that are not normally present. They are interpreted as indications of hyperfunction. It is noteworthy, however, that this parathyroid response was also seen in lizards in which the thyroid had been removed and then re-implanted (Drzewicki, 1927).

The ultimobranchial bodies (postbranchial bodies) were reported to undergo hypertrophy in thyroidectomized lizards (Drzewicki, 1929; Sembrat and Drzewicki, 1936). Eggert (1936b, 1937, 1938b) failed to confirm this response, but found instead that the ultimobranchial bodies show seasonal variations in secretory activity corresponding to those that occur in the thyroid. Moreover they respond to TSH administration in the same way as the thyroid. Long-continued treatment with TSH causes the formation of cysts. Eggert concluded that the ultimobranchial bodies of lizards are directly affected by TSH, but noted that hypophysectomy does not produce any detectable change in these structures. The ultimobranchial bodies of *Lacerta agilis* usually begin to undergo degenerative alterations during the second or third summer. Removal of ultimobranchial bodies causes no observable effect upon the behaviour or physiology of the lizard or upon the histology of its thyroid.

Removal of the parietal eye in *Sceloporus occidentalis* and *Uma ornata* results in thyroid stimulation (Stebbins and Eakin, 1958; Eakin *et al.*, 1959). Parietalectomized animals maintained in the laboratory at the mean temperature of their normal habitat show heightened thyroid epithelium and reduction of stored colloid within several months after operation. Lizards allowed to live free in the field after parietalectomy give histological evidence of elevated thyroid activity when collected in winter or spring but not when collected during the summer. The operation does not prevent the thyroid from going through an annual cycle of activity. It is suggested that the reptilian parietal eye may produce a hormone which exerts an inhibiting effect upon the bodily activity of the animal, probably via the pineal, pituitary, thyroid, and other endocrine glands. Studies of the histology and ultrastructure of the parietal eye seem to support the idea that it has a secretory function (Eakin and Westfall, 1959, 1960; Steyn, 1959; Steyn and Steyn, 1962).

Destruction of the epiphyseal region in the turtle, *Clemmys caspica leprosa*, by electro-cautery results in exophthalmia which can be relieved by the administration of lyophilized mammalian epiphysis (Aron *et al.*, 1960a and b).

The operated animals also show testicular inactivity and thyroid stimulation. There is a marked increase in neurosecretory material in the paraventricular nucleus of tortoises within five months after destruction of the epiphysis (Aron et al., 1960c). The ultrastructure of the epiphysis in turtles (*Pseudemys*) and snakes (*Natrix*) is consistent with secretory function (Vivien, 1964a and b).

XII. Miscellaneous Effects of Thyroid Hormone

Thyroidectomy is reported to result in formation of fluid-filled cysts in the thymus (Drzewicki, 1929, *Lacerta*), and injection of mammalian thymus extract is said to cause thyroid inactivity accompanied by increased frequency of ecdysis in a snake (Goslar, 1958b, *Natrix*).

Thyroidectomized *Lacerta* show a gradual decrease in physical activity and appetite and they die within three to eight months with indications of an anemia due to decreased blood-forming activity in the bone marrow (Eggert, 1933, 1936a). Thyroxin administration prevents the appearance of these symptoms. A relation between hematopoiesis and thyroid function is also indicated by the work of Charipper and Davis (1932) on *Pseudemys* and that of M. C. Saint Girons (1961) on *Vipera*. Maher and Levedahl (1959) concluded that the high mortality in their experiments with thyroxine-treated *Anolis* was related to involvement of the nervous system since the animals were subject to uncontrolled muscle contractions after tactile stimulation.

General pugnacity and territorial behaviour are increased by thyroxin or TSH in *Anolis* (Evans and Clapp, 1940) and thyroid feeding increases irritability in *Python* (Krockert, 1941).

XIII. Conclusion

During the past decade there has been a notable increase in researches concerning the thyroid of reptiles, and these have resulted in new insights into both the morphology and physiology of the gland in this group. In addition, these studies have served to indicate a number of promising areas for future investigation.

Newly developed histological techniques should be more fully applied to study of both the thyroid and pituitary in an effort to further elucidate questions concerning the secretory process, the precise identification of thyrotrophs, and the feedback mechanism involved in pituitary control. Autoradiographic determination of I^{131} localization in the cells of the thyroid epithelium and in the colloid under diverse conditions are not yet available for any reptile. Such studies would be of particular interest for the macrothyreocytes of snakes. Investigation of the ultrastructure of reptilian thyroid cells has made but a bare beginning, but there are indications that use of the electron microscope on such material will be most rewarding. Again, examination of the macrothyreocyte as a possible site of intracellular colloidogenesis seems especially needed. No work has been done on reptiles on the cellular biochemistry of the thyroid as revealed by study of enzyme systems, nor is there any information for this group concerning blood transport of thyroid hormones or their utilization in the peripheral tissues.

Although the origin and differentiation of the thyroid have been investigated for a number of reptiles, much remains to be done in the field of development. None of the lizards in which the thyroid is completely paired have been studied embryologically. It would be interesting to know when and how the originally single thyroid Anlage separates into two parts and to attempt to ascertain whether there is any mechanical explanation for this separation, as seems to be the case in anurans. Thus far there has been no approach to experimental study of reptilian embryology by microsurgical techniques. This is doubtless due to the lack of readily available embryonic material, but it would seem that the familiar methods that are so widely used in chick embryology could be adapted for reptilian eggs. Repetition of much of the classical work on avian embryology dealing with embryonic induction would then be possible and would be of special interest in reptiles, the only poikilothermous amniotes. With respect to the thyroid, a study of the differentiative capacity of the thyroid Anlage in chorioallantoic grafts immediately suggests itself. A related field of experimentation is the culture of embryonic thyroid tissue *in vitro*, another promising method for investigation of secretory function which remains to be exploited in these animals. The earliest beginning of iodide concentration by the cells of the embryonic thyroid, as indicated by uptake of I^{131}, has been studied for turtles only, and much more needs to be done in this area.

The relation between I^{131} metabolism and environmental temperature is known for several lizards, but more work is needed comparing this feature in reptiles living in regions in which optimal temperatures are widely different. The possible role of the thyroid in high temperature tolerance may be susceptible of elucidation by such studies, and this may be closely related to the mechanism of adaptation to special habitats.

Maher's (1961) recent studies on the metabolic effects of the thyroid hormone in lizards kept at high temperature have effectively disposed of the old question of whether the thyroid ever has any effect on metabolic rate in any poikilotherm. Such work must now be extended to other reptilian groups and to a wider variety of experimental treatments.

The extensive investigation by Eggert (1935, 1936a and c) concerning the role of the thyroid in ecdysis in *Lacerta* remains the classic in this area, and his findings are unequivocal. However, the conflicting results obtained in the few available studies on other lizards and the evidence for an opposite effect in snakes should lead to new comprehensive work on this phenomenon in other squamates.

The effect of the thyroid secretion upon bodily growth and differentiation is another subject that has been largely neglected. Much more work is needed directed towards accurate determination of effects of T_4 administration, thyroidectomy, and other experimental treatments in young animals and during embryonic stages. Such studies must concern not only general body growth but also growth and differentiation of various organ systems like the nervous system, skeletal system, and reproductive system which are known to be influenced by the thyroid in other animals.

The work of Eggert (1936b) on the thyroid-like responses of the ultimo-branchial bodies in *Lacerta* is an example of a particularly interesting early observation that deserves further attention. Effects of the thyroid upon hematopoiesis in reptiles have been indicated by several studies, but many other physiological relationships that are well demonstrated in mammals have not yet been explored in any reptile. These include renal function, secretory and muscular activity in the gastrointestinal tract, calcium metabolism, functioning of skeletal muscles, and wound healing.

Finally, the relation of thyroid function to behavioural patterns in reptiles is a field that is undoubtedly destined to develop rapidly. The studies of cyclic changes in the thyroid in connection with the reproductive cycle indicate that thyroid activity may play a part in sexual behaviour as well as in gonadal maturation and ovulation. The results of parietalectomy in lizards suggest a complex role of the parietal eye, the thyroid, and other endocrine organs in the behavioural patterns involved in seeking optimal conditions of light and temperature. There is currently much active interest in both of these aspects of reptilian behaviour, and the part played by the thyroid must certainly receive further evaluation.

GENERA CITED

TESTUDINES

Chelydra: Dimond, 1954.

Clemmys: Yamamoto, 1960; Giusti, 1931; Combescot, 1955, 1956; Aron et al., 1960a, b, c; Naccarati, 1922; Barchiesi, 1928.

Chrysemys: Evans and Hegre, 1940; Bileau, 1956.

Pseudemys: Shellabarger et al., 1956; Charipper and Davis, 1932; Waterman, 1961b; Vivien, 1964a.

Terrapene: Shellabarger et al., 1956.

Testudo: Herlant and Grignon, 1961; Voitkewitsch, 1944; Naccarati, 1922.

Lepidochelys: Yamamoto, 1960.

RHYNCHOCEPHALIA

Sphenodon: Lynn, 1960; Van Bemmelen, 1887; O'Donoghue, 1920; Adams, 1939.

SAURIA

Anolis: Evans and Clapp, 1940; Ratzersdorfer *et al.*, 1949; Kobayashi and Gorbman, 1959; Evans and Hegre, 1938; Maher and Levedahl, 1959; Nussbaum, 1963; Lynn *et al.*, 1965.

Phrynosoma: Mellish and Meyer, 1937.

Sceloporus: Wilhoft, 1958; Kobayashi and Gorbman, 1959; Eakin *et al.*, 1959; Chiu *et al.*, 1970.

Uma: Stebbins and Eakin, 1958.

Agama: Charnier and Dutarte, 1956.

Uromastyx: Viguier, 1911a, b.

Gekko: Yamamoto, 1960; Maderson, 1965b, 1966; Chiu *et al.*, 1967; Chiu and Phillips, 1969.

Hemidactylus: Noble and Bradley, 1933.

Tarentola: Viguier, 1909a, b.

Xantusia: Miller, 1948, 1955, 1963; Buckingham, 1970.

Chalcides: Viguier, 1911c.

Eumeces: Yamamoto, 1960; Maher, 1964, 1965.

Leiolopisma: Wilhoft, 1963, 1964.

Lacerta: Eggert, 1933, 1935, 1936a, b, c, 1937, 1938b; Weigmann, 1932; Maher, 1961; Sembrat, 1963; Drzewicki, 1926, 1927, 1929; Sembrat and Drzewicki, 1935, 1936; Adams and Craig, 1950; Viguier, 1911c.

Psammodromus: Viguier, 1911c.

Takydromus: Hatta, 1944.

Anguis: Raynaud and Raynaud, 1961; Raynaud *et al.*, 1963; Saint Girons, 1963b.

AMPHISBAENIA

Trogonophis: Gans and Lynn, 1965.

OPHIDIA

Python: Gabe, 1961; Krockert, 1941.

Chionactis: Chiu and Lynn, 1970.

Coluber: Francescon, 1929.

Elaphe: Yamamoto, 1960; Kurosumi, 1961.

Malpolon: Francescon, 1929.

Natrix: Yamamoto, 1960; Mason, 1938; Halberkann, 1953, 1954a, b; Vivien, 1964b; Thompson, 1910; Bragdon, 1953; Goslar, 1958a, b, 1964; Saint Girons and Duguy, 1966.

Ptyas: Maderson *et al.*, 1970.

Thamnophis: Schaefer, 1933; Siler, 1936; Hellbaum, 1936.

Naja: Chiu *et al.*, 1969; Tam *et al.*, 1967.

Agkistrodon: Yamamoto, 1960.
Cerastes: Gabe, 1961.
Vipera: Gabe, 1961; M. C. Saint Girons, 1961; H. Saint Girons, 1957;
Saint Girons and Duguy, 1962a, b; Duguy, 1958.
CROCODILIA
Alligator: Waterman, 1961a.

References

Adams, A. E. and Craig, M. (1950). Observations on normal, thyroidectomized, thiourea-
and thiouracil-treated *Lacerta agilis. Anat. Rec.* 106, 263 (Abstract).

Adams, W. E. (1939). The cervical region of the Lacertilia. *J. Anat.* 74, 57–71.

Aron, E., Combescot, C. and Demaret, J. (1960a). Thyréostimulation et repos sexuel
après destruction de la région épiphysaire chez *Emys leprosa* Schw. *C. r. Séanc. Soc.
Biol.* 154, 1856–1859.

Aron, E., Combescot, C. and Demaret, J. (1960b). Exophtalmie de la tortue d'eau *Emys
leprosa* Schw. produite par la destruction de la région épiphysaire. *C. r. hebd. Séanc.
Acad. Sci., Paris* 250, 3386–3387.

Aron, E., Combescot, C., Demaret, J. and Guyon, L. (1960c). Neurosécrétion chez la
tortue d'eau *Emys leprosa* Schw. après destruction de la région épiphysaire. *C. r. hebd.
Séanc. Acad. Sci., Paris* 251, 1914–1916.

Barchiesi, A. (1928). Ricerche istologiche sulla tiroide di *"Emys orbicularis* L." tenute a
diquino fino a ventisei mesi. *Bill. Soc. ital. Biol. sper.* 3, 1204–1206.

Berg, O., Gorbman, A. and Kobayashi, H. (1959). Thyroid hormones in invertebrates and
lower vertebrates. *In* "Comparative Endocrinology" (A. Gorbman, ed.), p. 302–319.
Wiley and Sons, New York.

Bern, H. A. and Nandi, J. (1964). Endocrinology of poikilothermic vertebrates. *In* "The
Hormones" (G. Pincus, K. V. Thimann and E. B. Astwood, eds), 4, 199–298. Academic
Press, New York.

Bileau, Sr. M. (1956). The uptake of I^{131} by the thyroid gland of turtles after treatment
with thiourea. *Biol. Bull. Mar. biol. Lab., Woods Hole* 111, 190–203.

Bragdon, D. E. (1953). A contribution to the surgical anatomy of the water snake, *Natrix
sipedon sipedon*; the location of the visceral endocrine organs with reference to ventral
scutellation. *Anat. Rec.* 117, 145–161.

Buckingham, M. B. (1970). Effects of TSH and thiourea upon thyroid function in the
lizard *Xantusia henshawi. Gen. Comp. Endocrinol.* 14, 178–183.

Chakrabarty, N. C. (1962). The thyroid in house lizards. *J. anat. Soc. India* 11, 39
(Abstract).

Charipper, H. A. and Davis, D. (1932). Studies on the Arneth count. XX. A study of the
blood cells of *Pseudemys elegans* with special reference to the polymorphonuclear
leucocytes. *Q. Jl exp. Physiol.* 21, 371–382.

Charnier, M. and Dutarte, J. P. (1956). Variations histo-physiologiques de la thyroïde
du lézard de la région de Dakar pendant le période de préhivernage. *C. r. Séanc. Soc.
Biol.* 150, 1387–1388.

Chiu, K. W., Lynn, W. G. and Leichner, J. P. (1970). Environmental temperature and
thyroid activity in the fence lizard, *Sceloporus occidentalis. Biol. Bull. Mar. biol. Lab.,
Woods Hole* (in press).

Chiu, K. W. and Lynn, W. G. (1969). The role of the thyroid in ecdysis in the shovel-
nosed snake, *Chionactis occipitalis. Gen. Comp. Endocrinol.* (in press).

Chiu, K. W. and Phillips, J. G. (1969). The effect of hypophysectomy and of replacement using TSH and ACTH on the sloughing cycle in the gecko, *Gekko gecko* L. (in preparation).

Chiu, K. W., Phillips, J. G. and Maderson, P. F. A. (1967). The role of the thyroid in the control of the sloughing cycle in the Tokay (*Gekko gecko*, Lacertilia). *J. Endocr.* 39, 463–472.

Chiu, K. W., Phillips, J. G. and Maderson, P. F. A. (1969). Seasonal changes in the thyroid gland in the male cobra, *Naja naja* L. *Biol. Bull. Mar. biol. Lab.*, *Woods Hole* 136, 347–354.

Combescot, C. (1955). L'hypophyse, la thyroïde et la surrénale de la tortue d'eau algérienne. *Bull. Soc. Hist. nat. Afr. N.* 46, 250–257.

Combescot, C. (1956). Sur les variations thyroïdiennes chez la tortue d'eau algérienne. *C. r. Séanc. Soc. Biol.* 149, 2169–2171.

Desmarais, A. and Laham, Q. N. (1960). The histophysiology of the thyroid. A review. *Revue can. Biol.* 19, 1–26.

Dimond, Sr. M. T. (1954). The reactions of developing snapping turtles, *Chelydra serpentina serpentina* (Linné), to thiourea. *J. exp. Zool.* 127, 93–115.

Dimond, Sr. M. T. (1963). Pituitary-thyroid relations in developing turtles. *Proc. 16th Intern. Congr. Zool.* 2, 159 (Abstract).

Drzewicki, S. (1926). Influence de l'extirpation de la glande thyroïde sur la mue du lézard (*Lacerta agilis* L.). *C. r. Séanc. Soc. Biol.* 95, 893–895.

Drzewicki, S. (1927). Examen histologique des lézards thyroïdectomisés (*Lacerta agilis* L.). *C. r. Séanc. Soc. Biol.* 97, 925–926.

Drzewicki, S. (1929). Über den Einfluss der Schilddrüsenexstirpation auf die Zauneidechse. (Hemmung des Häutungsprozesses, Veränderungen in der Haut, in den Augen und in den innersekretorischen Drüsen, Wachstumshemmung). *Arch. EntwMech. Org.* 114, 155–176.

Duguy, R. (1958). Le comportement de printemps chez *Vipera aspis*. *Vie Milieu* 9, 200–210.

Eakin, R. M. and Westfall, J. A. (1959). Fine structure of the retina in the reptilian third eye. *J. biophys. biochem. Cytol.* 6, 133–134.

Eakin, R. M. and Westfall, J. A. (1960). Further observations on the fine structure of the parietal eye of lizards. *J. biophys. biochem. Cytol.* 8, 483–499.

Eakin, R. M., Stebbins, R. C. and Wilhoft, D. C. (1959). Effects of parietalectomy and sustained temperatures on thyroid of lizard, *Sceloporus occidentalis*. *Proc. Soc. exp. Biol. Med.* 101, 162–164.

Eggert, B. (1933). Ueber die histologischen und physiologischen Beziehungen zwischen Schilddrüse und Häutung bei den einheimischen Eidechsen. *Zool. Anz.* 105, 1–9.

Eggert, B. (1935). Zur Morphologie und Physiologie der Eidechsen-Schilddrüse. I. Das jahreszeitliche Verhalten der Schilddrüse von *Lacerta agilis*, *L. vivipara* Jacq. und *L. muralis* Laur. *Z. wiss. Zool.* 147, 205–262.

Eggert, B. (1936a). Zur Morphologie und Physiologie der Eidechsen-Schilddrüse. III. Über die nach Entfernung der Schilddrüse auftretenden allgemeinen Ausfallserscheinungen und über die Bedeutung der Schilddrüse für die Häutung und für die Kaltstarre. *Z. wiss. Zool.* 148, 221–260.

Eggert, B. (1936b). Zur Morphologie und Physiologie des ultimobranchialen Körpers der Eidechsen. *Zool. Anz.* 114, 119–128.

Eggert, B. (1936c). Zur Morphologie und Physiologie der Eidechsen-Schilddrüse. II. Über die Wirkung von hohen und niedrigen Temperaturen, von Thyroxin und von thyreotropem Hormon auf die Schilddrüse. *Z. wiss. Zool.* 147, 537–594.

Eggert, B. (1937). Zur Morphologie und Physiologie der Eidechsen-Schilddrüse. IV. Über den Einfluss der Schilddrüsenexstirpation auf den ultimobranchialen Körper und auf die Keimdrüsen. *Z. wiss. Zool.* 149, 280–322.

Eggert, B. (1938a). "Morphologie und Histophysiologie der normalen Schilddrüse. Zwanglose Abhandlungen aus dem Gebiete der Inneren Sekretion," 3, 1–113. J. A. Barth, Leipzig.

Eggert, B. (1938b). Der ultimobranchiale Körper. *Endokrinologie* 20, 1–7.

Evans, L. T. and Clapp, M. (1940). The relation of thyroid extract to territorial behavior and to anoxemia in *Anolis carolinensis. J. comp. Psychol.* 29, 277–281.

Evans, L. T. and Hegre, E. (1938). The effects of ovarian hormones and seasons on *Anolis carolinensis.* I. The thyroid. *Anat. Rec.* 72, 1–9.

Evans, L. T. and Hegre, E. (1940). Endocrine relationships in turtles. Effects of seasons and pituitary extracts on the thyroid. *Endocrinology* 27, 144–148.

Francescon, A. (1929). Il corpo ultimobranchiale nei rettili. *Archo ital. Anat. Embriol.* 26, 387–400.

Gabe, M. (1961). Données histologiques sur les macrothyréocytes (cellules parafolliculaires) de quelques sauropsidés et anamniotes. *Acta anat.* 47, 34–54.

Gabe, M. and Rancurel, P. (1958). Particularités histologiques du complexe hypothalamo-hypophysaire chez *Crocodilus niloticus* Laurenti. *C. r. hebd. Séanc. Acad. Sci., Paris* 247, 522–524.

Galeotti, G. (1897). Beitrag zur Kenntniss der Sekretionserscheinungen in den Epithelzellen der Schilddrüse. *Arch. mikrosk. Anat. EntwMech.* 48, 305–328.

Gans, C. and Lynn, W. G. (1965). Comments on the thyroid structure of some acrodont amphisbaenids, with remarks on their systematic status. *Herpetologica* 21, 23–26.

Giusti, L. (1931). La tiroidectomia en una tortuga *Clemmys leprosa* (Schweig). *Revue Méd. vét.* 13, 16–19.

Goldsmith, E. D. (1949). Phylogeny of the thyroid: descriptive and experimental. *Ann. N. Y. Acad. Sci.* 50, 283–316.

Gorbman, A. (1959). Problems in the comparative morphology and physiology of the thyroid gland. *In* "Comparative Endocrinology" (A. Gorbman, ed.), pp. 266–282. Wiley and Sons, New York.

Gorbman, A. and Bern, H. A. (1962). "Textbook of Comparative Endocrinology." Wiley and Sons, New York.

Goslar, H. G. (1958a). Beiträge zum Häutungsvorgang der Schlangen. I. Mitteilung. Histologische und topochemische Untersuchungen an der Haut von *Natrix natrix* L. während der Phasen des normalen Häutungzyklus. *Acta histochem.* 5, 182–212.

Goslar, H. G. (1958b). Über die Wirkung eines standardisierten Thymusextraktes auf die Häutungsvorgang und auf einige Organe von *Natrix natrix* L. *Arch. exp. Path. Pharmak.* 233, 201–225.

Goslar, H. G. (1958c). Die Reptilienhaut als endokrines Testobjekt. *Endokrinologie* 36, 279–286.

Goslar, H. G. (1964). Beiträge zum Häutungsvorgang der Schlangen. II. Studien zur Fermenttopochemie der Keratogenese und Keratolyse am Modell der Reptilienhaut. *Acta histochem.* 17, 1–60.

Grignon, G. and Herlant, M. (1959). Les cellules du lobe glandulaire de l'hypophyse chez la tortue terrestre (*Testudo mauritanica*). *C.r. hebd. Séanc. Acad. Sci., Paris* 248, 3046–3048.

Gross, J. (1957). The dynamic cytology of the thyroid gland. *Int. Rev. Cytol.* 6, 265–288.

Halberkann, J. (1953). Untersuchungen zur Beeinflussung des Häutungzyklus der Ringelnatter durch Thyroxin. *Arch. Derm. Syph.* 197, 37–41.

Halberkann, J. (1954a). Zur hormonalen Beeinflussung des Häutungzyklus der Ringelnatter. *Z. naturf.* 96, 77–80.

Halberkann, J. (1954b). Der Häutungsablauf der Ringelnatter unter Methyl-Thiouracil. *Naturwissenschaften* 41, 237–238.

Halmi, N. S. (1961). Thyroidal iodide transport. *Vitams Horm.* 19, 133–163.

Hatta, K. (1944). Seasonal and experimental changes of Golgi body of the epithelial cells of the thyroid gland using *Takydromus. Dobutsugaku Tasshi* (Zool. Mag.) 56, 57–61.

Hellbaum, H. W. (1936). The cytology of snake thyroids following hypophysectomy, activation and ultra-centrifuging. *Anat. Rec.* 67, 53–67.

Herlant, M. and Grignon, G. (1961). Le lobe glandulaire de l'hypophyse chez la tortue terrestre (*Testudo mauritanica* Dumer.). Étude histochimique et histo-physiologique. *Archs Biol., Paris* 72, 97–151.

Jankowsky, H. D. (1964). Die Bedeutung der Hormone für die Temperaturanpassung im normalen Temperaturbereich. *Helgoländer wiss. Meeresunters.* 9, 412–419.

Kobayashi, H. and Gorbman, A. (1959). Thyroidal utilization of radioiodide in normal and dehydrated lizards. *Annotnes zool. jap.* 32, 179–184.

Krockert, G. (1941). Kontinuierliche Hyperthyreoidisierung und Epiphysierung an *Python bivittatus. Vitam. Horm., Lpz.* 1, 24–31.

Kroon, D. B. (1958). The macrothyrocyte as a functional stage of the thyroid cell. *Acta. Anat.* 33, 76–104.

Kurosumi, K. (1961). Electron microscopic analysis of the secretion mechanism. *Int. Rev. Cytol.* 11, 1–124.

Legait, H. and Legait, E. (1957). Les voies extra-hypophysaires des noyaux neuro-sécrétoires hypothalamiques chez les batraciens et les reptiles. *Acta Anat.* 30, 429–443.

Leloup, J. and Fontaine, M. (1960). Iodine metabolism in lower vertebrates. *Ann. N. Y. Acad. Sci.* 86, 316–353.

Licht, P. and Jones, R. E. (1967). Effects of exogenous prolactin on reproduction and growth in adult males of the lizard *Anolis carolinensis. Gen. Comp. Endocrinol.* 8, 228–244.

Lynn, W. G. (1960). Structure and functions of the thyroid gland in reptiles. *Am. Midl. Nat.* 64, 309–326.

Lynn, W. G. (1967). Thyroid morphology in lizards of the families Eublepharidae, Sphaerodactylidae, and Gekkonidae. *Copeia* 1967, 476–477.

Lynn, W. G. and Colorigh, Sr. M. L. (1967). Thyroid morphology in lizards of the families Anguidae, Chameleonidae, and Cordylidae. *Am. Midl. Nat.* 77, 247–250.

Lynn, W. G. and Komorowski, L. A. (1957). The morphology of the thyroid gland in lizards of the families Pygopodidae and Amphisbaenidae. *Herpetologica* 13, 163–172.

Lynn, W. G. and Wachowski, H. E. (1951). The thyroid gland and its functions in cold-blooded vertebrates. *Q. Rev. Biol.* 26, 123–168.

Lynn, W. G. and Walsh, G. A. (1957). The morphology of the thyroid gland in the Lacertilia. *Herpetologica* 13, 157–162.

Lynn, W. G. and Zmich, J. (1967). Thyroid morphology in lizards of the family Scincidae. *Am. Midl. Nat.* 77, 245–247.

Lynn, W. G., McCormick, J. J. and Gregorek, J. C. (1965). Environmental temperature and thyroid function in the lizard, *Anolis carolinensis. Gen. Comp. Endocrinol.* 5, 587–595.

Lynn, W. G., Fitzpatrick, Sr. A. M. and Kelly, Sr. M. (1966a). Thyroid morphology in lizards of the families Lacertidae and Teiidae. *Herpetologica* 22, 71–75.

Lynn, W. G., O'Brien, Sr. M. C. and Herhenreader, Rev. P. (1966b). Thyroid morphology in lizards of the families Iguanidae and Agamidae. *Herpetologica* 22, 90–93.

Maderson, P. F. A. (1965a). Histological changes in the epidermis of snakes during the sloughing cycle. *J. Zool.* 146, 98–113.

Maderson, P. F. A. (1965b). The structure and development of the squamate epidermis. *In* "Biology of the Skin and Hair Growth" (A. G. Lyne and B. F. Short, eds). Angus and Robertson, Sydney.

Maderson, P. F. A. (1966). Histological changes in the epidermis of the Tokay (*Gekko gecko*) during the sloughing cycle. *J. Morph.* **119**, 39–50.

Maderson, P. F. A. and Licht, P. (1967). Epidermal morphology and sloughing frequency in normal and prolactin treated *Anolis carolinensis* (Iguanidae Lacertilia). *J. Morph.* **123**, 157–172.

Maderson, P. F. A., Chiu, K. W. and Phillips, J. G. (1970). Histological changes in the sloughing cycle in the male rat snake, *Ptyas korros* (Schlegel). *J. Morph.* (in press).

Maher, M. J. (1961). The effect of environmental temperature on metabolic response to thyroxine in the lizard, *Lacerta muralis*. *Am. Zool.* **1**, 461 (Abstract).

Maher, M. J. (1964). Metabolic response of isolated lizard tissues to thyroxine administered in vivo. *Endocrinology* **74**, 994–995.

Maher, M. J. (1965). The role of the thyroid gland in the oxygen consumption of lizards. *Gen. Comp. Endocrinol.* **5**, 320–325.

Maher, M. J. and Levedahl, B. H. (1959). The effect of the thyroid gland on the oxidative metabolism of the lizard *Anolis carolinensis*. *J. exp. Zool.* **140**, 169–189.

Mason, E. M. (1938). Assay of thyrotropic hormone. *Nature, Lond.* **142**, 480–481.

Mellish, C. H. and Meyer, R. K. (1937). The effects of various gonadotropic substances and thyroxine on the ovaries of horned lizards (*Phrynosoma cornutum*). *Anat. Rec.* **69**, 179–189.

Miller, M. R. (1948). The gross and microscopic anatomy of the pituitary and the seasonal histological changes occurring in the pars anterior of the viviparous lizard *Xantusia vigilis*. *Univ. Calif. Publs Zool.* **47**, 225–246.

Miller, M. R. (1955). Cyclic changes in the thyroid and interrenal glands of the viviparous lizard, *Xantusia vigilis*. *Anat. Rec.* **123**, 19–31.

Miller, M. R. (1959). The endocrine basis for reproductive adaptations in reptiles. *In* "Comparative Endocrinology" (A. Gorbman, ed.). Wiley and Sons, New York.

Miller, M. R. (1963). The histogenesis of the endocrine organs of the viviparous lizard, *Xantusia vigilis*. *Gen. Comp. Endocrinol.* **3**, 579–605.

Naccarati, S. (1922). Contribution to the morphologic study of the thyreoid gland in *Emys europaea*. *J. Morph.* **36**, 279–297.

Noble, G. K. and Bradley, H. T. (1933). The relation of the thyroid and the hypophysis to the molting process in the lizard, *Hemidactylus brookii*. *Biol. Bull. Mar. biol. Lab.*, *Woods Hole* **64**, 289–298.

Nussbaum, N. (1963). Hypophysectomy and thyroid function in *Anolis* (Iguanidae). *Anat. Rec.* **145**, 340 (Abstract).

O'Donoghue, C. H. (1920). The blood vascular system of the tuatara, *Sphenodon punctatus*. *Phil. Trans. R. Soc.* **210**, 175–252.

Pitt-Rivers, R. (1961). Iodine metabolism in the thyroid gland. *Mem. Soc. Endocrinol.* **1961**(11), 71–78.

Rall, J. E., Robbins, J. and Lewallen, C. G. (1964). The thyroid. *In* "The Hormones" (G. Pincus, K. V. Thimann and E. B. Astwood, eds), **5**, 159–439. Academic Press New York.

Ratzersdorfer, C., Gordon, A. S. and Charipper, H. A. (1949). The effects of thiourea on the thyroid gland and molting behavior of the lizard, *Anolis carolinensis*. *J. exp. Zool.* **112**, 13–27.

Raynaud, A. and Raynaud, J. (1961). L'activité sécrétoire précoce des glandes endocrines de l'embryon d'orvet (*Anguis fragilis* L.). *C. r. hebd. Séanc. Acad. Sci., Paris* **253**, 2254–2256.

Raynaud, A., Raynaud, J. and Pieau, C. (1963). État d'activité des glandes endocrines chez les jeunes orvets (*Anguis fragilis* L.). *Gen Comp. Endocrinol.* **3**, 687 (Abstract).

Rivera Commers, F. (1955). Sueño invernal y tiroides en los reptiles. *Zooiatria* **5**, 12–20.

Saint Girons, H. (1957). Le cycle sexuel chez *Vipera aspis* L. dans l'ouest de la France. *Bull. Biol. Mar. biol. Lab.*, *Woods Hole* **91**, 284–350.

Saint Girons, H. (1959). Remarques histologiques sur l'hypophyse de *Vipera aspis* L. *C. r. Séanc. Soc. Biol.* **153**, 5–7.

Saint Girons, H. (1960). Particularités anatomiques et histologiques de l'hypophyse chez les Squamata. *C. r. hebd. Séanc. Acad. Sci.*, *Paris* **251**, 2584–2586.

Saint Girons, H. (1961). Particularités anatomiques et histologiques de l'hypophyse chez les Squamata. *Archs Biol.*, *Paris* **72**, 211–299.

Saint Girons, H. (1963a). Histologie comparée de l'adénohypophyse chez les reptiles. *Colloques int. Cent. natn. Rech. scient.* **1963**(128), 275–285.

Saint Girons, H. (1963b). Données histophysiologiques sur le cycle annuel des glandes endocrines et de leurs effecteurs chez l'orvet, *Anguis fragilis* L. *Archs Anat. microsc. Morph. exp.* **52**, 1–51.

Saint Girons, H. and Duguy, R. (1962a). Données histologiques sur le cycle annuel de la glande thyroïde chez les vipères. *Gen. Comp. Endocrinol.* **2**, 337–346.

Saint Girons, H. and Duguy, R. (1962b). Données histophysiologiques sur le cycle annuel de l'hypophyse chez *Vipera aspis* (L.). *Z. Zellforsch. mikrosk. Anat.* **56**, 819–853.

Saint Girons, H. and Duguy, R. (1966). Données histophysiologiques sur les variations de la glande thyroïde au cours du cycle annuel chez la couleuvre vipérine *Natrix maura* (L.). *Archs Anat. microsc. Morph. exp.* **55**, 345–362.

Saint Girons, M. C. (1961), Étude de l'érythropoïèse chez la vipère bérus (*Vipera berus* L.) en fonction de l'activité thyroidïenne et des phénoménes cycliques de la mue. *Bull. Soc. zool. Fr.* **86**, 59–67.

Schaefer, W. H. (1933). Hypophysectomy and thyroidectomy of snakes. *Proc. Soc. exp. Biol. Med.* **30**, 1363–1365.

Sembrat, K. (1963). I[131] accumulation rate in the thyroid of dogfish and lizard, with some remarks on the morphogenetic abilities of this gland. *Folia Biol.* **11**, 473–482.

Sembrat, K. and Drzewicki, S. (1935). Influence de la glande thyroïde des sélaciens sur la mue des lézards. *C. r. Séanc. Soc. Biol.* **118**, 1599–1602.

Sembrat, K. and Drzewicki, S. (1936). The influence of selachian thyroid upon the molting process of the lizards, with some remarks on the skin, the eyes, and the ultimo-branchial body of the thyroidectomized lizards. *Zoologica Pol.* **1**, 119–169.

Shellabarger, C. J., Gorbman, A., Schatzlein, F. C. and McGill, D. (1956). Some quantitative and qualitative aspects of I[131] metabolism in turtles. *Endocrinology* **59**, 331–339.

Siler, K. A. (1936). The cytological changes in the hypophysis cerebri of the garter snake (*Thamnophis radix*) following thyroidectomy. *J. Morph.* **59**, 603–623.

Simon, J. (1844). On the comparative anatomy of the thyroid gland. *Phil. Trans. R. Soc.* (134), 295–303.

Soetjipto, A. (1960). The morphology and histology of the thyroid gland in four lacertilian species from Bandung. *Treubia* **25**, 235–240.

Stebbins, R. C. and Eakin, R. M. (1958). The role of the "third eye" in reptilian behavior. *Am. Mus. Novit.* (1870), 1–40.

Steyn, W. (1959). Epithelial organization and histogenesis of the epiphysial complex in lizards. *Acta anat.* **37**, 310–335.

Steyn, W. and Steyn, S. (1962). Verdere lig-en elektronemikroskopie van die derde oog met aanmerkings oor sy termoregulatiewe funksie. *Cimbebasia* (4), 7–16.

Tam, W. H., Phillips, J. G. and Lofts, B. (1967). Seasonal variation in histology and in vitro steroid production by cobra (*Naja naja* Linn.) testis and adrenal gland. *Proc. 3rd Asia and Oceania Congr. Endocrinol. Manila.*

Thompson, F. D. (1910). The thyroid and parathyroid glands throughout vertebrates, with observations on some other closely related structures. *Phil. Trans. R. Soc.* **201**, 91–132.

Van Bemmelen, J. F. (1887). Die Halsgegend der Reptilien. *Zool. Anz.* **10**, 88–96.

Viguier, G. (1909a). Recherches sur le corps thyroïde de gecko (*Tarentola mauritanica* Lin.). *Bibliphie anat.* **19**, 92–97.

Viguier, G. (1909b). La structure du corps thyroïde du gecko (*Tarentola mauritanica* L.). *C. r. Séanc. Soc. Biol.* **66**, 1064–1065.

Viguier, G. (1911a). Modifications des parathyroïdes après thyroïdectomie chez un lézard (*Uromastix acanthinurus*, Bell). *C. r. Séanc. Soc. Biol.* **70**, 186–189.

Viguier, G. (1911b). Modifications de l'hypophyse après thyroïdectomie chez un lézard (*Uromastix acanthinurus* Bell). *C. r. Séanc. Soc. Biol.* **70**, 222–223.

Viguier, G. (1911c). Sur le corps thyroïde médian de quelques sauriens d'Algérie, *Lacerta ocellata* var. *pater* Lat., *Psammodromus algirus* Fitz. et *Gongylus ocellatus* Gm. *Bull. Soc. zool. Fr.* **36**, 135–140.

Vivien, J. H. (1964a). Structure et ultrastructure de l'épiphyse d'un chélonien, *Pseudemys scripta elegans*. *C. r. hebd. Séanc. Acad. Sci., Paris* **259**, 899–901.

Vivien, J. H. (1964b). Ultrastructure des constituents de l'épiphyse de *Tropidonotus natrix* L. *C. r. hebd. Séanc. Acad. Sci., Paris* **258**, 3370–3372.

Voitkewitsch, A. A. (1944). Thyroid function and its conditioning by the hypophysis having been activated by light. *Dokl. Akad. Nauk SSSR* **45**, 396–400.

Waterman, A. J. (1961a). Thyroid gland of the young alligator, *A. mississippiensis*. *Am. Zool.* **1**, 475 (Abstract).

Waterman, A. J. (1961b). Thyroid gland of the young "slider" turtle, *Pseudemys scripta*. *Am. Zool.* **1**, 475. (Abstract).

Weigmann, R. (1932). Jahrescyklische Veränderungen im Funktionszustand der Schilddrüse und im Stoffumsatz von *Lacerta vivipara* Jacq. *Z. wiss. Zool.* **142**, 491–509.

Wilhoft, D. C. (1958). The effect of temperature on thyroid histology and survival in the lizard, *Sceloporus occidentalis*. *Copeia* **1958**(4), 265–276.

Wilhoft, D. C. (1963). Seasonal changes in the gonads and thyroid in a tropical lizard, *Leiolopisma rhomboidalis*. *Diss. Abstr.* **24**, 1304–1305.

Wilhoft, D. C. (1964). Seasonal changes in the thyroid and interrenal glands of the tropical Australian skink, *Leiolopisma rhomboidalis*. *Gen. Comp. Endocrinol.* **4**, 42–53.

Yamamoto, Y. (1960). Comparative histological studies of the thyroid gland of lower vertebrates. *Folia anat. jap.* **34**, 353–387.

CHAPTER 7

The Parathyroid

NANCY B. CLARK

Department of Zoology,
The University of Connecticut,
Storrs, Connecticut, U.S.A.

I. Introduction

The parathyroid glands of mammals have been studied intensively because of their important role in calcium and phosphate homeostasis. Much less is known of the parathyroids of members of other vertebrate classes, and reptiles are among the least well studied in this respect. This paper is a review of our present knowledge concerning the location, structure, and function of the parathyroid glands of reptiles. For reviews of older literature concerning the location and embryological derivation of reptilian parathyroids, see Krause (1922), von Wettstein (1931, 1937, 1954), Pischinger (1937), Bargmann (1939) and Lüdicke (1962, 1964).

The structure of the reptilian parathyroid is similar to that found in mammals, birds, and urodeles, but is quite different from the whorl-like arrangement of cells in the parathyroid glands of anurans. Reptiles have two or four parathyroid glands, depending upon the group, species, or age of the animal studied. There is still confusion regarding the number of parathyroids in some species, as various epithelial glands described by early authors have sometimes been unreliably interpreted to be parathyroid tissue. The German term "Epithelkörper" has contributed to the confusion; in the early German literature the word referred to a variety of small nodules. Even more confusion has been caused over the years by calling the parathyroids or other epithelial structures "Carotiskörperchen" or "carotid bodies".

Studies of embryological development of the parathyroids of reptiles generally indicate that the rostral and caudal pairs of parathyroids are derived from pharyngeal pouches three and four respectively. The parathyroid glands are not associated with the thyroid glands, but are located nearer the thymuses or ultimobranchial bodies because, unlike the mammalian parathyroids, they do not migrate, but tend to retain their original relationship with the third and fourth aortic arches. In those animals having four parathyroids, the anterior (or rostral) pair is generally located near the branching of the carotid artery, except where, as in the Testudines, the definitive carotid bifurcation is developmentally a secondary one; the posterior (or caudal) pair is located near the aorta. When only a single pair of glands persists in adults, it is that derived from pouch three.

The parathyroid glands of reptiles are small, measuring about 0·5 to 1·0 mm in diameter, and are easily overlooked in dissections. Their structure is essentially similar in the various groups of reptiles, and parathyroid tissue is easily recognized in histological preparations. The parathyroids are surrounded by a substantial capsule of connective tissue and have a cellular, cord-like parenchymal structure with connective tissue and capillaries or sinusoids present between the cords. Most reports of their histology indicate that the glands contain a single type of cell, presumably homologous with the chief cell of mammals. Oxyphil cells appear to be absent.

A unique feature of the glands in several groups of reptiles is the presence of "follicles" consisting of cells surrounding a central lumen. In many cases these follicles contain a secretion which stains positively for carbohydrate content. There is speculation that this may represent stored parathyroid hormone, but experimental evidence is not yet available. Follicles occasionally occur in mammalian parathyroid tissue, but generally only in older animals, in which they have been considered an effect of age. However, follicles have been noted in the parathyroids of young turtles (Clark, 1965) and, therefore, cannot be dismissed as an aging phenomenon in reptiles.

Little work has been done to determine the function of the parathyroid glands of reptiles. However, the few studies performed indicate at least some similarities of reptilian and mammalian parathyroid function in the regulation of the concentrations of calcium and phosphate in body fluids.

II. Testudines

Although the literature before 1911 contains several conflicting reports (Table I), turtles possess two pairs of parathyroid glands, which develop from pharyngeal pouches three and four (Shaner, 1921a and 1921b; Johnson, 1922). The anterior pair of glands is embedded within the tissue of the thymus and is difficult to detect except upon histological investigation. The posterior pair of glands is more obvious, lying in connective tissue near the arch of the aorta and in close association with the tissues of the left ultimobranchial body (Fig. 1). Some early papers (Doyon and Kareff, 1904; Thompson, 1910) refer only to the more obvious posterior pair of glands; the anterior parathyroids, located within the thymus, were apparently overlooked. In 1911, Aimé commented that some earlier workers who per-

TABLE I

Species of Testudines Examined with Regard to Parathyroid Number

Family and subfamily	Species	Parathyroids Embryo	Adult	Authority
Kinosternidae	*Kinosternon subrubrum* (= *K. pennsylvanicum*)	–	4	Thompson (1910)
Chelydridae	*Chelydra serpentina*	4	4	Johnson (1922)
Testudinidae				
Testudininae	*Geochelone denticulata* (= *Testudo tabulata*)	4	4	Van Bemmelen (1888)
	Testudo graeca	4	4	Van Bemmelen (1888)
		–	4	Francescon (1929)
Emydinae	*Chrysemys picta*	–	2	Thompson (1910)
		4	4	Shaner (1921a and b)
		4	4	Johnson (1922)
		–	4	Clark (1965)
	Emys orbicularis	–	2	Afanassiew (1877)
	(= *E. europaea*)	6	6	Van Bemmelen (1886)*
		–	4	Francescon (1929)
	Graptemys pseudogeographica	–	4	Clark (1965)
	Pseudemys scripta	–	2	Thompson (1910)
		–	4	Clark (1965)
Cheloniidae	*Chelonia mydas*	4	4	Van Bemmelen (1888)
Trionychidae	*Trionyx* sp.	4	4	Johnson (1922)

*These glandlike nodules were not definitely identified as parathyroids.

formed parathyroidectomies in turtles failed to remove both pairs of parathyroid glands.

The parathyroid glands of turtles measure about 1 mm in diameter in adults and about half that size in hatchlings. The histology of the parathyroids varies somewhat from one species of fresh-water turtle to another. While the parathyroid parenchyma of all species studied consists of cellular cords, a conspicuous follicular arrangement of cells is characteristic of the slider, *Pseudemys scripta* (Thompson, 1910), and the false map turtle, *Graptemys pseudogeographica*. However, fewer follicles are found in parathyroid tissue of the painted turtle, *Chrysemys picta* (Clark, 1965; Figs 2 and 3). Some of the follicles contain a substance which stains with periodic acid Schiff (PAS) but is not glycogen.

The cells of the parathyroid glands of these three species of turtles, as seen with the light microscope, appear to be of a single type. They contain round or oval nuclei and a finely granular cytoplasm which stains faintly with PAS and eosin. Use of a technique that stains mammalian mitochondria did not

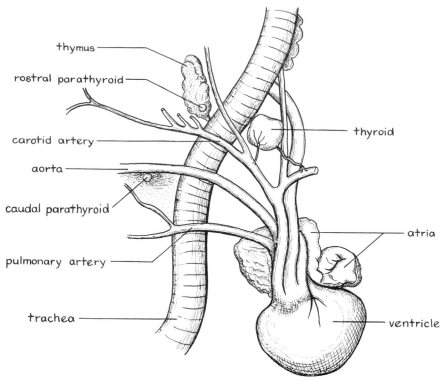

Fig. 1. Location of the right parathyroid glands in a freshwater turtle, *Emys orbicularis* (modified from Van Bemmelen, 1888).

demonstrate cells rich in mitochondria which might correspond to the oxyphil cells of mammals. In silverstained preparations, nerves were seen entering the thymus and ultimobranchial bodies of turtles, but no nerves were seen in connection with the parathyroid tissue. Accessory parathyroid glands were not found in histological sections of the region near the heart and major blood vessels in the turtles studied (Clark, 1965).

We have performed preliminary tests of the histochemistry and ultrastructure of the parathyroid glands of the freshwater turtles *Chrysemys picta* and *Pseudemys scripta* (Clark and Khairallah, 1969). Tissues for histochemical study were fixed in Bouin's fluid or formalin and embedded in paraffin or plastic, while tissues for electron microscopy were fixed in osmic acid (2%) or in glutaraldehyde and post-fixed in osmium and embedded in plastic. The following histochemical tests were performed for polysaccharides: alcian blue for acid mucopolysaccharides, toluidine blue for metachromasia and mucin, and periodic acid-Schiff. All but alcian blue were positive, indicating that a mucoid or mucopolysaccharide component may be

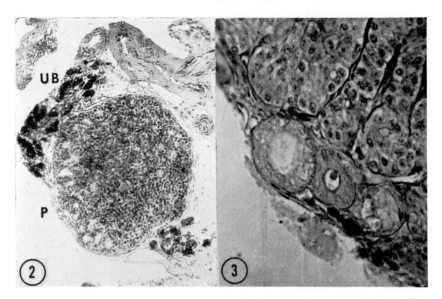

FIG. 2. Left parathyroid gland (P) of a hatchling turtle, *Graptemys pseudogeographica*, showing its follicular structure and close association with the ultimobranchial body (UB). Hematoxylin and eosin; × 120.

FIG. 3. Detail of parathyroid tissue of *Chrysemys picta* showing the structure of the cellular cords and the presence of several follicles, a rare occurrence in this species. Mallory's triple connective tissue stain; × 300.

present in the cytoplasm and in the contents of the follicular lumen. The mercury bromphenol blue test indicated a proteinaceous component in both cytoplasm and follicular lumen. The most striking histochemical finding was the demonstration, by the Sudan Black B method of McGee-Russell and Smale (1963), of large lipid droplets in the cytoplasm surrounding the nucleus (Fig. 4). This test gives a reversed or negative effect, in which the epon plastic becomes stained while the dense elements of the tissue (nuclei) do not; thus the nuclei appear white, the cytoplasm grey, and the lipid droplets black. Ultrastructural studies verify the presence of large lipid droplets in the cytoplasm, as can be seen in the low magnification of a cell cord (Fig. 5).

The cytoplasm of some of the parathyroid cells is electron lucent, while that of others is electron dense. It is not yet known if these represent different types of cells or different secretory stages of a single type. The light and dark cells are especially well seen in glutaraldehyde-fixed material (Fig. 6).

The cisternae of the endoplasmic reticulum of both the light and dark cells sometimes contain an electron dense material (Figs 6 and 7). Under high magnification, this material appears as parallel electron-dense bands which may represent crystalline material embedded within a less dense matrix; its

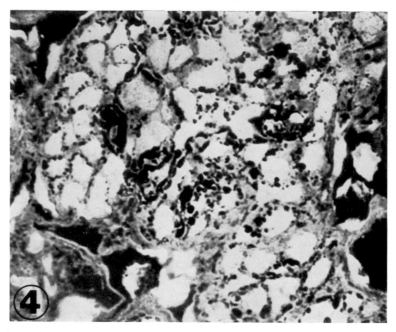

FIG. 4. Parathyroid tissue of *Chrysemys picta* treated with Sudan Black B method for demonstration of lipids. The lipid droplets in perinuclear region appear black, the nuclei white, and the cytoplasm grey; × 1,500.

structure is similar to that described for the endoplasmic reticulum of salamander liver (Hamilton *et al.*, 1966). Another feature of the parathyroid cells of both species of turtles is membrane bound, electron dense granules (Fig. 7) about 3000–4000 Å in diameter. The granules possess a substructure near the centre which closely resembles that seen within the endoplasmic reticulum (Clark and Khairallah, 1969). Further studies are in progress to determine the nature and function of the various cytoplasmic inclusions.

There have been only two studies of parathyroid function in turtles (Doyon and Kareff, 1904; Clark, 1965). The former performed parathyroidectomies on the "African tortoise" by removing a single pair of glands in the region of the aortic arch and pulmonary arteries. The result was paralysis and death of the animals. Removal of one gland was without effect. Since these authors did not measure blood calcium values, it is not certain that the results were due to parathyroid loss or innumerable other factors which might affect nerve function. It is impossible to repeat the experiment or to know if complete parathyroidectomies were performed, as the species of turtle used is not certain.

I was unable to induce tetany, paralysis, or significant alterations in total

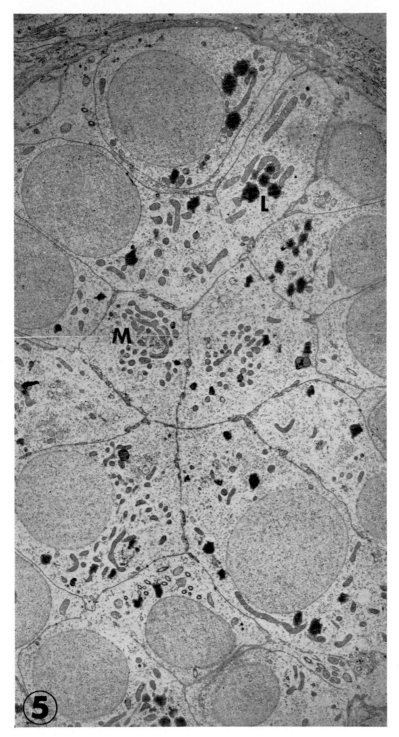

Fig. 5. Low power electron micrograph of a cellular cord in the parathyroid of *Chrysemys picta*, showing numerous mitochondria (M) and large, dark, lipid droplets (L). Osmium fixation, uranyl acetate and lead citrate staining; × 4000.

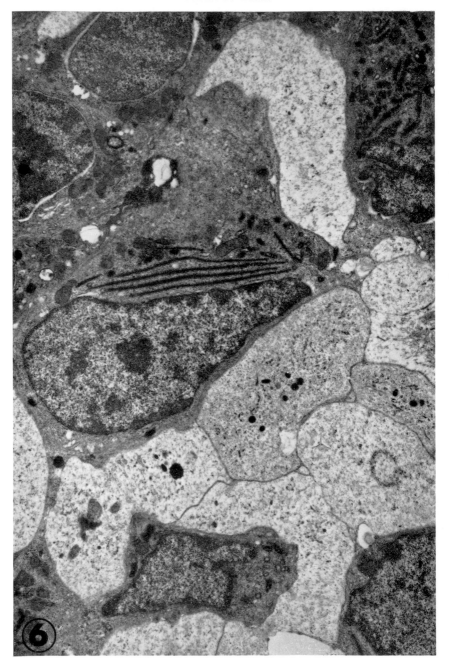

FIG. 6. "Dark" and "light" parathyroid cells of *Chrysemys picta*. The dark cell near the centre contains electron dense membranes of endoplasmic reticulum. Glutaraldehyde and osmium fixation, uranyl acetate and lead citrate staining; × 5700.

concentrations of calcium or inorganic phosphate in the serum of the fresh-water turtles *Chrysemys picta* or *Pseudemys scripta* after removal of both pairs of parathyroid glands (Clark, 1965). The concentration of calcium in the serum of parathyroidectomized and normal animals remained at about 2·5 mM/L, while that of inorganic phosphate was approximately 1·0 mM/L in both groups. There were considerable fluctuations in these values from day to day in an individual, whether parathyroidectomized or sham-operated.

The one parameter which was altered by parathyroidectomy of the turtles was urinary excretion of phosphate which decreased in parathyroidectoi-mized animals compared to its high levels in sham-operated controls. A similar hyperphosphaturia in sham-operated rats has been reported by Beutner and Munson (1960). Correlated with this was a significant rise in urinary excretion of phosphate in parathyroidectomized and normal turtles which received 100 IU or more of mammalian parathyroid extract (Lilly). After a three-day latent period, they excreted significantly higher amounts of phosphate, up to six times the normal amount by six days after the injection. The same animals had 20% higher concentration of calcium in their serum, again after a three-day latent period, but in this case the differences were not statistically significant ($P = 0·1$). There was no significant alteration of phosphate concentration in the serum or in the urinary level of calcium.

Administration of parathyroid extract did not affect the concentrations of calcium in fibulae as measured by wet-ash analysis. However, femurs of hatchling false-map turtles, *Graptemys pseudogeographica*, injected with parathyroid extract contained an average of one third more osteoclasts than control animals.

The reasons for the unresponsiveness of turtles to parathyroidectomy remain to be elucidated. It has been suggested that these animals might be able to obtain sufficient amounts of calcium and phosphate by means of a physico-chemical exchange between the large bony surface of the shell and the body fluids, or that they may have active transport systems for calcium in their pharyngeal or cloacal tissues (Clark, 1967).

III. Crocodilia

The best description of parathyroid location and embryological derivation in the Crocodilia is that of Van Bemmelen (1886 and 1888). He described a single pair of parathyroids derived from pouch three in specimens of *Alligator mississippiensis* and *Crocodylus porosus*. Hammar (1937) reported that two pairs of parathyroid glands were present in young crocodiles, but that the pair from pouch four disappeared in adults (Table II). The parathyroids of the Crocodilia are located just anterior to the heart, where the common carotid artery branches from the right innominate artery (Fig. 8). They are not intimately connected with the blood vessels.

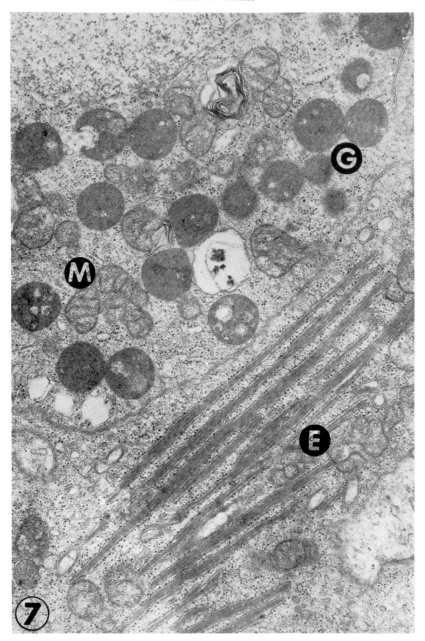

FIG. 7. Photomicrograph of parts of two adjacent cells of the parathyroid of *Chrysemys picta*, showing electron dense, membrane bound granules (G), mitochondria (M), and endoplasmic reticulum with possible crystalline inclusions (E). Glutaraldehyde and osmium fixation, uranyl acetate and lead citrate staining; × 22,000.

TABLE II

Species of Crocodilia Examined with Regard to Parathyroid Number

Species	No. of parathyroids Embryo	No. of parathyroids Adult	Authority
Alligator mississippiensis	2*	2	Van Bemmelen (1886, 1888)
	–	4–6	Reese (1931)
	–	2	Hammar (1937)
Caiman crocodilus	4†	–	Clark (present study)
Crocodylus porosus	2*	2	Van Bemmelen (1886, 1888)
	4	2	Hammar (1937)

*From examination of well-developed embryos.
†In hatchlings.

As there are no previously published accounts of the parathyroid histology of Crocodilia, four hatchling caimans (*Caiman crocodilus*; snout-vent length 13 cm) were examined. In all four animals, the parathyroid tissue on each side was composed of two glands surrounded by a single connective tissue capsule (Fig. 9). The size of the smaller gland ranged from about 0·25 to 0·5 mm in diameter, while the larger gland measured approximately 1 mm. It is probable that the double parathyroids represent the glands from pouches three and four described by Hammar (1937), and that later one pair (presumably the smaller) would have disappeared or fused with the other.

The parathyroid glands of the caimans lie near the branching of the right innominate artery and may sometimes be embedded within the thymic tissue. The glands are composed of cellular cords with connective tissue and blood vessels running between them. The cells have centrally located nuclei, and the cytoplasm stains with PAS and eosin. The few follicles do not form a conspicuous feature of the glands (Fig. 10).

I know of no studies of parathyroid function in the Crocodilia.

IV. Lepidosauria

A. RHYNCHOCEPHALIA

The parathyroids of the rhynchocephalian, *Sphenodon punctatus*, have been the object of only a few studies (Table III). Van Bemmelen (1887 and 1888) described a pair of "Carotiskörperchen" and a slightly more posterior pair of Aortakörperchen in adult *Sphenodon*. Later investigators have interpreted these as two pairs of parathyroid glands. Described as small, round bodies of epithelial structure, the Carotiskörperchen are located at the bifurcation of the carotid artery into internal and external carotids while the Aortakörperchen lie close to the posterior wall of the aortic arch (Fig. 11).

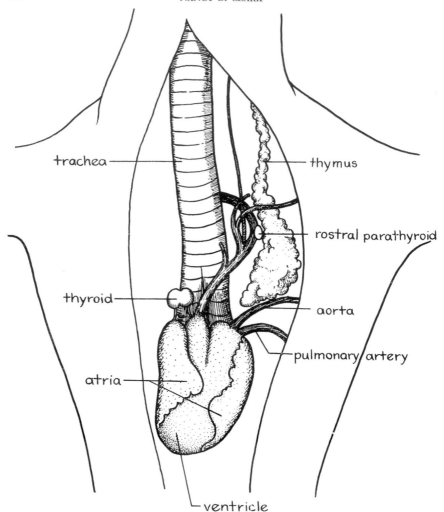

FIG. 8. Location of the left parathyroid gland in *Crocodylus porosus* (after Van Bemmelen, 1888).

From his studies of their development in *Lacerta*, Van Bemmelen (1887) decided that the glands in *Sphenodon* originate from pharyngeal pouches three and four respectively.

Only Gabe and Saint Girons (1964) have recently investigated parathyroid histology in *Sphenodon*. They confirmed the presence of four parathyroid glands in their two specimens. The parathyroids are structurally similar to those of other reptiles, being composed of cellular cords invested with connective tissue strands and capillaries (Fig. 12a). The parathyroid tissue contains only a single type of cell which measures about 12–15 μ in diameter, contains a central nucleus and has cytoplasm containing PAS-positive

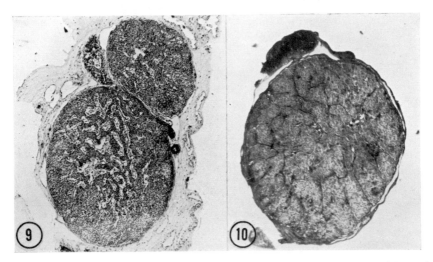

FIG. 9. Double parathyroid gland of *Caiman crocodilus*. The open areas between the cellular cords are artifacts caused by fixation approximately one day after the death of the animal. PAS and hematoxylin; × 90.

FIG. 10. Parathyroid gland of *Caiman crocodilus*, showing the structure of the cellular cords and the paucity of follicles. PAS and hematoxylin; × 130.

granules which were identified as glycogen by the malt diastase digestion technique (Fig. 12b). The parathyroid cells are not arranged in follicles (Fig. 12a–d).

The fact that *Sphenodon* possesses four parathyroid glands was, at first, interpreted as evidence of its primitive nature and was even regarded as a specific character (von Wettstein, 1931–1937), as most lizards have only a single pair. Subsequent investigations have shown that many other reptiles, including snakes, turtles and some lizards, also have four parathyroid glands.

There have been no physiological investigations of the parathyroid glands of *Sphenodon*.

B. SQUAMATA

1. *Ophidia*

Early work on the number, location, and embryological origin of the parathyroid glands in snakes was done by Van Bemmelen (1886 and 1888), Verdun (1898), Saint-Remy and Prenant (1904), and Harrison and Denning (1929). There is still confusion regarding their embryological derivation (see Clark, 1967).

The most complete description of parathyroid numbers, location, and histology has been provided by Herdson (1956; see Table III). In a study of seven species of snakes of the families Colubridae, Elapidae, and Viperidae, he found two pairs of parathyroids in every case, with no evidence

TABLE III

Species of Rhynchocephalia and Ophidia Examined with
Regard to Parathyroid Number

Family	Species	No. of Parathyroids		Authority
		Embryo	Adult	
Sphenodontidae	Sphenodon punctatus	4	4	Van Bemmelen (1887, 1888)
		–	4	Adams (1939)
		–	4	Gabe and Saint Girons (1964)
Colubridae	Carphophis amoenus vermis	–	4	Herdson (1956)
	Coluber constrictor	–	4	Neudeck (1969)
		–	4	Clark (present study)
	Coluber jugularis	–	4–10	Verdun (1898)†
	Coluber sp.	6	6	Saint-Remy and Prenant (1904)
	Dryophis prasinus (?)	–	4	Herdson (1956)
	Lampropeltis doliata	–	4	Neudeck (1969)
	Natrix natrix	6	6	Van Bemmelen (1886, 1888)*
		6	4	Saint-Remy and Prenant (1904)
		–	4	Herdson (1956)
	Natrix sipedon	–	4	Neudeck (1969)
		–	4	Clark (present study)
	Oligodon octolineatus	–	4	Herdson (1956)
	Thamnophis radix	10	4	Harrison and Denning (1929)
	Thamnophis sirtalis	–	4	Neudeck (1969)
		–	4	Clark (present study)
	Thamnophis sp.	–	4	Herdson (1956)
Elapidae	Notechis scutatus	–	4	Herdson (1956)
Viperidae	Agkistrodon contortrix	–	4	Herdson (1956)
	Crotalinae indet.	6	6	Van Bemmelen (1886, 1888)

*These glandlike nodules were not definitely identified as parathyroids.
†Usually two parathyroids on each side.

of accessory parathyroid tissue. The rostral pair of parathyroids lies at the bifurcation of the carotid arteries near the angle of the jaw, while the caudal pair lies a considerable distance away, between the lobes of the thymus just anterior to the heart (Figs 13 and 14). The caudal parathyroid glands of *Vipera berus*, located close to the thymus glands, are diagrammed by Boyd (1942). The parathyroids of snakes are not in intimate connection with the walls of the blood vessels and are not innervated. The glands possess connective tissue capsules and measure about 0·5 to 1·0 mm in diameter. Ophidian parathyroids are formed by cellular cords, with connective tissue and capillaries lying between the cords. The nuclei are large and the cytoplasm scanty.

Four species of snakes, *Thamnophis sirtalis*, *Coluber constrictor*, *Natrix sipedon*, and *Lampropeltis doliata*, have been studied in my laboratory. Their parathyroid glands are about 0·5 to 1·0 mm in diameter and have the typical parenchymal structure with cellular cords (Fig. 15). The cytoplasm stains faintly with PAS and contains PAS-positive granules, histochemical tests

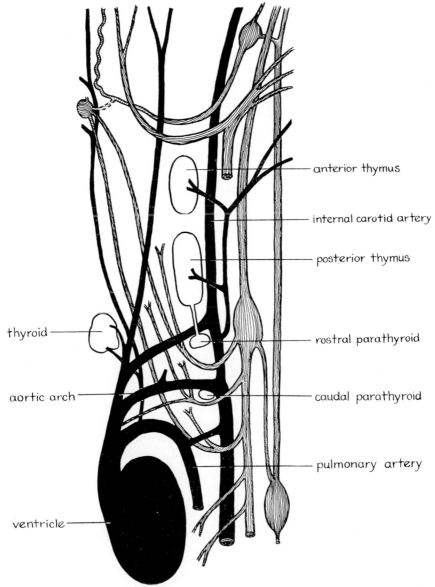

FIG. 11. Location of the left parathyroid glands in *Sphenodon punctatus* (after Van Bemmelen, 1888).

performed on the parathyroids of *N. sipedon* demonstrated the presence of protein in the cytoplasm but no evidence of lipids (Neudeck, 1969). Follicles are sometimes conspicuous in the parathyroid glands of *Thamnophis sirtalis*. The glands appear to be composed of a single type of cell, as noted by Herdson (1956). Their locations agreed with those reported by Herdson in all cases but one: in a young *Natrix* the caudal parathyroids were not conspicuous in gross dissection. However, when the thymuses were removed and sectioned, a parathyroid gland was found closely adhering to the surface of each thymus (Fig. 16). In this individual, the thymuses which were about 1 cm long, several times the size of those in older individuals, appear to have almost enveloped the caudal parathyroids. In an earlier paper, Thompson (1910) noted a parathyroid gland embedded in the head of the thymus in *Natrix sipedon*. Her finding that the parathyroid glands of this species lack follicles and lumina is confirmed by my observations.

We have recently parathyroidectomized the snake *Thamnophis sirtalis* in my laboratory. Blood samples were collected from the tail, ten days after the operation. Their values for concentration of total calcium were 30% lower than those of the sham-operated controls. The parathyroidectomized animal with the lowest blood calcium ($>50\%$ below normal) went into tetanic convulsions six days later. A snake from which three parathyroid glands had been removed went into tetany 51 days later, but none of the animals died as a result of the operation (Clark and Srivastava, 1970). The evidence suggests that these glands are important to the calcium metabolism of snakes.

2. *Sauria*

The parathyroids of lizards are better known than those of any other group of reptiles. Most adult lizards possess a single pair of parathyroid glands, the rostral pair derived from pharyngeal pouch three; a caudal pair, derived from pharyngeal pouch four, generally develops during the early embryonic stages and subsequently disappears. Recently, however, several species of lizards have been found to possess two pairs of parathyroid glands (Adams, 1953; Underwood, 1957; Underwood, cited by Greep, 1963; Clark, 1968), and possibly this condition will be found in other species as well (Table IV).

In those lizards possessing a single pair of parathyroids, the glands are

---

Fig. 12. Parathyroid of an adult female *Sphenodon punctatus*, fixed with Halmi's fluid. (Photomicrographs kindly provided by Dr. M. Gabe.)

    a. PAS and Groat's hematoxylin-picro-indigocarmine. Note the conspicuous sheath of connective tissue and the lobulation of the glandular tissue; × 230 (from Gabe and Saint Girons, 1964).

    b. Same slide as A. Note the PAS-positive intracellular glycogen granules; the histochemical significance of the PAS-reactivity is ascertained by malt diastase digestion performed on an adjacent slide; × 550.

    c. Groat's hematoxylin and van Gieson's picrofuchsin. Note the connective tissue (black) and the intercellular melanin granules; × 150.

    d. Same slide as C. Note the intercellular melanin granules; × 2000.

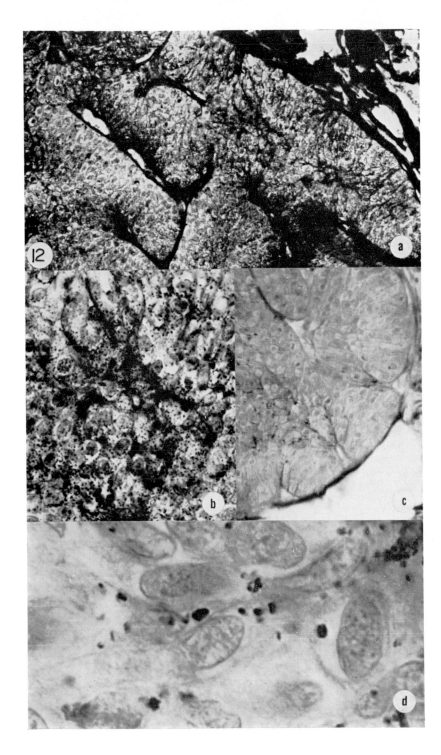

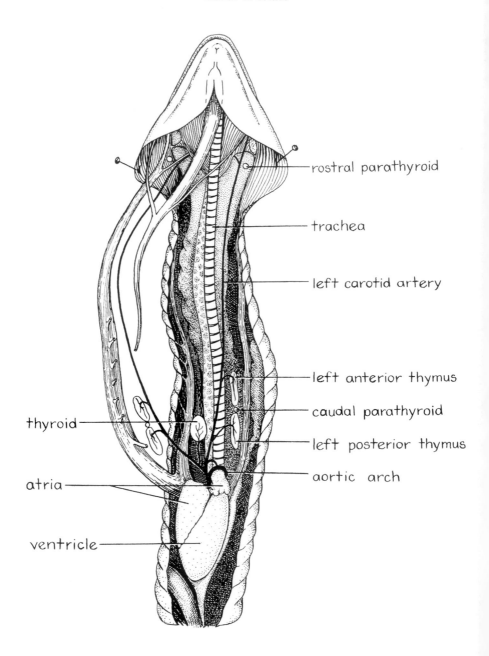

FIG. 13. Location of the parathyroid glands in the snake *Natrix natrix* (modified from Van Bemmelen, 1888).

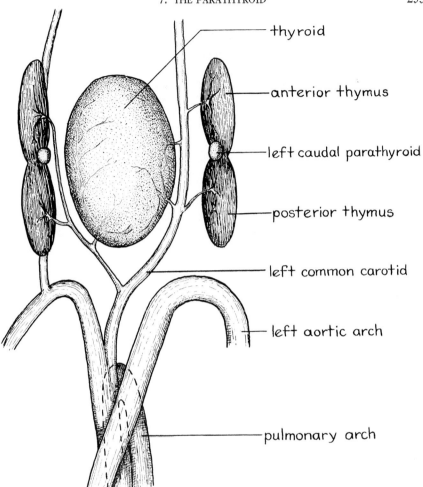

thyroid

anterior thymus

left caudal parathyroid

posterior thymus

left common carotid

left aortic arch

pulmonary arch

FIG. 14. Detail of the area of the thymus glands in the snake *Thamnophis*, showing the location of the caudal pair of parathyroid glands (from Herdson, 1956).

located near the bifurcation of the carotid arch in the cervical region. The glands are generally closely associated with the blood vessels and may be embedded in the adventitia (Fig. 17), thus making parathyroid removal rather difficult without damage to the blood vessels. When a second pair of parathyroids is also present, it is about half the size of the rostral pair (approximately 0·5 mm diameter) and located just posterior to them near the arch of the aorta on either side of the neck.

The histological appearance of the parathyroid glands has been described for many species of lizards (Weber, 1909; Peters, 1941; Adams, 1952; Rogers, 1963; Sidky, 1965; Clark, 1968) and resembles that of other reptiles.

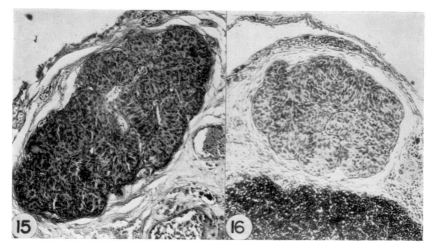

FIG. 15. Parathyroid gland of *Thamnophis sirtalis*, showing the structure of the cellular cords. PAS and hematoxylin; × 140.

FIG. 16. Caudal parathyroid gland of a young *Natrix sipedon*, demonstrating its close association with the thymic tissue. Hematoxylin and eosin; × 100.

The glands are composed of cellular cords, with capillary or sinusoidal networks between the cords, and are surrounded by a connective tissue capsule. The parathyroid cells have round or oval nuclei that are rather large relative to the amount of cytoplasm. The cytoplasm contains only faint granulation and stains weakly with PAS. A characteristic feature of some lacertilian parathyroids is the presence of follicles. The follicles often contain material which stains strongly with PAS. Figures 18 and 19 show the parathyroid structure in *Anolis carolinensis*.

Although light microscopy of the parathyroid suggests that there is only a single type of cell (Peters, 1941; Sidky, 1965; Clark, 1968), Rogers (1963), on the basis of the only histochemical investigation of lacertilian parathyroids, has distinguished three types of cells in these glands of the Australian skinks *Tiliqua occipitalis* and *Trachydosaurus rugosus*. The most common type of cell is compared with that of mammals, and given the same name, chief cell. Vacuolated chief cells are compared with the mammalian "water clear" variant and are not considered a separate type of cell. Two rare additional types are the "dark cells", containing smaller nuclei and cytoplasm which can be distinguished histochemically from that of chief cells, and the "epithelial cells", in which both cells and nuclei are fusiform and the cytoplasm is non-granular; the significance of these different cells is not known. Ultrastructural investigations would probably demonstrate whether different types of cells exist in these animals.

TABLE IV

Species of Sauria Examined with Regard to Parathyroid Number

Family	Species	No. of Parathyroids Embryo	Adult	Authority
Iguanidae	*Anolis carolinensis*	–	4	Clark (1968)
	Anolis garmani	–	4	Underwood (unpublished)
	Anolis grahami	–	4	Underwood (unpublished)
	Anolis lineatopus	–	4	Underwood (unpublished)
	Anolis opalinus	–	4	Underwood (unpublished)
	Cyclura carinata	–	2	Underwood (unpublished)
	Cyclura caymanensis	–	2	Underwood (unpublished)
	Iguana iguana	4	4	Van Bemmelen (1888)*
		–	2	Underwood (unpublished)
	Xiphocercus valencienni	–	4	Underwood (unpublished)
Gekkonidae	*Gekko gecko*	4	4	Van Bemmelen (1888)*
	Hemidactylus flavi-viridis	–	2	Bhatia and Dayal (1933)*
Pygopodidae	*Aprasia pulchella*	–	2	Underwood (1957)
	Delma fraseri	–	4	Underwood (1957)
	Lialis sp.	–	2	Underwood (1957)
Scincidae	*Chalcides ocellatus*	–	2	Sidky (1965, 1966)
	Scincus scincus	–	2	Sidky (1965, 1966)
	Tiliqua occipitalis	–	2	Rogers (1963)
	Trachydosaurus rugosus	–	2	Rogers (1963)
Lacertidae	*Lacerta agilis*	4	2	Verdun (1898)
		4	2	Maurer (1899)
		4	2	Peter (1901)
		4	2	Saint-Remy and Prenant (1904)
		–	2	Peters (1941)
	Lacerta muralis	6	6	Van Bemmelen (1886)*
		–	2	Peters (1941)
	Lacerta viridis	4	2	Saint-Remy and Prenant (1904)
		–	2	Peters (1941)
	Lacerta vivipara	–	2	Peters (1941)
	Lacerta sp.	4	2	Adams (1939)
Anguidae	*Anguis fragilis*	4	4	Van Bemmelen (1888)*
		4	2	Saint-Remy and Prenant (1904)
	Ophisaurus sp.	4	4	Van Bemmelen (1888)*
Varanidae	*Varanus griseus*	–	2	Sidky (1965, 1966)
	Varanus monitor	–	2	Chowdhary (1950)
	Varanus varius	–	2	Adams (1962)

*These glandlike nodules were not definitely identified as parathyroids.

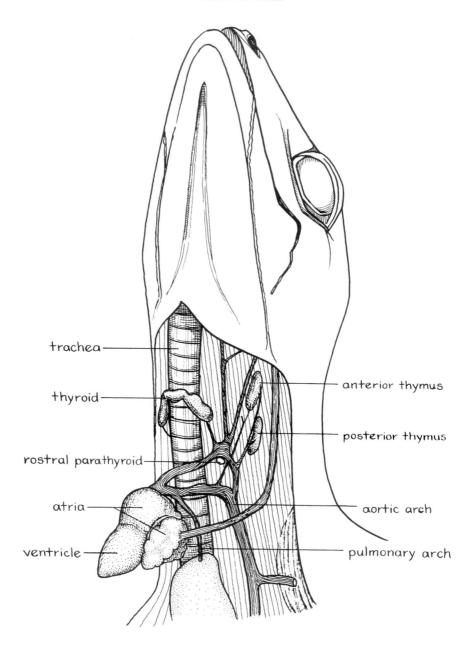

FIG. 17. Location of the left parathyroid in the lizard *Gekko verticillatus* (*Platydactylus guttatus*) (after Van Bemmelen, 1888).

Seasonal variation in the histological appearance of the parathyroids has been reported in several species of lizards. Peters (1941) noted some degenerative changes and occasional formation of cysts in *Lacerta viridis* in the winter. About half the parathyroid cells in the African skinks *Chalcides ocellatus* and *Scincus scincus* regressed and disappeared during the winter months and then regenerated during the summer (Figs 20 and 21; Sidky, 1965). Such seasonal changes also occur in several species of anurans, and von Brehm (1964) attributed these changes to winter temperatures as they could be induced by subjecting the animals to low temperature out of season. However, Sidky (1965) has attributed the degenerative changes in the parathyroids to failure of his lizards to feed, and has duplicated the effect by starvation of the lizards during the summer months.

Accessory parathyroid glands have occasionally been reported. The relatively frequent occurrence of accessory tissue in a species may reflect the occasional persistence of a second pair of parathyroid glands, as in *Lacerta viridis*, in which Peters (1941) found accessory parathyroid tissue in 6 out of 16 animals. On the other hand, Sidky (1965) found accessory glands in only one of over forty lizards (*Chalcides ocellatus* and *Scincus scincus*) examined and Adams (1939) noted the retention of a caudal parathyroid within the thymus in only one specimen of *Lacerta*.

Parathyroidectomy has been performed on several species of lizards, including *Lacerta viridis* (Peters, 1941), *Chalcides ocellatus* and *Varanus griseus* (Sidky, 1966), and *Anolis carolinensis* (Clark, 1968; Clark *et al.*, 1969). In all species, removal of the parathyroid glands (one pair in all except *A. carolinensis*, in which there are two pairs) resulted in hyperexcitability and tetanic convulsions, usually after a latent period of several days or more depending upon the environmental temperature. Peters (1941) found that some of his parathyroidectomized animals did not respond as described above, but in most cases histological investigation revealed accessory parathyroid tissue or remnants of the removed pair.

Sidky (1966) was the first to measure the concentration of calcium in the plasma of parathyroidectomized lizards, and found that this falls to approximately half the normal value of 3 mM/L. Blood samples which are taken from parathyroidectomized lizards in tetany fail to clot, indicating the low concentration of calcium ions in the body fluids. Unilateral parathyroidectomy has no effect on the behaviour of the animals or the concentration of calcium in their plasma and administration of calcium gluconate relieves the convulsions and tremors of parathyroidectomized animals.

In *Anolis carolinensis*, removal of three of the four glands usually does not affect the animal's behaviour (Clark, 1968). Removal of all four glands, however, results in tetanic convulsions and paralysis within one or two days after the operation. The attacks are induced when the animal does any sort of

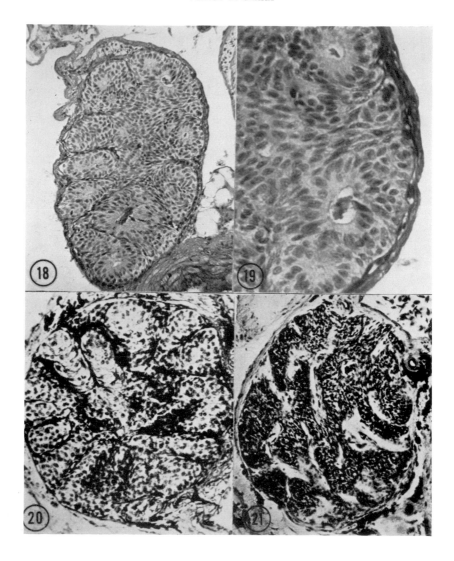

FIG. 18. Parathyroid gland of *Anolis carolinensis*, showing cellular cords and conspicuous follicular structure. PAS and hematoxylin; × 100. From Clark (1968).

FIG. 19. Detail of a portion of the gland shown in figure 18, showing two follicles containing PAS-positive material. PAS and Hematoxylin; × 275.

FIG. 20. Active parathyroid gland of the lizard *Chalcides ocellatus* during June, showing well formed cellular cords. Hematoxylin and acid fuchsin; × 135. From Sidky (1965).

FIG. 21. Parathyroid gland of the lizard *Chalcides ocellatus* during March, showing degeneration of the cellular cords. Hematoxylin and acid fuchsin; × 155. From Sidky (1965).

mild exercise, are of about a 30-second duration, and can be reinduced after approximately one hour.

Parathyroidectomized *A. carolinensis* have concentrations of calcium in the serum less than half those of sham-operated controls, and the concentrations of phosphate in their serum are 70% above normal. Parathyroid extract eliminates tetanic seizures of parathyroidectomized animals and causes the concentrations of calcium and phosphate in the serum to return to near-normal levels (Clark *et al.*, 1969).

Administration of parathyroid extract induces hypercalcemia, hypercalci-uria, and hyperphosphaturia in normal *Dipsosaurus dorsalis* and *Sceloporus grammicus* (McWhinnie and Cortelyou, 1968), but is without effect on the level of phosphate in the serum. I can demonstrate no significant effect of parathyroid extract on concentrations of calcium or phosphate in the serum of normal *Anolis carolinensis*.

In a study of lizard limb regeneration, Umanski and Kudokotzev (1951) demonstrated that the administration of parathyroid extract results in in-creased numbers of osteoclasts in the bone of *Lacerta agilis*.

Thus lizards yield the best evidence of parathyroid influence on the calcium and phosphate metabolism of reptiles.

V. Acknowledgements

I wish to thank Drs. M. Gabe, P. B. Herdson, H. Saint Girons, and Y. A. Sidky for kindly providing figures used in this paper. Mrs. Stephani Schaefer modified and redrew the figures from van Bemmelen (1888). I am indebted to Drs. Norman Scott and Michael W. Dix for their help in identification and revision of names of reptiles in the tables. The electron micrographs were prepared in the Department of Animal Diseases, University of Connecticut, under the direction of Drs. Lamia Khairallah and Carroll Burke. I am grate-ful to Dr. W. E. Adams for reading the manuscript and offering valuable suggestions. This study was supported in part by Grant GB 7619 from the National Science Foundation and grants from the University of Connecticut Research Foundation to me and to the Electron Microscope Laboratory of the Department of Animal Diseases.

References

Adams, W. E. (1939). The cervical region of the Lacertilia. *J. Anat.* 74, 57–71.
Adams, W. E. (1952). The carotid sinus complex and epithelial body of *Varanus varius*. *Anat. Rec.* 113, 1–27.
Adams, W. E. (1953). The carotid arch in lizards with particular reference to the origin of the internal carotid artery. *J. Morph.* 92, 115–155.
Adams, W. E. (1962). The carotid sinus-carotid body problem in the Chelonia (with a note on a foramen of Panizza in *Dermochelys*). *Arch. int. Pharmacodyn. Thér.* 139, 28–37.

Afanassiew, B. (1877). Weitere Untersuchungen über den Bau und die Entwicklung der Thymus und der Winterschlafdrüse der Säugetiere. *Arch. mikrosk. Anat. EntwMech.* 14, 343–389.

Aimé, P. (1911). Note sur les glandules parathyroides et parathymiques de la tortue grecque. *C.r. Séanc. Soc. Biol.* 70, 209–210.

Bargmann, W. (1939). Die Epithelkörperchen. *In* "Handbuch der mikroskopischen Anatomie des Menschen" (W. von. Möllendorff, ed.) 6 (2), 137–196. Springer, Berlin.

Beutner, E. H. and Munson, P. L. (1960). Time course and urinary excretion of inorganic phosphate by rats after parathyroidectomy and after injection of parathyroid extract. *Endocrinology* 66, 610–616.

Bhatia, M. L. and Dayal, J. (1933). On the arterial system of the lizard *Hemidactylus flaviviridis* Rüppel (the wall lizard). *Anat. Anz.* 76, 417–437.

Boyd, J. D. (1942). The nerve supply of the branchial arch arteries in *Vipera berus*. *J. Anat.* 76, 248–257.

von Brehm, H. (1964). Experimentelle Studie zur Frage der jahreszyklischen Veränderungen. Morphologische Untersuchungen an Epithelkörperchen (Glandulae parathyreoideae)von Anuren. II. *Z. Zellforsch. mikrosk. Anat.* 61, 725–741.

Chowdhary, D. S. (1950). A note on the carotid body and carotid sinus of *Varanus monitor*. *Anat. Rec.* 107, 235–241.

Clark, N. B. (1965). Experimental and histological studies of the parathyroid glands of fresh-water turtles. *Gen. Comp. Endocrinol.* 5, 297–312.

Clark, N. B. (1967). Parathyroid glands in reptiles. *Am. Zool.* 7, 869–881.

Clark, N. B. (1968). Effect of parathyroidectomy in the lizard, *Anolis carolinensis*. *Gen. Comp. Endocrinol.* 10, 99–102.

Clark, N. B. and Khairallah, L. H. (1969). Histochemistry and ultrastructure of the parathyroid glands of the turtle, *Pseudemys scripta*. *Am. Zool.* 9, 1083.

Clark, N. B. and Srivastava. (1970). Parathyroidectomy in the garter snake, *Thamnophis sirtalis*. *Am. Zool.* 10 (in press).

Clark, N. B., Pang, P. K. T. and Dix, M. W. (1969). Parathyroid glands and calcium and phosphate regulation in the lizard, *Anolis carolinensis*. *Gen. Comp. Endocrinol.* 12, 614–618.

Doyon, M. and Kareff, N. (1904). Les parathyroides chez la tortue (Tortue d'Afrique). *C.r. Seanc. Soc. Biol.* 56, 719–720.

Francescon, A. (1929). Il corpo ultimobranchiale nei rettili. *Arch. ital. Anat. Embriol.* 26, 387–400.

Gabe, M. and Saint Girons, H. (1964). "Contributions a l'Histologie de *Sphenodon punctatus* Gray." Centre National de la Recherche Scientifique, Paris.

Greep, R. O. (1963) Parathyroid glands. *In* "Comparative Endocrinology", (U.S. von Euler and H. Heller, eds.) 1, 325–370. Academic Press, New York.

Hamilton, D. W., Fawcett, D. W. and Christensen, A. K. (1966). The liver of the slender salamander *Batrachoseps attenuatus*. I. The structure of its crystalline inclusions. *Z. Zellforsch. mikrosk. Anat.* 70, 347–363.

Hammar, J. A. (1937). Zur Bildungsgeschichte der Kiemenderivate der Krokodile. *Z. mikrosk.-anat Forsch.* 41, 75–87.

Harrison, B. M. and Denning, N. E. (1929). Embryonic development of the pharyngeal region in *Thamnophis radix*. *Anat. Rec.* 44, 101–116.

Herdson, P. B. (1956). "The cervical region of the Ophidia with especial reference to the parathyroids and carotid arteries." Thesis, University of Otago, New Zealand.

Johnson, C. E. (1922). Branchial derivatives in turtles. *J. Morph.* 36, 299–329.

Krause, R. (1922). "Mikroskopische Anatomie der Wirbeltiere in Einzeldarstellungen. II Vögel und Reptilien." de Gruyter, Berlin.

Lüdicke, M. (1962, 1964). Ordnung der Klasse Reptilia: Serpentes. *In* "Handbuch der Zoologie", (W. Kükenthal and T. Krumbach, eds.) 7, (5–6), 1–298. de Gruyter, Berlin.

Maurer, F. (1899). Die Schilddrüse, Thymus und andere Schlundspalten-derivate bei der Eidechse. *Morph. Jahrb.* 27, 119–172.

McGee-Russell, S. M. and Smale, N. B. (1963). On colouring epon-embedded tissue sections with Sudan black B or Nile blue A for light microscopy. *Q. Jl. Microsc. Sci.* 104, 109–115.

McWhinnie, D. J. and Cortelyou, J. R. (1968). Influence of parathyroid extract on blood and urine mineral levels in iguanid lizards. *Gen. Comp. Endocrinol.* 11, 78–87.

Neudeck, L. D. (1969). Histological investigation of snake parathyroid glands. *Am. Zool.* 9, 1083–1084.

Peter, K. (1901). Mitteilungen zur Entwicklungsgeschichte der Eidechse. II. Die Schlundspalten in ihrer Anlage, Ausbildung und Bedeutung. *Arch. mikrosk. Anat. EntwMech.* 57, 705–765.

Peters, H. (1941). Morphologische und experimentelle Untersuchungen über die Epithelkörper bei Eidechsen. *Z. mikrosk.-anat. Forsch.* 49, 1–40.

Pischinger, A. (1937). Kiemenanlagen und ihre Schicksale bei Amnioten – Schilddrüse und epitheliale Organe der Pharynxwand bei Tetrapoden. *In* "Handbuch der vergleichende Anatomie der Wirbeltiere" (L. Bolk, E. Göppert, E. Kallius, and W. Lubosch, eds) 3, 279–348. Urban und Schwarzenberg, Berlin and Wien.

Reese, A. M. (1931). The ductless glands of *Alligator mississippiensis. Smithson. misc. Collns.* 82, (16), 1–14.

Rogers, D. C. (1963). A cytological and cytochemical study of the "epithelial body" on the carotid artery of the lizards, *Trachysaurus rugosus* and *Tiliqua occipitalis. Q. Jl. microsc. Sci.* 104, 197–205.

Saint-Remy, G. and Prenant, A. (1904). Recherches sur la développement des dérivés branchiaux chez les sauriens et les ophidiens. *Archs. Biol., Paris* 20, 142–216.

Shaner, R. F. (1921a). The development of the pharynx, and the histology of its adult derivatives, in turtles, *Anat. Rec.* 21, 81.

Shaner, R. F. (1921b). The development of the pharynx and aortic arches of the turtle, with a note on the fifth and pulmonary arches of mammals. *Am. J. Anat.* 29, 407–429.

Sidky, Y. A. (1965). Histological studies on the parathyroid glands of lizards. *Z. Zellforsch. mikrosk. Anat.* 65, 760–769.

Sidky, Y. A. (1966). Effect of parathyroidectomy in lizards. *Gen. Comp. Endocrinol.* 7, 22–26.

Thompson, F. D. (1910). The thyroid and parathyroid glands throughout vertebrates with observations on some other closely related structures. *Phil. Trans. R. Soc.* (B) 104, 91–132.

Umanski, E. E. and Kudokotzev, V. P. (1951). Stimulation of the regenerative process in the limb of reptiles with parathyroid hormone. (In Russian). *Dokl. Akad. Nauk. SSSR* 77, 533–536.

Underwood, G. (1957). On lizards of the family Pygopodidae (A contribution to the morphology and phylogeny of the Squamata.). *J. Morph.* 100, 207–268.

Van Bemmelen, J. F. (1886). Die Visceraltaschen und Aortenbogen bei Reptilien und Vögeln. *Zool. Anz.* 9, 528–532 and 543–548.

Van Bemmelen, J. F. (1887). Die Halsgegend der Reptilien. *Zool. Anz.* 10, 88–96.

Van Bemmelen, J. F. (1888). Beiträge zur Kenntniss der Halsgegend bei Reptilien. *Bijdr. Dierk.* 16, 101–146.

Verdun, M. P. (1898). Glandules branchiales et corps postbranchiaux chez les reptiles. *C.r. Séanc. Soc. Biol.* 50, 1046–1048.

Weber, A. (1909). Recherches cytologiques sur la sécrétion des glandes parathyroides du gecko. *C.r. Séanc. Soc. Biol.* **67**, 17–18.

Wettstein, O. von (1931–1937). 1. Ordnung der Klasse Reptilia: Rhynchocephalia. *In* "Handbuch der Zoologie," (W. Kükenthal and T. Krumbach, eds) 7, (1–3), 1–235. de Gruyter, Berlin.

Wettstein, O. von (1937–1954). 2. Ordnung der Klasse Reptilia: Crocodilia. *In* "Handbuch der Zoologie," (W. Kükenthal and T. Krumbach, eds) 7, (3–4), 236–424. de Gruyter, Berlin.

CHAPTER 8

The Adrenal

MANFRED GABE

Laboratoire d'Évolution des Êtres Organisés, Paris, France

I. Introduction

The adrenal gland of reptiles has been known since its description by Perrault (1676) and Morgagni (1763), but its real significance only became recognized in the 19th century. The relatively small number of papers dealing with the reptilian adrenal contrasts markedly with the enormous amount of research that has been devoted to it in eutherian mammals.

The classical publications of the early 19th century (Cuvier, 1805; Bojanus, 1819–21; Retzius, 1830; Nagel, 1836; Ecker, 1846, 1847; Rathke, 1839, 1866; Günther, 1867) give the first detailed descriptions of the microscopic anatomy of the organ and establish its homology with the mammalian adrenal gland. Leydig (1853), Braun (1879), Pettit (1896), Vincent (1896), Minervini (1904) and Poll (1904a, 1904b, 1906) review the numerous histological investigations of the reptilian adrenal, the details of its vascularization, and its interspecific differences. The brief statements these offered seem to have been considered sufficient by herpetologists to establish the topographic position of the reptilian adrenal gland. Those workers interested in histophysiological or physiological approaches seem to have hesitated to study animals difficult to capture, to manipulate, and to maintain live in the laboratory, and have consequently experimented mainly with small mammals. As a result, the number of publications on the adrenal gland of reptiles diminishes sharply at the beginning of the twentieth century (cf. the reviews of Berkelbach van der Sprenkel, 1934; Wettstein, 1931–1937, 1937–1954; Hartman and Brownell, 1949; Bachmann, 1954). Even Chester Jones (1957b) cites but few recent studies of the reptilian adrenal (see addendum).

Attempts to combine modern techniques with an adequate sampling of reptilian groups have been made by Hebard and Charipper (1955), Gabe and

Martoja (1961, 1962), Gabe and Rancurel (1964) and Gabe and Saint Girons (1964a, 1964b). Recent reviews are furnished by Bern and Nandi (1964), Gabe *et al.* (1964) and Matty (1966). Several books on comparative endocrinology (see especially Barrington, 1963; Gorbman and Bern, 1962) contain chapters on the reptilian adrenal.

The lack of information is even more obvious when one attempts to review the physiology of this organ. The two hormones, adrenalin and noradrenalin, produced by the adrenomedullary tissue of the mammals have also been identified in reptiles. The biosynthesis of the corticosteroids in reptiles and the interrelations of their adrenal gland with other endocrine glands are particularly poorly known. Their seasonal and other cyclic changes have been explored in only a very few species.

It is useful to start by stating the nomenclature to be utilized. The term "adrenal gland" must be maintained since it is universally used, but it is misleading. Except among the turtles, the reptilian adrenal lacks any clear anatomical relation to the kidney; in contrast to other vertebrates its relations are much closer to the gonads and to the gonoducts.

The names of the two parts of the organ are even more difficult. Many authors attempt to maintain the nomenclature used for eutherian mammals and designate the cytological and physiological equivalent of their adrenal cortex as "adrenocortical tissue" in reptiles. They also describe a reptilian "medullary" tissue. This approach is clearly inappropriate.

The "medullary" tissue of all reptiles examined occupies a peripheral position, and the "adrenocortical" tissue is centrally placed. The two types of tissue are often mixed, but there are examples in which transverse sections of the organ show a cortex entirely constituted by "medullary" tissue, and a medulla formed of "adrenocortical" tissue only (Gabe *et al.*, 1964). A comparable anatomical position makes the term "adrenocortical tissue" equally inappropriate in birds and anamniotes. It seems preferable to refer to this tissue as "interrenal", a term created by Balfour (1876) for the cytological and functional equivalent in other vertebrates of the adrenal cortex of mammals.

The term "medullary" is, fortunately, less often applied to the reptilian adrenal; most workers refer to chromaffin tissue, but use of this term also presents problems (see especially Poll, 1906). The terms "chromaffin" or "phaeochrome" tissue designate all those cells derived from the neural crest and specialized for the production of sympathomimetic catecholamines independent of their localization. However, the homologies of the mammalian adrenomedullary tissue are not with topographical equivalents in other vertebrates. The term "adrenal tissue" (Balfour, 1876–1878) is most nearly adequate since it simultaneously defines the nature and the localization of the tissue, and it is hence adopted here.

II. Embryonic Development

A. GENERAL

The duality of embryonic origin of the two tissues that form the adrenal gland of reptiles was well established by the classical works published during the end of the 19th and the beginning of the 20th century and agrees with that in all other vertebrates. However, even some of the most recent works contain categorical contradictions concerning the embryology of the reptilian adrenal gland (see Table I), and the number of species studied in detail is yet small; thus new investigations utilizing the techniques of experimental embryology are still desirable.

TABLE I

Sources on the embryonic origin of reptilian interrenal tissue

Species	Origin of interrenal tissue	References
Caretta caretta	coelomic epithelium	Kuntz, 1912
Chrysemys picta marginata	coelomic epithelium	Allen, 1905
Emys orbicularis	coelomic epithelium	Mihalkovics, 1885; Poll, 1905
Sternotherus odoratus	coelomic epithelium	Risley, 1933
Anguis fragilis	mesonephros (*pro parte*)	Raynaud, 1960
Anolis carolinensis	coelomic epithelium	Forbes, 1956
Calotes cristatellus	coelomic epithelium	Simkins and Asana, 1930
Chalcides ocellatus	coelomic epithelium	Bimmer, 1950
Lacerta agilis	mesonephros	Hoffmann, 1889
Lacerta agilis	coelomic epithelium	Bimmer, 1950
Lacerta muralis	mesonephros	Weldon, 1885
Lacerta muralis	coelomic epithelium	Soulié, 1903
Lacerta sicula campestris	coelomic epithelium	Marin and Sabbadin, 1859
Lacerta vivipara	coelomic epithelium	Bimmer, 1950
Xantusia vigilis	coelomic epithelium	Miller, 1963
Natrix natrix	coelomic epithelium	Braun, 1879, 1882
Alligator mississippiensis	coelomic epithelium	Forbes, 1940

Two fundamental questions about the ontogeny of the adrenal gland are: what is the origin of the cells constituting the two tissues, and when do they switch from the embryonic to the functional state? The first of these seems to have attracted the attention of most of the authors mentioned in Table I, but our knowledge of both of these must be reviewed.

B. Origin and Early Ontogeny of the Interrenal Tissue

All authors agree that the reptilian interrenal tissue, like that of all verte-brates, is of mesodermal origin. Yet there are at least two distinct views regarding the establishment of the Anlage of the organ.

Most authors concur (see Table I) that the interrenal tissue is derived from the coelomic epithelium. It differentiates either within the epithelium proper or in the underlying mesenchyme. Proliferation occurs in the pro-longation of the genital crest, between this and the root of the mesentery, or on the lateral or medial border of this crest. Some descriptions mention a continuous proliferation; others refer to the production of a series of buds which secondarily fuse.

Weldon (1884) and Hoffmann (1889) presented a very different concept. According to these authors the Anlage of the interrenal tissue derives from the internal wall of the Malpighian corpuscle of the mesonephros; the dorsal part of the resulting blastema develops between the mesonephros and the vena cava and becomes the interrenal tissue, while its ventral portion reaches into the genital crest and forms the testicular net. The connection between the two Anlagen could be noted until a relatively advanced stage of develop-ment. Only Raynaud (1962; *Anguis fragilis*) among recent authors reaches conclusions similar, in part, to those of Weldon and Hoffmann.

Miller's (1963) description of the development of the adrenals of *Xantusia vigilis* is typical of the first and more widely held view. According to him, in 2 mm long embryos of *Xantusia vigilis*, cells, destined to form the interrenal tissue in the intermediate mesoderm, proliferate between the future positions of the gonad and the mesonephros. The first identifiable elements seem to derive from mesenchymatic cells located just below the peritoneum lateral to the gonadal Anlage and ventromedial to the mesonephros. Groups of these cells occur on both sides of the midline, lateral to the root of the dorsal mesentery. In 3 mm embryos the interrenal cells have become considerably more numerous, and osmiophilic droplets appear in their cytoplasm. By the 5 mm stage the mass of interrenal tissue has gradually increased and ex-tended posteriorly, and has almost contacted the adrenal element extending from the zone of the paravertebral ganglia. By the 6 mm stage this contact is realized, and the osmiophilic droplets are much more abundant in the in-terrenal cells. Later developmental stages show a progressive organization of the adrenal cells into a dorsal cap on the surface of the osmiophilic, lipid–rich interrenal tissue which is penetrated by many adrenal cells. Near the time of hatching (22 mm stage) the interrenal tissue and the gonads start to separate, continuing to do so during the first six months of life, as the mesonephros regresses.

Raynaud's (1962) description of the development of *Anguis fragilis* is typical of the second view. In 4·5 to 5·2 mm embryos he notes a proliferation of the external wall of Bowman's capsule of the mesonephric glomerulus lying on the medial side, near the junction of the atrophied nephrostomal duct with the metanephritic vesicula. The proliferation produces a cluster of cells between the medial border of the mesonephros, the peritoneum, and the aorta. By the following stage (embryos from 5 to 6 mm), the cluster has increased in volume, the cells are migrating dorsally, and proliferation of the peritoneum occurs at the contact of its ventral border with the cluster of cells. After this developmental stage it is impossible to determine from cross sections whether the cellular cluster of mesonephritic origin remains autonomous or whether it incorporates peritoneal cells. The interrenal Anlage, however constituted, shows a segmental pattern, and its lateral border adjoins the medial surface of each Malpighian corpuscle of the mesonephros. As development proceeds, the interrenal Anlage shifts progressively away from the peritoneum and reaches a position dorsal to the gonad. Lying between the internal veins of the mesonephros and the medial border of that organ, the Anlage begins to detach from the Malpighian corpuscles in embryos weighing 40 to 60 mg; the separation of the two organs is complete when the embryo reaches 80 to 100 mg.

Both Raynaud (1962) and Miller (1963) comment that only the techniques of experimental embryology might permit a decision between the above two hypotheses. This suggests that no conclusion is now possible. It is, nevertheless, interesting that the mesonephritic origin of the interrenal Anlage is claimed only by authors who studied saurian embryos (*Lacerta muralis*, Weldon, 1884; *Lacerta agilis*, Hoffmann, 1889; *Anguis fragilis*, Raynaud, 1962); no embryological work on the interrenal tissue of Testudines, Crocodilia, or Ophidia mentions this mode of ontogeny. Also, the last claim for a mesonephritic origin of the interrenal tissue (Raynaud, 1962) is much less strongly stated than are the older studies (Weldon, 1885; Hoffmann, 1889); the possibility of a *mixed* origin, involving both peritoneal *and* mesonephritic tissues, is not excluded.

C. Start of Interrenal Activity

I know of no papers presenting physiological data concerning the start of activity in the embryonic interrenal tissue, and the morphological studies provide no more than a first approximation. Indeed, the only technique other than descriptive microscopical anatomy that has been applied to the embryology of the reptilian adrenal gland is the identification of lipid globules revealed by their osmiophilic reaction or by staining with dyes of the Sudan series. No workers seem to have attempted specific tests for steroids or for Δ^5-3-β-hydroxysteroido-dehydrogenase.

Particulate lipids appear in the interrenal cells of saurians in a relatively early embryonic stage (Bimmer, 1950; Raynaud and Raynaud, 1961; Miller, 1963). The interrenal cells of *Lacerta* contain lipids as soon as the Anlage has fused into a continuous interrenal cord (Bimmer, 1950), while 120 to 150 mg embryos of *Anguis fragilis* show particulate lipids in the interrenal cells (Raynaud and Raynaud, 1961). Even 3 mm embryos of *Xantusia* contain osmiophilic lipids (Miller, 1963).

D. Embryonic Development and Start of Activity in the Adrenal Tissue

Opinions differ about the origin of reptilian interrenal tissue, but there is a complete agreement that reptilian adrenal tissue has the same origin as that of other vertebrates and that this tissue forms and begins to function relatively late in ontogeny.

Earlier authors (see summaries of Poll, 1904a, 1904b, 1906) noted the presence of small clusters of sympathopheochromoblasts in the connective tissue between the notochord, aorta and mesonephros of reptilian embryos. These cells were identified by the intense coloration of their cytoplasm, but did not yet yield a chromaffin reaction, specific for polyphenolic components. The chromaffin cells begin to differentiate after the interrenal tissue is clearly differentiated and already contains particulate lipids; the contact between the interrenal and adrenal tissue develops only in late ontogenetic stages, or after hatching.

Modern investigations confirm these results entirely. Bimmer (1950) shows that the differentiation of the adrenal tissue of *Lacerta* and *Chalcides* embryos occurs in an area that extends considerably posterior to the interrenal tissue and that the chromaffin reaction only occurs just before hatching. Adrenal cells of *Xantusia vigilis* first appear in 3 mm embryos (Miller, 1963). At this time the interrenal tissue still contains osmiophilic lipids; the time of contact for the two tissues was noted above in the description of interrenal development. Cytological signs of secretion only appear with the approach of hatching, and the topographic relations between adrenal and interrenal tissues become fixed only after the first months of life.

III. Macroscopic Anatomy

The first investigators noted the great variability of form and size in reptilian adrenal glands, and all recent reviews emphasize this. Its topographic position tends to vary with the systematic position of the animals studied, but certain of its relations are relatively constant.

Quantitative data concerning the size of the adrenals are rare and cannot easily be compared because of such parameters as the sex and age of the animals, as well as their stage in the annual cycle. The lack of homogeneity probably magnifies the inherent variability (Table II). In general the two adrenals weigh between 10 and 60 mg for each 100 g of body weight.

TABLE II

Some data on the relative weight of reptilian adrenal glands
(after Chester Jones, 1957b, simplified)

Species	Relative weight of the adrenals (mg/100g)
Caretta caretta	33
Emys orbicularis	10
Geochelone chilensis	9.5
Testudo sp.	10
Heloderma suspectum	24.96
Lacerta viridis	40
Tupinambis teguixin	33.7
Varanus salvator	14
Coluber sp.	40
Natrix natrix	50
Thamnodynastes sp.	24.15–55.6
Tomodon sp.	15.43–34.2
Caiman latirostris	19

The color of the adrenal gland also varies from light yellow to reddish, not only from one species to another but also during the annual cycle of a single species. This color is produced, at least in part, by the relative abundance of particulate lipids in the interrenal cells and by the amount of blood in the organ.

The shape and the relations of the adrenal with adjoining organs are quite variable and differ with the major systematic groups, so that they must be treated separately.

The adrenal gland of turtles is dorsoventrally flattened, has more or less regular borders, and lies against the kidney (Fig. 1). The dorsal limit of the gland is difficult to see, since only the basement membranes of the cellular strands separate the gland from the renal parenchyma. The islets of interrenal and adrenal tissue regularly penetrate a short distance into the parenchyma. The ventral sides of the glands are covered by the parietal folds of the peritoneum. A peritoneal fold, attached to the ventrolateral side of the adrenal gland, ensheathes each gonad and the proximal part of each gonoduct to form the mesorchium of the male and the mesovarium of the female. The gland also lies close to the kidney and the proximal segments of the genital system and is crossed by the efferent renal veins.

The adrenal gland of *Sphenodon punctatus*, the only Recent rhynchocephalian, lacks a direct relation with the kidney (Fig. 2). Its topographical

MANFRED GABE

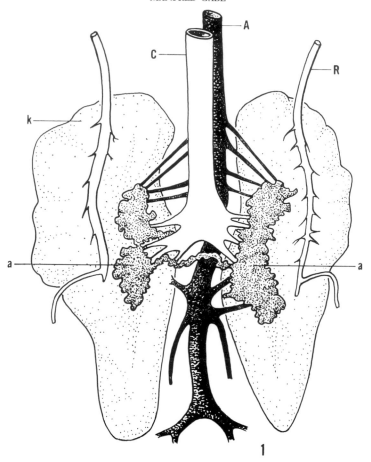

FIG. 1. Location of the adrenal glands at the ventral surface of the kidneys in *Pseudemys scripta* (after Hartman and Brownell, 1949). A, aorta; a, adrenal gland; C, vena cava posterior; k, kidney; R, vena renalis afferens.

relations with the genital system are even closer than in turtles, since the adrenal is entirely incorporated in the mesorchium of the male or mesovarium of the female. It is impossible to separate the adrenal gland of the male from the epididymis or that of the female from the Wolffian vestiges, since a common sheath of connective tissue covers both (Osawa, 1897). The anteroposterior extension of the organ is considerable, with the anterior pole applied to the gonad and the posterior pole terminating some distance from the kidney. The transverse diameter of the adrenal is, on the contrary, relatively small, so that the organ has the shape of an elongate spindle.

The adrenal gland of the Squamata is also incorporated in the mesorchium or mesovarium of the gonad (Fig. 3). The gland's relations with the testes or

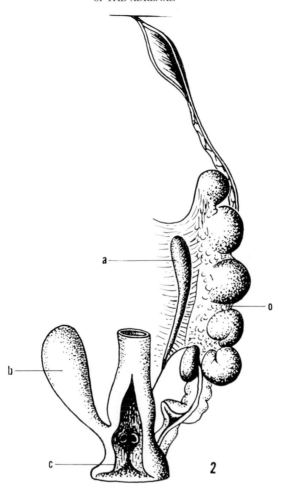

FIG. 2. Diagrammatic representation of the adrenal gland in a female *Sphenodon punctatus* (after Osawa, 1897). a, adrenal gland; b, bladder; c, cloaca; o, ovary.

ovaries and the gonoducts are very similar to those noted in *Sphenodon*. The transverse diameter of the gland is generally relatively small. Some lizards have globular or cylindric adrenal glands, but in snakes the adrenal is pronouncedly elongate and filiform. Its relations to the mesonephric derivatives are as close as in *Sphenodon*.

The adrenal gland of crocodilians is entirely retroperitoneal (Fig. 4); the rather massive cylindric organ lies dorsal to the gonad and lateral to the genital duct. Its posterior pole is insinuated into the parietal peritoneum along the ventral side of the kidney.

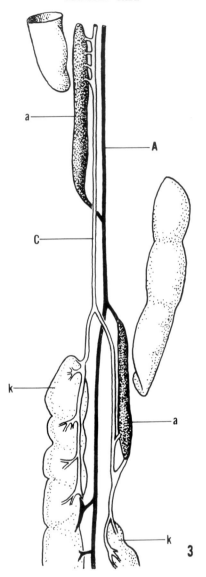

FIG. 3. Location of the adrenal gland in *Thamnophis sirtalis* (after Hartman and Brownell, 1949). A, aorta; a, adrenal gland; C, vena cava posterior; k, kidney.

In spite of the differences in the form of their adrenals and in their intra-mesenteric position in lepidosaurs and in contrast to their retroperitoneal position in turtles and crocodilians, all reptilian adrenal glands share several common macroscopic characteristics. Thus they always lie dorsal to the gonads and in close proximity to the genital ducts, the latter being medial or ventral to the gland.

The adrenal glands of all reptiles except turtles are markedly asymmetric. The right gland lies well anterior to the left so that its anterior pole may, in certain Squamata, approach the posterior part of the liver (Fig. 3).

The blood supply of the reptilian adrenal gland was shown by Gratiolet (1853) to contain a venous portal system, so that it receives venous as well as

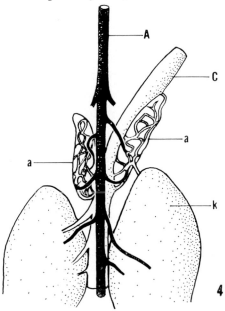

FiG. 4. Location of the adrenal gland in *Alligator mississippiensis* (after Pettit, 1896). A, aorta; a, adrenal gland; C, vena cava posterior; k, kidney.

arterial blood. This peculiarity has been confirmed by all subsequent workers.

The arterial blood reaches the adrenal gland via branches of the dorsal aorta, genital arteries (testicular in males, ovarian in females), and renal arteries. The relative importance of the different blood vessels is group specific. The works of Pettit (1896), Beddard (1904a, 1904b, 1904c, 1904d, 1906a, 1906b), Spanner (1929) and Hebard and Charipper (1955), as well as other papers cited in the general reviews mentioned in the introduction, show that in turtles arterial blood is supplied via the renal arteries. Branches of the dorsal aorta are most important in the arterial irrigation of crocodilian adrenal glands, while branches from the dorsal aorta and genital arteries furnish arterial blood to lepidosaurian adrenal glands. The aortic supply is much more important in lizards than in snakes. One special case is worth mentioning: in *Gerrhonotus multicarinatus* branches of the several large arteries in the vicinity, including the mesenteric arteries contact the adrenal gland and ramify on it (Retzlaff, 1949).

The afferent vessels of the adrenal portal system are of a venous type, and their origin varies with the systematic position of the species. In turtles the three, very short, afferent veins of this portal system arise from the renal portal veins (Spanner, 1929). The afferent adrenal vein of *Sphenodon punctatus* arises from the anterior part of the kidney and, in adult specimens, follows the derivatives of the Wolffian body to reach the adrenal gland and ramify on it (O'Donoghue, 1921). The trunk of the afferent vein also receives parietal and vertebral veins. Two afferent adrenal veins occur in snakes and both arise from the dorsal body wall. The adrenal portal system varies greatly in lizards. Some forms have only one afferent adrenal vein that passes from the dorsal wall of the body, touches the posterior extremity of the adrenal gland, and ramifies on it (*Phrynosoma cornutum*, Hebard and Charipper, 1955). Other species have two afferent adrenal veins passing from the dorsal body wall (*Agama agama, Lacerta viridis*, Chester Jones, 1957b), and in still other species the number of afferent adrenal veins varies from one to three. In crocodilians one vein, arising from the dorsal body wall, forms the afferent portion of the adrenal portal system (Pettit, 1896; Spanner, 1929; Hebard and Charipper, 1955).

All the blood from the adrenal gland, whether derived from the adrenal arteries or from the afferent veins of the portal system, drains to the vena cava posterior. The pattern of the venous return is determined by the relations of the adrenal gland to the vena cava, which is formed by the junction of the efferent renal veins. In turtles, the latter may receive the adrenal drainage while they cross the middle of the adrenal parenchyma. Distinct efferent adrenal veins join the spermatic veins in the male of *Sphenodon punctatus* (O'Donoghue, 1921); the homologous veins of the females have not been studied. In squamates and crocodilians, the venous blood flows directly from the right adrenal gland into the vena cava posterior, while the left gland is drained by veins entering the renal vein.

Less precise information is available about the innervation of the reptilian adrenal gland than about its vascularization. Most authors report that the nerves to the organ originate in the lateral sympathetic ganglia of the paravertebral chain, but the structure seems to be very variable, especially in the number of ganglia which participate in this innervation. Clusters of ganglion cells have, furthermore, been reported in the immediate proximity of the adrenal gland or in contact with it in all reptiles thus far studied, but the origin and terminations of the nerve fibers to the organ have never been studied systematically. Hebard and Charipper (1955) mention the very rich innervation of the glandular parenchyma, but give no information about the extraglandular course of these fibers.

IV. Microscopic Anatomy

A. General

Comparison of the descriptions in the classic papers of Braun (1882), Vincent (1896), Minervini (1904), and Poll (1906) discloses the fundamental similarity of the adrenal histology in all reptiles and confirms its morphological resemblance to that of birds. However, noticeable differences do exist between representatives of different orders of reptiles. These differences are sometimes reflected in the histology of the organ, while in other cases they are in the relative abundance of connective tissue and glandular parenchyma, in the distribution of interrenal and adrenal tissues, or in the presence or absence of chromatophores and neurons in the gland. Hence it is necessary to consider the major groups separately.

B. Testudines

Histological investigations of the testudinian adrenal gland are not numerous; Table III lists the species described in the literature.

TABLE III

Turtles for which the structure of the adrenal gland has been described

Family	Species
Testudininae	*Testudo graeca* (Ecker, 1846, 1847; Gabe and Martoja, 1962; Pettit, 1896; Thompson, 1932); *Geochelone sulcata* (Pettit, 1896).
Emydinae	*Clemmys guttata* (Hebard and Charipper, 1955); *C. caspica leprosa* (Gabe and Martoja, 1962); *Chrysemys picta* (Hebard and Charipper, 1955); *Pseudemys scripta* (Hebard and Charipper, 1955); *Terrapene carolina* (Hebard and Charipper, 1955).
Chelydridae	*Chelydra serpentina* (Hebard and Charipper, 1955).
Kinosternidae	*Kinosternon flavescens* (Hebard and Charipper, 1955); *Sternotherus odoratus* (Hebard and Charipper, 1955).
Cheloniidae	*Lepidochelys olivacea* (Gabe and Martoja, 1962); *Caretta caretta* (Holmberg and Soler, 1942).
Trionychidae	*Trionyx ferox* (Hebard and Charipper, 1955); *T. sinensis* (Liu and Maneely, 1959).

As noted under macroscopic anatomy, the adrenal gland of Testudines is not strictly delimited dorsally, and renal and adrenal parenchyma may intermingle there. Nodules of interrenal or adrenal tissue may be scattered along the walls of efferent renal veins at the ventral side of the gland.

A connective tissue capsule of variable thickness covers the ventral face of the gland. Dorsally, this sheath is represented only by capsular expansions, extending from the ventral and lateral faces of the gland and limiting the cellular cords. The development of the ventral wall of the capsule is proportional to the size of the animal; the capsule is thin in *Testudo graeca*, well developed in *Clemmys caspica leprosa*, and very thick in *Lepidochelys olivacea* (Gabe and Martoja, 1962). In *Caretta caretta* the connective tissue capsule forms an uninterrupted plate bridging the median line and resulting in a median coalescence of the two adrenal glands (Holmberg and Soler, 1942).

The capsule is formed mainly of randomly oriented, collagenous fibers. Hebard and Charipper (1955) claim that the fibers are thickest in the external zones of the capsule, where it connects to the neighboring connective tissue. The internal zones, in contact with the parenchyma, contain thinner collagenous and reticular fibers. Elastic fibers are rare in the capsule, but frequent in the walls of blood vessels crossing it. Most cells of the connective tissues are fibrocytes; mast cells are rather rare. The texture of the gland is produced by expansions of the internal layers of the capsule that contain rather thin collagenous and reticular, but no elastic fibers.

Within this capsule the interrenal tissue forms a net of anastomosed cords (Figs 5 and 6). Each cord is composed of radially arranged cells. One pole of an interrenal cell contacts an adjoining cell, while the opposite pole contacts the capsular expansion that separates the cord from the blood vessels. Consequently a cross section passing exactly along the longitudinal axis of a cord shows two rows of cells. The orientation of cords in the organ is variable, but the cellular arrangement is very uniform and rarely shows regional differentiation. In *Chrysemys picta* the peripheral cords of the adrenal contain narrower and more elongate cells than do the central cords (Hebard and Charipper, 1955).

The adrenal tissue of the Testudines consists of cellular clusters distributed irregularly in the gland (references in Table III). Some of these clusters are in contact with the connective tissue capsule; other, larger ones, lie in the middle of the parenchyma. Capsular expansions, comparable to those which delimit the interrenal cords, cover the more or less globular, ovoid, or irregularly shaped clusters of adrenal cells. In contrast to the condition frequently observed in lepidosaurians, the clusters do not expand between the interrenal cords.

There seem to be no quantitative data about the relative volumes of the two tissues in turtles; subjective statements, of course, represent only a first approximation. Volumetric differences may occur, since Hebard and Charipper (1955) note the particular abundance of adrenal tissue in the gland of *Clemmys guttata*.

Neurons are common in the adrenal glands of all Testudines studied. Small clusters of neurons are often included in the capsule or in the space between it and the glandular parenchyma. Isolated nerve cells or small groups of them are also found in the parenchyma; most are in contact with

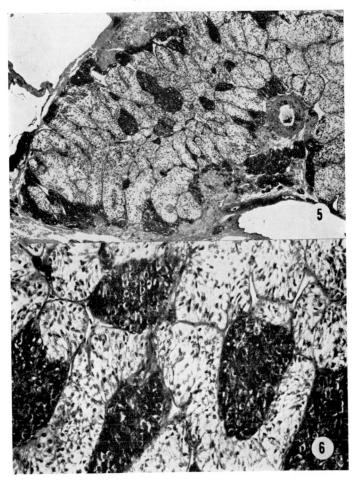

FIGS 5 and 6. Cross section of the left adrenal gland of *Clemmys caspica leprosa*. Bouin's fluid, one-step trichrome, × 30 (Fig. 5) and × 150 (Fig. 6), green filter. Note the intermingled interrenal cords and clusters of adrenal tissue (dark).

groups of adrenal cells. Nerve fibers, which are often quite large, may be seen amid the clusters of adrenal cells, even when these are only stained for topography. Neurofibrillar impregnations show an abundance of nerve fibers along the capsular expansions and neuronal penetration into the clusters of adrenal cells. Penetration of nerve fibers into the interrenal cords is much rarer (Hebard and Charipper, 1955).

Dendritic melanophores are found in the peritoneum, the connective tissue capsule, and even the parenchyma of the adrenal gland in some species. They are particularly noticeable in *Testudo graeca* (Gabe and Martoja, 1962).

C. RHYNCHOCEPHALIA

The adrenal gland of *Sphenodon* lies within the gonadal mesentery (Osawa, 1897) and is consequently easier to recognize than that of Testudines.

A generally quite thin connective tissue capsule containing collagenous and reticular fibers totally ensheathes the gland (Gabe and Saint Girons, 1964a, 1964b). Since the adrenal gland lies adjacent to the vas deferens, the connective tissue sheaths of both organs are continuous. In females the capsule of the adrenal gland is less closely united to the connective tissue of the proximal segments of the genital system. As in other reptiles, partitions, formed of very slender collagenous and reticular fibers and projecting inward from this capsule, subdivide the organ and form its supporting framework. The thinness of the capsule explains the impossibility of determining whether it has both external and internal layers like those of turtles.

The interrenal cords anastomose and are, as in other reptiles, constituted of radially arranged cells. One pole of each cell is applied to the capsular expansion that separates it from the blood vessels. The orientation of the cords is irregular within the parenchyma, and no regional differences occur.

The adrenal gland of *Sphenodon punctatus* differs from those of all other reptiles in the disposition of the adrenal tissue. The interrenal cords are dorsally covered by a relatively thick, ventrally concave, trough-shaped mass of adrenal tissue (Figs 7 and 8). As in other lepidosaurs, expansions from this mass penetrate between the interrenal cords into the interior of the organ. Variably sized islets of adrenal cells occur within the parenchyma. The adrenal gland of *Sphenodon* is fundamentally distinct by having more or less voluminous clusters of this tissue on its ventral surface, although this surface never contains adrenal tissue in any other lepidosaur (Gabe and Saint Girons, 1964a and 1964b). Only in the lateral regions of the gland and at certain points in the ventral zone do the interrenal cords touch the capsule.

The accumulations of nerve cells are rather frequent near the dorsal surface of the adrenal gland, but they are smaller than in Testudines. These cell groups either contact the capsule or lie in the dorsal layer of the adrenal tissue. The much rarer nerve cells embedded in the parenchyma are often isolated. In cross sections stained for topography, the nerve fibers seem to be much rarer and thinner than those in the adrenal glands of turtles.

Dendritic melanophores occur in the capsule as well as in the parenchyma of the adrenal gland. They are rarer than in *Testudo* as are mast cells.

D. SQUAMATA

The adrenal gland of the Squamata lies within the gonadal mesentery near the gonad and the proximal parts of the gonoducts, as does that of *Sphenodon punctatus*. The right gland is attached to the vena cava posterior.

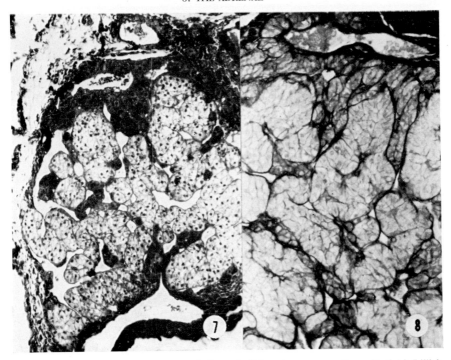

Fig. 7. Cross section of the adrenal gland of a male *Sphenodon punctatus*. Regaud's fluid, Lillie's ferric ferricyanide method, haematoxylin counterstain × 100, orange filter. Note the light interrenal cords, the dorsal layer of adrenal tissue, and the clusters of adrenal cells scattered among the interrenal cords.

Fig. 8. Section of another fragment of the same adrenal gland as in Fig. 7. Bouin's fluid, PAS, methyl green counterstain, × 150, green filter. Note the capsular expansions limiting the interrenal cords and the clusters of adrenal cells.

The microscopic anatomy of the adrenal has been studied in numerous squamates (Table IV).

TABLE IV

Squamates for which the structure of the adrenal gland has been described

Family	Species
Gekkonidae	*Coleonyx variegatus* (Gabe et al., 1964); *Gehyra variegata* (Gabe et al., 1964); *Gonatodes fuscus* (Hebard and Charipper, 1955); *Hemidactylus turcicus* (Gabe and Martoja, 1961; Hebard and Charipper, 1955); *Hoplodactylus pacificus* (Gabe et al., 1964); *Quendenfeldtia trachyblepharus* (Gabe and Martoja, 1961); *Sphaerodactylus cinereus* (Hebard and Charipper, 1955); *Tarentola mauritanica* (Gabe and Martoja, 1961; Hebard and Charipper, 1955); *Phelsuma madagascarensis* (Gabe et al., 1964).

TABLE IV—*cont.*

Family	Species
Xantusiidae	*Xantusia vigilis* (Miller, 1952); *Xantusia henshawi* (Gabe *et al.*, 1964).
Pygopodidae	*Delma fraseri* (Gabe *et al.*, 1964); *Lialis burtonis* (Gabe *et al.*, 1964).
Iguanidae	*Anolis carolinensis* (Gabe and Martoja, 1961; Hartman and Brownell, 1949; Hebard and Charipper, 1955); *Dipsosaurus dorsalis* (Gabe *et al.*, 1964); *Phrynosoma cornutum* (Hebard and Charipper, 1955); *Phrynosoma maccallii* (Gabe *et al.*, 1964); *Sceloporus graciosus* (Gabe *et al.*, 1964); *Sceloporus occidentalis* (Gabe *et al.*, 1964); *Sceloporus undulatus* (Hebard and Charipper, 1955); *Uma inornata* (Gabe *et al.*, 1964); *Uta stansburiana* (Gabe *et al.*, 1964).
Agamidae	*Agama agama* (Wright and Chester Jones, 1957); *Agama impalearis* (Gabe and Martoja, 1961); *Amphibolurus reticulatus* (Gabe *et al.*, 1964); *Draco volans* (Gabe *et al.*, 1964); *Calotes cristatellus* (Gabe *et al.*, 1964); *Physignatus longirostris* (Gabe *et al.*, 1964); *Uromastyx hardwickii* (Vincent, 1896).
Chamaeleonidae	*Chamaeleo chamaeleon* (Schoof, 1888; Vincent, 1896); *Chamaeleo lateralis* (Gabe and Martoja, 1961).
Scincidae	*Ablepharus boutonii* (Gabe *et al.*, 1964); *Chalcides mionecton* (Gabe and Martoja, 1961); *Chalcides ocellatus* (Bimmer, 1950; Gabe and Martoja, 1961); *Eumeces algeriensis* (Gabe and Martoja, 1961); *Eumeces fasciatus* (Hebard and Charipper, 1955); *Eumeces obsoletus* (Hebard and Charipper, 1955); *Leiolopisma rhomboidalis* (Wilhoft, 1964); *Leiolopisma zelandica* (Gabe *et al.*, 1964); *Lygosoma laterale* (Hebard and Charipper, 1955); *Tiliqua scincoides* (Gabe *et al.*, 1964).
Feyliniidae	*Feylinia currori* (Gabe *et al.*, 1964).
Lacertidae	*Acanthodactylus erythrurus* (Gabe and Martoja, 1961); *Acanthodactylus pardalis* (Gabe and Martoja, 1961); *Acanthodactylus* sp. (Schoof, 1888); *Lacerta agilis* (Bimmer, 1950; Radu, 1934); *Lacerta muralis* (Gabe and Martoja, 1961; Soulié, 1903; Vincent, 1896); *Lacerta lepida* (Nagel, 1836); *Lacerta sicula* (Bimmer, 1950); *Lacerta viridis* (Gabe and Martoja, 1961; Pettit, 1896; Vincent, 1896; Wright and Chester Jones, 1955); *Lacerta vivipara* (Bimmer, 1950; Panigel, 1956); *Psammodromus algirus* (Gabe and Martoja, 1961).
Teiidae	*Cnemidophorus tessellatus* (Hebard and Charipper, 1955); *Cnemidophorus tigris* (Gabe *et al.*, 1964); *Teius teyou* (Houssay *et al.*, 1962).
Anguidae	*Anguis fragilis* (Gabe and Martoja, 1961; Vincent, 1896); *Gerrhonotus coerulescens* (Hebard and Charipper, 1955); *Gerrhonotus multicarinatus* (Gabe *et al.*, 1964; Retzlaff, 1949); *Ophisaurus koellikeri* (Gabe and Martoja, 1961); *Ophisaurus ventralis* (Hebard and Charipper, 1955).
Anniellidae	*Anniella pulchra* (Gabe *et al.*, 1964).
Helodermatidae	*Heloderma suspectum* (Gabe *et al.*, 1964; Hartman and Brownell, 1949).
Varanidae	*Varanus exanthematicus albigularis* (Spanner, 1929); *Varanus griseus* (Gabe and Martoja, 1961); *Varanus niloticus* (Arvy, 1962; Gabe and Martoja, 1961; Pettit, 1896); *Varanus salvator* (Pettit, 1896).

TABLE IV—*cont.*

Family	Species
Amphisbaenidae	*Blanus cinereus* (Gabe and Martoja, 1961).
Trogonophidae	*Trogonophis wiegmanni* (Gabe and Martoja, 1961).
Typhlopidae	*Typhlops punctatus* (Gabe and Martoja, 1961); *Typhlops vermicularis* (Gabe *et al.*, 1964).
Leptotyphlopidae	*Leptotyphlops dulcis* (Gabe and Martoja, 1961).
Boidae	*Charina bottae* (Hebard and Charipper, 1955); *Eryx jaculus* (Gabe and Martoja, 1961); *Lichanura roseofusca* (Gabe *et al.*, 1964); *Python regius* (Gabe and Martoja, 1961).
Colubridae	*Coronella austriaca* (Gabe and Martoja, 1961; Radu, 1934); *Elaphe longissima* (Gabe and Martoja, 1961; Vincent, 1896); *Elaphe scalaris* (Gabe and Martoja, 1961); *Lampropeltis doliata* (Hebard and Charipper, 1955); *Lioheterodon geayi* (Gabe and Martoja, 1961); *Macroprotodon cucullatus* (Gabe and Martoja, 1961); *Natrix maura* (Gabe and Martoja, 1961); *Natrix natrix* (Arvy, 1962; Gabe and Martoja, 1961; Radu, 1934; Vincent, 1896; Wright and Chester Jones, 1957); *Natrix sipedon* (Hebard and Charipper, 1955); *Opheodrys v. vernalis* (Hebard and Charipper, 1955); *Philodryas* sp. (Junqueira, 1944); *Thamnophis elegans* (Fox, 1952); *Thamnophis sirtalis* (Hebard and Charipper, 1955); *Xenodon merremii* (Houssay *et al.*, 1962; Tramezzani *et al.*, 1964).
Elapidae	*Acanthophis antarcticus* (Gabe *et al.*, 1964); *Bungarus fasciatus* (Gabe *et al.*, 1964); *Denisonia signata* (Gabe *et al.*, 1964); *Naja naja* (Gabe *et al.*, 1964); *Oxyuranus scutellatus* (Gabe *et al.*, 1964); *Pseudechis australis* (Gabe *et al.*, 1964).
Hydrophiidae	*Microcephalophis gracilis* (Gabe *et al.*, 1964); *Laticauda colubrina* (Gabe *et al.*, 1964); *Laticauda laticaudata* (Gabe *et al.*, 1964).
Viperidae	*Vipera aspis* (Gabe and Martoja, 1961); *Vipera berus* (Gabe and Martoja, 1961); *Cerastes cerastes* (Gabe and Martoja, 1961), *Cerastes vipera* (Gabe and Martoja, 1961). *Crotalus viridis* (Hebard and Charipper, 1955).

The connective tissue capsule, again formed of collagenous and reticular fibers, is generally thicker in the larger glands. The fibrous constituents of the connective tissue capsule are not oriented. Smaller glands lack zonation in the capsule; larger ones have the thicker collagenous fibers externally and the reticular and thinner collagenous fibers located internally in contact with the parenchyma. Connective tissue cells morphologically similar to fibrocytes are rare. Dendritic melanophores have been found in only a few lizards (especially in the Diploglossa). Mast cells are very rare.

As in other reptiles, capsular expansions, of collagenous and reticular fibers, partition the glandular parenchyma.

The interrenal cells are arranged in cords as in other reptiles (Figs 9 to 13).

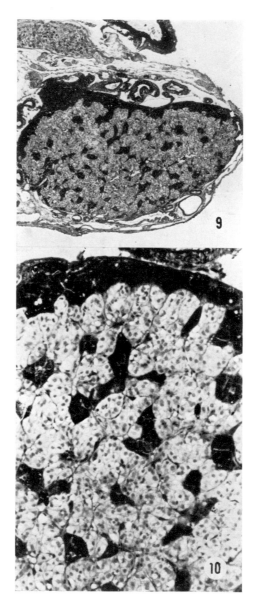

Figs 9 and 10. Cross sections of the adrenal gland of a male *Chamaeleo lateralis*. Regaud's fluid, Lillie's ferric ferricyanide method, haematoxylin counterstain, ×30 (Fig. 9) and ×150 (Fig. 10), orange filter. Note the conspicuous dorsal layer of adrenal tissue and the clusters of adrenal cells scattered among the interrenal cords.

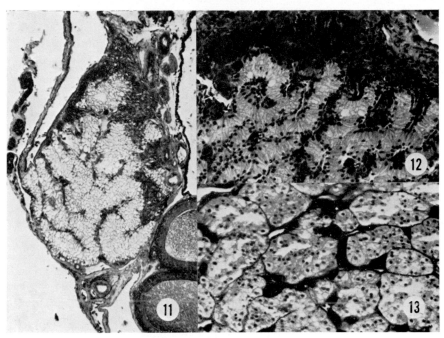

FIG. 11. Cross section of the adrenal gland of a female *Tarentola mauritanica*. Bouin's fluid, one-step trichrome, × 100, green filter. Note the regular disposition of interrenal cords, the dorsal layer of adrenal tissue, and the small clusters of adrenal cells located among the interrenal cords.

FIG. 12. Part of a section of the adrenal gland of *Lacerta muralis*. Bouin's fluid, Masson-Goldner's stain, × 150, green filter. Note the conspicuous dorsal layer of adrenal cells and the expansions intermingling with the interrenal cords.

FIG. 13. Part of a section of the adrenal gland of *Elaphe scalaris*. Regaud's fluid, PAS, haematoxylin counterstain, × 150, green filter. Note the dark clusters of adrenal cells scattered among the interrenal cords.

The cords are oriented randomly and show no regional differentiation in structure. Hebard and Charipper (1955) recognize three patterns of cells within the interrenal cords of lizards. The first is found in the Gekkota and Scincomorpha, including the Gekkonidae, Dibamidae, Pygopodidae, Xantusiidae and Scincidae, the second in the Diploglossa, and the third in the Iguania.

The essential morphological character of the first, gekkotan and scincomorphan type of interrenal tissue is a radial disposition of tall conical cells with the nuclei generally located towards the periphery of the cords. In the Diploglossa prismatic cells, lower than those of the Gekkota, are irregularly distributed and the cords lack regular rows of cells. The Iguania have regularly arranged double rows of interrenal cells with central nuclei.

Actually the position of the nuclei in the interrenal cells is so variable, even in a single individual, that it cannot be utilized as a criterion (Figs 14 to 17). The variations in the position of the nuclei presumably correspond to stages in the secretory cycle and are discussed below.

The adrenal tissue of all Squamata thus far studied consists of a compact dorsal layer from which extensions penetrate into the parenchyma, and of isolated islets that lie within the parenchyma on the border of the interrenal cords in immediate proximity to the blood sinuses.

The thickness of the dorsal layer varies in different regions of the gland. Its center is well developed, while its edges are thinner in most snakes; the layer is thick anteriorly and becomes thin posteriorly in Scincomorpha. The layer is particularly well developed in amphisbaenians, but very poorly so in Leptotyphlopidae. Similarly the extensions derived from the dorsal layer of the adrenal tissue differ in their development in different groups. The snakes, Diploglossa, Gekkota and Iguania are characterized by rather short but thick extensions of adrenal tissue which do not deeply penetrate the interrenal tissue, while the extensions of the Scincomorpha are longer and thinner. In amphisbaenians the extensions are so numerous that parasaggital sections, far from the median plane, seem to show complete mixing of the two tissues like that in crocodilians and birds.

The number and size of the islets of adrenal tissue included within the parenchyma and lacking connections with the dorsal layer also vary. Quantitative studies are rare, and even when the relative volumes of the interrenal and the adrenal tissue are given (notably by Bimmer, 1950), no distinction is made between the dorsal layer and the isolated islets. The latter are generally numerous but small in the Squamata. Clusters of adrenal cells as large as those found in turtles are very rare.

In squamates, nerve cells, isolated or grouped into small ganglia, almost always occur at the dorsal face of the adrenal gland, either in contact with the connective tissue capsule or in the dorsal mass of the adrenal tissue. Ganglia rarely occur within the parenchyma, but isolated nerve cells, which are almost always in contact with islets of adrenal cells, are common.

In Diploglossa the parenchyma of the adrenal gland contains only few dendritic melanophores and pigmented macrophages histologically similar to hepatic and splenic macrophages. Mast cells are also rare.

E. CROCODILIA

The adrenal gland of crocodilians is sharply defined; not only is its anterior part distinct from the adjoining gonad and genital ducts, but its posterior end is also clearly separated from the ventral face of the kidney. Histological investigations on *Crocodylus niloticus* (Rathke, 1866; Arvy and Bonichon, 1958a, 1958b; Gabe and Rancurel, 1964), *Alligator mississippiensis* (Rathke, 1866; Pettit, 1896; Reese, 1931; Lawton, 1937; Forbes, 1940;

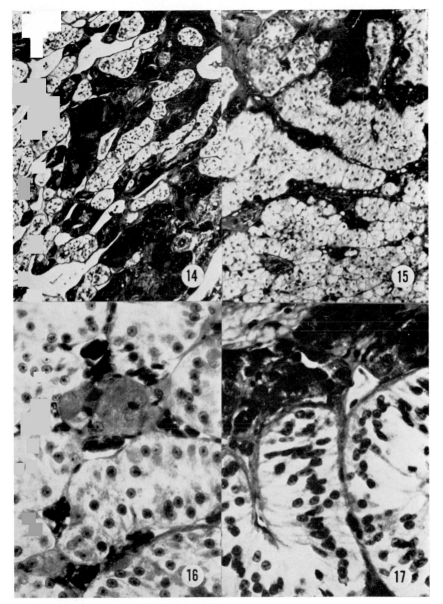

FIG. 14. Interrenal cords (light) and clusters of adrenal cells (dark) of *Testudo graeca*. Regaud's fluid, PAS, haematoxylin counterstain, × 100, green filter.

FIG. 15. Interrenal cords and clusters of adrenal cells of *Python regius*. Regaud's fluid, PAS haematoxylin counterstain, × 150, green filter.

FIG. 16. Interrenal cords and a group of adrenal cells of *Eumeces algeriensis*. Bouin's fluid, Heidenhain's azan, × 375, green filter. Note the feebly granular cytoplasm of the interrenal cells and dense cytoplasmic granulations of the adrenal cells.

FIG. 17. Peripheral part of a section of the adrenal of a young *Crocodylus niloticus*. Regaud's fluid, PAS, haematoxylin counterstain, × 375, green filter. Note the peripheral layer of adrenal cells (top) and the light interrenal cords (bottom).

Hebard and Charipper, 1955) and *Caiman crocodilus* (Rathke, 1866; Pettit, 1896; Hebard and Charipper, 1955) prove that the structure of the organ is very uniform within this order.

The connective tissue capsule, which completely ensheathes the adrenal, is relatively thicker than that of other reptiles. Its external layers, formed of bundles of thick collagenous and reticular fibers, send sheets inward to partition the parenchyma (Hebard and Charipper, 1955). Only the tunics covering blood vessels crossing this capsule contain elastic and muscular fibers.

The interrenal cords resemble those of other reptiles and touch the capsule in some places (Figs 18 and 19). In other regions the cords are separated from the capsule by a discontinuous layer of adrenal tissue that sends extensions to the center of the organ, so that the two tissues are closely intermingled throughout the adrenal gland. This arrangement is exactly like that noted in birds.

Nerve cells, isolated or grouped into small ganglia, frequently lie in contact with the dorsal face of the gland, but they generally remain outside the capsule. Crocodilians have fewer nerve cells in the parenchyma than do any other reptiles.

F. Structural Types of Adrenal Glands

Three structural arrangements of the adrenal tissue and interrenal cords may be distinguished in sauropsids.

In the first, found in turtles, the adrenal tissue is dispersed in irregular or ovoid clusters. These clusters are randomly spread throughout the organ. Different species of turtles contain variable quantities of adrenal tissue associated with the interrenal cords in both the periphery and the center of the adrenal gland.

The second type, found in lepidosaurs, is characterized by a clear tendency for aggregation of the adrenal tissue. In *Sphenodon punctatus* much of the tissue is arranged in a dorsal layer which covers the mass of interrenal cords, while isolated islets of adrenal tissue occur within the parenchyma and on the ventral face of the gland. The pattern seems to be the same in squamates, but there the concentration is more pronounced, and the isolated islets of adrenal tissue have practically disappeared from the ventral face of the adrenal gland. Most of the adrenal tissue is located in the dorsal layer, and the total volume of the extensions and of the isolated islets within the parenchyma is small.

The third adrenal type, characteristic of archosaurs, is found in crocodilians and birds. Almost all the adrenal tissue is arranged in bands which, in cross section, seem to alternate with the interrenal cords. Histological

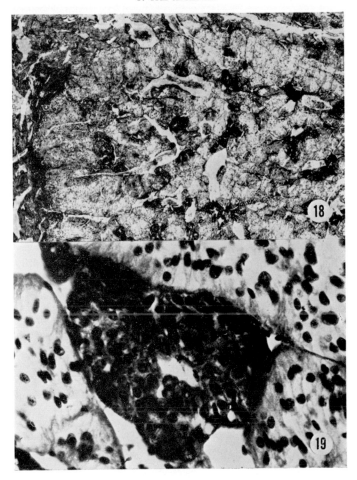

FIG. 18. General view of the adrenal gland of an adult male *Crocodylus niloticus*. Regaud's fluid, Lillie's ferric ferricyanide method, haematoxylin counterstain, × 30, orange filter. Note the intermingling cords of interrenal and adrenal tissue.

FIG. 19. Part of the same section as in Fig. 18, × 375. Note the dark cord of adrenal cells, surrounded by light interrenal cords.

sections of crocodilian adrenal glands do not indicate a zonation, although those of certain birds do, uniquely, show indications of such a zonation (Hartman and Brownell, 1949; Knouff and Hartman, 1951).

The microscopic anatomy of the sauropsid adrenal gland thus supports the accepted subdivisions of the reptiles and the present conceptions of their phyletic relations.

G. Aberrant Clusters of Interrenal Tissue and of Chromaffin Cells

As already noted, the adrenal tissue does not include all the chromaffin elements, either of vertebrates in general or of reptiles in particular, nor does interrenal tissue occur only in the adrenal gland. Knowledge of their embryology explains the frequent cases of aberrant nodules of interrenal or adrenal tissue.

No systematic inventory of the aberrant sites of these two reptilian tissues has yet been compiled though some incidental observations are reported by Poll (1906). Such nodules are particularly common dorsal to the adrenal gland *sensu strictu*, in the connective tissue that surrounds blood vessels of this region, and in the paravertebral connective tissue. In turtles and crocodilians even the kidney may contain islets of adrenal or interrenal tissue that have lost contact with the body of the gland.

These islets generally represent only a relatively small mass of tissue superficially of little importance. However, their presence must be considered by physiologists, especially when interpreting the consequences of surgical adrenalectomy.

V. Cytological and Histochemical Characteristics of Interrenal Cells

Though the adrenal gland of reptiles is anatomically very diverse, the cytological and histochemical characteristics of its parenchymal elements are remarkably uniform. Hence only a general description seems necessary. Modifications observed in some species are mentioned in the course of the description.

The interrenal cells of all reptiles thus far studied are generally prismatic. Their mean height varies from 15 to 30 μ; size variations in different species cannot be easily interpreted because the interrenal cells may vary in size within one animal. The basal pole of each cell is in contact with the capsular expansion that separates it from a blood vessel; the apical pole meets another interrenal cell. The position of the nucleus in the cells is similarly variable. Though older works generally report that it lies in basal position, near the capillaries, this is not universally true. Gabe *et al.* (1964) have shown that the nucleus often lies near the capillary pole in the Scincomorpha, yet in all reptiles certain interrenal cords show obviously central nuclei. Detailed analysis of the sections proves that the position of the nuclei varies considerably in different cords of the same adrenal. The nuclei occasionally lie in an apical position with the basal pole occupied by lipidic droplets, as described for the interrenal cords of *Thamnophis sirtalis* (Hebard and Charipper, 1955). It is highly probable that the several different positions of the nuclei correspond to functional stages of the cells, but the available histo-physiological data do not yet permit unequivocal interpretations.

The nuclei also vary in form and structure. Extreme variants include nuclei of oval or circular cross section with rather small, diffuse, irregularly distributed blocks of chromatin, and crumpled nuclei with irregular contours and dense chromatin. The nucleoli are very easy to recognize in the first case and difficult to distinguish in the second.

The structural differences in the nuclei correlate directly with the abundance of particulate lipids in the cytoplasm. Cells with clear nuclei and a well defined nucleolus are poor in particulate lipids, while cells with a crumpled nucleus contain great quantities of lipids. Cross sections suggest that the pressure of the lipid inclusions has deformed the nuclei.

The hyaloplasm of the interrenal cells is feebly acidophilic; the general color is very variable and depends on the abundance of the particulate lipids which are dissolved during paraffin embedding. If the inclusions of the hyaloplasm are abundant, the cross sections show only a fine, slightly colored cytoplasmic net, with gaps corresponding to the lipid inclusions. When the cell is poorer in particulate lipids the hyaloplasm will, on the contrary, be well developed and its acidophily stronger. The ultrastructure of the chondriome of reptilian interrenal cells is yet unknown, though this organelle has been described from fresh tissue, and both Janus Green vital staining and the classical mitochondrial techniques have been applied (Retzlaff, 1949; Hebard and Charipper, 1955; Liu and Maneely, 1959; Gabe and Martoja, 1961; Gabe and Rancurel, 1964; Gabe and Saint Girons, 1964a, 1964b). All data agree about the form of the chondriome, represented by rather short chondrioconts and by mitochondria. All these organelles are concentrated in thin cytoplasmic pillars in cells that are rich in lipids. A perinuclear location of the chondriome has been reported in *Alligator mississippiensis* (Hebard and Charipper, 1955), and in *Trionyx sinensis* (Liu and Maneely, 1959). No particular orientation of the chondrioma has been described in other species. The chondrioma of the interrenal cells are more easily demonstrated when particulate lipids are scarce.

Little is known about the Golgi apparatus of the interrenal cells and its ultrastructure has not been described. Scattered dictyosomes occur in the interrenal cells of *Gerrhonotus multicarinatus* and there is no "Golgi zone" (Retzlaff, 1949). Liu and Maneely (1959), on the other hand, report a Golgi apparatus at one pole of the nucleus of the interrenal cells of *Trionyx sinensis*. Light microscopy cannot show ergastoplasm in the interrenal cells of reptiles, and ribonucleic acids are demonstrable only in the nucleoli.

The interrenal cells are quite uniform in structure and show few species specific differences. Cells of a special form have been reported among the Squamata only in the Diploglossa (Gabe and Martoja, 1961; Gabe *et al.*,

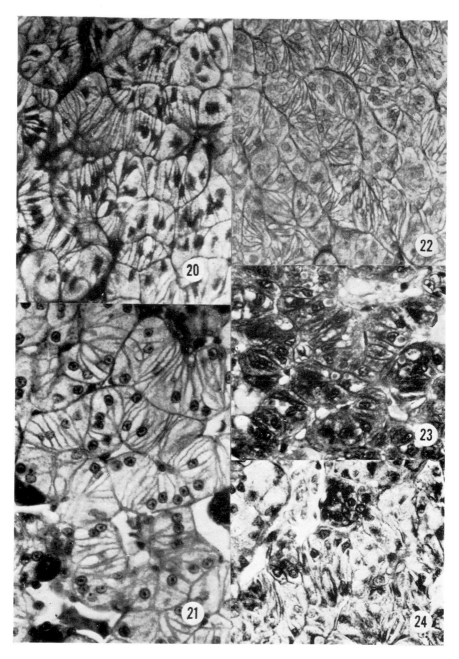

FIGS 20 to 24. Cell types of the diploglossan interrenal tissue. Bouin's fluid, one-step trichrome, ×375, green filter. (Fig. 20) *Anguis fragilis*; (Fig. 21) *Ophisaurus koellikeri*; (Fig. 22) *Varanus griseus*; (Fig. 23) *Gerrhonotus multicarinatus*; (Fig. 24) *Heloderma suspectum*. Note the columnar and conical interrenal cells.

1964). These diploglossan cells are as high as the ordinary prismatic cells among which they are interspersed, but their conical rather than prismatic shape permits rapid recognition of the adrenal glands of diploglossan lizards (Figs 20–24). The bases of these elements face the centers of the cords, and their apices are in contact with the capsular extensions. The cells do not otherwise differ in histology nor in histochemical reactions.

Conical cells have been observed in *Anguis fragilis*, *Ophisaurus koellikeri*, *Gerrhonotus multicarinatus*, *Anniella pulchra*, *Heloderma suspectum*, *H. horridum*, *Varanus griseus*, and *V. niloticus*. No other reptiles are known to have any interrenal cells of this type. Histological study thus confirms remarkably and unexpectedly the current concept of the systematic position of the Diploglossa which is, of course, derived from arguments of a totally different kind (McDowell and Bogert, 1954).

There are numerous recent studies of the histochemistry of reptilian interrenal cells. Glycogen has been found in Squamata (Gabe and Martoja, 1961), Testudines (Gabe and Martoja, 1962), *Crocodylus niloticus* (Gabe and Rancurel, 1964), and *Sphenodon punctatus* (Gabe and Saint Girons, 1964a, 1964b). The abundance of this polysaccharide differs in different species and in different regions of the gland, but it is never very great (Fig. 25). The interrenal tissue of the Squamata and the Testudines is generally richer in glycogen than is that of *Crocodylus niloticus*, while *Sphenodon punctatus* has the most glycogen of all the reptiles studied; indeed, glycogen is extremely abundant in many organs of *Sphenodon* (Gabe and Saint Girons, 1964b). The

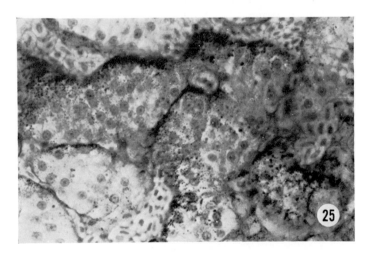

FIG. 25. Interrenal tissue of adult female *Eumeces algeriensis*. Bouin's fluid, PAS, haematoxylin counterstain, × 375, green filter. Note the dark (red in the slide) granules of glycogen. The amylase test has been performed with a positive result on an adjacent section.

amount of glycogen clearly varies during the annual cycle (see below).

The first report of ascorbic acid in reptilian interrenal tissue is that of Knab (1942) for *Lacerta agilis*, *L. muralis*, and *L. viridis*. Knab emphasizes the high individual variability, the absence of any preferential localization in the cell, and the low rate of enrichment of the interrenal tissue after subcutaneous injections of ascorbic acid in *Lacerta agilis*, *L. muralis* and *L. viridis*. This absence of a preferential localization has been confirmed in *Agama agama* and *Natrix natrix* (Wright and Chester Jones, 1957; Chester Jones, 1957a, 1957b) and various squamates and three species of turtles (Gabe and Martoja, 1961, 1962). Only Liu and Maneely (1959; *Trionyx sinensis*) report a "Golgian" localization of the ascorbic acid in the interrenal cells. No one has yet checked for ascorbic acid in the interrenal tissue of the crocodilians or *Sphenodon*. No histochemically detectable acid mucosubstances occur in reptilian interrenal cells.

Histochemically detectable lipids are common in the interrenal tissue of reptiles and have been known since the classic works of the beginning of the

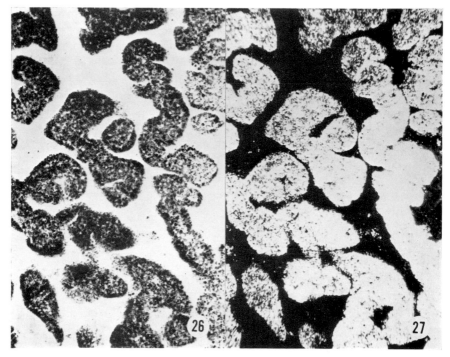

FIGS 26 and 27. Adjacent frozen sections of the adrenal of *Testudo graeca*. Formalin fixation, BZL blue staining (Fig. 26), and photomicrography taken in polarized light (Fig. 27); ×100. Note the identical distribution of sudanophilic (Fig. 26) and anisotropic (Fig. 27) lipids (from Gabe and Matoja, 1962).

twentieth century. The lipids form droplets or larger plaques which are osmiophilic and stain with all the usual lipid dyes. Their histochemistry has been studied for representatives of all the reptilian orders of the class (Hebard and Charipper, 1955; Wright and Chester Jones, 1957; Gabe and Martoja, 1961, 1962; Martoja *et al.*, 1961; Gabe and Saint Girons, 1964a, 1964b). Generally the neutral lipids stain rose with Nile blue sulfate (method of Lorrain Smith) and represent only a small fraction of the globular lipids; this observation explains the abundance of birefringent lipidic inclusions that produce the black cross phenomenon in polarized light (Figs 26–33). Variants of the reactions of Liebermann and of Windaus for cholesterides always yield positive results. The occurrence of lipidic carbonyles is shown by the positive results of pseudoplasmal reactions and by those of Ashbel and Seligman (Hebard and Charipper, 1955; Chester Jones, 1957b). Thus the lipids of the reptilian interrenal tissue agree in their histochemical characteristics with

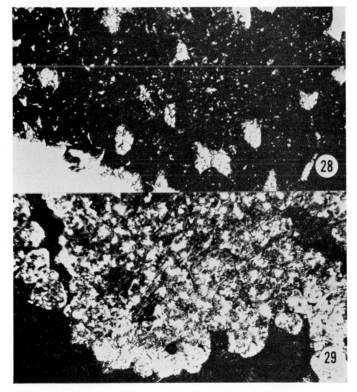

FIGS 28 and 29. Adjacent frozen sections of the adrenal gland of *Chamaeleo lateralis*. Formalin fixation, Sudan black B staining (Fig. 28) and photomicrograph taken in polarized light (Fig. 29), × 100. Note the unstained islets of adrenal cells in Fig. 28 and the identical distribution of sudan-ophilic and anisotropic lipids.

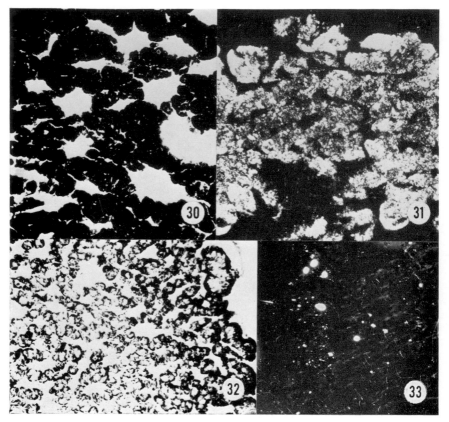

Figs 30 to 33. Frozen sections of formalin-fixed adrenal glands of *Cerastes cerastes*. Specimens killed in October (Figs 30 and 31) and in April (Figs 32 and 33). Sudan black B staining (Figs 30 and 32) and photomicrography in polarized light (Figs 31 and 33), × 100. Note the great seasonal variation in both sudanophilic and anisotropic lipids (after Gabe and Martoja, 1961).

those of other vertebrates (Hebard and Charipper, 1955; and many more recent workers).

Hebard and Charipper (1955) describe three patterns of distribution of the lipidic inclusions in interrenal cells. In the first, lipidic droplets are found at the vascular pole of the cells, while the nuclei lie at the opposite pole, near the central part of the cord. This pattern has only been found in *Thamnophis sirtalis*.

The second situation is the reverse of the first, and the nuclei are then found at the vascular pole of the cell. This situation occurs in certain lizards, especially *Eumeces obsoletus*. In the third case, all parts of the cell contain lipidic inclusions, while the nuclei are central. This pattern occurs in all turtles and crocodilians and in some lizards.

This classification is obviously schematic. Only the relative frequency of the several cell types varies, since careful search of cross sections shows all three types in any one individual.

Besides particulate lipids, the interrenal tissue of different species and individuals contains variable amounts of oxidative derivatives of lipids (Fig. 34). These granules belong to the group of the chromolipoids and, in all their

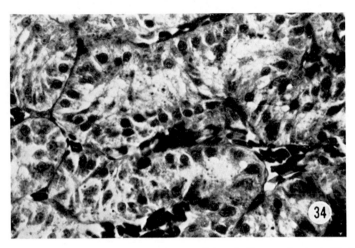

FIG. 34. Part of a section of the adrenal gland of an adult male *Eumeces algeriensis*. Bouin's fluid; Heidenhain's azan, × 375, green filter. Note the lipofuscin globules scattered through the cytoplasm of the interrenal cells.

histochemical properties, correspond to the lipofuscins of the reticular zone of the mammalian adrenal cortex. These inclusions are circular in cross-section, yellow in unstained sections, without melanins, and more frequent in turtles than in lepidosaurs and crocodilians.

Protids are rare in the reptilian interrenal cells, and there are no reports of accumulation of these compounds. Cytoplasmic ribonucleins have already been noted to be undetectable by light microscopy. The total mineral contents of the cells is quite low. Ionic iron is absent, which is remarkable since it is rather frequent in the reticular zone of the mammalian adrenal cortex.

The presence of a non-specific alkaline phosphomonoesterase (Fig. 35) has been observed in representatives of all reptilian orders (Arvy and Bonichon, 1958a, 1958b; Gabe and Martoja, 1931; Gabe and Saint Girons, 1964a, 1964b) which is in accord with data for the mammalian adrenal cortex (see the bibliography of Arvy, 1963). Liu and Maneely (1959), however, could not demonstrate alkaline phosphatase in the interrenal tissue of *Trionyx sinensis*. The works cited earlier also document the absence of non-specific

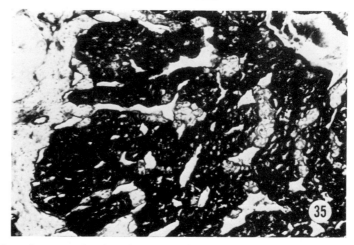

FIG. 35. Part of a cross section through an acetone-fixed adrenal gland of an adult male *Sphenodon punctatus*. Gomori's method for alkaline glycerophosphatase, iodine green counterstain, ×150, green filter. Note the intense reactivity of the interrenal cords (black); the adrenal tissue (dorsal layer at the left edge and clusters scattered among the interrenal cords) does not react.

acid phosphomonoesterase in reptilian interrenal tissue. Strong Δ^5-3-β-hydroxysteroido-dehydrogenase activity has been noted in the interrenal tissue of *Emys orbicularis*, *Varanus niloticus* and *Natrix natrix* (Arvy, 1962). Similar enzymatic activity occurs in the adrenal cortex of mammals and, more generally, in all tissues involved in active steroidogenesis.

A unique case of "colloidogenesis" of the interrenal tissue in an adult male *Gerrhonotus multicarinatus* is reported by Gabe *et al.* (1964). While none of the other organs proved anomalous in macroscopic or microscopic study, a great number of the interrenal cells of this animal were rich in spherical inclusions, clearly larger than the granules of chromolipoids (Fig. 36). Acidophilic in paraffin embedded material and strongly PAS-positive, these inclusions closely resemble the adrenal "colloid" of mammals. Unfortunately it is not known whether this phenomenon is widespread.

The physiological observations on the zonation of the mammalian adrenal cortex explain why most recent authors consider the possibility of a similar zonation of the reptilian interrenal tissue. No physiological data suggest a functional specialization of different regions of the reptilian interrenal tissue, and there are only isolated and irregular indications of morphological zonation. Yet its existence cannot be disproven; the cells of the peripherical interrenal cords are distinctly smaller than those of the central cords in *Philodryas* sp. (Junqueira, 1944) and *Gerrhonotus multicarinatus* (Retzlaff, 1949). Hebard and Charipper (1955) report differences in staining properties of the central and the peripheral interrenal cords of *Gerrhonotus coeruleus*.

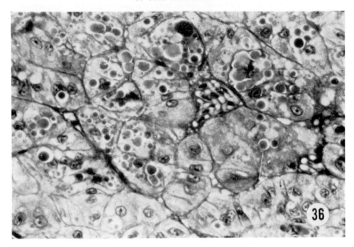

FIG. 36. Colloidogenesis in the interrenal cells of an adult male *Gerrhonotus multicarinatus*. Bouin's fluid; Masson-Goldner's stain, × 375, orange filter. Note the colloid droplets in many interrenal cells.

"Atrophic" cells in the peripherical interrenal cords of *Agama agama* and *Natrix natrix* show shrunken cytoplasm after paraffin embedding (Wright and Chester Jones, 1957). Their "vacuoles", reflecting dissolved lipidic inclusions, are more numerous than those in the cells of the central cords. This observation is confirmed by the histochemical results. Especially in the Scincomorpha (Fig. 37) and Ophidia, the peripherical zones of the adrenal

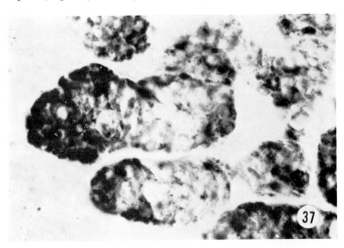

FIG. 37. Frozen section of a formalin-fixed adrenal gland of an adult male *Eumeces algeriensis*; BZL blue stain, × 375, orange filter. Note the accumulation of sudanophilic lipids in the most peripheral cells of the interrenal cords (left side). The dorsal layer of adrenal tissue (left edge) remains unstained.

tissue are richer in particulate lipids than the central zones (Gabe and Martoja, 1961). Furthermore the Δ^5-3-β-hydroxysteroido-dehydrogenase activity
is weaker in the peripheral than in the central interrenal cords of *Emys
orbicularis*, *Varanus niloticus* and *Natrix natrix* (Arvy, 1962). In spite of these
incidental observations, the zonation of reptilian interrenal tissue is never so
clearly established as is that of certain birds (Knouff and Hartmann, 1951).

VI. Cytological and Histochemical Characters of the Adrenal Cells

A. GENERAL

The adrenal cells, whose topographic position has already been noted in
the section on microscopic anatomy, are generally smaller than the interrenal
cells. When preparations are stained for topography, the cells may be distinguished by the stronger reaction of their cytoplasm, which is related to the
absence or scarcity of particulate lipids and to the presence of cytoplasmic
granules noted after fixation in most of the standard solutions. In contrast,
the cytoplasmic granules of the mammalian adrenomedullary cells are only
shown well when the gland is fixed in solutions containing potassium
bichromate.

Certain histological characters are common to all reptilian adrenal cells, as
well as to the chromaffin elements lying outside the adrenal gland proper.
Other cytological and histochemical characters permit the division of
adrenal cells into two groups, corresponding to the noradrenalin and the
adrenalin cells recognized in the adrenal medulla of mammals.

B. HISTOLOGICAL CHARACTERISTICS SHARED BY THE TWO TYPES OF ADRENAL CELLS

All isolated adrenal cells are oval or spherical in general shape. They
become polyhedric when grouped in clusters (Figs 38–47). The cellular
dimensions vary with the greatest diameter ranging from 12 to 18 μ. The
nuclei are central, spherical, rather clear, and provided with one or more
clearly visible nucleoli, even after a topographical staining. Acidophilic
intranuclear inclusions, different from the nuceolus and visible under the
light microscope, have been observed in squamate adrenal tissue (Gabe and
Martoja, 1961). They are rarer in Testudines (Gabe and Martoja, 1962) and
exceptional in *Crocodylus niloticus* (Gabe and Rancurel, 1964). They appear
to be absent in the adrenal tissue of *Sphenodon* (Gabe and Saint Girons,
1964a, 1964b). Electron microscopic observations would be essential for a
correct interpretation of the relations of these structures with the intranuclear inclusions of mammalian adrenomedullary tissue (see references in
Bachmann, 1954 and Picard and Vitry, 1959).

There is insufficient ribonucleic acid in the cytoplasm of the adrenal cells

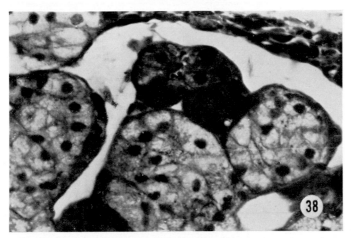

FIG. 38. Part of a cross section of the adrenal gland of a male *Sphenodon punctatus* (same slide as in Fig. 7). × 375, orange filter. Note the two kinds of adrenal cells in the dark cluster.

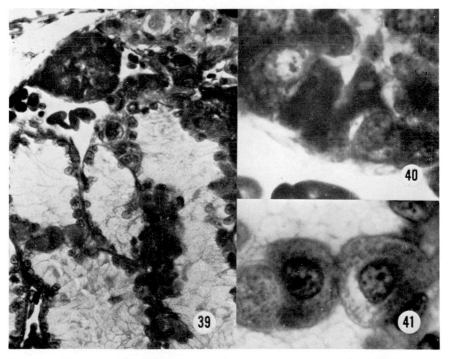

FIGS. 39 to 41. Cross sections through the adrenal gland of an adult male *Quedenfeldtia trachyblepharus*. Bouin's fluid; Heidenhain's azan, × 375 (Fig. 39) and × 1500 (Figs 40 and 41); green filter. Note the dorsal layer of noradrenalin cells (Figs 39 and 40), the small group of sympathetic neurons (Fig. 39, top edge) and the adrenalin cells scattered among the interrenal cords (Figs 39 and 41).

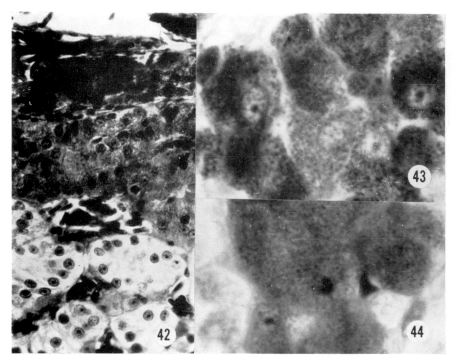

FIGS 42 to 44. Cross sections through the adrenal gland of an adult male *Eumeces algeriensis*. Bouin's fluid; Heidenhain's azan, ×375 (Fig. 42) and ×1500 (Figs 43 and 44); green filter. Note the dorsal layer of noradrenalin cells (Figs 42, top, and 43) and the adrenalin cells scattered among the interrenal cords (Figs 42 and 44).

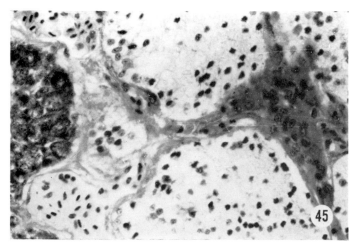

FIG. 45. Cross section through the adrenal gland of an adult male *Chalcides ocellatus*. Bouin's fluid; Mann's stain, ×375, orange filter. Note the light interrenal cords, the noradrenalin (left edge) and adrenalin (right edge) cells.

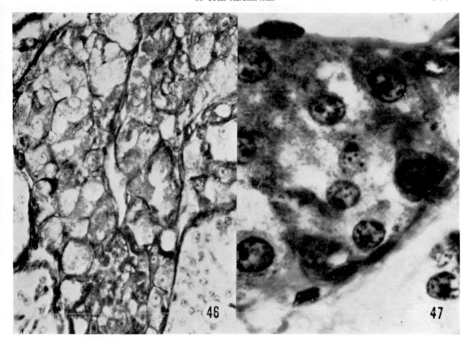

FIG. 46. Detail of cross section of the adrenal gland of a young female *Crocodylus niloticus*. Bouin's fluid, PAS, haematoxylin counterstain, × 375, green filter. Note the "light" and "dark" cells in the adrenal tissue cord.

FIG. 47. Detail of a section of another fragment of the same adrenal gland as in Fig. 46. Regaud's fluid, Lillie's ferric ferricyanide method, haematoxylin counterstain, × 1500 orange filter. Note the two types of adrenal cells.

to be demonstrated by light microscopy. The chondriomes are difficult to reveal because of the abundance of secretory granules of similar staining properties; the short chondrioconts and mitochondria lack clear orientation within the cytoplasm. The Golgi apparatus of reptilian adrenal cells has never been methodically studied with the electron microscope. In *Gerrhonotus multicarinatus* there are grouped dictyosomes, located at one of the poles of the nucleus of certain adrenal cells, in contrast to their diffuse location in interrenal cells (Retzlaff, 1949). The silver impregnation of these structures by the method of DaFano seems easy. Liu and Maneely (1959) report a juxtanuclear net representing the Golgi apparatus in the adrenal cells of *Trionyx sinensis* fixed in osmium.

The secretory granules of the adrenal cells are strongly acidophilic when preserved in all the usual fixatives and take up hematoxylin lac. In crocodilians the latter reaction is the clearest. Numerous staining methods demonstrate the differences between the two cell types (Figs 38–47). It is quite

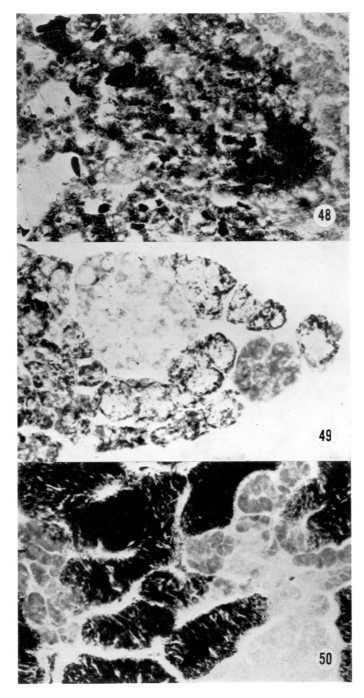

understandable that different authors (Reese, 1931; Radu, 1934; Retzlaff, 1949; Miller, 1952) postulated the duality of the reptilian adrenal cells before study of other vertebrates suggested that these two types represent nor-adrenalin and adrenalin cells. This distinction is now definitely established and confirmed biochemically (Wright and Chester Jones, 1955, 1957; Chester Jones, 1957b; Gabe and Martoja, 1961, 1962; Wassermann and Tramezzani, 1961, 1963; Houssay et al., 1962; Wasserman et al., 1963; Gabe et al., 1964; Gabe and Rancurel, 1964; Gabe and Saint Girons, 1964a, 1964b; Tramezzani et al., 1964), while the ultrastructural characteristics of the secretory granules have also been determined (Wassermann and Tramezzani, 1963).

C. Histological Characteristics of the Noradrenalin Cells

The size of reptilian noradrenalin cells varies within certain limits depend-ing on their systematic position. In all orders except the Crocodilia the largest diameter approximates 12 μ. In *Crocodylus niloticus* the noradrenalin cells have a greatest diameter that reaches or surpasses 15 μ and are consequently larger than the adrenalin cells. This dimensional relation of the adrenal cells is quite unusual, since the noradrenalin cells are smaller than the adrenalin cells, not only in other reptiles, but also in all other classes of vertebrates.

The noradrenalin cells have large secretory granules dispersed throughout their cytoplasm. They are easily recognized, even under low magnification and correspond well to the definition of "rhagiochrome" cells (see references in Picard and Vitry, 1959). The secretory granules are acidophilic with all trichrome stains and take up ferric hematoxylin. They are less abundant than the cytoplasmic granules of the adrenalin cells and thus may be the cells referred to as "light" (see especially Hebard and Charipper, 1955). Evidently the term refers to the general coloration of the cell rather than the staining intensity of the individual granules.

The most obvious histochemical characteristic of reptilian noradrenalin cells is the strongly positive classical pheochrome (chromaffin) reaction. Treatment with liquids containing potassium bichromate stains the granules of these cells a more or less intense brown, though they maintain the capacity to react to P.A.S. and to ferric ferricyanide. The granules of the noradrenalin cells develop a dark brown color after Hillarp and Hökfelt's (1955) methods with potassium iodate (Figs 48–50). After fixation in formaldehyde they show a white fluorescence, similar to that described for mammals (Eränkö,

---

FIGS 48 to 50. Detection of noradrenalin and adrenalin cells by means of Hillarp and Hökfelt's method in the adrenal tissue of *Varanus salvator* (Fig. 48), *Clemmys caspica leprosa* (Fig. 49), and *Crocodylus niloticus* (Fig. 50); BZL blue counterstain, × 150, yellow filter. Interrenal cells black, noradrenalin cells dark gray (right edge, Fig. 48, Fig. 49; top, Fig. 50), adrenalin cells light gray or unstained (left edge, Fig. 48; top, Fig. 49; bottom, Fig. 50).

1955), yet retain the capacity for azo and argentaffin reactions. The pattern thus resembles that well established for all other vertebrates.

The ultrastructure of the secretory granules of noradrenalin cells has only been studied in the snakes *Xenodon merremii*, *Bothrops alternatus* and *B. neuwiedi* (Wassermann and Tramezzani, 1963). The granules may appear spherical, oval, polygonal, or comma-shaped with the polymorphism very characteristic of this type of cell. Each granule is surrounded by a very thin membrane which is difficult to fix. The average diameter of the granules is approximately 2000 Å, but the polymorphism produces considerable variation in size. The internal structure of the granules varies with different fixations, but their heterogeneity is always evident. Fixation by Caufield's method often produces "cristalline" structures in the granules which are evidently artifacts (Wassermann and Tramezzani, 1963).

The cytoplasm of the noradrenalin cells is slightly acidophilic and lacks ribonucleic acids and particulate lipids, but demonstrates a variable quantity of glycogen. All reptilian adrenal cells studied thus far contain a small quantity of ascorbic acid (Knab, 1942; Gabe and Martoja, 1961, 1962).

The histo-enzymological characteristics of the noradrenalin cells are identical to those of the adrenalin cells, so that the two types of cells cannot now be distinguished on the basis of their enzymatic activities (which are summarized in the next section). In contrast, the noradrenalin cells of the adrenal medulla of mammals can be detected by their feeble or nonexistent acid phosphomonoesterase activity, since the adrenalin cells show this strongly.

D. HISTOLOGICAL CHARACTERISTICS OF THE ADRENALIN CELLS

The adrenalin cells are larger (largest diameter approximately 18 μ) than the noradrenalin cells, except in the Crocodilia in which they are smaller (approximately 12 μ). Except for *Crocodylus niloticus*, the morphology of the secretory granules contained in the adrenalin cells resembles that described in the "hyalochrome" cells of the mammalian adrenal medulla. The granules are small, numerous, and very densely packed, giving the cytoplasm a homogenous appearance under low magnification. The abundance of secretory granules explains the stronger acidophilia in trichrome stains and why the adrenalin cells have been described as "dark cells" (Hebard and Charipper, 1955). The secretory granules of the adrenalin cells of *Crocodylus niloticus* are as large as, but more numerous than, those of the noradrenalin cells.

The secretory granules give strong classical pheochrome reactions, but they are not revealed by the potassium iodate method of Hillarp and Hökfelt (1955) nor by that of Eränkö (1955).

Wassermann and Tramezzani (1963) described the ultrastructure of the almost always regularly rounded secretory granules of the adrenalin cells.

These granules have a diameter of approximately 1600 Å, and the variance is smaller than that of the noradrenalin granules. A space of low electron density separates a single membrane from the homogenous or finely granular center. The dimensions of this clear space vary according to the technique of fixation. No cristallization artifacts have been observed.

In most histochemical characteristics, the cytoplasm of the adrenalin cells resembles that of the noradrenalin cells. Both show equivalent amounts of glycogen and ascorbic acid and lack ribonucleic acids. In contrast to noradrenalin cells, adrenalin cells generally contain small quantities of particulate lipids, which are isotropic and "acidic" according to the present nomenclature. Chromolipids have also been reported (Gabe *et al.*, 1964), but their histophysiological significance has not yet been established.

As noted above, the histo-enzymological properties are indentical to those of the adrenalin cells. No alkaline-phosphatase activities are found in *Sphenodon punctatus* (Gabe and Saint Girons, 1964a, 1964b), Squamata (Gabe and Martoja, 1961), or *Crocodylus niloticus* (Arvy and Bonichon, 1958a, 1958b). Gabe and Martoja (1962) found no reactivity in Testudines, but Liu and Maneely (1959) claim that the adrenal tissue of *Trionyx sinensis* has an alkaline phosphatase activity. The material should certainly be re-examined and the question settled.

The acid phosphatase activity of reptilian adrenal tissue is very strong (Figs 50–52). It permits quick detection of both groups of adrenal cells, but does not distinguish between them. No non-specific esterase activities have been found, and the localization of acetylcholinesterase and butyrylcholinesterase corresponds to that of the acid phosphatases (Arvy, 1962; Arvy and Bonichon, 1958a, 1958b).

E. Distribution of the Two Types of Adrenal Cells

The orders of the reptiles clearly differ in the localization of the two types of tissues in the adrenal gland.

As noted in the section on microscopic anatomy, the clusters of adrenal tissue in the Testudines are randomly distributed. They may contain adrenalin cells, noradrenalin cells, or a mixture of the two types (Gabe and Martoja, 1962). Any of these three types of islets of adrenal tissue may be found at any point in the organ (Fig. 53).

The dorsal layer of adrenal tissue, which surrounds the interrenal cords of *Sphenodon punctatus*, contains primarily noradrenalin elements. The ventral islets, which are in contact with the capsule of the organ, are either mixed or constituted exclusively of one of the two cellular types (Gabe and Saint Girons, 1964a, 1964b) (Fig. 54). The same is true for the islets included within the parenchyma.

The distinction between the two cellular types is much more pronounced

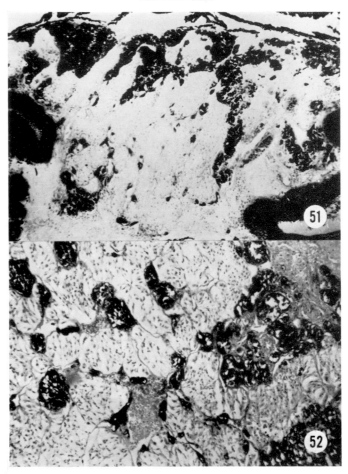

FIG. 51. Part of a longitudinal section through the acetone-fixed adrenal of an adult male *Blanus cinereus*. Gomori's method for acid glycerophosphatase, methyl green counterstain, × 100, green filter. Note the strong reaction in the adrenal tissue (dorsal layer and expansions) and its absence in the interrenal cords.

FIG. 52. Part of a section through the acetone-fixed adrenal of an adult male *Testudo graeca*. Same method as in Fig. 51. Note the strong reaction in the clusters of adrenal cells and its lack in the interrenal cords.

in the Squamata. The dorsal layer of adrenal tissue consists exclusively of noradrenalin cells as do the digitations which penetrate between the internal cords. The clusters of adrenal tissue, incorporated in the parenchyma, contain only adrenalin cells (Wright and Chester Jones, 1955, 1957; Chester Jones, 1957a, 1957b; Gabe and Martoja, 1961; Wassermann and Tramezzani, 1961, 1963; Houssay *et al.*, 1962) (Fig. 55).

FIG. 53. Diagrammatic cross section through the adrenal gland of *Testudo graeca*. Adrenal tissue clusters containing only noradrenalin cells hatched, clusters containing only adrenalin cells stippled, mixed clusters black (after Gabe *et al.*, 1964).

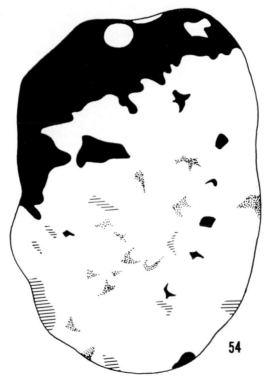

FIG. 54. Diagrammatic cross section through the adrenal gland of *Sphenodon punctatus*; notation as in Fig. 53 (after Gabe *et al.*, 1964).

This anatomical separation enabled Houssay and his co-workers to make a fluorometrical and chromatographical study of the two types of adrenal cells. Their results give a splendid confirmation of the histochemical data. In *Xenodon merremii* $96 \cdot 77 \pm 0 \cdot 89$ per cent of the catecholamines extracted from the peripheral layer of the adrenal appear to be noradrenalin; in contrast,

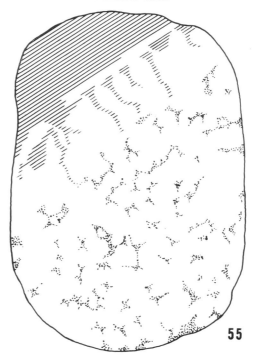

FIG. 55. Diagrammatic cross section through the adrenal gland of *Vipera aspis*; notation as in Fig. 53 (after Gabe *et al.*, 1964).

FIG. 56. Diagrammatic cross section through the adrenal gland of *Crocodylus niloticus*; notation as in Fig. 53 (after Gabe *et al.*, 1964).

85 ± 3.12 per cent of the catecholamines extracted from the central part appear to be adrenalin. Chromatographic analysis indicates only a single spot, corresponding to noradrenalin, for extracts from the periphery, while extracts from the center indicate both a large spot corresponding to adrenalin and a slight spot corresponding to noradrenalin. Since noradrenalin is a normal precursor of adrenalin, these results do not contradict the morphological observation that the central part of the adrenal gland lacks noradrenalin cells (Wassermann and Tramezzani, 1963).

In *Crocodylus niloticus* (Fig. 56), all the cords of adrenal tissue are mingled with the interrenal cords and contain adrenalin as well as noradrenalin cells (Gabe and Rancurel, 1964); the same situation is found in birds (Wright and Chester Jones, 1955).

The cytological data, therefore, agree well with current ideas on reptilian classification. Turtles, lepidosaurs, and archosaurs show quite distinct patterns, while that of crocodilians resembles the pattern seen in birds.

VII. Histophysiology

A. General

In the introduction I noted the meager utilization of reptiles in physiological studies. This explains the lack of data that would allow the definition of the histological modifications of the adrenal gland in different physiological states. Most of the results here presented concern the Squamata.

B. Effects of Hypophysectomy

Only the interrenal tissue shows modifications after hypophysectomy. Direct adenohypophysial control of the reptilian adrenal tissue of reptiles and the mammalian adrenal medulla is commonly lacking.

In *Thamnophis sirtalis* and *T. radix* hypophysectomy produces a significant diminution of the adrenal glands and a reduction of the volume of the interrenal cells (Schaefer, 1933). In *Xantusia vigilis* the amount of the lipidic droplets is reduced in part of the interrenal tissue after hypophysectomy (Miller, 1952). This decrease in lipids is accompanied by degenerative phenomena, such as nuclear pycnosis and a decrease in the size of the cells. During the weeks following the operation, the modified cells occur only in certain regions, while other zones in the same cross section show normal interrenal parenchyma. Hypophysectomy also induces a reduction of the cellular dimensions and of the lipidic droplets in the interrenal tissue of *Lacerta vivipara* (Panigel, 1956); according to Wright and Chester Jones (1959) hypophysectomy causes the adrenal glands to lose up to 60 per cent of the weight shown by the controls in *Agama agama* in 30 days. During the same period the mean weight loss of the testis is 90 per cent. The adrenal tissue shows no histological modifications, but in the interrenal tissue the lipidic inclusions coalesce into "vacuoles" of great size, certain cells atrophy with pycnosis of their nuclei, and in some cases the cytoplasm is reduced to a thin perinuclear layer. These changes mainly affect the peripheral cords. One month after hypophysectomy of *Natrix natrix*, during the winter, the adrenal gland atrophies by 80 per cent (Wright and Chester Jones, 1957), and similar degenerative phenomena are seen in *Agama agama*. The distinctness of the effects increases proportionally with the interval between surgical intervention and post mortem examination, but zones of normal interrenal tissue persist for at least 40 days after hypophysectomy.

C. COMPENSATION FOR THE EFFECTS OF HYPOPHYSECTOMY

Data concerning the compensation for the atrophy produced by hypophysectomy are reported by Schaefer (1933) and Wright and Chester Jones (1957).

In two species of *Thamnophis* the atrophy disappears after implantation of hypophyses of the same species (Schaefer, 1933). Injections of mammalian ACTH produce the same effect (Wright and Chester Jones, 1957). Actually the weight of the adrenal glands in *Natrix natrix* (mean weight approximately 60 g) is not modified by hypophysectomy if the animals receive daily injections of 0·5 I.U. of this hormone for the ten days preceding the autopsy. Histological examination confirms the normal state of the interrenal parenchyma, but often reveals an important thickening of the basement membrane.

D. EFFECTS OF ACTH INJECTIONS ON THE ADRENAL GLAND

The effects of ACTH injections on *Xantusia vigilis* (Miller, 1952) and on *Natrix natrix* (Wright and Chester Jones, 1957) are similar. Both species react to small doses of ACTH by depletion of lipids in the interrenal cells. In *Xantusia* injection of higher doses produces degenerative modifications of the interrenal parenchyma, nuclear pycnosis, and a diminution of cellular size. After a prolonged treatment, the basement membrane of the interrenal cords of *Natrix natrix* shows the same thickening as is observed after the injection of ACTH into hypophysectomized snakes.

As Chester Jones (1957b, p. 181) notes, interpretation of the degenerative modifications is not easy, since most of the commercial preparations of ACTH are contaminated by neurohypophysial hormones which might be responsible for some alteration of the corticotrophic effects. However, the reality of an effect due to high doses of ACTH, that is to a too strong stimulation of the interrenal parenchyma, cannot be excluded.

E. Injection of Corticosteroids

The only descriptions of corticosteroid effects are those of Miller (1952) and Wright and Chester Jones (1957). In *Xantusia vigilis* and *Natrix natrix*, the injection of desoxycorticosterone or of cortisone produces degenerative modifications of the interrenal tissue. These are indicated by a great increase of blood flow through the gland, a depletion of lipid in the cells, and even by atrophy which can be as pronounced as that following hypophysectomy. Cortisone is much more efficient than desoxycorticosterone in diminishing the size of the organ.

F. Changes in the Adrenal Gland During the Annual Cycle

Modifications of the adrenal gland during the annual cycle have been studied only in Squamata. Their interpretation is particularly difficult because few authors have associated histological examinations with physiological or biochemical tests which could have supported their conclusions.

Studies of such changes in the adrenal tissue are especially rare. Panigel (1956) claims that this tissue undergoes no notable modification during gestation in females of *Lacerta vivipara*, but his conclusions are based on preparations treated only with topographical staining methods. Techniques adequate for the study of chromaffin elements, especially the pheochrome reaction, clearly show inactivation of the adrenal cells during the first half of hibernation in *Vipera aspis*, *V. berus*, and *Anguis fragilis* (Martoja et al., 1961; Saint Girons and Martoja, 1963; Saint Girons, 1963). Signs of histological activity appear long before the end of the hibernation in these three species, and the strong histological indications of activity of the adrenal tissue correspond to a clear increase of glycemia (Agid et al., 1961). The onset of vernal activity coincides chronologically with a strong depletion of chromaffin granulations, the adrenal cells being clearly hypertrophied. The period of aestivation is accompanied by a diminution in size of the adrenal cells. The secretory granules are again abundant, but the modifications are much less pronounced than those accompanying winter involution. A new period of activity corresponds to the fall peak of sexual activity that precedes hibernation.

There are more studies of the modifications of the interrenal tissue, and these agree that the gland hypertrophies and the cell volume increases during sexual activity (Bimmer, 1950; Fox, 1952; Miller, 1952; Panigel, 1956; Martoja et al., 1961; Saint Girons, 1963; Saint Girons and Martoja, 1963; Wilhoft, 1964). Those authors who have studied the whole annual cycle note a decrease in the size of the interrenal cells at the start of the hibernation similar to that reported in the adrenal tissue. The nuclei become small and chromophilic, while the cytoplasm contains abundant lipidic inclusions, formed mainly by neutral lipids. As the gland enters its active phase, its size characteristically increases and there is a distinct lipidic depletion. Periods of sexual inactivity are marked by a new accumulation of particulate lipids in the interrenal cells. The validity of the histological criteria of the functional states of the adrenal gland has been demonstrated experimentally in mammals. In the latter, and presumably also in reptiles, the accumulation of particulate lipids in the interrenal cells is a sign of functional inactivity and lipidic depletion is a sign of activation. Furthermore, the activation of the interrenal tissue is paralleled by a decrease in the amount of glycogen within it (Martoja et al., 1961). This suggests parallels to the comparable changes in the glycogen content of the adrenal cortex of mammals (Planel and Guilhem, 1960).

VIII. Conclusion

The adrenal gland of reptiles exhibits a pattern very similar to that known in other vertebrates; there are, nevertheless, some pecularities of this class.

Some doubt remains about the exact origin of the cells that form the interrenal cords. Most authors think that they derive from the coelomic epithelium; others that they derive from the wall of the Malpighian corpuscles of the mesonephros. The definitive histological characters of the interrenal cells appear at relatively early ontogenetic stages. The adrenal cells, which, according to all authors, have their origin in the sympatheticoblasts, only develop their definitive characters at a much later ontogenetic stage.

The adrenal gland of the Testudines resembles that of anuran amphibians in macroscopic anatomy, since it is closely adpressed to the ventral face of the kidney. In all other reptiles the relations of the gland with the metanephros are looser, and instead those with the gonad and gonoducts are closer. Similar relations also occur in birds.

At the microscopic level, the reptilian adrenal gland is characterized by the intermingling of the interrenal and the adrenal tissues. The modalities of this intermingling are different in the turtles, the lepidosaurs, and crocodilians.

All of the histological characters of the interrenal and the adrenal cells resemble those described in other vertebrates. Two types of adrenal cells have been found in all orders of reptiles, and their distribution within the adrenal gland is diagnostic. In spite of the paucity of experimental studies, this morphological similarity permits the application in reptiles of the histological criteria for the functional stages of the adrenal gland established in other vertebrates.

IX. Acknowledgements

The author is greatly indebted to Dr. E. Boesiger (Laboratoire de Génétique Évolutive du C.N.R.S., Gif/Yvette, France) for the accurate translation of the French manuscript of this contribution and to Dr. C. Gans (Dept. of Biology, State University of New York at Buffalo) for the careful revision of the English text.

References

Agid, R., Duguy, R. and Saint Girons, H. (1961). Variations de la glycémie, du glycogène hépatique et de l'aspect histologique du pancréas chez *Vipera aspis*, au cours du cycle annuel. *J. Physiol., Paris* 53, 807–824.

Allen, B. M. (1905). The embryonic development of the rete-cords and sex-cords of *Chrysemys. Am. J. Anat.* 5, 79–94.

Arvy, L. (1962). Présence d'une activité stéroïdo-3-β-ol-déshydrogénasique chez quelques Sauropsidés. *C.r. hebd. Séanc. Acad. Sci., Paris* 255, 1803–1804.

Arvy, L. (1963). "Histo-enzymologie des Glandes Endocrines." Gauthier-Villars, Paris.

Arvy, L. and Bonichon, A. (1958a). Contribution à l'histoenzymologie de la glande surrénale chez *Crocodylus niloticus* Laur. *C.r. hebd. Séanc. Acad. Sci., Paris* 246, 1759–1761.

Arvy, L. and Bonichon, A. (1958b). Contribution à l'histoenzymologie de *Crocodylus niloticus* Laur. *Z. Zellforsch. mikrosk. Anat.* 48, 519–535.

Bachmann, R. (1954). Die Nebennieren. *In* "Handbuch der Mikroskopischen Anatomie des Menschen" (W. v. Möllendorff, ed.). Springer, Berlin. Vol. 5, part 6.

Balfour, F. (1876–1878). On the development of elasmobranch fishes. *J. Anat. Physiol., Lond.* 10, 377–411, 517–570, 672–688; (1877) 11, 128–172, 406–490, 674–706; (1878) 12, 177–216.

Barrington, E. J. W. (1963). "An Introduction to General and Comparative Endocrinology." Clarendon Press, London.

Beddard, F. E. (1904a). Contributions to our knowledge of the circulatory system in the Ophidia. *Proc. zool. Soc., Lond.* 1, 331–370.

Beddard, F. E. (1904b). Contributions to the anatomy of the Lacertilia. 1. On the venous system in certain lizards. *Proc. zool. Soc., Lond.* 1, 436–450.

Beddard, F. E. (1904c). Contributions to the anatomy of the Lacertilia. 3. On some points in the vascular system of *Chamaeleon* and other lizards. *Proc. zool. Soc., Lond.* 2, 6–22.

Beddard, F. E. (1904d). Notes upon the anatomy of certain snakes of the family Boidae. *Proc. zool. Soc., Lond.* 2, 107–121.

Beddard, F. E. (1906a). Contributions to the anatomy of the Ophidia. I. Notes on the vascular system of the Anaconda, *Eunectes notaeus. Proc. zool. Soc., Lond.* 1, 12–44.

Beddard, F. E. (1906b). Contributions to the knowledge of the vascular and respiratory systems in the Ophidia and to the anatomy of the genera *Boa* and *Corallus. Proc. zool. Soc., Lond.* 2, 499–532.

Berkelbach van der Sprenkel, H. (1934). Nebenniere und Paraganglien. *In* "Handbuch der Vergleichenden Anatomie der Wirbeltiere" (L. Bolk, E. Göppert, E. Kallius and W. Lubosch, eds). Urban und Schwarzenberg, Berlin and Vienna. Vol. 2, 777–816.

Bern, H. A. and Nandi, J. (1964). Endocrinology of poikilothermic vertebrates. *In* "The Hormones" (G. Pincus, K. V. Thimann and E. B. Astwood, eds). Academic Press, New York. Vol. 4, 199–298.

Bimmer, A. (1950). Metrische Untersuchungen über die Entwicklung der Nebenniere und der ihr benachbarten Organe bei Eidechsen. *Anat. Anz.* 97, 276–311.

Bojanus, L. H. (1819–1821). "Anatomie Testudinis Europaeae." Vilno, (also reprint 1970 *Fascim. Repr. Herpetology* (26) Soc. Stud. Amph. Rept.).

Braun, M. (1879). Über Bau und Entwicklung der Nebenniere bei Reptilien. *Zool. Anz.* 2, 238–239.

Braun, M. (1882). Bau und Entwicklung der Nebenniere bei Reptilien. *Arb. zool. Inst. Würzburg* 5, 1–30.

Chester Jones, I. (1957a). Comparative aspects of adrenocortical-neurohypophysial relationships. *In* "The Neurohypophysis" (H. Heller, ed.). Academic Press, New York.

Chester Jones, I. (1957b). "The Adrenal Cortex." Cambridge University Press.

Cuvier, G. (1805). "Leçons d'Anatomie Comparée Recueilles et Publieés." Duvernoy, Paris. 5 Vols.

Dufaure, J. P. (1969). Ultrastructural features of Steroid-secreting cells of reptiles. *Gen. comp. Endocrinol.* 13, 502.

Dufaure, J. P. (1970). Quelques caractères ultrastructuraux des cellules interrénales chez un reptile, Le Lézard Vivipare. *J. Microscopie, Paris.* 9(1), 89–98.

Ecker, A. (1846). "Der feinere Bau der Nebenniere beim Menschen und den vier Wirbel-thierklassen." Braunschweig.

Ecker, A. (1847). Recherches sur la structure intime des corps surrénaux. *Annls Sci. nat. Zool.* ser. 8, 3, 103–118.

Eränkö, O. (1955). Distribution of adrenaline and noradrenaline in the adrenal medulla. *Nature, Lond.* 175(4445), 88–89.

Forbes, T. R. (1940). Studies on the reproductive system of the alligator. IV. Observations on the development of the gonad, the adrenal cortex and the Müllerian duct. *Carnegie Inst. Publ.* (518), 129–155.

Forbes, T. R. (1956). The development of the reproductive system of a lizard, *Anolis carolinensis. Am. J. Anat.* 98(1), 134–158.

Fox, W. M. (1952). Seasonal variation in the male reproductive system of Pacific coast garter snake. *J. Morph.* 90, 481–553.

Gabe, M. and Martoja, M. (1961). Contribution à l'histologie de la glande surrénale des Squamata. *Archs. Anat. microsc.* 50, 1–34.

Gabe, M. and Martoja, M. (1962). Contribution à l'histologie de la glande surrénale des chéloniens. *Archs Anat. microsc.* 51, 107–128.

Gabe, M., Martoja, M. and Saint Girons, H. (1964). État actuel des connaissances sur la glande surrénale des reptiles. *Année biol.* 3, 303–376.

Gabe, M. and Rancurel, P. (1964). Contribution à l'histologie de la glande surrénale de *Crocodylus niloticus* Laur. *Archs Anat. microsc.* 53, 225–240.

Gabe, M. and Saint Girons, H. (1964a). Particularités histologiques de la glande surrénale chez *Sphenodon punctatus* Gray. *C.r. hebd. Séanc. Acad. Sci., Paris* 258, 3559–3562.

Gabe, M. and Saint Girons, H. (1964b). "Contribution à l'Histologie de *Sphenodon punctatus* Gray." Editions du Centre National de la Recherche Scientifique, Paris.

Gorbman, A. and Bern, H. A. (1962). "Textbook of Comparative Endocrinology." Wiley and Sons, New York.

Gratiolet, P. (1853). Système veineux des reptiles. *L'Inst.* (*Paris*). 21, 60–62; and *Société Philomatique de Paris. Extraits des Verbaux des Seances, pendant l'annee* 1853, p. 7 (cited from Chester Jones, 1957b).

Günther, A. (1867). Contribution to the anatomy of *Hatteria* (*Rhynchocephalus* Owen). *Phil. Trans. R. Soc.* 157, 595–630.

Hartman, F. A. and Brownell, K. A. (1949). "The Adrenal Gland." Kimpton, London.

Hebard, W. B. and Charipper, H. A. (1955). A comparative study of the morphology and histochemistry of the reptilian adrenal gland. *Zoologica* **40**, 101–123.

Hillarp, N. A. and Hökfelt, B. (1955). Histochemical demonstration of noradrenaline and adrenaline in the adrenal medulla. *J. Histochem. Cytochem.* **3**, 1–5.

Hoffmann, C. K. (1889). Zur Entwicklungsgeschichte der Urogenitalorgane bei den Reptilien. *Z. wiss. Zool.* **48**, 260–300.

Holmberg, A. D. and Soler, F. L. (1942). Some notes on the adrenals. Presence of an united adrenal in the marine tortoise. *Contrib. Lab. Anat. Physiol. Univ. Buenos Aires* **20**, 457–469; 667–675.

Houssay, B. A., Wassermann, G. F. and Tramezzani, J. H. (1962). Formation et sécrétion différentielles d'adrénaline et de noradrénaline surrénales. *Archs int. Pharmacodyn. Thér.* **140**, 84–91.

Junqueira, L. C. U. (1944). Nota sôbra i morfologia das adrenais des ofidios. *Revta bras. Biol.* **4**, 63–67.

Knab, J. (1942). Untersuchungen über den histochemischen Nachweis von Vitamin C in der Niere und Nebenniere von Sauropsiden. *Z. mikrosk.-anat. Forsch.* **52**, 418–439.

Knouff, R. A. and Hartman, F. A. (1951). A microscopic study of the adrenal of the brown pelican. *Anat. Rec.* **109**(2), 161–187.

Kuntz, A. (1912). The development of the adrenal in the loggerhead turtle, *Thalassochelys caretta. Am. J. Anat.* **13**, 71–89.

Lawton, F. E. (1937). The adrenal-autonomic complex in *Alligator mississippiensis. J. Morph.* **60**, 361–370.

Leydig, F. (1853). "Anatomisch-histologische Untersuchungen über Fische und Reptilien." Reimer, Berlin.

Liu, H. C. and Maneely, R. B. (1959). Some aspects of adrenal histology and histochemistry in the soft-shelled turtle of South China (*Chelonia amyda*). *J. Endocrinol.* **19**, 1–9.

Marin, G. and Sabbadin, A. (1959). Sviluppo e differenziamenti della gonadi in *Lacerta sicula campestris. Atti Accad. naz. Lincei Rc.* **26**, 59–62.

Martoja, M., Duguy, R. and Saint Girons, H. (1961). Données histologiques sur les variations de la glande surrénale au cours du cycle annuel chez *Vipera aspis* L. *Archs Anat. microsc.* **50**, 233–250.

Matty, A. J. (1966). Endocrine glands in lower vertebrates. *Int. Rev. gen. exp. Zool.* **2**, 43–138.

McDowell, S. B., Jr. and Bogert, C. M. (1954). The systematic position of *Lanthanotus* and the affinities of the anguinomorphan lizards. *Bull. Am. Mus. nat. Hist.* **105**, 1–142.

Mihalkovics, G. V. v. (1885). Die Anlage der Zwischenniere bei der europäischen Sumpfschildkröte nebst allgemeinen Bemerkungen über die Stammes- und Entwicklungsgeschichte des Interrenalsystems der Wirbeltiere. *Int. Mschr. Anat. Histol.* **2**, 41–62; 65–106; 284–306; 307–339; 348–385; 387–433; 435–485.

Miller, M. R. (1952). The normal histology and experimental alteration of the adrenal of the viviparous lizard, *Xantusia vigilis. Anat. Rec.* **113**, 309–323.

Miller, M. R. (1963). The histogenesis of the endocrine organs of the viviparous lizard, *Xantusia vigilis. Gen. comp. Endocrinol*, **3**, 579–605.

Minervini, R. (1904). Des capsules surrénales. Développement, structure, fonction. *J. Anat. Physiol., Paris* **40**, 449–492; 634–667.

Morgagni, J. B. (1763). "Opuscula Miscellanea." Simoniana, Napoli.

Nagel, C. F. (1836). Über die Struktur der Nebennieren. *Müllers Arch. Anat. Physiol.* (1836) 365–383.

O'Donoghue, C. H. (1921). The blood vascular system of the tuatara, *Sphenodon punctatus. Phil. Trans. R. Soc.* B210, 175–252.

Osawa, G. (1897). Beiträge zur Lehre von den Eingeweiden der *Hatteria punctata. Arch. mikrosk. Anat. EntwMech.* 49, 113–226.

Panigel, M. (1956). Contribution à l'étude de l'ovoviviparité chez les Reptiles: gestation et parturition chez le Lézard vivipare *Zootoca vivipara. Annls Sci. nat. Zool.* Ser. 18, 11, 569–668.

Perrault, C. (1676). "Suite de Mémoires pour Servir à l'Histoire Naturelle des Animaux." Imprimerie Royale, Paris. 2 Vols.

Pettit, A. (1896). Recherches sur les capsules surrénales. *Robin Jl. Anat.* 32, 301–362; 369–419.

Picard, D. and Vitry, G. (1959). "Histophysiologie de la Médullo-surrénale. 5e Réunion des Endocrinologistes de Langue francaise." Masson and Cie, Paris.

Planel, H. and Guilhem, A. (1960). Le glycogène de la glande surrénale. *Pathol. Biol., Paris* 8, 1861–1871.

Poll, H. (1904a). Allgemeines zur Entwicklungsgeschichte der Zwischenniere. *Anat. Anz.* 25, 16–23.

Poll, H. (1904b). Die Anlage der Zwischenniere bei der europäischen Sumpfschildkröte (*Emys europaea*) nebst allgemeinen Bemerkungen über die Stammes-und Entwicklungsgeschichte des Interrenalsystems der Wirbeltiere. *Int. Mschr. Anat. Physiol.* 21, 195–291.

Poll, H. (1906). Die vergleichende Entwicklungsgeschichte der Nebennierensysteme der Wirbeltiere. *In* "Handbuch der vergleichenden und experimentellen Entwickelungslehre der Wirbeltiere" (O. Hertwig, ed.). G. Fischer, Jena. 3(1), 443–618.

Radu, V. (1934). Les glandes surrénales des reptiles (note préliminaire). *Ann. Univ. Jassy* 19, 378–381.

Rathke, H. (1839). "Entwicklungsgeschichte der Natter (*Coluber natrix*)." Gebrüder Bornträger, Königsberg (cited from Chester Jones, 1957b).

Rathke, H. (1866). "Untersuchungen über die Entwickelung und den Körperbau der Krokodile" (W. von Wittich, ed.). F. Vieweg and Sohn, Braunschweig.

Raynaud, A. (1962). Les premiers stades de la formation du cortex surrénal chez l'embryon d'orvet (*Anguis fragilis* L.). *Bull. Soc. zool. Fr.* 87, 98–120.

Raynaud, A. and Raynaud, J. (1961). L'activité sécrétoire précoce des glandes endocrines de l'embryon d'orvet (*Anguis fragilis*). *C.r. hebd. Séanc. Acad. Sci. Paris*, 253, 2254–2256.

Reese, A. M. (1931). The ductless glands of *Alligator mississippiensis. Smithson. misc. Collns* 82, 1–14.

Retzius, A. J. (1830). Anatomisk undersökning öfver nagra delar *Python bivitatus* jemte comparativa an markningar. *Stockholm Akad. Handl.* 81–116 (cited from Chester Jones, 1957b).

Retzlaff, E. W. (1949). The histology of the adrenal gland of the alligator lizard, *Gerrhonotus multicarinatus. Anat. Rec.* 105, 19–28.

Risley, P. L. (1933). Contributions on the development of the reproductive system in *Sternotherus odoratus* (Latreille). 2. Gonadogenesis and sex differentiation. *Z. Zellforsch. mikrosk. Anat.* 18, 493–543.

Saint Girons, H. (1963). Données histophysiologiques sur le cycle annuel des glandes endocrines et de leurs effecteurs chez l'orvet, *Anguis fragilis* L. *Archs Anat. microsc.* 52, 1–51.

Saint Girons, H. and Martoja, M. (1963). Données histophysiologiques sur le cycle annuel de la glande surrénale chez *Vipera berus* (L.) en montagne. *C.r. Séanc. Soc. Biol.* 167, 1928–1930.

Schaefer, W. H. (1933). Hypophysectomy and thyroidectomy of snakes. *Proc. Soc. exp. Biol. Med.* 30, 1363–1366.

Schoof, F. (1888). Beiträge zur Kenntniss des Urogenitalsystems der Saurier. *Zool. Anz.* 11, 189–190.

Sheridan, M. N. (1963). Fine structure of the interrenal cell of the garter snake (*Thamnophis sirtalis*). *Anat. Rec.* 145(2), 285.

Simkins, C. S. and Asana, J. (1930). Development of the sex glands in *Calotes*. 1. Cytology and growth of the gonads prior to hatching. *Q. Jl microsc. Sci.* 74, 133–149.

Soulié, A. H. (1903). Recherches sur le développement des capsules surrénales chez les vértébrés supérieurs. *J. Anat. Physiol., Paris* 39, 197–293; 390–425; 492–533; 634–662.

Spanner, R. (1929). Über die Wurzelgebiete der Nieren-, Nebennieren-und Leber-pfortader bei Reptilien. *Morph. Jb.* 63, 314–358.

Thomson, J. (1932). The anatomy of the tortoise. *Proc. R. Soc. Dublin* 20, 359–461.

Tramezzani, J. A., Chiocchio, S. and Wassermann, G. F. (1964). A new technique for light and electron microscopic localization of noradrenaline. *Acta physiol. latinoam.* 14, 122–123.

Varano, L. and Della Corte, F. (1969). Fine morphology of the Interrenal cells of *Lacerta s. sicula Raf. Gen. comp. Endocrinol.* 13, 536.

Vincent, S. (1896). The suprarenal capsules in the lower vertebrates. *Proc. Bgham nat. Hist. phil. Soc.* 10, 1–26.

Wassermann, G. F. and Tramezzani, J. H. (1961). Complete separation of adrenaline and noradrenaline secreting cells in a snake's adrenal gland. *Acta physiol. latinoam.* 11, 148–149.

Wassermann, G. F. and Tramezzani, J. H. (1963). Separate distribution of adrenaline and noradrenaline secreting cells in the adrenal of snakes. *Gen. comp. Endocrinol.* 3, 480–489.

Wassermann, G. F., Tramezzani, J. H. and Donoso, A. S. (1963). Adrenal veins of the snake *Xenodon merremii*. Differential secretion of adrenaline and noradrenaline. *Acta physiol. latinoam.* 13, 290–292.

Weldon, W. F. R. (1884). Note on the origin of the suprarenal bodies of vertebrates. *Proc. R. Soc.* 37, 422–425.

Wettstein, O. v. (1931–1937). Rhynchocephalia. *In* "Handbuch der Zoologie" (W. Kükenthal and T. Krumbach, eds). de Gruyter, Berlin. Vol. 7 (1), 1–235.

Wettstein, O. v. (1937–1954). Crocodilia. *In* "Handbuch der Zoologie" (W. Kükenthal and T. Krumbach, eds). de Gruyter, Berlin. Vol. 7(1), 236–424.

Wilhoft, D. C. (1964). Seasonal changes in the thyroid and interrenal glands of the tropical Australian skink, *Leiolopisma rhomboidalis. Gen. comp. Endocrinol.* 4, 42–53.

Wright, A. and Chester Jones, I. (1955). Chromaffine tissue in the lizard adrenal gland. *Nature, Lond.* 175, 1001–1002.

Wright, A. and Chester Jones, I. (1957). The adrenal gland in lizards and snakes. *J. Endocrinol.* 15, 83–99.

Note added in Proof

A short note on the fine structure of the interrenal cells of *Thamnophis sirtalis* (Sheridan, 1963) escaped the author during the preparation of the manuscript. Several more recent papers also deal with the fine structure of reptilian interrenal cells. Among these is a preliminary note on *Lacerta l. sicula* (Varano and Della Corte, 1969). A short note (Dufaure, 1969) and more detailed paper (Dufaure, 1970) give a description of the same cells in *Lacerta vivipara*. These papers all document that the infrastructure of reptilian interrenal cells approximates that of mammalian adrenocortical cells. The mitochondria are numerous and large, with mainly tubular cristae; the smooth endoplasmic reticulum is well developed and one sees many free ribosomes, a typical and moderately developed Golgi complex, and a great number of lipid droplets.

CHAPTER 9

The Pancreas

MALCOLM R. MILLER AND MICHAEL D. LAGIOS

Departments of Anatomy and Pathology
University of California
School of Medicine
San Francisco, California, U.S.A.

I. Introduction

A growing interest in comparative cytology and physiology has expanded our comprehension of reptilian pancreatic anatomy in the past decade, and recent contributions regarding the fine structure of the pancreatic islets of several species have been particularly prominent. However, the work of Thomas, published in 1942, remains the bulwark of our knowledge of reptilian pancreatic exocrine (acinar) tissue.

Very little has been published specifically pertinent to the gross anatomy or detailed features of the reptilian pancreas. Even Broman's account in Bolk's Handbuch (1937) offers little in this respect. Much more detailed studies of its structure and arrangement are needed, as is indeed true for other visceral organs of reptiles as well.

We have attempted to supplement this review with original observations of the gross anatomy, histology, and ultrastructure of the reptilian pancreas, using living specimens whenever possible. Thorough examination of every major group of reptiles in such perspective would require a lifetime. Reptilia as a group have suffered from lack of scientific attention, and the vast part of the attention they have received has been devoted to their bones and scales rather than to any of their viscera. The present account, accordingly, devotes greatest emphasis to those areas that we could review firsthand; the intervening areas will, therefore, appear incomplete reflecting the scanty relevant literature.

II. Embryology

Thoughtful discussion and extensive reviews of the literature on the origin and cytogenesis of reptilian pancreatic islet cells are found in the papers of

Frye (1958; 1959), Bencosme (1955) and Bargmann (1939), while the more general problems of pancreatic histogenesis are treated by Siwe (1926).

The pancreas in reptiles is usually derived from one dorsal and two ventral diverticula of the foregut which evaginate just anterior to the hepatic rudiments. While the dorsal pancreatic rudiment always develops, there is considerable specific variation in contributions to the definitive pancreas by the ventral Anlagen. Either both ventral diverticula contribute, or one or the other may be short-lived and disappear without forming part of the adult gland. These variations were discussed by Broman (1937). In the lizard *Xantusia vigilis* both ventral Anlagen appear, while only one, usually the left, contributes to the definitive pancreas. The late appearance of small islets in the anterior end of the pancreas, largely derived from the ventral Anlagen, suggests the possible existence of an islet contribution from that primordium on morphologic grounds alone (Miller, 1963).

III. Topography and Structure

A. General

Differences observed in the detailed gross anatomy of the pancreas in reptiles are largely dependent upon structural modifications of various portions of the gut, or relate to narrowing or broadening of the body cavity coincident with alterations in body form. Probably to a lesser, and as yet undetermined, extent, gross structural modifications of the pancreas may be phylogenetically explained.

B. Turtles

The gross form of the pancreas has been depicted in very few species of turtles (Broman, 1937; Ashley, 1955). In *Pseudemys scripta* (Fig. 1), the stomach and duodenum form a large "C"-shaped loop stretching across the wide center of the body cavity. Commencing at the pylorus and attached to the mesenteric border of the duodenum, the pancreas extends to the right and gradually enlarges as it approaches the right end of the latter organ; it follows the anterior, dorsal, and finally posterior duodenal loops, and terminates by leaving the duodenum and splaying out over the spleen, which is located more dorsally and usually more posteriorly than the terminal duodenal portion.

Anatomic arrangements in the soft-shelled turtle *Lissemys punctata* are similar to those in *P. scripta*. The pancreas lies along the mesenteric border of the wide duodenal loop (Fig. 5), and a small part of the pancreas, connected by a thin shell of tissue to the mid-portion of the main body of the gland, is closely applied to the splenic capsule. The main body of the pancreas is vascularized by the pancreatic-duodenal artery which originates

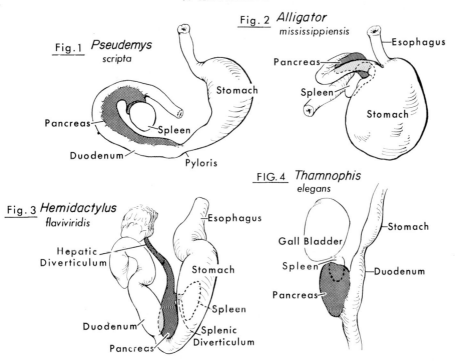

FIGS 1–4 are diagrammatic representations of the gross anatomy of the pancreas in various living reptiles.

FIG. 1. *Pseudemys scripta*, a cryptodiran turtle.

FIG. 2. *Alligator mississippiensis*, a crocodilian.

FIG. 3. *Hemidactylus flaviviridis*, a lizard.

FIG. 4. *Thamnophis elegans*, a snake.

from the common left-gastric-pancreatic trunk arising from the left aorta. Branches of this vessel supply the pancreas, duodenum, gall bladder, cystic duct, and also a portion of the right hepatic lobe. The spleen and the portion of pancreas applied to its capsule are independently vascularized by a splenic artery, also arising from the left aorta.

We were able to examine only a single living pleurodire, *Podocnemis unifilis*, in addition to poorly preserved museum specimens of *Podocnemis* sp., *Chelodina longicollis*, *Chelus fimbriatus* and *Emydura latisternum*. The arrangement in *P. unifilis* (Fig. 6) is remarkably similar to that described for the cryptodiran turtles: a wide duodenal loop has the pancreas lying on the mesenteric surface, supplied by a pancreatic-duodenal artery derived from the left aorta. However, the lack of association between the pancreas and spleen is a prominent difference. The latter organ lies dorsal to the gastric curvature, with a left-sided retroperitoneal attachment, and is vascularized by a left gastro-splenic artery supplying the spleen and lesser curvature of stomach. Other pleurodiran turtles examined were museum specimens in all of which the spleen was located on the left side of the peritoneal cavity in close association with the gastric curvature. In *C. longicollis*, the pancreas splayed out over the spleen, but in its most proximal portion, at the level of the pyloro-duodenal junction; in contrast *P. scripta* has the most distal portion of the pancreas in close contact with the spleen.

These preliminary observations suggest the utility of a more thorough comparison of the anatomic arrangements of pancreas and spleen in crypto-diran and pleurodiran turtles. No comprehensive statement on these two groups should be attempted on the basis of the present limited material.

C. Crocodilians

In *Alligator mississippiensis* (Fig. 2), the stomach is large and spherical. The duodenum arises from the crop-like stomach at a point adjacent, but slightly anterior and ventral to the esophago-gastric junction. To the right of the stomach, the duodenum loops first ventrally and then dorsally. The ventral portion of the pancreas lies between the limbs of the ventral duodenal loop, binding them together. The dorsal duodenal loop is formed by the sharp dorsad- and caudad-turning ascending limb. Following the dorsally turning duodenum, the body of the pancreas finally terminates upon the spleen, which is attached to the descending limb of the dorsal duodenal loop.

D. Lizards

Lizards generally have a pancreas with three limbs, one running along the bile duct towards the gall-bladder, one running to the small intestine, and a usually slender limb, often terminating in a distinct lobe, which runs back to the spleen (Underwood, 1967). In *Hemidactylus* (Fig. 3), the duodenum originates at the posterior end of the stomach, curves sharply to the right, and then turns anteriorly to form an ascending loop. A ventral portion of the pancreas lies between the stomach and the ascending duodenal loop, and, stretching dorsally from this portion, a thin extension of pancreatic tissue (splenic portion) ends near or upon the spleen. Extending anteriorly from the ventral pancreas is a thin diverticulum of pancreatic tissue (hepatic portion) encircling the common bile duct. This diverticulum may reach or actually enter the hepatic parenchyma, a feature commonly seen in teleost fish.

E. Snakes

In snakes somewhat greater attention has been given to the gross anatomy of the pancreas, but no detailed descriptions have yet been published. The relative position of the pancreas in numerous snakes was mapped by

Bergman (1961 and earlier), but his reports provide no other anatomical details. Underwood (1967) reported some highly significant and interesting positions of the snake pancreas, but did not deal with the organ's histology.

Because of the potential significance of anatomic variations in the pancreas of snakes, we examined several different types of snakes and were largely able to confirm Underwood's (1967) findings. In many cases, only fixed museum specimens were available for study and their abdominal viscera were sometimes decomposed due to inadequate fixation. This suggests caution in interpreting splenic-pancreatic relationships from such museum material. It should also be stressed that the location, exact form, and anatomic relationships of the pancreas vary markedly even within a single species. Hence studies of the gross anatomy of the ophidian pancreas, should be based upon sizeable samples.

The pancreas of snakes is generally a well consolidated, often pyramidal mass of tissue affixed to the first portion of the duodenum (Fig. 4). The pancreas lies posterior to the spleen, though they may be in contact. The pancreas may be just posterior to, or at the same level as, the gall bladder; almost always it lies somewhat posterior to the caudal tip of the liver. Underwood (1967) recognized several structural patterns in snakes which he summarized as: *Cylindrophis*, *Platyplectrurus* and a number of Boidae have a limb of the pancreas running forwards to the spleen. In *Xenopeltis* this isthmus of the pancreas is interrupted. In some species of *Eryx*, in *Sanzinia*, and in *Corallus caninus* there is a distinct gap between the body of the pancreas and the spleen while a splenic limb is missing. *Leptotyphlops* has the spleen applied to the body of the pancreas which has a folded splenic limb. A few lower snakes have the spleen closely applied to the compact pancreas (*Typhlops*, *Boa*, Acrochordidae); all Caenophidia show this condition.

Some of our observations on gross structure suggest modifications. The pancreas of *Typhlops punctatus* was pear-shaped, with the larger portion extending caudally to the right while the spleen lay several millimetres anterior to it, near the anterior end of the gall bladder. The pancreas of *Typhlops proximus* was a spherical, compact body attached to the duodenum but separate from the spleen.

In the single specimen of *Cylindrophis rufus* the pancreas was elongated and divided into three portions. We could not ascertain whether or not there was an interconnecting piece of pancreatic tissue. In *Xenopeltis unicolor*, the pancreas was a solid, pyramidal structure lying against the cranial surface of the duodenum and separate from the spleen.

In the boid *Lichanura roseofusca*, the pancreas was elongate, extending anteriorly from the duodenum between the gall bladder and the stomach, and terminating upon the spleen. In some specimens of *Charina bottae* the pancreas was a single solid mass, but in others it may be divided into distinct portions. It is always in contact with the spleen. The pancreas of *Calabaria reinhardtii* is elongate, extends anteriorly from its duodenal attachment, and lies between the stomach and gall bladder. The anterior end is not in contact with the spleen. The pancreas of *Eryx johnii* was a solid pyramidal body lying ventral in close contract with the duodenum. The spleen was not identified in our specimens.

As noted by Underwood (1967), the pancreata of typhlopids, leptotyphlopids, boids and anillids often appeared to be separated from the spleen. In addition, it appears that in these primitive snakes the pancreas tends to be more elongate and less compact than in boids and Caenophidia. We also confirm Underwood's (1967) report that in the species of Caenophidia the pancreas was usually a compact pyramidal body fixed to the duodenum and in contact with the spleen. Yet in the sea snake, *Lapemis hardwickii*, the pancreas was elongated and lay between the gall bladder and stomach. Its spleen was most unusual in that it was also elongate and wrapped about the entire right edge of the pancreas.

F. Amphisbaenians

The gross structure of pancreata has been noted in only a few species of this problematic group. In the amphisbaenid *Amphisbaena caeca*, the pancreas is a compact, pyramidal organ resting on the cranial surface of the duodenum, closely adjacent to the spleen. In the trogonophid *Diplometopon zarudnyi*, a compact truncate part of the pancreas is attached to the duodenum, but in addition irregularly-shaped extensions of the pancreas are loosely wrapped about the duodenum.

Thus while the gross pancreatic anatomy of *Amphisbaena caeca* reminds one of that of higher snakes, the arrangement seen in *Diplometopon zarudnyi* is unusual. Definitive statements concerning the amphisbaenian pancreas must await the study of more species and specimens.

IV. Histology

A. Exocrine Pancreas

The exocrine parenchyma of the reptilian pancreas consists of branching tubules rather than the typical acini observed in mammals. Light and electron microscopic examinations of longitudinally sectioned glands revealed parallel rows of polarized zymogen cells facing a small, uniform lumen, while transversely sectioned glands exhibited a histology not unlike that of a true acinus (Fig. 7).

First-order exocrine ducts merged abruptly with the tubular parenchyma. In transverse sections, epithelial cells of the duct simply replaced zymogen cells in the parenchymal tubule for a short distance (Fig. 9). There is no

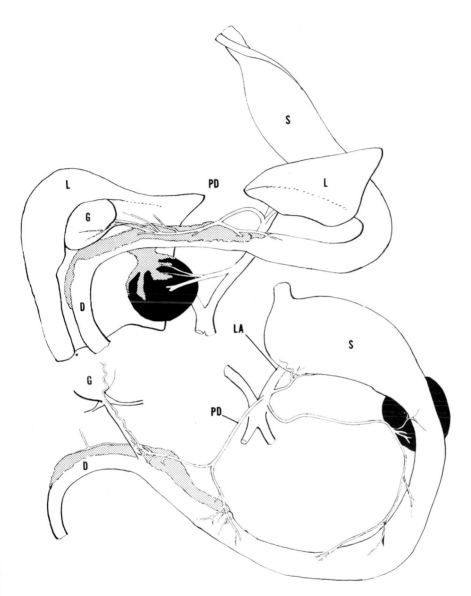

Fig. 5. (Top), *Lissemys punctata*, a cryptodiran turtle, showing the spleno-pancreatic relationships and vascularization in ventral view.

Fig. 6. (Bottom), *Podocnemis unifilis*, a pleurodiran turtle, showing the non associated pancreas and spleen in ventral view.

Solid black spleen; gray shading, pancreas; D, duodenum; G, gallbladder; L, liver; LA, left aortal; PD, pancreatic-duodenal artery; and S, stomach.

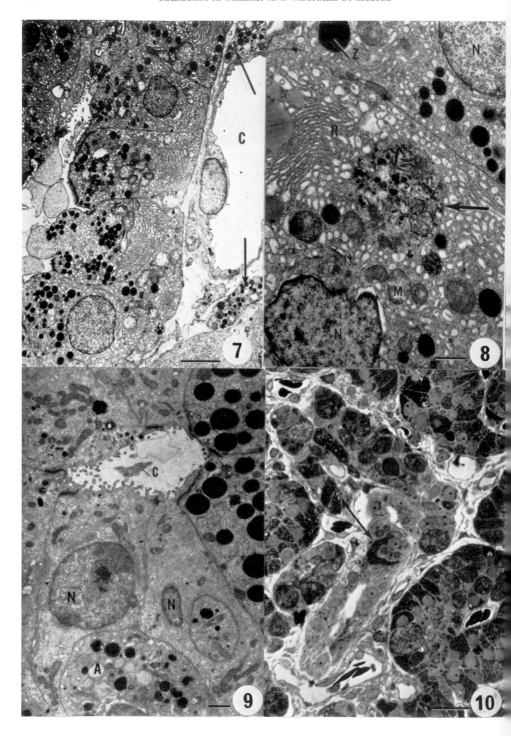

intercalated or transitional segment or centro-acinar cell as in the mammalian pancreas (Thomas, 1942).

The cytology of zymogen cells in reptiles is similar to that described for all other vertebrates. Zymogen cells are arranged in a polarized position about the glandular lumina: there is an apical portion which is usually packed with eosinophilic zymogen granules, and a basal portion containing the spherical nucleus with a prominent nucleolus. The basal portion of the cell has an intense affinity for basic dyes such as hematoxylin, and lies adjacent to a capillary surface. Ultrastructurally the basophilia is associated with uniform, closely stacked cisternae of the rough-surfaced or ribosome-studded endoplasmic reticulum, known to be the protein-synthesizing intracellular organelle. The apical cytoplasm is often nearly filled with uniform oval profiles of electron-dense, membrane-bound zymogen granules and less electron-dense, somewhat larger precursors or protozymogen granules. The latter granules are formed by condensation of the protein content of the rough-surfaced endoplasmic reticulum in several specialized clusters of cisternae (the Golgi apparatus) with which they are connected. The mature zymogen granule is discharged by fusion of the membrane envelope of the granule with that of the cell surface (emiocytosis). The luminal border of the zymogen cell contains microvilli and stereocilia; adjacent cells are bound by junctional complexes.

The process of protein secretion, granule formation, and granule discharge is basically similar in zymogen cells of all vertebrates, as well as in other protein-producing endocrine cells, e.g., those of the islets of Langerhans, the adenohypophysis, and the juxtaglomerular granular epithelioid cells. Accordingly there were few significant differences in the histologic organization or ultrastructural cytology of the exocrine pancreas in the reptiles examined from that described for the Mammalia.

Microscopic examination of poorly nourished animals characterized by lean appearance, atrophy of the dorsal musculature, and resorption of fat bodies, reveals thin, irregular, dilated exocrine glands. Zymogen cells are atrophic, without apical granulation or the characteristic basal basophilia, and contain numerous cytoplasmic vacuoles and dense basophilic bodies.

FIG. 7. *Elaphe vulpina*. Electronmicrograph of exocrine tubule and adjacent capillary (C) cut longitudinally. Arrows indicate macrophages in pericapillary space. Scale = 5·0 μ.

FIG. 8. *Elaphe vulpina*. Electronmicrograph of exocrine secretory cells. M, mitochondrion; N, nucleus; R, parallel arrays of rough-surfaced endoplasmic reticulum, Z; zymogen granule. Arrow indicates membrane-bound area of intracellular lysis, autophagosome. Scale = 1·0 μ.

FIG. 9. *Contia tenuis*. Electronmicrograph of junction of exocrine secretory tubule and first order duct, transverse section. A, alpha cell intercalated at base of duct; C, cilia in lumen of duct; N, duct cell nucleus.

FIG. 10. *Alligator mississippiensis*. Paraffin section. Arrow indicates islet cell in second order duct.

At the ultrastructural level, numerous large autophagosomes (cytolysosomes) incorporate portions of parallel cisternae of the rough-surfaced endoplasmic reticulum (RER), zymogen granules, and mitochondria (Fig. 8). Some zymogen cells were almost completely replaced by these membrane-bound autophagosomes and residual bodies. Cannibalization of cell organelles of the digestive organs of starving animals may represent a method of utilizing endogenous protein (Agid *et al.*, 1961). Focal areas of degenerating exocrine glands were infiltrated by foamy phagocytes and inflammatory cells. Thomas (1942) reported similar degenerative changes in zymogen cells of numerous North American snakes, and comparable light and electron microscopic pathology has been observed in experimental pancreatic atrophy induced by protein-deficient diets in mammals (Weisblum *et al.*, 1962; Lazarus and Volk, 1965; Racela *et al.*, 1966) and in severe protein malnutrition in infants or kwashiorkor (Blackburn and Vinijchaikul, 1969).

B. ISLET TISSUE

Reptilian islet tissue, unlike that of most mammals, lacks a sharp demarcation from the exocrine pancreatic tissue. It is typically associated with first-order exocrine ducts and tubules, and lacks a capsule (Thomas, 1942; Miller, 1962; Titlbach, 1967). Ophidian islet tissue, in particular that of more advanced snakes such as the Colubridae, is essentially restricted to the splenic pole of the pancreas, where semi-confluent giant islets are associated with numerous first-order exocrine ducts. Many of these ducts seem to end blindly in islet tissue (Thomas, 1942). Not only are isolated endocrine islet cells intercalated in the epithelium of pancreatic ducts (Fig. 10), but better organized, larger masses of islet tissue also lack fibrous or basement membranes separating them from the exocrine tubules. Titlbach (1966) noted a similar dual distribution in turtles. Tight junctions are often observed between exocrine and endocrine cells at the ultrastructural level.

Two general histologic patterns are apparent in reptilian islet tissue. In the first, seen in the Squamata, islet tissue is localized primarily in the splenic portion of the pancreas. Large, irregularly branching cords of islet tissue characteristically occur just beneath the pancreatic capsule, adjacent to the spleen, and, occasionally in some snakes, within the spleen itself (Thomas, 1942; Miller, 1962; Hellerström and Asplund, 1966). The cords are composed of tall columnar cells with pronounced perivascular polarization, basal nuclei, and apical secretory granules (Fig. 11). In contrast to islet organization in mammals (Munger *et al.*, 1965), and in some birds and fish (Watanabe, 1960; Fujita, 1964; Patent and Eppel, 1967), no segregation of alpha and beta cells exists in the Squamata: these two cell types lie adjacent to each other in an alternating pattern along vascular spaces. The amphisbaenians examined in this study (*Amphisbaena caeca*, *Diplometopon zarudnyi*, *Bipes biporus*) did not deviate significantly from this pattern. In snakes belonging to the Boidae and Typhlopidae (*Charina bottae, Lichanura roseofusca, Typhlops* sp.), however, the islet tissue is more compact with fewer branching cords extending into the exocrine pancreas. Beta cells of *Lichanura roseofusca*, appear to be restricted to the periphery of globose islets along perivascular borders, while the more avascular central portion is formed almost exclusively of alpha cells. A similar arrangement occurs in *Vipera* (Hellerstrom and Asplund, 1966).

In contrast to the specialized morphology of the Squamata, representatives of the more "conservative" reptilian orders, the crocodilians and turtles, exhibit a marked segregation of alpha and beta cells (Fig. 12), reminiscent of similar degrees of segregation observed in fish (see above), in some birds (Miller, 1942) and in mammals.

The islet tissue of *Alligator mississippiensis* is arranged in loose, globose masses, frequently associated with first-order exocrine ducts at the periphery. Beta cells are often aggregated in the central portion of the islet, while alpha cells cluster peripherally. Segregation is not as pronounced as in some rodents, but is as well developed as in many other mammals, including man. Cytologically, the endocrine cells are more cuboidal than those of Squamata and lack their strong perivascular polarization. Chelonian islet tissue is similarly segregated to a greater (*Geoemyda pulcherrimma*) or a lesser (*Pseudemys scripta*) degree, and there is no concentration of islet tissue in the splenic pole of the pancreas. Titlbach (1966) described peripheral localization of alpha cells in *Emys orbicularis* and *Testudo graeca* as similar to that in *Alligator*.

Only two types of cells with known endocrine functions occur in islet tissue. These are characterized by specific histochemical and immunofluorescent staining reactions, specific ultrastructural configuration of secretory granules and organelles, and experimental identification based on response to cellular toxins or physiologically altered states (Thomas, 1942; Burton and Vensel, 1966). The three di-cystine linkages in the insulin molecule form the basis for a number of histochemical procedures, some relying on oxidation of the cystine, which then reacts with the stain. The latter techniques include performic acid–alcian blue, and similar methods for the demonstration of SS/SH groups. Aldehyde fuchsin and chrome alum hematoxylin behave alike after oxidation, but the histochemical basis for these reactions is less well known. In addition, metachromasia produced by the fluorescent dye pseudoisocyanin is used empirically to tag insulin-containing secretory granules in beta cells. Pseudoisocyanin requires oxidized cystine bonds, thus resembling reagents used for identifying SS/SH groups (Coalson, 1966). Alpha cells secrete glucagon in birds and mammals, and apparently in reptiles, and their massed secretory granules impart in acidophilia which is demonstrable with acid dyes (eosin, phloxine, ponceau d'xylidine). Glucagon has recently been identified in pancreatic extracts

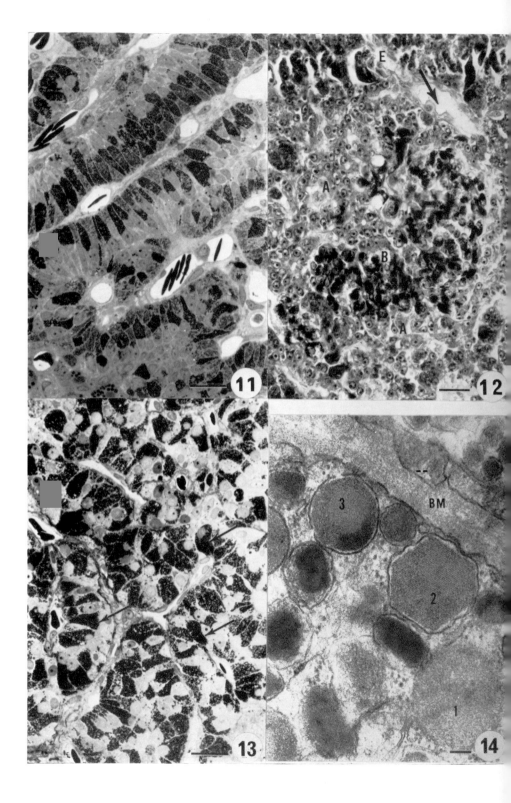

from turtles (Marques and Karenber, 1968) in amounts similar to those found in mammalian extracts, and is apparently immunochemically related to the mammalian hormone. The alpha secretory granule also possesses a variable affinity for metallic silver and phosphotungstic acid after oxidation. This argyrophilia of the alpha granule has given rise to claims that two types of alpha cells may be differentiated in many vertebrate pancreata (Hellerstrom and Hellman, 1960). A2 alpha cells are non-agyrophilic and in many species represent the predominant type of alpha cell. Recently several investigators (Fujita, 1964, 1968; Munter *et al.*, 1965; Patent and Eppel, 1967) concluded that the agyrophilic alpha cell (or A1 cell) is identical to the D cell of Bloom (1931), while others (Hellerström and Asplund, 1966) have demonstrated exactly the reverse situation in snakes and lizards: the major alpha cell is agyrophilic and a D cell is nonagyrophilic. We have confirmed the agyrophilia of alpha cell in *Leiocephalus* (Fig. 13) using the method of Lee (1967), who similarly reported rabbit alpha cells to be agyrophilic. In the chimaeroid fish *Hydrolagus*, all but 5% of the non-beta-cell islet elements, alpha, D and X, can be agyrophilic, depending on the silver staining method used (Patent and Eppel, 1967). Despite arguments supporting the unitary nature and constant agyrophilia of the A1/D cell (Fujita, 1968), the body of evidence suggests that the ability to deposit silver in proteinaceous secretory granules is probably not dependent upon any basic structural similarity of the molecule. These capricious techniques differ significantly in kind from those which rely on the known di-cystine links in insulin to characterize beta cells. Honma and Tamura (1968) discuss the non-specificity of the silver impregnation methods.

D cells (Bloom, 1931) comprise a proportionately small component of islet tissue. They do not react to the usual staining methods for beta cells nor to acid dyes, but will stain with Light Green. They have a variable affinity for silver impregnation (see above). Gomori (1941) noted the distinction between these cells and typical alpha cells, as well as the preferential localization

---

FIG. 11. *Drymarchon corais*. Plastic (Araldite) section, 0.5μ. Tall columnar islet cells with perivascular polarization exemplify the morphology in the Squamata.

FIG. 12. *Geoemyda pulcherrimma*. Paraffin section, chrome alum hematoxylin-phloxine. Darkly stained beta cells, B, are segregated in the central portion of the islet; lighter stained alpha cells, A, occur peripherally. E, exocrine tissue. Arrow indicates a first order duct at periphery.

FIG. 13. *Leiocephalus carinatus*. Plastic section, 0.5μ, modified silver methenamine reaction. Numerous positively-staining alpha cells (arrows) alternate with clear beta cells.

FIG. 14. *Drymarchon corais*. Electronmicrograph of portion of a beta cell adjacent to a basement membrane, bm. Beta secretory granules exhibit several types of profiles: (1) spherical uncondensed; (2) hexagonal with crystalline substructure; (3) form with peripheral condensation. Scale $= 0.1 \mu$.

of both cell types together in the acini of human pancreas. He suggested that the D cell was an altered alpha cell, and ultrastructural studies have supported this early observation (Sato et al., 1966; Like, 1967).

Some recent investigators (Cavallero et al., 1967; Epple, 1968; Fujita, 1968) have suggested on the basis of reported tinctorial similarities to a gastrin-producing human islet cell neoplasm, that the delta cells secrete a third pancreatic hormone. However, ultrastructural studies of these tumors do not support this viewpoint (Greider and Elliot, 1964; Greider et al., 1963; Toker, 1967). Certainly some human endocrine neoplasms retain the ability to synthesize the original hormone. However it should be noted that others, particularly bronchogenic carcinoma and islet cell tumors, can produce de novo a host of hormones normally synthesized elsewhere (Bower and Gordon, 1965); these include ACTH and parathormone, gastrin, and, as recently suggested, secretin (Zollinger et al., 1968) in the case of islet cell tumors. Yet there is no physiologic evidence that the human pancreas normally produces ACTH, parathormone, gastrin, or secretin. Neoplastic hormone production should not be strictly interpreted to imply that the normal parent tissue synthesizes that hormone.

Very recently Lomsky et al. (1969) demonstrated by an indirect fluorescent antibody technique that mammalian islet cells, identifiable as agyrophilic D or A, cells, correspond to cells which bind rabbit anti-porcine gastrin. This preliminary work, as noted by the authors, contradicts earlier attempts to isolate gastrin from a number of normal mammalian pancreata (Gregory et al., 1960; Zollinger et al., 1962). In addition, McGuigan (1968), using a similar fluorescent antibody technique to identify gastrin-containing cells in hog antrum, was unable to demonstrate agyrophilia in these cells. The singular finding of cells ultrastructurally consistent with enterochromaffin type II cells in rabbit islets (Parilla et al., 1969) lends substance to the theory that rare heterotopic gut elements can be present in islet tissue (Zollinger et al., 1968). To what extent these heterotopic elements exist, and to what degree they correspond to gastrin producing and/or agyrophilic D or alpha cells remains to be seen.

Considerable variation occurs in the amount of stainable granules in representatives of any one cell-type, and some cells appear "clear" or devoid of granules. Recent studies (Caramia et al., 1965; Munger et al., 1965) tend to subdivide alpha and beta cells according to the degree of granulation, usually on the basis of the intensity of the staining reaction. While such subdivision is useful in characterizing types in terms of the animal's physiologic state, the misinterpretation that different types secrete different protein hormones should be avoided.

To help clarify the morphologic classification of reptilian islet cell types, we have studied the fine structure of the pancreatic islets of Leiocephalus *carinatus, Contia tenuis, Drymarchon corais, Elaphe vulpina, Alligator mississippiensis,* and *Pseudemys scripta.* Fixation for electron microscopy was achieved by canulation and perfusion of the left aorta in anaesthetized animals. In turtles the pancreatico-duodenal arterial trunk was used. The perfused fixative was 1·5% distilled glutaraldehyde in 0·067M sodium cacodylate buffer and 1 gm % sucrose at pH 7·4, 310 mOsm and 32–35°C. Tissue became fixed within a minute of perfusion.

Osmium tetroxide was used as a post fixative. Araldite imbedded tissue was sectioned at 800 Å, sections were stained with uranyl acetate and lead citrate and viewed with a Siemens Elmiskop I electronmicroscope. Araldite sections for light microscopy were sectioned at 0·5 μ and stained with toluidine blue. Only the general features of reptilian pancreatic islet ultrastructure derived from these observations are considered here, in relation to a general discussion of the fine structure of this tissue in reptiles.

The ultrastructural morphology of secretory granules best distinguishes the cell-types of endocrine islet tissue (Lacy, 1957). Beta secretion granules are unit-membrane-bound and characteristically contain polyhedral crystalloid condensations within a lighter matrix (Fig. 14). Such condensations are peculiar to the beta secretory granule and permit identification when the size, density and unit-membrane profile of alpha granules are similar. The condensations present tetrahedral, trapezoidal, hexagonal, and irregularly polyhedral profiles. Greater magnification frequently discloses a substructure of stacked, parallel, linear densities or plates (Sato *et al.*, 1966; Titlbach, 1968), clearly shown in *Drymarchon* in which a constant periodicity of 62 Å was measured (Fig. 15). This measurement compares with plate periodicities of 36 and 18 Å in the salamanders *Amphiuma* and *Ambystoma*, respectively, and 15 Å in the dog (Sato *et al.*, 1966). Differences in the periodicities in the crystalloidal substructure of granules in beta cells may reflect differences in the molecular size of the insulin. In a similar problem with another protein, Lessin (1968) found a close correspondence between the measured periodicity of crystalloidal aggregates of hemoglobin in red cells obtained by freeze-etching electron-microscopy and those obtained by X-ray diffraction, confirming that individual plates correspond to single bimolecular layers. He notes that the usual fixation and embedding procedures cause considerable artefactual shrinkage of the plate width, apparently due to dehydration and polymerization. Further, the abnormal human hemoglobins, types S and C, which differ by only one amino acid in composition from the normal type A, produce a small but reproducible difference in their crystalloidal periodicity. The difference observed in the crystalloidal substructure of reptilian beta granules may, indeed, reflect differences in the amino acid sequence of reptilian insulins, as well as considerable but at present unassessed artefact. But aside from fish (Wilson and Dixon, 1961; Smith, 1966) differences in amino

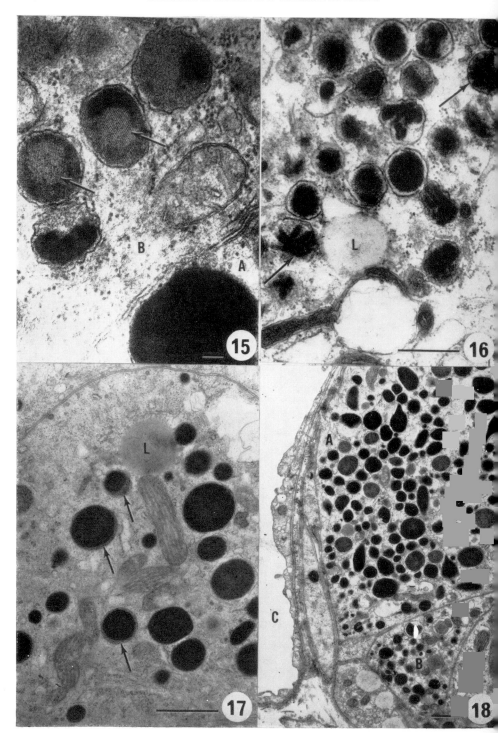

acid sequence are small, particularly in mammals (Prout, 1963); while chicken insulin differs from that of the Sei whale by only two amino acid residues in the A and three in the B chain. Unfortunately the molecular size, weight, amino acid composition, and sequence is not yet known for any reptilian insulin, although an educated, but incautious guess would make them similar to the insulins of chickens and other birds. In the snake, *Drymarchon*, the periodicity of beta plates does not vary with the size, shape, or density of the secretory granule in which it occurred.

Other, presumably less condensed or immature, beta secretory granules have large spherical profiles and a homogeneous flocculant content. In *Drymarchon*, the less condensed granules exhibit a complete series of transitional forms toward the dense crystalloid granule. These forms develop areas of marginal electron-density, which in other profiles reveal circumferential confluence of dense areas with a residual, less dense, central matrix. The polyhedral aspect of the secretory granule may appear before any peripheral condensation has occurred, implying that a crystalloid structure is present even before condensation begins. In beta cells with strong perivascular polarization, no preferential stratification of one or the other type of granule was noted. We found multiple, discrete, polyhedral condensations in beta secretion granules of *Alligator* and *Pseudemys* (Fig. 16). A similar morphology was evident in *Lacerta* (Titlbach, 1967), while in certain Squamata (*Drymarchon, Elaphe, Contia* and *Leiocephalus*) beta secretory granules contain a single crystalloid condensation.

In contrast to beta secretory granules, the granules of alpha cells are indistinguishable from many proteinaceous secretory granules found in non-islet secretory cells. Alpha granules characteristically have round profiles; they are usually homogeneous, but occasionally reveal a paracrystalline substructure and nearly fill the unit membrane. A thick zone of lesser electron-density lies between the granule and the unit membrane (Fig. 17). Although the condensed portion of the beta secretory granule is often smaller than the alpha granule, mean diameters of the profiles of alpha and beta unit membranes are almost identical in all species examined except *Drymarchon*, in

---

FIG. 15. *Drymarchon corais*. Electronmicrograph of junction of alpha cell, A, and beta cell, B. Note parallel linear plates in center of condensing beta granules (arrows). Scale = 0·1 μ.

FIG. 16. *Pseudemys scripta*. Electronmicrograph of beta cell with secretory granules displaying multiple bar-like condensations arranged in a sunburst configuration (arrows). L, lipid vacuole. Scale = 0·5 μ.

FIG. 17. *Contia tenuis*. Electronmicrograph of alpha cell with spherical secretory granules. Arrows indicate less dense marginal zone of secretory granule. L, lipid vacuole. Mitochondrial profiles of two types are evident. Scale = 1·0 μ.

FIG. 18. *Contia tenuis*. Electronmicrograph of alpha, A, and beta, B, cells adjacent to a capillary, C. Note pleomorphic alpha secretory granules. Scale = 1·0 μ.

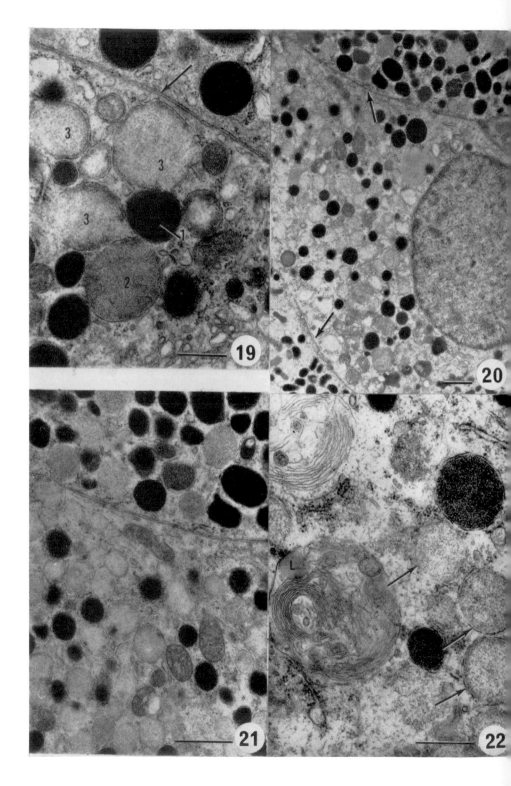

which profiles of alpha unit membranes are twice the diameter of beta profiles. Elongate spheroids and rod-like profiles of alpha granules also occur (Fig. 18).

Almost every alpha cell contains unit-membrane-bound granules of low electron-density, without central dense cores. In fact many contain only a slight electron-dense peripheral condensation on the inner surface of the unit membrane, similar to the peripheral condensation zone of typical alpha granules. A central portion of the granule consists of loose fibrillar material indistinguishable from that of typical D cell granules (Fig. 19) reported by Sato *et al.* (1966) and Fujita (1968). A continuous gradation was observed between the condensed alpha granule and the loose fibrillar form within single cells. In addition, individual alpha cells vary considerably in the proportion of loose, fibrillar or dense-type granules (Figs 20 and 21). Some cells contain only one or two typical dense alpha granules, while the remaining ones are of the loose, fibrillar D-type (figure as a D cell in *Lacerta* in Titlbach's, 1967, Fig. 10). Finally, some cells, indistinguishable from previously described D-cells in reptiles, contain only the loose, fibrillar-type granule. The genera with D cell type of morphology studied by us (*Leiocephalus*, *Contia* and *Alligator*), always showed a complete range of intergrades between typical dense alpha and loose, D cell granular profiles. Cells with a granular morphology typical of D cells, commonly occur in association with alpha cell clusters, as noted previously by Gomori (1941), Sato *et al.* (1966) and Honma and Tamura (1968). Conversely, beta cell clusters rarely reveal a morphology characteristic of D cells. In *Leiocephalus*, the frequency of profiles of the loose fibrillar D type granule in alpha cells is paralleled by the frequency of autophagosomes and complexes of membrane-bound lipids and myelin figures (Fig. 21). Some alpha D cell intergrades are filled with autophagosomes and contain few granules. Since these cells border well-perfused capillaries and lie adjacent to well-fixed alpha cells, they are probably not artefacts.

Unquestionably, granules with the D type of ultrastructure can occur and

FIG. 19. *Contia tenuis*. Electronmicrograph of two adjacent alpha cells. Arrow indicates apposed cell membranes. Several forms of alpha secretory granules are present: (1) electron-dense; (2) homogeneous and of lesser electron density; and (3) indistinguishable from granules of D cells. Scale = 0·5 μ.

FIG. 20. *Leiocephalus carinatus*. Electronmicrograph of three adjacent alpha cells. Arrows indicate cell membranes (borders). Numerous D-type secretory granules are apparent in the middle alpha cell. Scale = 1·0 μ.

FIG. 21. Enlargement of an area of Fig. 20. Scale = 1·0 μ.

FIG. 22. *Leiocephalus carinatus*. Electronmicrograph of alpha cell with few electron-dense secretory granules and many D-type granules (arrows) of very low electron density. Two membrane-bound vacuoles contain whorled membranes and lipid, L. Scale = 0·5 μ.

presumably can be synthesized in otherwise unmistakable alpha cells. We have demonstrated a complete gradation between alpha cells and D cells in some reptiles, like that previously reported in man (Gomori, 1941; Like, 1967). However, Machino and Sakuma (1967) and Machino *et al.* (1966) have presented clear evidence of active emiocytosis, discharge of secretory product, in D type granules of chick embryos, thus suggesting a functional cell, and Przybylski (1967) found similar granular profiles in differentiating alpha cells in the chick embryo. The fortuitous occurrence of autophago-somes and D type cells in *Leiocephalus* may suggest a common functional condition in such cells which is not shared by typical alpha cells. This association should not be misinterpreted as a general indication of a moribund state; the majority of such cells in other species we studied lacked such lysosomal activity.

A recent paper by Kobayashi and Fujita (1969) which appeared during revision of this manuscript confirms our own impressions of the artefactual nature of most descriptions of D-cell ultrastructure. These authors also employed perfusion fixation and their figure number 5 described as a D and A cell side by side we interpret as the type of *inter*grade observed in our own studies. We would interpret both as A cells.

In *Alligator*, columnar cells bordering the pericapillary spaces but lacking specific secretory granules resemble in their ultrastructure the C cells described by Munger *et al.* (1965) and Sato *et al.* (1966). In the former, however, these cells possess a villous apical surface partially forming the wall of a small first-order exocrine duct. Adjacent zymogen cells display ciliated surfaces, and zymogen granules are emptied into the duct, which is filled with granular electron-dense material (Fig. 23). In *Contia* numerous addi-tional examples of the epithelium of first-order ducts are intercalated be-tween islet cells bordering a pericapillary space. Although some mammalian C-cells may be degranulated or quiescent endocrine cells (Sato *et al.*, 1966; Lee, 1967), and despite attempts to equate all C-cells with granular D-cells (Fujita, 1968), reptilian C-cells may form the epithelium of first-order duct, even though the luminal border does not appear in all sections examined.

Aside from secretory granules, some islet cells contain certain other distinguishing organelles. Mitochondrial profiles in beta cells are curved and tubular, with irregularly disposed, transverse cristae and granular, electron-dense matrices. Alpha cells contain similar mitochondria, but the snake *Contia* possesses numerous large, relatively rigid mitochondrial profiles with longitudinally-oriented, parallel cristae. A few sections reveal abrupt tran-sitions between the longitudinal and transverse cristae within a single mitochondrion (Fig. 24). At higher magnification, the cristae are seen to bear a beaded fuzz of rigid periodicity; in transverse section, the cristae themselves have triangular profiles with coronae of small (ca. 60–80 Å)

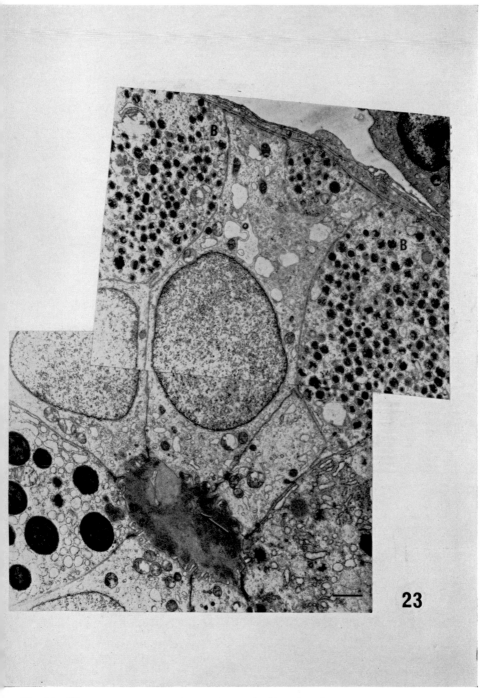

Fig. 23. *Alligator mississippiensis.* Electronmicrograph of junction of first order duct and exocrine tissue. Duct cell is intercalated in the islet capillary surface between two beta cells, B. An additional beta cell is cut tangentially, its profile appearing in the cytoplasm of the duct cell. Arrows indicate cilia in the lumen of the duct. Scale = 1·0 μ.

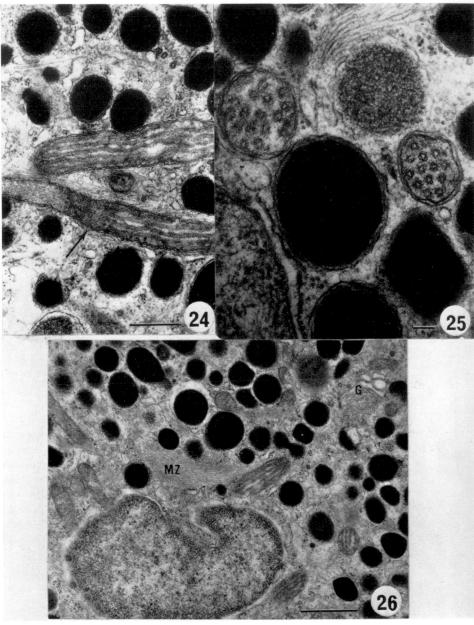

Fɪɢ. 24. *Contia tenuis*. Electronmicrograph of two prismatic mitochondria within an alpha cell. Arrow indicates junction of transverse and longitudinal cristae. Note the pleomorphic alpha secretory granules with less dense periphery. Scale = 0·5 μ.

Fɪɢ. 25. *Contia tenuis*. Electronmicrograph of alpha cell. Two prismatic mitochondria with transversely sectioned triangular cristae are visible. Scale = 0·1 μ.

Fɪɢ. 26. *Contia tenuis*. Electronmicrograph of alpha cell at low magnification. Prismatic and regular mitochondrial profiles and fibrils of macular zone, MZ, are evident. G, Golgi zone. Scale = 1·0 μ.

beaded densities (Fig. 25). The repeating fuzz on these specialized reptilian mitochondria resembles the repeating particle associated with the inner membrane of mitochondrial cristae reported by Fernandez-Moran *et al.* (1964). Similar prismatic cristae in the mitochondria of specialized reptilian alpha cells were described by Burton and Vensel (1966), but mitochondria with similar rigidly parallel, longitudinal cristae have been reported in the beta cells of toads and mammals (Kobayashi, 1966), in neurons of fish (Braak, 1967), and in the cricothyroid muscle of bats. The periodicity of intracristal and intercristal mitochondrial suborganelles was reviewed by Suzuki and Mostofi (1967). In *Contia*, there is a filamentous, paranuclear macular zone similar to that described in the beta cells of toads and mammals (Kobayashi, 1966) and mammalian alpha cells (Fujita and Matsuno, 1967). We saw no strict association of specialized mitochondria with the macular zone in *Contia* (Fig. 26).

Bencosme (1959) first described secretomotor innervation of islet tissue, and recent studies have revealed both adrenergic and cholinergic secretomotor innervation of alpha and beta cells in some mammals (Legg, 1967; Esterhuizen *et al.*, 1968; Watari, 1968) and in toads (Kobayashi, 1966). Physiologically, corroboration of this innervation is not yet complete (Kaneto *et al.*, 1967 and 1968; Nelson *et al.*, 1967; Ezdinli *et al.*, 1968). We ourselves observed secretomotor innervation only in snakes (*Drymarchon* and *Contia*), and then only in beta cells (Fig. 27). The secretomotor synapses often lie depressed in the surface of the beta cell, beneath the parenchymal basement membrane (Fig. 28). Clear synaptic vesicles measuring ca. 500 Å occur in clusters, while there are relatively few large, dense-cored vesicles 1200–1500 Å in diameter (Fig. 29). Such morphology suggests that the synaptic ending is *adrenergic* (Richardson, 1964; Watari, 1968). In addition to secretomotor synapses, multiple unmyelinated nerve profiles were observed in the pericapillary spaces of all species. Fenestrated endothelium of the islet capillaries and their perivascular connective tissue spaces are characteristic of endocrine organs (Farquhar, 1961).

V. Conclusion

In this brief review of the reptilian pancreas we attempt to collate the existing literature and our own limited direct observations in a form which reflects current areas of research in this field. We hope the report provides strong support for the theory that any such study benefits from a comparative viewpoint: many of our observations of reptilian pancreatic morphology become relevant only by reference to literature dealing strictly with mammals or for that matter, with fishes.

In numerous instances, we have postulated our own interpretation, particularly in regard to the ultrastructure of islet tissue, where we hope to

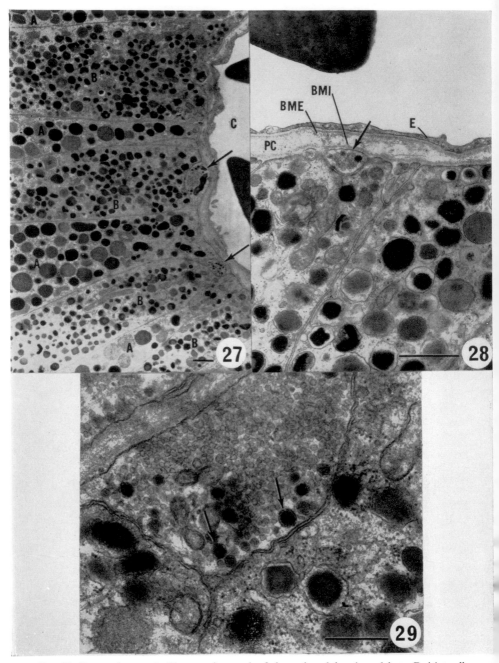

FIG. 27. *Drymarchon corais*. Electronmicrograph of alternating alpha, A, and beta, B, islet cells palisaded along capillary space, C. Arrows indicate two unmyelinated nerve profiles. Scale = 1·0 μ.

FIG. 28. *Drymarchon corais*. Higher magnification of islet. Small unmyelinated nerve (arrow) lies adjacent to one of two beta cells. E, endothelium; PC, pericapillary space; bme, endothelial basement membrane; bmi, islet basement membrane. Scale = 1·0 μ.

FIG. 29. *Drymarchon corais*. Electronmicrograph of unmyelinated nerve profile adjacent to beta cell. Arrows indicate large dense-cored vesicles. Scale = 0·5 μ.

provide a re-examination of some prevailing notions. Though strongly worded, our interpretations are not intended to masquerade as ultimate or definitive statements, but rather to stimulate further investigation in this area.

VI. Acknowledgements

The authors are indebted to Miss Michiko Kasahara for skilled technical assistance, to Mr. Wayne Emery for execution of Figures 1–4, to Miss Rosamunda Holly for sound editorial help, and to Dr. Alan Leviton, Curator of Herpetology at the California Academy of Sciences, San Francisco, for his generous loan of museum material. This work was supported in part by USPH Service Grants Nos. NB-05532, AM-11182 and 5T01-GM00349.

References

Agid, R., Duguy, R. and Saint Girons, H. (1961). Variation de la glycémie, du glycogène hépatique et de l'aspect histologique du pancréas, chez *Vipera aspis*, au cours du cycle annuel. *J. Physiol.* 53, 807–824.

Ashley, L. M. (1955). "Laboratory Anatomy of the Turtle." W. C. Brown, Dubuque, Iowa.

Bargmann, W. (1939). Die Langerhansschen Inseln des Pankreas. *In* "Handbuch der mikroskopischen Anatomie des Menschen" (W. von Möllendorff, ed.), vol. 6, pt. 2, pp. 197–288. J. Springer, Berlin.

Bencosme, S. A. (1955). The histogenesis and cytology of the pancreatic islets in the rabbit. *Am. J. Anat.* 96, 103–152.

Bencosme, S. A. (1959). Studies on the terminal autonomic nervous system with special reference to the pancreatic islets. *Lab. Invest.* 8, 629–646.

Bergman, R. A. M. (1961). The anatomy of some Viperidae. *Acta morph. neerl.-scand.* 4, 195–230.

Blackburn, W. R. and Vinijchaikul, K. (1969). The pancreas in Kwashiorkor, an electron microscopic study. *Lab. Invest.* 20, 651–658.

Bloom, W. (1931). A new type of granular cell in the islets of Langerhans of man. *Anat. Rec.* 49, 363–371.

Bower, B. F. and Gordon, G. S. (1965). Hormonal effects of non-endocrine tumors. *A. Rev. Med.* 16, 83–118.

Braak, H. (1967). Elektronenmikroskopische Untersuchungen am Catecholaminkern im Hypothalamus vom Goldfisch (*Carassius auratus*). *Z. Zellforsch. mikrosk. Anat.* 83, 398–415.

Broman, I. (1937). Das Pankreas. *In* "Handbuch der vergleichenden Anatomie der Wirbeltiere" (L. Bolk, E. Göppert, E. Kallius, W. Lubosch, eds), 3, 715–796. Urban und Schwartzenberg, Berlin.

Burton, P. R. and Vensel, W. H. (1966). Ultrastructural studies of normal and alloxan-treated islet cells of the pancreas of the lizard, *Eumeces fasciatus*. *J. Morph.* 118, 91–118.

Caramia, F., Munger, B. L. and Lacy, P. E. (1965). The ultrastructural basis for the identification of cell types in the pancreatic islets. I. Guinea pig. *Z. Zellforsch. mikrosk. Anat.* 67, 533–546.

Cavallero, C., Solcia, E. and Sampietro, R. (1967). Cytology of islet tumours and hyperplasias associated with the Zollinger-Ellison syndrome. *Gut* 8, 172–177.

Coalson, R. E. (1966). Pseudoisocyanin staining of insulin and specificity of empirical islet cell stains. *Stain Technol.* **41**, 121–129.

Epple, A. (1968). Comparative studies on the pancreatic islets. *Endocr. jap.* **15**, 107–122.

Esterhuizen, A. C., Spriggs, T. L. B. and Lever, J. D. (1968). Nature of islet-cell innervation in the cat pancreas. *Diabetes* **17**, 33–36.

Ezdinli, E. Z., Javid, R., Owens, G. and Sokal, J. E. (1968). Effect of high spinal cord section on epinephrine hyperglycemia. *Am. J. Physiol.* **214**, 1019–1024.

Farquhar, M. G. (1961). Fine structure and function in capillaries of the anterior pituitary gland. *Angiology* **12**, 270–292.

Fernandez-Moran, H., Oda, T., Blair, P. V. and Green, D. E. (1964). A macromolecular repeating unit of mitochondrial structure and function. *J. Cell. Biol.* **22**, 63–100.

Frye, B. E. (1958). Development of the pancreas in *Amblystoma opacum*. *Am. J. Anat.* **102**, 117–139.

Frye, B. E. (1959). The development of function in the islets of Langerhans. *In* "Comparative Endocrinology" (A. Gorbman, ed.), pp. 681–696. Wiley, N.Y.

Fujita, H. and Matsuno, Z. (1967). Some observations on the fine structure of the pancreatic islet of rabbits, with special reference to B cell alteration in the hypoglycemic state induced by alloxan treatment. *Archvm. histol. jap.* **28**, 383–398.

Fujita, T. (1964). The identification of the argyrophil cells of pancreatic islets with D-cells. *Archvm. histol. jap.* **25**, 189–197.

Fujita, T. (1968). D cell, the third endocrine element of the pancreatic islet. *Archvm. histol. jap.* **29**, 1–40.

Gomori, G. (1941). Observations with differential stains on human islets of Langerhans. *Am. J. Path.* **17**, 395–406.

Gregory, R. A., Tracy, H. J., French, J. M. and Sircus, W. (1960). Extraction of a gastrin-like substance from a pancreatic tumour in a case of Zollinger-Ellison syndrome. *Lancet* **1960** (1), 1045.

Greider, M. H. and Elliott, D. W. (1964). Electron microscopy of human pancreatic tumors of islet cell origin. *Am. J. Path.* **44**, 663–678.

Greider, M. H., Elliott, D. W. and Zollinger, R. M. (1963). An electron microscope study of islet cell adenomas. *J. Am. med. Ass.* **186**, 566–569.

Hellerström, C. and Asplund, K. (1966). The two types of A-cells in the pancreatic islets of snakes. *Z. Zellforsch. mikrosk. Anat.* **70**, 68–80.

Hellerström, C. and Hellman, B. (1960). Some aspects of silver impregnation of the islets of Langerhans in the rat. *Acta Endocr.* **35**, 518–532.

Honma, Y. and Tamura, E. (1968). Studies on the Japanese chars of the genus *Salvelinus*. V. Cytology of the pancreatic islets in the Nikko-iwana, *Salvelinus leucomaenis pluvius* (Hilgendorf). *Bull. Jap. Soc. Scient. Fish.* **34**, 555–561.

Kaneto, A., Kosaka, K. and Nakao, K. (1967). Effects of stimulation of the vagus nerve on insulin secretion. *Endocrinology* **80**, 530–536.

Kaneto, A., Kajinuma, H., Kosaka, K. and Nakao, K. (1968). Stimulation of insulin secretion by parasympathomimetic agents. *Endocrinology* **83**, 651–658.

Kobayashi, K. (1966). Electron microscope studies of the Langerhans islets in the toad pancreas. *Archvm. histol. jap.* **26**, 439–482.

Kobayashi, S. and Fujita, T. (1969). Fine structure of mammalian and avian pancreatic islets with special reference to D cells and nervous elements. *Z. Zellforsch. mikrosk. Anat.* **100**, 340–343.

Lazarus, S. S. and Volk, B. W. (1965). Ultrastructure and acid phosphate distribution in the pancreas of rabbits. *Archs Path.* **80**(2), 135–147.

Lacy, P. E. (1957). Electron microscopic identification of different cell types in the islets of Langerhans of the guinea pig, rat, rabbit and dog. *Anat. Rec.* **128**, 255–267.

Lee, D. H. (1967). Identification of argyrophilic cells in pancreatic islets by light and electron microscopy in osmium-fixed plastic-embedded sections. *Z. Zellforsch. mikrosk. Anat.* **77**, 1–7.

Legg, P. G. (1967). The fine structure and innervation of the beta and delta cells in the islet of Langerhans of the cat. *Z. Zellforsch. mikrosk. Anat.* **80**, 307–321.

Lessin, L. S. (1968). Structure moléculaire de l'hémoglobine cristallisée d'erythrocytes de rat, étudiée par cryo-décapage.*Nouv. Revue fr.Hemat.* **8**(4), 423–463.

Like, A. A. (1967). The ultrastructure of the secretory cells of the islets of Langerhans in man. *Lab. Invest.* **16**, 937–951.

Lomsky, R., Langr, F. and Vortel, V. (1969). Immunohistochemical demonstration of gastrin in mammalian islets of Langerhans. *Nature, Lond.* **223**, 618–619.

Machino, M. and Sakuma, H. (1967). Electron microscopy of islet alpha cells of domestic fowl. *Nature, Lond.* **214**, 808–809.

Machino, M., Sakuma, H. and Onoe, T. (1966). The fine structure of the D-cells of the pancreatic islets in the domestic fowl and their morphological evidence of secretion. *Archvm. histol. jap.* **27**, 407–418.

Marques, M. and Kraemer, A. (1968). Extractable insulin and glucagon from turtle's (*Chrysemys d'orbignyi*) pancreas. *Comp. Biochem. Physiol.* **27**, 439–446.

McGuigan, J. E. (1968). Gastric mucosal intracellular localization of gastrin by immuno-fluorescence. *Gastroenterology* **55**, 315–327.

Miller, M. R. (1962). Observations on the comparative histology of the reptilian pancreatic islet. *Gen. Comp. Endocrinol.* **2**, 407–414.

Miller, M. R. (1963). The histogenesis of the endocrine organs of the viviparous lizard, *Xantusia vigilis. Gen. Comp. Endocrinol.* **3**, 579–605.

Miller, R. A. (1942). Effects of anterior pituitary preparations and insulin on islet cells of pigeon pancreas. *Endocrinology* **31**, 535–544.

Munger, B. L., Caramia, F. and Lacy, P. E. (1965). The ultrastructural basis for the identification of cell types in the pancreatic islets. II. Rabbit, dog and opossum. *Z. Zellforsch. mikrosk. Anat.* **67**, 776–798.

Nelson, N. C., Blackard, W. G., Cocchiara, J. C. and Labat, J. A. (1967). Influence of the vagus nerves on pancreatic insulin secretion. *Diabetes* **16**, 852–857.

Parilla, R., Gomez-Acebo, J. and R-Candela, J. L. (1969). Ultrastructural evidence for the presence of enterochromaffin type II cells in the pancreatic islets of the rabbit. *J. Ultrastruct. Res.* **26**, 1–7.

Patent, G. J. and Eppel, A. (1967). On the occurrence of two types of argyrophil cells in the pancreatic islets of the holocephalan fish, *Hydrolagus colliei. Gen. Comp. Endocrinol.* **9**, 325–333.

Prout, T. E. (1963). The chemical structure of insulin in relation to biological activity and to antigenicity. *Metabolism* **12**, 673–686.

Przybylski, R. J. (1967). Cytodifferentiation of the chick pancreas. I. Ultrastructure of the islet cells and the initiation of granule formation. *Gen. Comp. Endocrinol.* **8**, 115–128.

Racela, A. S., jr., Grady, H. J., Higginson, J. and Svoboda, D. J. (1966). Protein deficiency in Rhesus monkeys. *Am. J. Path.* **49**(3), 419–443.

Reid, K. B. M., Grant, P. T. and Youngson, A. (1968). The sequence of amino acids in insulin isolated from islet tissue of the Cod (*Gadus callarias*). *Biochem. J.* **110**, 289–296.

Richardson, K. C. (1964). The fine structure of the albino rabbit iris with special reference to the identification of adrenergic and cholinergic nerves and nerve endings in its intrinsic muscles. *Am. J. Anat.* **114**, 173–205.

Sato, T., Herman, L. and Fitzgerald, P. J. (1966). The comparative ultrastructure of the pancreatic islet of Langerhans. *Gen. Comp. Endocrinol.* 7, 132–157.

Siwe, S. A. (1926). Pankreasstudien. *Morph. Jb.* 57, 84–308.

Smith, L. F. (1966). Species variation in the amino acid sequence of insulin. *Am. J. Med.* 40, 662–666.

Suzuki, T. and Mostofi, F. K. (1967). Intramitochondrial filamentous bodies in the thick limb of Henle of the rat kidney. *J. Cell. Biol.* 33, 605–623.

Thomas, T. B. (1942). The pancreas of snakes. *Anat. Rec.* 82, 327–345.

Titlbach, M. (1966). Licht- und elektronenmikroskopische Untersuchungen der Langerhansschen Inseln von Schildkröten (*Testudo graeca*). *Z. Zellforsch. mikrosk. Anat.* 70, 21–35.

Titlbach, M. (1967). Licht- und elektronenmikroskopische Untersuchungen der Langerhansschen Inseln von Eidechsen (*Lacerta agilis* L., *Lacerta viridis* Laurenti). *Z. Zellforsch. mikrosk. Anat.* 83, 427–440.

Titlbach, M. (1968). Licht- und elektronenmikroskopische Untersuchungen der Langerhansschen Inseln von Nattern (*Natrix natrix* L., *Natrix tessellata* Laurenti). *Z. Zellforsch. Mikrosk. Anat.* 90, 519–534.

Toker, C. (1967). Some observations on the ultrastructure of a malignant islet cell tumor associated with duodenal ulceration and severe diarrhea. *J. Ultrastruct. Res.* 19, 522–531.

Underwood, G. (1967). "A Contribution to the Classification of Snakes." British Museum of Natural History, London.

Watanabe, A. (1960). Histologische, cytologische und elektronenmikroskopische Untersuchungen über die Langerhansschen Inseln der Knochenfische, insbesondere des Karpfens. *Archvm. histol. jap.* 19, 279–330.

Watari, N. (1968). Fine structure of nervous elements in the pancreas of some vertebrates. *Z. Zellforsch. microsk. Anat.* 85, 291–314.

Weisblum, B., Herman, L. and Fitzgerald, P. J. (1962). Changes in pancreatic acinar cells during protein deprivation. *J. Cell. Biol.* 12(2), 313–327.

Wilson, S. and Dixon, G. H. (1961). A comparison of cod and bovine insulins. *Nature, Lond.* 191, 876–879.

Zollinger, R. M., Elliott, D. W., Endahl, G. L., Grant, G. N., Goswitz, J. T. and Taft, D. A. (1962). Origin of the ulcerogenic hormone in endocrine induced ulcer. *Ann. Surg.* 156, 570–576, 578.

Zollinger, R. M., Tompkins, R. K., Amerson, J. R., Endahl, G. L., Kraft, A. R. and Moore, F. T. (1968). Identification of the diarrheogenic hormone associated with non-beta cell tumors of the pancreas. *Ann. Surg.* 168, 502–518, 521.

Author Index

The numbers in *italics* indicate the pages on which names are mentioned in the reference lists.

A

Abdel-Messeih, G., 12, 15, 30, *63*
Ackerman, G. A., 118, 121, *130*
Adams, A. E., 221, 227, *228*
Adams, W. E., 112, 113, 118, *130*, 203, 227, *228*, 248, 250, 253, 255, 257, *259*
Afanassiew, B., 115, 118, 120, *130*, 237, *260*
Agee, J. R., 39, *68*
Agid, R., 11, 18, 20, 21, *54*, 311, *313*, 328, *343*
Aime, P., 236, *260*
Alder, A., 11, *54*, 95, 96, 97, *108*
Aldred, P., 14, *54*
Allen, B. M., 265, *313*
Allison, A. C., 40, 42, *61*
Allison, W. S., 46, *71*
Altland, P. D., 11, 38, *54*, 56, 95, 98, 100, *108*, 135, *196*
Altman, P. L., 73, *89*, 95, 96, 97, 98, *108*
Amerson, J. R., 332, *346*
Amin, A., 49, *64*
Andersen, H. T., 11, 13, 17, 18, *54*
Andersson, K., 27, 29, *70*
Andreen-Svedberg, A., 11, 19, *54*
Anson, M. L., 40, *54*
Appleby, E. C., 26, *54*
Archer, O. K., 111, 127, *130*
Aron, E., 29, 38, *54*, 223, 224, 226, *228*
Arvy, L., 280, 281, 284, 295, 296, 298, 305, *313*
Asana, J., 265, *317*
Ashley, L. M., 320, *343*
Asplund, K., 328, 329, 331, *344*
Attleberger, M. H., 35, *60*
Auerbach, R., 118, *130*
Augustinsson, K., 29, *54*, *55*
Austin, J. H., 11, 14, 16, 19, *55*
Austin, S., 33, *68*

B

Babudieri, B., 73, *89*, 95, 96, 97, 98, 101, 102, 104, *108*
Bachmann, R., 263, 298, *313*
Baker, C. M. A., 42, *65*
Baker, E. G. S., 99, *108*
Balfour, F., 264, *313*
Baltac, M., 20, 21, 22, 23, *71*
Bamberger, J. W., 88, *90*
Banerjee, V., 82, *89*
Barber, A. A., 12, 32, 38, 39, *55*, *69*
Barchiesi, A., 208, 226, *228*
Barcroft, J., 40, *54*
Bargmann, W., 111, 120, 121, *130*, 137, 142, *196*, 235, *260*, 320, *343*
Baril, E. F., 27, 30, *55*
Barrington, E. J. W., 264, *313*
Barros, M., 20, 21, 22, 23, *64*
Bartel, A. H., 27, 30, 35, 49, *55*, *64*, *68*
Bartholomew, G. A., 21, *55*
Barwick, R. E., 21, 30, 45, 46, *55*
Bassot, J. M., 135, *199*
Bauer, C. B., 17, *65*
Baumgartner, E. A., 135, 159, 160, *196*
Beard, D., 120, *132*
Beard, J. W., 120, *132*
Bearn, A. G., 46, *71*
Beaudreau, G. S., 120, *132*
Beck, A. B., 32, *55*
Beck, H., 45, *64*
Becker, C., 120, *132*
Beddard, F. E., 273, *313*, *314*
Beebe, J. L., 45, *57*
Beer, G. R. de, 159, *196*
Belkin, D. A., 17, 18, *55*
Bellamy, D., 17, *55*
Bencosme, S. A., 320, 341, *343*

347

C

Subject Index

A

A band, 124
A1 alpha cell, 331
A2 alpha cell, 331
Ablepharus, adrenal, 280
  pituitary, 175
Aboral lobe of adenohypophysis, *see* Posterior lobe of adenohypophysis
Ac-globulin, *see* Proccelerin
Acanthodactylus, adrenal, 280
  blood cell morphology, 74, 76
  blood cell numbers, 96
  pituitary, 145, 153, 155, 173, 192
  thymus, 113
Acanthophis, adrenal, 281
  pituitary, 148
Accessory parathyroid gland, 238, 248, 257
Accessory pectoral vein, 203
Acetate, 46
Acetazolamide, 45
Acetic acid, 41
Acetone, 296, 306
Acetylcholinesterase, 305
Acid fuchsin, 258
Acid glycerophosphatase, 306
Acid mucopolysaccharide, 156, 238
Acid phosphatase, 46, 305
Acid phosphomonoesterase, 296, 304
Acidity, *see* pH
Acidophils, *see* Eosinophils
Acidophily, *see* Eosinophily
  see also Erythrophily
Acini of exocrine pancreas, 324, 332
Acrochordidae, pancreas, 323
ACTH, *see* Corticotrophic hormone
Adeleiina, blood cell morphology, 88
Adenohypophysis, 135, 137, 142–159, 161,
    163, 169, 170, 172, 173, 174, 176, 178,
    181, 183, 190, 192, 193, 194, 327
Adenosine triphosphate, 46

Adrenal colloid, 296, 297
Adrenal gland, 13, 210, 263–317
  capsule, 275, 276, 277, 278, 279, 281,
    286, 305
  degeneration, 309, 310, 311
  embryology, 265–268
  histophysiology, 309–312
  macroscopic anatomy, 268–274
  microscopic anatomy, 275–288
  structural types, 286–287
  zonation, 296, 298
Adrenal portal system, 273, 274
Adrenal tissue, 264, 266, 268, 275, 277, 278,
    279, 282, 283, 285, 286, 287, 288, 296,
    297, 298–309, 310, 311, 312
  cytology and histochemistry, 298–309
  development, 268
Adrenalectomy, 288
Adrenalin, 264, 309
Adrenalin cells, 298–303, 304–309
Adrenergic secretomotor innervation, 341
Adrenocortical tissue, *see* Interrenal tissue
Adrenomedullary tissue, *see* Adrenal tissue
Aestivation, 216, 311
Afferent adrenal vein, 274
Afferent renal vein, 270
Agama, adrenal, 274, 280, 292, 297, 309,
    310
  blood cell morphology, 76, 82, 88
  blood cell numbers, 96, 103
  blood chemistry, 5, 13
  pituitary, 138, 148, 149, 171
  thymus, 113
  thyroid, 216, 227
Agamidae, adrenal, 280
  blood cell morphology, 76
  blood chemistry, 15, 28, 31, 50, 52
  pituitary, 136, 138, 143, 145, 146, 149,
    151, 154, 157, 169–170, 171, 192, 194
  thyroid, 204, 205

Y

Z